cyclical city

cyclical city

Five Stories of
Urban Transformation

JILL DESIMINI

University of Virginia Press

CHARLOTTESVILLE AND LONDON

University of Virginia Press
© 2021 by the Rector and Visitors of the University of Virginia
All rights reserved
Printed in the United States of America on acid-free paper

First published 2021

9 8 7 6 5 4 3 2 1

Library of Congress Cataloging-in-Publication Data

Names: Desimini, Jill, author.
Title: Cyclical city : five stories of urban transformation / Jill Desimini.
Description: Charlottesville : University of Virginia Press, 2021. | Includes bibliographical references and index.
Identifiers: LCCN 2021016942 (print) | LCCN 2021016943 (ebook) | ISBN 9780813946320 (hardback) |
    ISBN 9780813946337 (ebook)
Subjects: LCSH: Land use, Urban—Case studies. | Urban renewal—Case studies. | Terrain vague.
Classification: LCC HD1391 .D47 2021 (print) | LCC HD1391 (ebook) | DDC 711/.4—dc23
LC record available at https://lccn.loc.gov/2021016942
LC ebook record available at https://lccn.loc.gov/2021016943

Furthermore:
a program of the J. M. Kaplan Fund

Publication of this volume was assisted by a grant from Furthermore: a program of the J. M. Kaplan Fund.

Cover illustration by the author with Taylor Baer.

To Daniel, Nora, and Arlo Bauer

There's a place between two stands of trees where the grass grows uphill
and the old revolutionary road breaks off into shadows
near a meeting-house abandoned by the persecuted
who disappeared into those shadows.

I've walked there picking mushrooms at the edge of dread, but don't be fooled
this isn't a Russian poem, this is not somewhere else but here,
our country moving closer to its own truth and dread,
its own ways of making people disappear.

I won't tell you where the place is, the dark mesh of the woods
meeting the unmarked strip of light—
ghost-ridden crossroads, leafmold paradise:
I know already who wants to buy it, sell it, make it disappear.

And I won't tell you where it is, so why do I tell you
anything? Because you still listen, because in times like these
to have you listen at all, it's necessary
to talk about trees.
—Adrienne Rich, "What Kind of Times Are These" from *Collected Poems: 1950–2012*

CONTENTS

ACKNOWLEDGMENTS

I have many people to thank.

My past and present colleagues at the Harvard Graduate School of Design: Sarah Whiting, Mohsen Mostafavi, Anita Berrizbeitia, Charles Waldheim, Francesca Benedetto, Silvia Benedito, Eve Blau, Joan Busquets, Danielle Choi, Daniel D'Oca, Gareth Doherty, Craig Douglas, Peter del Tredici, Sonja Dümpelmann, Edward Eigen, Rosetta S. Elkin, Susan Fainstein, Richard Forman, Teresa Gali Izard, Toni Griffin, Gary Hilderbrand, Michael Hooper, Jane Hutton, Rosalea Monacella, Niall Kirkwood, John Peterson, Sergio Lopez-Pineiro, Monserrat Bonvehi Rosich, Kiel Moe, Robert Pietrusko, Jackie Piracini, Antoine Picon, Chris Reed, Patricia Roberts, Martha Schwartz, John Stilgoe, Michael van Valkenburgh.

My colleagues who provided or reviewed content: Michael R. Allen, Julie Bargmann, Silvia Benedito, Sean Burkholder, João Castro, Sonja Dümpelmann, Rosetta S. Elkin, Maria Jose Fundavilla, João Gomes da Silva, Jane Hutton, Almut Jirku, Erin Kelly, Ingo Kowarik, Jens Lachmund, Christopher Marcinkoski, Manuela Raposo Magalhães, Brent Ryan, Martin Schaumann, Anne Whiston Spirn, Ed Wall, Tim Waterman, Jane Wolff, and the anonymous reviewers, among others.

Research assistants: Taylor Baer, Senta Burton, Emmanuel Coloma, Tiffany Dang, Michelle Arevalos Franco, Michael Luegering, Ailyn Mendoza, Angela Moreno-Long, Ambrose Luk, Lane Raffaldini Rubin, Megan Jones Shiotani, Ruth Siegal, Ui Jun Song, Hannah van der Eb, A. Gracie Villa, Timothy Wei.

Seminar and thesis students: Madeleine Aronson, Michelle Benoit, Yash Bhutada, Dan Bier, Travis Bost, Ryn Burns, Anna Cawrse, Nina Chase, Amna Rafi Chaudhry, Elena Clarke, Rachael Cleveland, Daniel Daou, Alexis Del Vecchio, Hana Disch, Terence Fitzpatrick, Ana Garcia, Laura Gomez, Emily Gordon, Laura Haak, Keith Hartwig, Diana Jih, Je Sung Lee, Frankie Leung, Grace McInery, Nathalie Mitchell,

Stephanie Morrison, Sara Newey, Avery Normandin, Laura Stacy Passmore, Paul Fletcher Phillips, Greta Ruedisueli, Zephaniah Ruggles, Moritz Schudel, Megan Jones Shiotani, Alec Spangler, Elaine Stokes, AJ Sus, Catherine Tang, Héctor Tarrido-Picart, Seok Min Yeo, Jessica Yurkofsky, Menghi Zhang.

Editors and publishers: Jane M. Curran, Anne Hegeman, Mark Mones, Ellen Satrom, Cecilia Sorochin, Boyd Zenner.

And: Linda and Donald Desimini; Sam, Louise, Suzanne, and Robert Sullivan; Rachel, Marjorie, and Mark Bauer.

This project received critical funding from the Dean's Junior Faculty Grant programs at the Harvard Graduate School of Design.

cyclical city

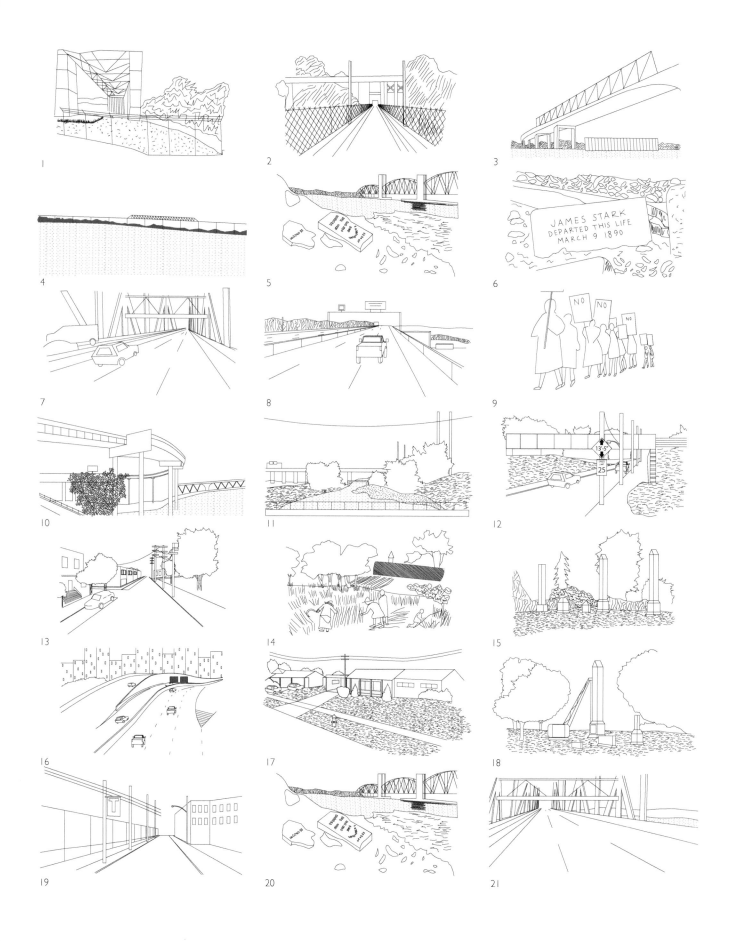

1

2

3

4

5

6

7

8

9

10

11

12

13

14

15

16

17

18

19

20

21

PROLOGUE

About a decade ago, in the Bridesburg neighborhood of Philadelphia, I took a long walk along the forgotten and largely inaccessible Frankford Creek diversion channel, starting out near Delaware Avenue, one of the few at-grade crossings. At some point along an overgrown path, I passed through an open chain-link fence that opened to the wide prospect of the Delaware River. The broad scale of the river was framed and augmented by the enormous buttresses of the highway bridge above; the eye drawn out and up and away from the ground, and only when I looked back down into the water was I snapped out of a kind of sky-daze. Along the water's edge, the riprap, I soon realized, bore names. Broken, unclaimed headstones, it turns out, were helping to support the interstate. Cars racing by hundreds of feet above depended on these old lost souls.

Creek, channel, fence, river, highway, water, granite carved to the specifications of an undertaker and the next of kin: these juxtapositions—some based on ingrained histories of urban development, others unique and peculiar—manifest layers of urban change. The specific types of changes, their stages and dates, can be peeled back to tell a story. The waterfront, marginalized by industrial development gone defunct, became a location of a transportation megaproject in the late 1960s and early 1970s.[1] The project included a new bridge across the Delaware River and a connecting highway to bring the bridge traffic to the nearby interstate. This highway portion, constructed at a perpendicular to the river, bisected a neighborhood that was already isolated, sandwiched between a major interstate and the river. The interstate itself, realized with Federal Highway Act of 1956 funds, was still a recent addition to the area when the bridge project was initiated. Neighborhood protests eventually stopped some roadway construction—a planned continuation of the bridge highway to meet another highway over 2.5 miles away. The project was literally cut off, leaving naked columns in

Figure 1. Sequencing the cyclical city, Philadelphia, 1999–2019: a hypothetical drive over, under, and around the Betsy Ross Bridge.

the middle of the interstate, planned to carry the load of the highway, and two flyover ramps truncated and unconnected. These ghost ramps remain a visual reminder of the disconnect between the preexisting fabric of the city and the ensuing transportation construction efforts. The giant spaghetti of concrete ramps sits atop the old and current beds of the Frankford Creek itself partially realigned, diverted, and sewered between the late 1800s and 1956. The concrete ramps also fly over an adjacent rail line, which runs along the creek built in the late 1800s, again during a time of major transportation investments. The freight and regional passenger rail, too, crosses the Delaware River on the first bridge constructed over the river in Philadelphia, completed in 1896. The various systems—waterway, railway, highway—are layered on top of each other and placed at different elevations, each representing different eras of city building. Driving along the local industrial byway of Richmond Street, the car moves under the railroad embankment, over the creek, past the on-ramp to the bridge, and under its roadway connection to eventually arrive at a residential neighborhood of 1920s row houses. These houses, built for white European immigrants, sit next to a Catholic cemetery from 1887 and on the previous trapping grounds and farmlands of the Swedish settlers who first displaced the homelands and altered the watershed of the Taconick Indians, a tribe of the Lenni Lenape. The Swedish were in turn displaced by Dutch, British, German, Irish, Polish, and American claims.

About seven miles away in another neighborhood, around the time of the bridge construction, an old inner-city cemetery in disrepair was condemned by the city. Ownership was transferred to a nearby university looking to build a parking lot to attract commuting students. Car travel was increasing, and parking was difficult. The cemetery, built in 1839 in the Victorian garden style, had been slowly modified with time. When it was built, the area was not yet developed. As the city expanded, streets were cut through the original plot. The cemetery reached capacity in 1920, and by the 1950s, maintenance was at a bare minimum. The neighborhood around it was also transitioning, as incentives such as the Servicemen's Readjustment Act of 1944, or the GI Bill, and new housing construction were pulling white families to the suburbs. The Levittown, Pennsylvania, development opened twenty-five miles away in 1958. Homes were not sold to African Americans. The city struggled to keep up, and lending practices discouraged investment in older, racially heterogeneous neighborhoods such as the one where the cemetery was located. The cemetery was destroyed, or nearly destroyed. Eight thousand bodies were claimed and moved individually. The remaining twenty thousand were transferred en masse to a cemetery nine miles north in another jurisdiction. The headstones were sold to the construction company responsible for the bridgework, filling a need for limestone and granite riprap for the bridge substructure. The cemetery was paved over and converted to a parking lot. The alignment of a nearby high school reflects the angle of the old cemetery's perimeter—a skew taken off an adjacent street that follows an old Indian trail along a ridge in the city rather than one following the later city grid. In addition, a few stone walls and a couple of London plane trees remain, indicating the original grade of the cemetery and the city, nearly ten feet above some of the lowered streets around it. As for the parking lot, much of it has been converted to athletic facilities, reflecting the changing priorities of American universities.

The destruction of the cemetery and construction of the bridge are still united forty years later, on a literal margin, at the interface of land, water, and infrastructure. In this littoral zone, a new rocky habitat is created. It is an unfathomable yet also sadly routine story. The details and particular circumstances are unique—few bridge abutments are constructed with headstones—but the overall storylines—building infrastructure along creeks and in valleys, investing in massive road construction projects, delaying or halting projects as a result of citizen protests, isolating or destroying fallow cemeteries and parklands, expanding campuses and institutions, paving urban surfaces, investing differentially in different urban areas, engaging in policies that lead to racial segregation, causing populations to shift either through forced relocation or as a result of political and economic decisions, leaving behind other populations—are present in many places. These registrations manifest physically in the urban landscape, where the layers overlap, and where previous occupations are never fully cleared: centenarian walls and trees frame a small remnant sexagenarian parking lot and expansive athletic facilities built in the last decade.

INTRODUCTION

The Underlying Condition

This book focuses on the sites, circumstances, and contexts of abandonment as well as the political, social, economic, ecological underpinnings, and the designed responses to these conditions. It examines the differentially shifting urban landscape over long time cycles, uncovering dramatic shifts in the landscape, that can be both singular and episodic. It argues that history matters, and that past actions and policies have played a fundamental role in producing and sustaining abandonment. It also counters the notion that change is unidirectional, toward advancement and progress, and debunks myths that seek to generalize geographic and temporal situations. It looks at patterns of growth and decline and their periodic and potentially repetitive nature. It reveals the emergent properties of the shrinkage landscape, or the resultant landscapes of economic decline. In doing so, the book tests the idea of cycles with regard to long-term transformation, to place the problematic narrative of growth and decline in a relative and contingent lens. The cycles refer to both the evolution of the cities and sites themselves and the alterations to the specific material conditions present. Water, plant, crop, and material cycles exist at the elemental level and within the built environment as development promotes and resists these cycles and these cycles promote and resist development.

The work builds on design literature around the void but challenges the implication that the land is empty.[1] Instead, the terms abandoned, and fallow are adopted to emphasize the deliberate jettisoning of the land (metaphorically speaking, of course, as land cannot be thrown away) and the potential of a pause to nurture, restore and allow for inventive futures for these latent landscapes.[2] Ultimately, this book develops a framework to understand these abandoned and fallow landscapes beyond their aesthetic qualities in order to posit a fundamental role for spatial design practice to transform these spaces through time. It pushes against the fetishization of voids and ruins,

Figure 2. Dissonance, Youngstown, 2011: a mismatch of GPS map and view, where the view is not what one might imagine when looking at the map.

demanding accountability to and reparations for the local inhabitants. It looks at the deep physical and social topographies of five cities, each layered with diverse material and cultural memories over centuries, as a thick substrate primed for a radical shift in modes of living with the landscape. It critiques the singular, parcel-level strategies that seek to replace one use with the next, that rely on technofixes that focus solely on the logics of capital markets: efficiency, monetary returns, short-term evaluation.[3] Finally, it argues conversely for the potential of aggregation and slow incremental transformation, and the ability to empower and build communal wealth through land reform and spatial design. It develops a design approach and methodology that confronts histories of colonization and systemic failure and foregrounds the specific affordances of the land itself (hydrology, vegetation, topography, geology, infrastructural capacity, occupation potential); the importance of cyclical change; and the particularities of the cultural, political, and physical context. These themes are explored in depth through changing landscapes in five cities—Philadelphia, Berlin, Lisbon, Amsterdam, and

St. Louis—across centuries, from periods of great upheaval to ones of relative stability and even growth.

The framework and methodology combine text and original visuals. Each city and its projects are researched, visited, and drawn in a particular manner. The fallow and abandoned landscapes are put into cartographic dialogue with the key urban structuring elements (waterways and floodplains in Philadelphia; rails and forest reserves in Berlin; valleys and soils in Lisbon; interstices and canals in Amsterdam; and highways, levees, and bridges in St. Louis). The fallow ground and projects are juxtaposed with an urban plan and a planning history. A set of itinerant sections relates the plans from above

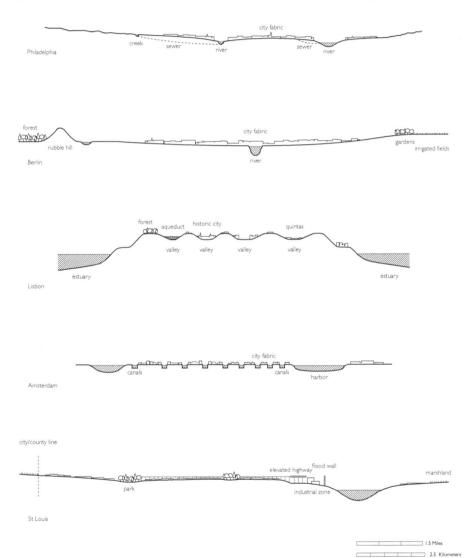

Figure 3. City profiles: sections through Philadelphia, Berlin, Lisbon, Amsterdam, and St. Louis showing key structuring elements.

to the movement through the city and call out the particular project locations. These sites are drawn in plan and section over time, as well as in an axonometric view to give a three-dimensional understanding of the sites and chosen topographical moments. In addition, the rudimentary materials (stormwater meadow, *Robinia pseudoacacia,* shed and *Arundo donax* teepee, sand, brick, *Helianthus annuus*) are photographed and illustrated to provide textural quality and scalar understanding. In the end, the history and design cycles are shown, intertwined in a complex wheel of interdependency where events and statistics are related temporally. The techniques relate history and space, analysis and imagination dynamically through time.

Abandonment

The idea of abandonment is complex. The term is rooted etymologically in loss and exuberance, devotion and surrender, relinquishment of property and freedom of inhibition. Abandon and abandonment represent the full cycle of inhabitation and the attendant care models. Abandonment is both the state of being left behind and the action of relinquishing.

The cultural and economic value of a landscape is dependent on context, both the physical surroundings (location matters) and the cultural history (lineage matters). The economic value of land varies significantly depending on its situation within a city, a region, or the country as a whole, and this value fluctuates with time and market cycles. The price of housing, for example, is split between the cost of the structure and the value of the land. The land value varies widely; in 2014 it ranged from 5 percent to 34.4 percent of the total price in Detroit and from 72.3 percent to 88.9 percent in San Francisco.[4] Economic values change with circumstance, but so does cultural appreciation. The swaths of meadows occupying abandoned city neighborhoods are perceived very differently than the seeded meadows that flow across suburban campuses or even those that replace fallow agricultural lands at the urban periphery. The differences in species mix and ecological characteristics may be indiscernible, but the contextual differences override the similarities. A zoom-in renders the meadows comparable whereas a zoom-out reveals the disparities. The thin vegetative cover cannot hide the past site narratives nor the distinctions in long-term investment.

It is crucial to return to this idea of abandonment and the notion that the level of abandonment that a site incurs becomes part of its essence and ascribed value. Analogous to the hybridity between nature and nurture in human development, the site is governed both by its physical characteristics and its cultural history—and to some degree these cannot be separated.[5] Take, for example, three sites along the Emerald Necklace in Boston, Massachusetts: the Arnold Arboretum, the Bussey Brook Meadow (now part of the Arboretum) and Franklin Park. Nearly contiguous and all recognized as part of an important and valued corridor within the city, the three sites have evolved separately, as triplets separated at conception.

As part research institution for Harvard University and part public park for the city of Boston, the Arnold Arboretum is a horticultural display grounds. Established in 1872 and designed in collaboration with the landscape architect Frederick Law Olmsted, the Arnold Arboretum has been continuously operated as a living collection of trees, shrubs, and woody vines—meticulously documented, studied, and maintained by researchers and staff.[6] The plants are deliberately placed and carefully maintained. Human touch is everywhere.

By contrast, the Bussey Brook Meadow, prior to its unification and total adoption by the Arnold Arboretum in 1996, has been subjected to multiple owners and multiple transgressors throughout its postcolonial history.[7] The site, now a research ground for urban ecology, has been cut off from the surrounding fabric by roadways and rail berms and crisscrossed by utilities. Its hydrology has been significantly altered both inadvertently and deliberately. It has served as an impromptu landfill, a stormwater impoundment area, and the site of neighborhood controversy. It has housed community gardens and has been home to transient populations. The vegetation is spontaneous—an arboretum gone wild with its lushness an indicator of resiliency.[8] Human abuse is everywhere.

Franklin Park represents a middle ground, between active management and active neglect, emblematic of the struggle for funding for public park maintenance especially in neighborhoods with chronic public and private disinvestment. Also designed by Frederick Law Olmsted as his large masterpiece at the end of the Emerald Necklace, the park faced immediate pressure for alteration after it opened in the late 1880s. A golf course had replaced the country park within ten years of construction. And there were further appropriations: it served as home to a zoo, a stadium, and a hospital. Alongside these large encroachments, to borrow Olmsted's term, many of the original structures have deteriorated or disappeared. The circulation system has been significantly altered; some plantings have gone wild while others are dying en masse. Ecological succession and crude maintenance drive the vegetal transformations. The park has its major bones, but the tissue is fragmented. Human touch is varied.

The three sites reflect their diverse lineages. They represent a gradient from tamed to wild, maintained to neglected, restrained to abandoned. The differences work at the site level, but within each site, nuance prevails. Locations within the arboretum are wild enclaves perfect for rebellious parties of teenagers; well-kept, monumental granite gates enclose Bussey Brook Meadow; and the recreational areas within Franklin Park are self-sustaining and revenue-generating. These differences underscore a need for close and critical spatial reading, for a long gaze at the individual materials and properties of the sites themselves as well as an interrogation of the governing political, economic, environmental, and cultural structures and systems at play. The three sites do differ in their physical properties—properties formed over millions of years—but these differences have been enhanced through the past four hundred years of development. This is, of course, old news, but a deep look at the specific outcomes of recent history is astonishing. The physical residues reflect both the care internal to the sites, as described above, and the larger patterns of structural disinvestment that result in the inequitable distribution of resources across municipal, regional, and national landscapes.

Time

It is with time that the effects of abandonment become evident, that the results of human care and neglect register profoundly through the urban landscape. It can be argued that the time scale of urban abandonment is both shorter and longer than that of occupation. The systems are governed by economics. On the one hand is the issue of

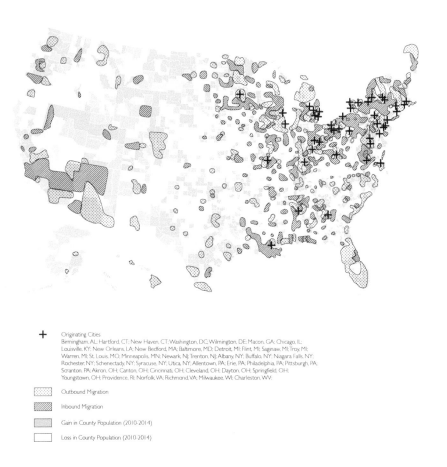

+ Originating Cities
Birmingham, AL; Hartford, CT; New Haven, CT; Washington, DC; Wilmington, DE; Macon, GA; Chicago, IL; Louisville, KY; New Orleans, LA; New Bedford, MA; Baltimore, MD; Detroit, MI; Flint, MI; Saginaw, MI; Troy, MI; Warren, MI; St. Louis, MO; Minneapolis, MN; Newark, NJ; Trenton, NJ; Albany, NY; Buffalo, NY; Niagara Falls, NY; Rochester, NY; Schenectady, NY; Syracuse, NY; Utica, NY; Allentown, PA; Erie, PA; Philadelphia, PA; Pittsburgh, PA; Scranton, PA; Akron, OH; Canton, OH; Cincinnati, OH; Cleveland, OH; Dayton, OH; Springfield, OH; Youngstown, OH; Providence, RI; Norfolk, VA; Richmond, VA; Milwaukee, WI; Charleston, WV.

Outbound Migration

Inbound Migration

Gain in County Population (2010-2014)

Loss in County Population (2010-2014)

Figure 4. Translocations, after Benton MacKaye and borrowing the idea of inflow and outflow or in-migration and out-migration.

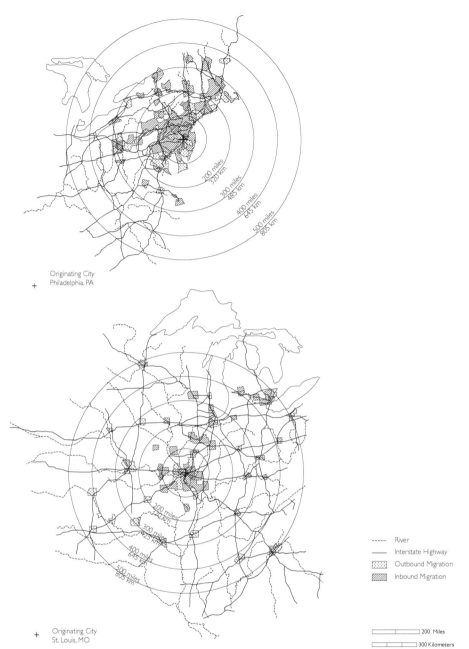

200 miles
320 km

300 miles
485 km

400 miles
645 km

500 miles
805 km

Originating City
+ Philadelphia, PA

200 miles
320 km

300 miles
485 km

400 miles
645 km

500 miles
805 km

+ Originating City
St. Louis, MO

----- River
——— Interstate Highway
▓▓▓ Outbound Migration
▨▨▨ Inbound Migration

200 Miles

300 Kilometers

Figure 5. Regional flows, after Benton MacKaye and
again borrowing the idea of inflow and outflow or
in-migration and out-migration.

durable goods: buildings are erected quickly with demand and removed slowly without it. On the other is the relatively quick evacuation of populations due to conflict, weather, or geologic events (storms or earthquakes) as well as economic and political change. The measure of transformation depends on the mobility of the actors and agents and the physical characteristics and scale of the site. Programs and people shift, capable of flowing like a river, to use the American planner and conservationist Benton MacKaye's analogy to describe American migrations from Westward Expansion to metropolitan sprawl.[9]

But this type of change is more aptly defined as translocation rather than transformation. The movement is rapid and fluid, rather than slow and halting. Empty receptacles are left behind, dry riverbeds without the water that shaped them. And it is these dry riverbeds—the residual urban formations—that are resistant to change. Adaptation of the built fabric to new models of inhabitation, new environmental conditions, and new support systems is a project of decades and centuries. Given the slow process of change and abandonment, how do we address the residual landscape? How do we see it again as something other than derelict? How do we come to appreciate this kind of fallow? To do so, it is necessary to look closely at the relatively slow change that is happening, to embrace the pause required for invention, to make room for the idea of zero growth to flourish, and to understand the longer histories at play in order to change the dominant, destructive story lines.[10] We cannot be lured by the physical forms and blind to the underlying discriminatory factors that led to their existence. These are sites of incredible environmental and social trauma that demand renewed investment. But at the same time, we cannot be paralyzed by their legacies or nostalgic for their heyday so as to repeat the single-minded models of the past. Instead, these sites hold the potential for true transformation, for new spatial forms, new material expressions, and new modes of collective governance whereby those left out of past plans and projects have a role in writing the next chapters.

Growth and Decline (and Growth and Decline)

Abandoned, previously built-upon urban land is a feature of any city, an evolutionary conceit of urbanization. Yet while pervasive and nearly universal, abandoned land reserves are nonetheless correlated with cities facing population and economic loss, where the conundrum of growing reserves of underutilized land is further exacerbated by decreasing financial resources and monetary land values. Governmentally operated land banks are becoming the adoption agencies for unwanted urban land, but land banks offer no clear direction, leaving an enigmatic terrain. The use and value of the land (and the land bank) seem vague to the general public.[11] Attempts have been made toward holistic quantification and qualification.[12] Yet a critical question remains: what

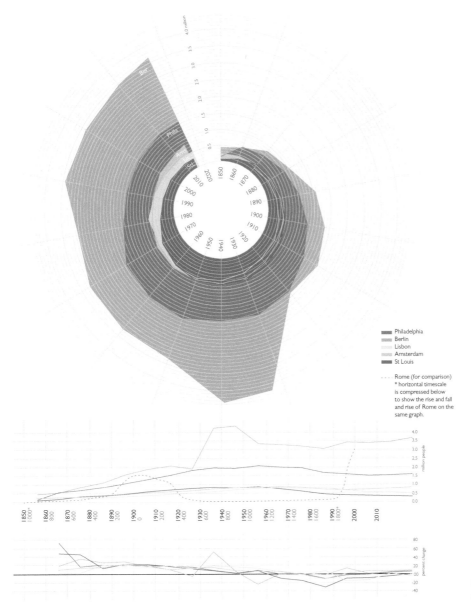

Philadelphia
Berlin
Lisbon
Amsterdam
St Louis

Rome (for comparison)
* horizontal timescale
is compressed below
to show the rise and fall
and rise of Rome on the
same graph.

Figure 6. Population fluctuations in the five cities over time

can become of this land inventory that is so rich despite its neglect, despite the derision it inspires?

In Western capitalist culture, we are obsessed with growth, to such an extent that it is the only story we hear in most cities. Growth narrative dominates the collective imagination, but cycles of both growth and decline are a part of the overall urban trajectory.[13]

Again, the physical fabric of cities is enduring, but its response to economic growth and decline is not equal. In times of increased demand, new buildings are constructed quickly. New subdivisions are platted. New urban plans are concocted. The response to decreased demand, on the other hand, is slow. With oversupply of housing, buildings, and plots, entropy ensues. The built environment is often left to unfettered structural atrophy or unencumbered vegetal growth, depending on your perspective. Either way, when development falters, abandonment occurs, and anxiety follows. It becomes difficult to imagine a turnaround when deep within the recesses of contraction, just as it is hard to foresee decline in times of growth. In 1930, the *New York Times* reported, "Detroit was able to cut down trees and plant skyscrapers." Today, wild urban woodlands are emerging in the vicinity of crumbling skyscrapers. Even when the city appears stagnant, it is changing. Yet, the patience for this slow, perhaps invisible transformation does not exist. Inertia masks a different kind of growth, but this isn't to say that a city merely returns to its previous state: from forest back to forest. Rather as it travels though time the city is layered, gathering materials and knowledge, like a snowball. The goal is not to dwell on past lost but to see the urban landscape as capable of evolution, and not just in spite of its ups and downs but because of them.

Though cities may appear to have died in the short term, history has shown us that many urban centers do ultimately come back as transformed versions of their former selves, over the course of years or decades or even centuries. Take Rome, the classic example. At its height in 100 AD, the city boasted a population of over 1,000,000 people. By 400 AD, the population began to fall. By 500 AD, a mere 100,000 people were estimated to remain Romans; by the end of the Gothic Wars in 554 AD, 30,000 people.[14] Yet Rome rebounded, gaining population steadily from the 1800s onward, to once again surpass 1,000,000 in the 1930s, and 2,750,000 in 2010.[15] Now we look to Venice, one of 350 global cities that have experienced a steep decline in population since the 1950s.[16] In the context of the climate crisis, its prospects look dire. In the context of the longer cycles of cities, Rome represents some hope for places such as Venice or St. Louis, whose present-day situation is unsettling.

Cycles

Evolution is a difficult idea when it comes to the design project. Nostalgia is a cultural value that poses a formidable barrier to evolution. Yet, to take a non-nostalgic approach to the evolution of the built environment and its designed interventions is refreshing. To imagine that what we make will inevitably change, for better and worse, relieves a kind of pressure and embraces a necessary reality. Designs, even good ones, are fleeting.

To this end, it is also refreshing to consider nonlinear models and longer periods of time. Here, it is possible to push back on the often destructive forward march of growth and progress, to investigate the periodic, the cyclical, and the recursive.

Something periodic happens again at regular intervals or intermittently. Something cyclical returns to itself, or an altered form of its former self. It is complete, reaching a momentary resolution. It is like a line closing on itself to form a circle. Something cyclical can also be defined as having a specific chronological period, for example, a solar or lunar cycle. Thus, a cycle has a period, and both the cyclical and the periodic are recursive.

In this volume, I consider the overall trajectories of growth and decline, not as either growing or declining, but rather as part of the same cyclical transformations. At the same time, I investigate recurrence related to landscape characteristics and design rudiments: the water, vegetal, crop, material, and life cycles. In the end, through each project, these transformations come together to expose the persistent qualities and potentials of the urban landscape. These changes are understood critically relative to other metric and decision-making cycles that often lead to structural disinvestment and limited readings of vitality. Cities are evaluated on three-month fiscal periods, leaders can shift with political elections every two and four years, and some resources are allocated based on decennial census counts.

Returning to the example of the Detroit skyscrapers and woodlands—the city was booming in 1930, rapidly felling trees for buildings. Those buildings are crumbling 80 years later, when seedlings are being deployed by the tens of thousands with the hopes of building an urban forest. Those trees will mature in 40–50 years. The period of change is, if all goes as currently planned, 125 years—a long time in human years and a relatively short one on a geological time scale. This cycle—from forest to forest—is understood in terms of the overall landscape, as well as the various changes in vegetal growth, political will, and social investment. In addition, it is also understood as an accruing condition, where difference over time is emphasized. The evolution is not clean; the new forest registers all of the events and mini-cycles that contributed to its existences. It is not a return to the past. It is like a dust ball that rolls and collects more dust in its path. In the end it is still a ball, but definitely not the same ball as when it started. It is a ball that evolves, but with an understanding of its past, and a position relative to how its future is being guided. The projects in this book emphasize a design process and a potential equitable distribution of power to drive a common project. To go from forest to forest is not to say that trees are inherently good or that just letting volunteer saplings grow can undo our climatic woes or societal ills. Rather, the argument is for a critical reflection on what constitutes progress—to not uproot a tree for the promise of capital economic opportunity and conversely to not plant a tree when the tree represents a speculative foreign investment or a predatory land grab.[17] Instead, the point is to interrupt flat and linear thinking, and to slowly evolve our cultural biases, undo our perverse and narrow means of evaluation, and to expand our collective tools to reform property and space alike.

To understand how design can critically engage with the cycles of abandonment,

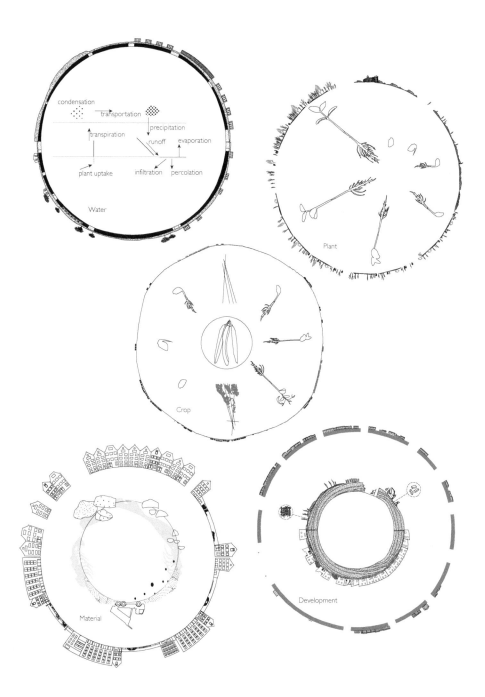

Figure 7. Cycles: Water, plant, crop, material, development.

I look at many different periods and intervals, through the lens of five specific urban conditions and four emblematic landscape characteristics in order to arrive at a set of methodological principles to engage this common and recursive predicament.

Shrinkage Landscapes

In doing so, I offer a complimentary yet critical perspective to what is sometimes referred to as a shrinking city or, here, a shrinkage landscape. The Shrinking Cities project, a German Federal Cultural Foundation project directed by the architect Philipp Oswalt and published in two thick volumes in 2005 and 2006, presents a near-comprehensive catalog of research, theory, and interventions related to places facing population decline. Despite its daunting length, the project is a breath of fresh air. It counters the demographically driven planning accounts. It does not ignore the undisputable, quantifiable population losses that have hit so many shrinking cities, but in addressing them, it examines the nuanced and problematic underpinnings of the phenomenon. For Oswalt's team, the focus is on the artistic, the fleeting, the nonphysical; they pay attention to the social activity of the cities. Refreshingly, cultural practice is divorced from the slowly changing physical properties of the urban landscape. The two are considered as interrelated, but not co-dependent. Cultural vibrancy can exist in a place of physical decline. This is a crucial turning point to counter the negative narratives of population loss, to espouse the people that remained, and to see opportunity for new modes of cultural practice. At the same time, there is a warning to issue: to say that even if people are resilient and creative, this does not lessen the need to address the broken systems that produce the inequities. The solution cannot be to place the care of the city and the supply of services into the hands of its citizen volunteers. The burden of government's failure to provide cannot be borne by those historically left behind. In fact, the failure of the government is like another pressure in itself; its absence is an additional pressure.

The Shrinking Cities work is an important repository of possibilities to be mined, critiqued, and expanded upon, especially with regard to the landscape condition. The volumes focus on architecture, planning and cultural practice and barely touch the role of landscape architecture, ecology and related fields.[18] For those interested in land transformation, the place to begin is the section entitled "Feral City,"[19] which examines the landscapes where urban wildness meets urban agriculture, where social networks engage spaces designed out of abandonment, where "rurbanity"[20] describes civic transformation. The thirty-two pages represent a broad spectrum of issues and projects briefly. The section opens inquiries and leaves room for elaboration. A broad net is cast, and the challenge is set for deeper engagement with the ideas presented.

In this book, I take on the challenge of a deep investigation. I build on the proposition of debunking the loss-centered narrative and tackle, in depth, one question at the core of the "Feral City" section: What can landscape-driven design approaches bring to previously occupied and currently abandoned landscapes, both in the shrinking city and beyond? Instead of presenting a catalog of approaches represented by many examples, devoid of a historical context and divorced from issues of social and environmental justice, I identify four fundamental properties of abandoned land through which to uncover political, social, environmental, cultural, and design narratives. These include its tendency to be low-lying and flood-prone, in the Black Bottoms of our cities; its innate habitat for spontaneous vegetal growth and animal activity that points to the possibility for curation as a design practice; its availability for food production in places where there is little access to fresh provisions; and its ability to attract land-impoverished people to use it, whereby new models of labor, economy, and occupation are possible.[21] In response, I see these characteristics as the key and expansive rudiments that designers have to engage with the social and spatial territory of urban abandonment: water, wild plants, cultivated crops, extended surfaces, and occupations.[22] I investigate how these elements and materials can be assembled and leveraged to create collective design projects for the city. Like the strategy of the Shrinking City project, the idea is not to imagine any one solution for the complexity and varied nature of abandoned sites but rather to understand the common design approaches operating in a context of neglect and abuse. Plurality is embraced.

Unlike the Shrinking City project, the cases are highly curated and the historical contexts are intensely specific. Each type of project is explored through the municipal actions of an emblematic city, chosen because the underlying topic can be associated clearly with that place. For example, hydrological innovation and stormwater management is central to Philadelphia's development and on-going land management. Wild plants are everywhere in Berlin, and wastelands, derided elsewhere, are recognized as culturally and ecologically significant landscapes for design to engage with proactively in the creation of viable civic space. Soil protection and cultivation are valued in Lisbon as means to organize and occupy the urban landscape. Interstitial paved plazas and playgrounds proliferate in Amsterdam's interior courtyards and exterior streetscapes. The found condition is embraced but highly altered to foreground participatory and incremental models of design and care. Human abuse turns into touch, everywhere.

I take inspiration from my walk under the bridge in Bridesburg[23] and from my many walks and drives through abandoned and neglected urban environments when arguing that cultural context matters. Specific places tell specific stories, stories dependent on locale and time period. Yet, through these stories, general themes arise. By understanding the history of water management in Philadelphia, it is possible to glean the importance and potential of water as a means to engage abandoned landscapes in other places. By exploring how Berlin came to love wild plants and design innovative park structures, it is possible to imagine how a similar process might or might not be appropriate elsewhere. By appreciating the collective efforts to integrate informal urban farms into Lisbon's ecological structure, it is possible to see how urban agriculture becomes a formidable part of a city's ecological strategy. By looking beyond the formal acumen of the playgrounds in Amsterdam and instead seeing them as a relevant time- and site-specific means of urban activation, it is possible to understand how this might take place in another context while taking an anti-nostalgic view toward the changes to the individual sites. Demise is indication, in this case, that the stigma of previous abandonment has dissipated. The city, perhaps like all cities, continues to evolve. This brings us to St. Louis, a city in flux, with numerous initiatives aimed at addressing abandonment, disinvestment, and racism. The city is divided, but the energy occasionally crosses that political, economic, and cultural boundary—and proposals graze all of the rudiments discussed: absorption, spontaneous and curated growth, tended cultivation, and social engagement through art, music, play, and other sponsored activity.

Stormwater: 350 Years of Hydrology in Philadelphia

Abandoned land tends to have great hydrological importance, and in Philadelphia, the use of fallow landscapes to absorb stormwater is a key piece in the city's potential transformation. The land often occurs in low-lying areas prone to flooding or along hardened and constricted water edges;[24] and land-use strategies have the potential to engage these erratic waters. Aqueous interventions range from full impoundment—lakes for storage and recreation—to small installations of vegetated infrastructure designed to catch, cleanse, and slow stormwater. Even paved plazas are designed to hold water within a thickened surface. Often, water-based strategies address coastal and riverine properties, enhancing protective marshes and providing room for expansion along what are typically constrained urban river sections. But they also operate within the inland city, occupying local low points on residual lands as ways to address water excess from storm events. Cities are only prone to more erratic hydrological experiences—with periods of storm and flood and periods of drought—the more its surfaces can act as scattered sponges, the more excess and scarcity can be balanced. The climatic crisis, marked by this epoch of warming, is here, and the ability to manage water is a fundamental component to adaptation.

Intentional, constructed projects on abandoned land are still rare and experimental. The risk is higher, as the impermeability of the surface is untested, and the character of the soil underneath is unknown. Fill happened a long time ago, before environmental monitoring. Materials—such as the bridge headstones—moved freely across the city. The dubious history makes contamination a threat. The low-profile status of the abandoned lands and their disenfranchised neighborhoods drives political dollars elsewhere. Sometimes the untested potential is a deterrent. When considering a place to collect stormwater, the abandoned landscape—while seemingly an opportunity with its undesignated program, its often-vegetated surfaces, and its unclaimed status—is subject to the same political and economic constraints that hinder the land's adoption by other programs and constituencies. In Philadelphia, there are hints of another approach — one important to consider given the role of urbanization in the climate crisis.

But if we are serious about adapting our cities to respond to potential inundation and drought, we must open our eyes to all landscapes. Design provocations have posited hydrological projects for the unclaimed urban territory, recognizing that limiting the potential acreage to well-known and well-loved landscapes is myopic. Water falls everywhere. It does not discriminate, even if the ground it falls on is shaped by discriminatory practices. As more hydrological infrastructure is returning to land-based systems, with water captured and cleansed on the surface instead of piped into large tunnels, the extensive inventories of low-lying vacant lands become places to accommodate excess stormwater. This is not a new idea but one being slowly implemented. These designed systems offer frameworks within which to explore how a common infrastructure, in this case the stormwater initiatives in Philadelphia, can extend to the forgotten territories of the city to create aqueous terrains for abandoned lands. These landscapes, while existing within a funded imperative to improve urban water management, are also social. They are located in the core landscapes of the lived human experience — the street, the house, the school, the workplace, the community garden, to name a few. Unlike the old pipes, surficial hydrological landscapes are seen and visited frequently. As such, they represent a way to both drain the city of water and fill it with many types of places for people, plants, and animals to be. Here, the social co-benefits of infrastructural projects are considered in relation to the social needs found in abandoned urban territories.

In the first chapter, I explore stormwater cycles and the history of water and water infrastructure in Philadelphia, from Lenni Lenape times to the contemporary *Green City, Clear Waters* program. Through this long lens, I argue that the manipulation of water resources is fundamental to the identity of the city and its works of landscape architecture. The city, often strapped for resources, has invested locally in sourcing and shedding its drinking, storm, and sanitary waters. Drinking water still comes from the rivers within its political boundary, and stormwater is now being managed through direct infiltration into the ground. More specifically, the capture of stormwater proposed for the city's many fallow lands is framed as part of this larger story. The hydrological story is further understood in relation to the political, economic, and social circumstances of the city while the projects are explained across scales, from the watershed to the individual basin.

In Philadelphia, through projects such as Liberty Lands, a balance between the top-down deployment and regulation of a citywide initiative and the local management of its individual projects adds a collective layer to the civic realm. In moving from resource to utility to commons, the banal and distributed hydrological infrastructure is leveraged once again — but this time as a means to use fallow and open landscapes to transform how, for whom, and by whom the urban environment looks and works.

Gleiswildnis: 200 Years of Ecology in Berlin

Another attribute of abandoned spaces is the materialization of a suite of vibrant, spontaneously growing plants. The disappearance of human use allows the explosion of plants—weeds to some and the species of rich ecosystems to others—that are adapted to disturbed sites filled with toxins, building remains, rubble piles, and detritus. A plant whose habitat of origin is a limestone cliff is quite at home in the cracking walls of an old concrete train platform.[25] The ruderal species, whose name comes from the fact that it grows on rubble and detritus, is an early adaptor of disturbed sites. These volunteer plants tend to be ones that spread quickly and crowd out the more sensitive. This affects their cultural reputation. They are often reviled and in turn settle in and define reviled urban spaces.

Proponents of the urban wild and intrepid field ecologists have documented the spread of wild plants in abandoned landscapes. They offer a different characterization of the species as having cultural importance and measurable ecological benefit. The plants are indicators of the history of the spaces that they occupy. If left to grow, they develop to create an amalgamation of interesting species—species that add biological and aesthetic diversity to the urban environment. The sites have rich vegetal structures that, with design, curation, and care, can be integrated into a compendium of urban public spaces. Reemergent grasslands and woodlands offer places of respite within the city for ambling, for dog walking, for exploration. They are spaces that are cultivated over time, through the efficient management of inherent resources. The plants that emerge on sites thrive, sometimes in ways that planted species, which require different soils and nutrients, do not. Wild plants, instead of being obliterated in the face of new development, can be integrated into the design of the public realm.

The greatest case for the incorporation of wild spontaneous ruderal vegetation into urban form through curatorial management is in Berlin, Germany. This is a place where urban design and ecology have come together to create a specific spatial and cultural experience. Ecology requires curation and translation to be harnessed as a process for city making, and in Berlin, there are wonderful examples of curated and constructed urban natures. The city has embraced wastelands—and wild plants—considering them to have ecological value worthy of protection. As a result, a series of projects have tested the incompatibility of ecological and recreational landscapes. In the second chapter, I evaluate several of these designs for public landscapes occupying former rail infrastructure on the west side of the city for their ability to integrate many layers of history and accommodate an evolving coexistence between human and nonhuman species. The projects offer a range of design approaches and public experiences. The first, Grünanlage Hallesche Straße, was protected in 1988, paving the way for the adaptation of architecture, landscape architecture, and infrastructure to include wastelands, rather than obliterating them. These so-called wastelands include a rich suite of *Gleiswildnis* or rail wildernesses.[26] The nomenclature is specific and inclusive of the site history. The abandoned rail infrastructure is habitat for a particular urban nature.

Drawing from the work of urban ecologist Herbert Sukopp, the urban design speculations of O. M. Ungers, and the contemporary designs of Ingo Kowarik, Ökoplan, Atelier Loidl, and others, I argue for the urban wild as a viable design response to fallow landscapes in Berlin and beyond. What emerges from these cases is a suite of options for how to deliberately and palatably include wild vegetation in the city—how to consider it an important element of the common urban experience rather than an unfortunate by-product of neglect to be cleared as soon as possible. Overall, the richness of the captured wild is championed as a design material innate to the rough and visceral qualities of the abandoned landscape. As the city cycles, with more adoption and less abandonment, the qualities of the field-grown species register the past history—histories that only decades earlier were deemed insignificant and obliterated. The variety of vegetal form and species adds cultural character while being economically, ecologically, and, when done right, socially responsive.

Hortas: 500 Years of Agronomy in Lisbon

Allotment gardening, especially when focused on food production, has a long history as a practice during periods of economic downturn, proliferating in moments of collective need.[27] In this sense, it is a widespread programmatic successor to urban vacancy. If the emergence of wild vegetation is a de facto condition following human neglect of the urban landscape, and the fence, seed, and mow approach is the most basic form of temporary maintenance, then the community garden or urban farm, together with the temporary recreational space, is the next level of intervention. Faced with social pressure, and a desire to do something, creating a simple, productive field becomes a temporary panacea. The most common gardens and farms are small, operating at the scale of a single lot or a few contiguous parcels, falling into the trap of the lot-level conversion. They are a low-cost and low-impact solution, with quickly erected raised beds laid over a preexisting ground condition. The insertions rarely engage their full systematic needs or potential. In many places, there is little municipal support for urban agriculture. Growing crops in the city is seen as regressive. Many urban lands used to be agricultural, and in some places, as the city grew, zoning laws were changed to prohibit agricultural use. In other places, long-term leases on property are not available, limiting uses—like agriculture—that require significant start-up costs. Without support, cultivation is limited, and small community gardens disappear as fast as they arise, propelling cycles of abandonment rather than promoting cycles of agriculture.

There are, of course, important exceptions, places where cultivation is accepted at a convincing scale and on a longer term as a viable urban practice. In these cases, the adoption of specific sites is driven by participation and advocacy. The sites require active care, both from people cultivating the sites and the ones organizing and managing the land. For this reason, the sites tend to be in places either with organized constituencies who value gardening, or with populations who depend on farming for subsistence.[28] In either case, agriculture is an ingrained part of the local culture.

Lisbon, Portugal, is a great example of a city where crop cultivation, as a means to organize territory, has historical significance and contemporary relevance. Located in an alluvial valley, the city has been actively farmed since pre-Roman times. While agriculture has been suppressed with centuries of development, it remains extremely active at the edges and in the margins where recent immigrants tend plots as a means of subsistence and economic livelihood. With pressure, the city has begun programs to elevate the status of farming as a cultural and socioeconomic project, integrating agronomic practices with other forms of ecological and recreational landscapes. Under the *Plano Verde de Lisboa,* or Green Plan for Lisbon, proposed in 1996 and adopted in 2007 to reinforce the ecological structure and performance of the city, the city has designated and designed a series of hybrid agricultural sites with *hortas,* or allotment gardens and recreational amenities.[29] The first one opened in 2011, with plans for twenty more. The city project takes a spontaneous and unplanned cultural practice, operating at the fringes of the city, at times to the detriment of public health, and integrates it with other projects to create larger ecological corridors in the urban valleys.[30] The sites are organized, with restrained materials, as a way to improve the farming conditions for the participants—the largely immigrant population previously using the site to grow vegetables—and to elevate the public perception of farming in the city. Instead of eradicating the squatter practice, the goal is to integrate it though acts of design, negotiation, and trust building. Cultivation becomes a means of adopting fallow urban sites, ones, in this case, with steep topographies but workable soils.

In the third chapter, I explore this symbiotic relationship between residual landscapes and agronomy in Lisbon's Chelas valley. Here, the entangled and cyclical histories of development and cultivation are exemplified. The protection of the fertile soil is a charged political, socioeconomic, and ecological project of the past, present, and future. Cultivation represents both cultural patrimony and contemporary struggle.

I argue that the Lisbon hortas or allotment vegetable gardens are a means to organize and occupy the city's abandoned spaces as well as express its underlying landscape structure. They articulate a specific heritage, one that includes the work of consummate Portuguese landscape architect Gonçalo Ribeiro Telles and his team with a more generalizable strategy widely used to activate unclaimed landscapes. Again, urban gardening thrives in conditions of economic downturn and in places of disinvestment. In the case of Lisbon, the common social practice is transcendent. It starts with the garden path and shed but extends to define a new landscape that renders soil and valley visible and performative.

Speelplaatsen: 100 Years of Play in Amsterdam

The abandoned, urban ground is not always open. If flat, it is often sealed beneath pavements, capped under a thick layer designed to keep potentially unruly vegetation and contaminants at bay while offering a surface for parking, building, or programs. In many cases, when coming upon these spaces, it is unclear if the abandonment preceded the pavement or vice versa. But it is clear that hard surfaces, especially those that invite social activation and use, can be instrumental in the organization of the abandoned urban landscape. Best-suited to small and scattered sites—those nested within the urban fabric and with nearby consistencies—paved surfaces can provide a civic and recreational amenity. When converted to a network of plazas, the spaces can address the lack of connection between available recreational spaces in a city and the needs of its population. As abandonment occurs, social spaces, built based on the location of previous inhabitants, are rarely adequate for the remaining citizenry. Parks and playgrounds, for example, are far from where people currently live. Changing demographics—proportionally fewer or more children, for example—require adjustments in the types of available recreational spaces. Finally, different use trends—perhaps more skateboards, better acoustics, mobile dining, eco-lighting, group exercise—might drive different spatial needs or change the way certain spaces are valued. A residual space under a highway overpass might become an active hangout space. A corner lot in an underserved commercial area might attract a food stand. An open space far from a park might become a neighborhood playground. These shifts have the potential to address inequity and uneven access, as well as contribute beneficially to people's health and well-being. It is known that places of disinvestment have higher instances of both acute and chronic illness, and the rise of pathogens and disease associated with climate collapse demand proximal open space.

Underlying the concept of abandonment, of course, is the social activation and deactivation of space. It is the loss of economic and social function that breeds anxiety and the desire for engagement that in turn drives many new initiatives. Often the social activation of abandoned space is short-lived, with the investment rarely significant enough to override the underlying structural issues. The use, then, either disappears and the land returns to its previous state, or the use continues indefinitely but without the intended reverberating response. Some projects are temporary from the outset, with stated end goals, and last for that set duration. Others have nebulous guidelines and exist until interest wanes. A select few continue longer—lasting for years or decades—supported by strong leadership and community interest.

Here, the focus is on the latter, on projects that have a significant and longer-term impact on their physical environment. In these projects, the physical space has a profound presence. It is designed for people in the city—and is enticing both when unoccupied and occupied. It is structured, contained, and given identity. The social use is not only achieved through event but also through constructed, measured alterations to the existing cityscape. Here, the possibility that the use is temporary is acknowledged, but space is still designed to last. The present is considered as important as the future.

In the fourth chapter, I explore the potentials and limitations for exertion and play to reignite the surfaces of the city as well as for the hard surfaces of the city to adapt with age. There is a strong correlation between recreational program and the so-called vacant lot, tracing back to the advent of the public playground in cities. The introduction of play into the unclaimed landscape addresses urban health on two fronts: it provides a place for children to exercise outside as well as stewardship for the wayward lots. This fruitful marriage was understood by the Amsterdam public works department, under designers Cornelis van Eesteren, Aldo van Eyck, Jakoba Mulder, and others. Over seven hundred *Speelplaatsen* or playgrounds were constructed in the forty-year period following World War II.[31] The projects were inserted into multiple parcel-sized gaps in the existing residential fabric, carved out of roadways, and used to define the amorphous open space in newly designed communities. Wherever there is a sliver of land, there can be a playground. The projects share a common and powerful language and a set of understated, inexpensive, durable, and transformative materials. They create a clear physical and experiential identity for the city. But they are also temporary means to activate the landscape, responsive to a particular time and cultural need. The ideals remain, but many of the spaces have transitioned. I place the Amsterdam project in its specific context—a thirty-year urban cycle—and also within a larger idea of play as a means to inhabit the abandoned landscape and address the well-being of an urban citizenry. Through expression and use, the landscapes gain value and livelihood and, ultimately, grow and evolve with the city.

Fallow Land: 150 Years of Disinvestment in St. Louis

The fallow landscape is powerful—and in all of these projects the goal is to understand its potential.[32] The idea is to place abandonment within a cyclical context and to explore the emergence, disappearance, and reemergence of water, plants, crops, soils, mineral, animals, and humans. The first four chapters tell the long histories of urban transformation and design intervention. At present, these stories are somewhat resolved, with known, if intermediary, conclusions. Of course, the cities and projects are ever changing, subject to the uncertainty of climate, politics, economics, and human will. By contrast, the conditions explored in the fifth chapter are unresolved. The history is equally complex, sordid, and interesting, full of cycles without closure.

Thus, the fifth chapter extends the ideas expressed in the first four chapters to address abandonment in a city in the throes of disinvestment. St. Louis has a growing inventory of fallow land and, relatively speaking, no clear vision for its care. There are numerous small-scale experiments in the city, undertaken by motivated individuals, philanthropic institutions, and responsible political entities.

Here, I investigate the St. Louis terrain—with its sinkholes, floods, mounds, and woodlands—and its divided socioeconomic and racial conditions to frame a reading of contemporary urban abandonment. I then critically evaluate some of the large and small strategies and endeavors at play in the city against the more coherent and context-specific approaches to water management, cultivation, and recreation found in other places. In the end, the fifth chapter posits an approach to thinking about and designing within the St. Louis context specifically and resource-strapped, land-rich communities more generally. It synthesizes the various approaches and underscores the need to develop different design methods for places of abandonment. Without alternative design methodologies and forms of critical evaluation, we are stuck within a nearly singular narrative of capital accumulation, of uneven wealth production whereby success is determined by monetary gain regardless of social and environmental context. Further, we risk design being solely at the behest of fee-paying clients, and design services to be a luxury reserved for the elite. There are entwinned social and spatial consequences. As designers operating in a public realm, we need to invent mechanisms to create capacity for project delivery, means to empower communities with tools to build quality civic space. This involves a deep understanding of history, of policy, of ecology, of culture, and of design. It necessitates moving beyond the before and after drawing to understand the steps of transformation and the nonlinear notions of time endemic to understanding failure and promoting change. The goal is to break unidirectional moves toward immediate gratification and extreme excess, to curtail fast, capital-driven marches into a social and climatic abyss. A thorough interrogation of the fallow landscape offers a slow point of entry.

1

STORMWATER

350 Years of Hydrology in Philadelphia

Water and the Metropolis

Ian McHarg, the Scottish landscape architect and educator whose influential legacy can still be felt in his adopted city of Philadelphia, was a complex individual—a romantic at heart—with a penchant for dramatic words and overly rational methods to fight what he saw as indiscriminate urbanization. Early on in his career, he and his collaborators developed and tested these planning methods to study the Philadelphia area. In the late 1950s, as head of the Institute of Environmental Studies of the Graduate School of Fine Arts at the University of Pennsylvania (Penn), McHarg was principal investigator on a study of Metropolitan Open Space and Natural Process for the region.[1] In this work, he and his colleagues proposed a reversal of the planning norm. Instead of the prevailing practice considering building development first and using the real estate market to dictate the form of urbanization, McHarg and his team suggested a method where the creation of open space could drive the pattern of future growth as the city expanded to its periphery. In this strategy, open space is no longer the residual outcome of city making but the driver.

McHarg's work on the Metropolitan Open Space and Natural Process proposal was a reaction to his prior experience on the West Philadelphia study. The West Philadelphia work was conducted with Penn graduate students and directed by professors from the departments of architecture, planning, and landscape architecture. In this collaborative investigation, McHarg was struck by the utter disregard for environmental and social concerns. Despite being engaged with some of the preeminent thinkers in architecture and planning, he felt there was no consideration either for the bio-geophysical properties of land or the concerns of its existing residents.[2] It can be said that in this observation were the seeds of McHarg's ecological planning ideas, and that a dominant

Figure 8. The Basin, Passyunk
Avenue, Philadelphia, 2015.

branch of American ecological planning was born, or at least reincarnated in the West
Philadelphia landscape.

If West Philadelphia was the site of conception, then hydrological function was a defining agent. The Metropolitan Open Space and Natural Process proposal was simple.
McHarg, along with landscape architects Donald Phimister and Frank Shaw, mapped
eight constituent phenomena as a means to assess key environmental processes in the
metropolitan region: surface water, flood plains, marshes, aquifers, aquifer recharge
areas, steep slopes, forests and woodlands, and prime agricultural land. Water and the
physiographic region became the signifiers of ecological function. As McHarg explained, "a gross perception of natural process may be revealed through the selection of
water as a unifying process."[3] To inform metropolitan development decisions, McHarg
generated a rereading of the Philadelphia landscape through a hydrological lens. He
used his mapping overlays to understand the function of water in the region and from
here to recommend where development might be prohibited or constrained. Water
was brought to the forefront again and given primary agency in the structuring of the
landscape. It is the return to an old practice of water as a driver of human settlement,
a practice with a long and prominent history in Philadelphia. It is a history that takes
many forms and can be told through multiple vantages.

A Trip through the Urban Watershed

Another good way to imagine Philadelphia's hydrological history is to take a trip through the Mill Creek watershed. The creek begins as open waters in Merion Township and then runs down into Philadelphia's sewer system underground to its outlet into the Schuylkill River. Above ground, in West Philadelphia, is its residual topography, both the valley of the former creek bed and the dry depressions of the former millponds. It is a trip with many stops, all linked, of course, by a common hydrological thread. The itinerary follows a jagged line through the landscape: stopping at key moments to discover places where the Mill Creek basin is still visible. This visibility is, at times, literal (often even a surprise). Other times, it is merely implicit. Adjacent the Merion Friends Meeting House is one of the last places where Mill Creek waters can be seen, as the creek literally runs underneath the structure.[4] Near the Overbrook train station, the creek is seen by peering into the tunnel below City Avenue, very near the creek's unceremonious entrance into the Philadelphia Sewer System. The visibility can also be less literal; often the creek basin is expressed in large expanses of abandoned parcels, where the watery underground has made building difficult or even dangerous (the ground above the sewer lines has caved in more than once). The visibility is also reactionary, as advocates push for better management of the city's stormwater: small demonstration gardens and rain barrels are attached to residential downspouts dotted along the creek's route, protest by gray water.

On one long trip through the Mill Creek watershed—a graduate school tour in the early 2000s—we perched on a bright and sunny sidewalk above the Sulzberger Middle School, listening to a representative from the Philadelphia Water Department talk about promoting stewardship of the city's watersheds. A short walk away from the school's playground there is a panoramic view of the city, and I was struck by the fact that a core sample taken nearly anywhere in this view would reveal an alternating stratigraphy of pavement and water—the social and environmental landscape mixing like pollen spores in ice cores. On this particular trip through the Mill Creek watershed, we ended in the prominent bowl-shaped landscape of Clark Park, a depression created by the filled-in Mill Creek–fed pond and now integrated into the park's design. This last stop was oddly shy of the point at which the still-sewered creek flows into the Schuylkill River. Approximately one-half mile away it exits through a giant outfall pipe, a callous departure on par with its brutal Overbrook entrance. In by tunnel under a large arterial road, out by contained pipe again passing under significant road and rail infrastructure. This largely inaccessible outlet can be seen from a distance, from the Gray's Ferry Bridge in winter, much as it was in an old engraving from the 1920s, or from the new trail on the Schuylkill River's eastern edge.[5] From either view, it is aesthetically anticlimactic, to say the least.

The subject of this tour, Mill Creek, was not happenstance but rather an obvious choice driven by the work of the landscape architect and educator Anne Whiston Spirn. Spirn had left Philadelphia by the time I discovered the Mill Creek, but her thirty-year-plus obsession with increasing the legibility and care of the Mill Creek landscape has endured.[6] My graduate school tour reflected this. The tour also invoked issues central to Spirn's work as an advocate for linking the ecological and social function of landscapes, of seeing both the impact of and potential to address hydrology in abandoned urban landscapes. This advocacy is an indirect descendent of planning decisions in the late nineteenth century to set aside large tracts of land within cities. It is in turn reignited in the face of growing concerns over postwar environmental and social devastation and today by mounting fears of ecological and economic scarcity. Our current cycle is one of climate crisis whereby land use, development, and resource management practices require drastic change and quick action. In Mill Creek, this need has been evident for decades, but in other places, it has gone unseen. We have been ignorantly guilty of gross malpractice.

On the tour, I sometimes found it difficult to imagine or even comprehend a lasting dedication to such a mundane landscape. There is nothing particularly dramatic or impressive about any one of the sites along Mill Creek. What is impressive is the whole basin taken as a paradigm, as a means of exploring the manipulation of local hydrology over time. It is like a dull ache rather than a sharp pain, an old and persistent injury that flares up in foul weather. The creek is always there. On a recent visit, a giant and celebrated sinkhole in the middle of the intersection at 43rd Street and Baltimore Avenue brought this home once again.[7] In this way, the Mill Creek landscapes embody a particular yet common narrative, a story to be told through the lens of a constructed profile of water. The historical cycles are legible in the physical territory of the city. The ecological and social layers of the city cannot be separated. In other words, this is an intertwined tale of poverty and potential, one played out through the lenses of water, of design, of property, of time.

Why Water? Why Philadelphia?

Abandoned and residual lands have hydrological intrigue more often than not. Just look at a map of the parcels identified as vacant and the urban topography and waterways. Water is not just a part of the development history; it is part of the present transformation, and it determines the future. Hydrology and urbanization are intertwined, and in the cases of early urbanized centers in North America such as Philadelphia, water is an ecological, social, economic, and political foundation for the city. The use of water in the city has changed with time, but the interdependence of city and water is a constant. The history of urbanization, in Philadelphia and elsewhere, can be told through the history of the human control of water. Water is a resource, a utility, as well as a means of transport, a means of power, a line of waste conveyance, a drainage system, a recreational amenity, and a form of identity.

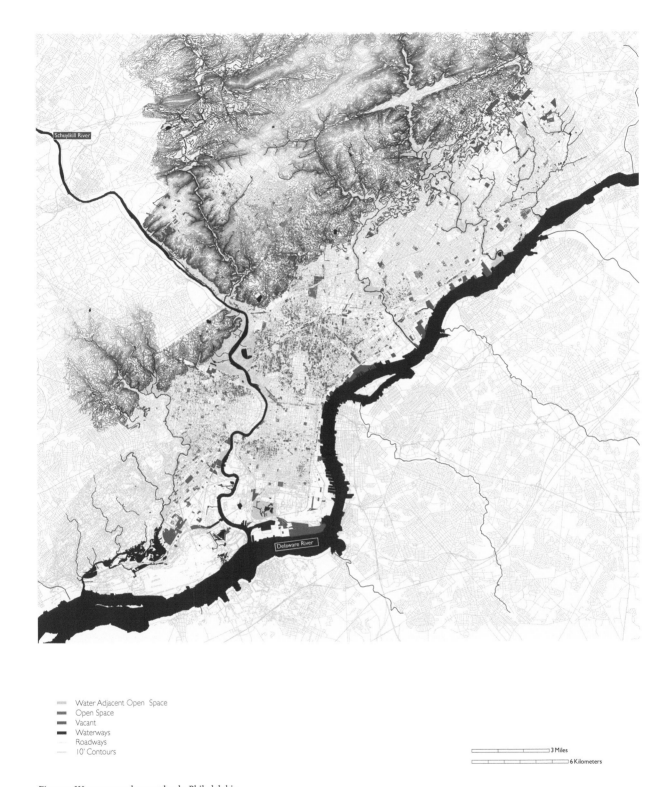

Schuylkill River

Delaware River

Water Adjacent Open Space
Open Space
Vacant
Waterways
Roadways
10' Contours

3 Miles

6 Kilometers

Figure 9. Waterways and vacant lands, Philadelphia.

This history drives the overall condition of the city, from its original location and orientation to its differential development over time. Property is affected by water, and the hydrological characteristics of a given terrain are a core part of its societal and environmental valuation. As a result, the residual landscapes of the city often share common hydrological parameters. For example, on lowlands in the city's interior, topographic and soil conditions make development prone to subsidence and flooding. On bank lands, the proximity to a water source attracts industry, and, subsequently, the abandonment of industry leaves polluted and difficult-to-integrate landscapes. Lastly, on infrastructural lands, the proximity to water treatment and sewerage conveyance systems (with their attendant fumes) has obvious negative effects on communities and development. In one way or another, water makes the land what it is, in the eyes of the city and its citizens, even if that relationship is not immediately obvious.

As cities everywhere strive to address the pressures of increasingly impermeable landscapes, frequent storm events, flooding, changing climatic conditions, and development, the abandoned and residual parcels have become places to investigate a different hydrological role for the future.[8] The once low-lying and buffer landscapes return to the center of the hydrological debate. Philadelphia looks again to its riverine landscape, its tributary creeks, its endemic basins, its pervasive parklands, and its fallow landscapes as a means to increase watershed function and stormwater storage capacity.[9]

Philadelphia has long been a hydrological innovator, from claiming one of the first municipal water supply systems in the United States, to creating parkland buffers that attempt to protect its watershed, to devoting its own waters to supply its population, to reinvesting in its landscape to address water quality issues, to considering the marriage of abandoned property and stormwater management.[10] The city provides an excellent case to investigate the shared relationships between hydrology and geography, between fallow lands and polluted waters, between poverty and promise. Herein, the river, the creek, the sewer, the marsh, and the basin form a common urban landscape, one of interrelated continuous flows, interrupted courses, disconnected basins, and scattered points. Again, the map shows the interrelation of stream and sewer, an environmental disaster born out of an engineering logic. Let's follow the history.

Philadelphia's Hydrological Geography: The Inputs

The city of Philadelphia's story is a riverine one, beginning with the Lenni Lenape, who lived seasonally in bankside encampments. Their displacement through colonial war and disease began with the early European cultivators and continued with William Penn's landing on the North Delaware riverfront in 1682. Penn, with his surveyor Thomas Holme and others, envisioned a garden city. The colonial settlement was bracketed between the Delaware and Schuylkill Rivers. Early maps and city views were drawn from the perspective of the Delaware, and these views show intense activity at

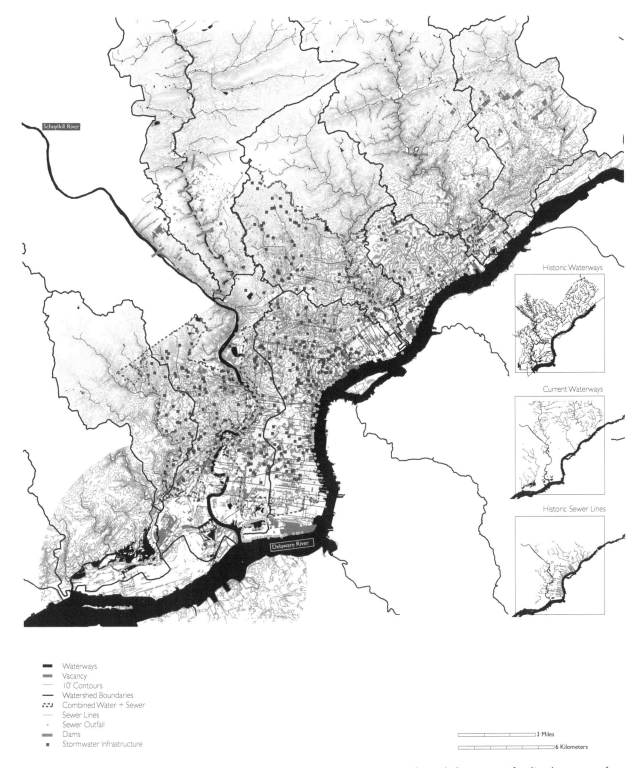

Schuylkill River

Delaware River

Historic Waterways

Current Waterways

Historic Sewer Lines

■ Waterways
▬ Vacancy
  10' Contours
▬ Watershed Boundaries
▬▬▬ Combined Water + Sewer
  Sewer Lines
· Sewer Outfall
▬ Dams
■ Stormwater Infrastructure

3 Miles

6 Kilometers

Figure 10. Water management, Philadelphia, showing rivers, streams, sewers, stormwater capture, and watersheds as a means of reading the structure of the city.

the river's edge, activity that dissipates toward the horizon, denoting the expanding city footprint. The boats that populate the foreground drive the hardening of the river's edge, a measure of the transformation brought by transport, trade, and industry.

Eventually, Philadelphia begins to turn its back on its dirty rivers, like many other East Coast cities.[11] But unlike New York and Boston, when Philadelphia faced a public health crisis attributed to well water contamination in the late 1700s and subsequent concerns of drinking water quality and supply in the 1800s, city officials invested in their local rivers. It was not a one-time question but an on-going debate: whether to continue to use the rivers as a water source or to look to the surroundings for a cleaner supply. The discussion first surfaced in 1865, when the city investigated alternative sources for its drinking water. Subsequently, a 1924 report detailed an aqueduct system to bring water from Upper Lehigh and Delaware Watersheds, a costly endeavor that was ultimately rejected.[12] The last proposal to look elsewhere for clean water dates from 1947, when the city conclusively opted for chemical treatment to address the sewage overflows into the Schuylkill and Delaware Rivers. Through intercepting canals and treatment plants, the city manages its hydrological inputs and outputs, drawing clean water upstream and expulsing overflow downstream.

What this means is that the water supply infrastructure is not pushed outward into the cleaner and less polluted environs, the standard solution elsewhere. Instead, the city commits to providing public drinking water for its citizens, using its own Schuylkill River. By the mid-1800s, cast iron pipes delivered water throughout the city from the elaborate neoclassical pumping station, the Fairmount Water Works, built at a high point on the riverbank, just over 1.5 miles from City Hall. In addition to this hard infrastructure, the cleanliness of the water is addressed through the management of the city's non-aqueous landscape. In an early example of green infrastructural planning, the lands adjacent to the Schuylkill River, on both banks, were set aside as parkland beginning in 1844. This is a notable foreshadowing of the city's contemporary initiatives to manage its watersheds through surface treatments.

The city appropriated numerous farms, small industries, and private lots through an Assembly Act in 1868 to protect the quality of its water source. The 9,200-acre Fairmount Park provides a wide buffer for the valuable river. Though the plan initially failed to improve water quality—and the river suffered from pollution—this is still an early and prototypical beginning to continuous investment in improving the city's hydrological system through both land and watershed management. The investment created one of the largest municipal park systems while simultaneously recognizing the interrelationship between public health, development, and water. If the two rivers play the leading roles in this story, the tributaries and adjacent lands—especially those that hold water as reservoirs or absorb water through permeable ground materials—are the underrecognized support cast.

Philadelphia's Hydrological Geography: The Outputs

As Philadelphia was deciding to continue its practice of using river water as drinking water, the city was also developing a system of storm and wastewater conveyance to combat the ill effects of unsanitized city life. The city began to convert its small streambeds into an elaborate network of constructed sewer lines to address health and drainage issues across the city (see figure 10). Starting in the 1850s, city engineers used the city's existing drainage lines and basins to construct infrastructure to support its growing populations. By the 1880s, drainage plans existed, and by 1895, the city had already constructed numerous sewer lines. The sewer lines took two forms, as interceptors designed to move waste further downstream to protect drinking water supplies or as combined pipes to collect storm and sewer water from populated areas and translocate the problematic waters, again downstream from its citizenry, albeit into the same river system. In some areas, with a longer history of settlement, the giant pipes were inserted below existing streets. In others, creek beds were filled, twenty-foot-diameter pipes constructed, and roadways added atop the previous valley condition.

A photograph of the Mill Creek sewer construction is a well-known and often reproduced example used to illustrate the construction of nineteenth-century sewer systems across the United States.[13] In the photograph, the creek bed is visible, workmen give scale to the infrastructure, on-looking children demonstrate the contemporary intrigue of such a monstrous work, and adjacent buildings show the push of the city, quickly meeting the edge of the construction, driving its very completion. The Mill Creek sewer is a several-mile-long system that runs from the Overbrook neighborhood on the city's border to the Schuylkill River, making maze-like turns underneath the road infrastructure. It took thirty years to complete, beginning in 1869 and ending around 1900. The sewer is still active; its presence is felt periodically through roadway collapses and basement flooding.[14] The system is not invisible, but rather is reflected in the differential morphology of buildings and blocks on the surface, demonstrating the power of water to shape this urban section—both for the advancement and the retreat of the city it supports.

Nineteenth-century engineers were given the reigns to transform the city, to build giant infrastructures designed to bring health and order to the city. This steers interest from the two-dimensional layout of streets and properties alone to the three-dimensional thickness of the city, to the support systems that lie beneath the surface. These support systems do heavy lifting, in every sense, to support the city above. Once the sewer systems were set in place, the valleys were filled—in the case of parts of Mill Creek with thirty feet of fill—to create a navigable road network and a relatively flat ground for building.

From Marsh to Sewer to Sewer and Marsh: Historical Cycles

In many ways, the transformation of the city is a hydrological and topographical story, played out through cartographic representation. The earliest known maps of the Philadelphia area were associated with the creation of the Pennsylvania Colony. Produced by the surveyor Thomas Holme, they were a means to document the territory, understand its ownership patterns, and plan its future development. The drawings were almost diagrammatic and focused on the ideal street grid as well as its juxtaposition with the other property delineations, expropriated lands, and the loose indication of unclaimed territory. The 1687 map was concerned with property—and by association, the relationship of *improved* land and the river systems supporting it.[15] Thus, the rivers are dominant in the map, with heavy engraved lines defining their banks, lighter lines representing their watery surfaces. They also drive the patterning of the land, with older properties extending perpendicularly from their banks and the surnames of the owners oriented thusly on the map itself. The most watery, marshy lands are also indicated, both through the absence of human improvement and a drawing hachure derived from that used to describe the water, one that abruptly ends at the edge of the claimed territory. The marshlands are visible, but the lines of property and the blank spaces that indicate the city to come already mask their extents. The grid gives way to the liberty lands, or semi-urban lands, that mediate between the formal means devised to control the territory and the preexisting agricultural estates beyond. Penn was keen to include free-form property and even commonly held lands in his early endeavors, but the commons disappeared by the mid-1680s in favor of more clearly articulated and controlled measures of land acquisition.[16]

In the early history of Philadelphia, and its maps, the rivers remain a strong constant. In a remarkable 1778 military map from publisher Peter Force's collection, the city is circumscribed by water, an island under development, crisscrossed by the diagonal ridge-line routes of its First Nation inhabitants and the small tributaries of the Schuylkill and Delaware.[17] Several creeks are visible, including the previously mentioned Mill Creek and the soon to be discussed Cohocksink Creek located just northeast of Center City. The city itself is a set of bourgeoning reddish-color blocks on the map—the classic color for urban development—shown with suburban property owners and military activities. As Philadelphia advances, the rivers are tamed representationally and, while always present, become lost amid the rapid rail, road, and building networks. By 1828, guidebooks show the plan of the city of Philadelphia to include the rivers and even some marshlands adjacent to the Schuylkill, but the emphasis is on the expanding blocks and built fabric. The topography and hydrology are visually eclipsed by the heavy streets and are only visible where road infrastructure is absent. As the new ground is built, the underlying ground conditions are erased from the map.

This brings us back to McHarg and his Metropolitan Open Space from Natural

Process project maps. Here McHarg and his team reacted strongly to this trend of overplaying roads and underplaying rivers.[18] While McHarg was arguably anti-urban in his motivation—a chapter on cities in his seminal text *Design with Nature* is called "The Plight"—he also embraced the urban condition as part of his work and even as the impetus behind his methodology. His maps were polemical overlays, yielding a fundamentally different representation of the urban condition. Instead of differentiating the city from its periphery, McHarg used his ecological inventories to describe the entire terrain, including the metropolis. His maps focus on the city as a biome, a physiographic region, and a river basin (see figure 11 with a McHarg map overlaid with contemporary fallowness). The typical interrelated layers (climate, geology, hydrology, soils, vegetation, and wildlife) are pulled out, while the layers of direct human occupation (transportation infrastructure, buildings, and boundaries) practically disappear. The argument, as demonstrated by the cartographic technique, was reactionary, yet effective.

If in the years prior the city had been described primarily as an urban plan, as a road map, as a type of figure-ground of built and unbuilt, McHarg's 1969 map positioned the city in a larger hydrological and vegetative network (again see the underlay in figure 11). If the previous maps underplayed the city's geological base, McHarg underrepresented the built fabric. His map, with its few major routes in grey and its full representation of the water system, recalls the hierarchy of maps from the late 1700s. In McHarg's case, however, it is not that the city is yet to be developed, but rather that it has been supplanted. His point was clear. The city is a place of previously underrepresented and often-maligned rivers and greenways, entities McHarg both championed and understood as co-opted by the forces of urban development. "Can you find the river that first made the city?" McHarg asked in a Wordsworthian tone. "Look behind the unkempt history, across the grassy railroad tracks and you will find the rotting piers and there is the great river, scummy and brown, wastes and sewage bobbing easily up and down with the tide, endlessly renewed."[19]

The way that rivers are remembered and the way that they are as a result considered in the present, both follow particular trends and respond to specific local geology and culture. The McHargian system with its extensive inventories, maps, and matrices—created in the same predetermined order—is universal rather than responsive to geographical conditions. Its application to the Philadelphia region produces a revolutionary and rhetorically anti-architectural reading of the city, yet the methodology is not tuned to the different sociological, cultural, political, or economic conditions of an urban environment. The same layers are used everywhere, regardless of context, implying false neutrality to the method as well as universality to the place of study.

Anne Whiston Spirn, a student and collaborator of McHarg's, embraced the challenge of adapting the McHargian methodology to the urban condition. *The Granite Garden* (1985) is a look at the relationship between cities and natural systems. Her

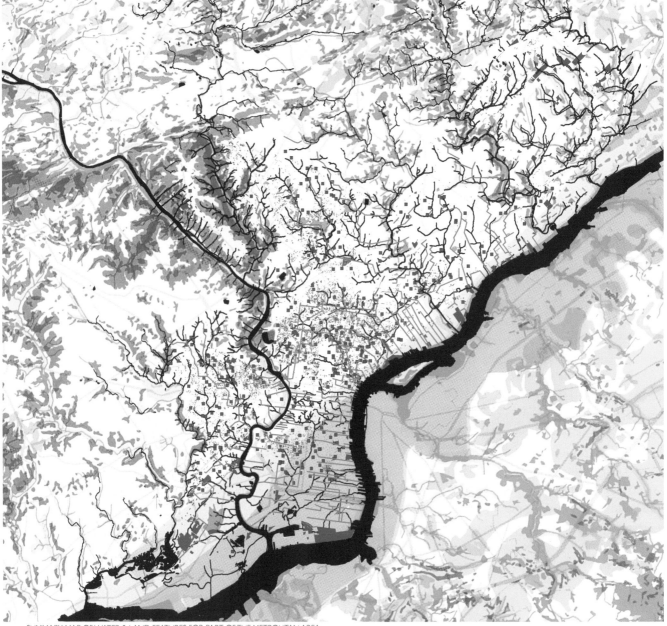

SUMMARY MAP OF WATER & LAND FEATURES FOR PART OF THE METROLITAN AREA

PHENOMENA	Surface water and riparian lands	Marshes	50-year floodplains	Aquifers	Aquifer recharge areas	Prime agricultural lands	Steep lands	Forests and woodlands
RECOMMENDED LAND USES	Ports, harbors, marinas, water-treatment plants, water-related industry, open space for institutional and housing use, agriculture, forestry and recreation.	Recreation.	Ports, harbors, barinas, water-treatment plants, water-related and water-suing industry, agriculture, forestry, recreation, institutional open space, open space for housing.	Agriculture, forestry, recreation, industries athat do not produce toxic or offensive effluents. All land uses within limits set by peroclation.	As aquifers.	Agriculture, forestry, recreation, open space for instituions, housing at 1 house per 25 acres.	Forestry, recreation, housing at maximum density of 1 house per 3 acres, where wooded.	Forestry, recreation, housing at densities not highter than 1 house per acre.

■ Waterways
— Historic Sewer
■ Vacant
▪ Stormwater Infrastructure

Adapted from Ian McHarg, Design with Nature, p. 63

⊏⊐⊏⊐⊏⊐⊐ 3 Miles
⊏⊐⊏⊐⊏⊐⊐ 6 Kilometers

design advocacy work in Philadelphia and Boston fights both social disinvestment and environmental degradation in the city. In both instances, a consideration of urban hydrology underlies Spirn's work. She exposes the relationships between water systems and cities and for decades has addressed the opportunities for coupling water management and design of the public realm. Regarding the abandoned lands in Mill Creek in West Philadelphia, she has articulated a fundamental correlation: "vacant land is concentrated in former floodplains, bogs, and marshes that were sewered and filled in the nineteenth century."[20] With this fundamental correlation comes a fundamental opportunity: to claim this land as a watery land and to use it to absorb and cleanse storm water and combat flooding.

Stormy Waters

The Philadelphia Water Department (PWD), which began its water service in 1801, is primarily charged with purveying high-quality clean drinking water to the city, a mission that, in a very practical way, brings with it the added responsibility of environmental stewardship.[21] In recent years, Howard Neukrug, a past engineer, consultant, and commissioner of the agency, and his colleagues embraced this charge with innovative environmental thinking and planning. As a revenue-generating entity and one charged with meeting EPA-mandated levels of water quality, the Water Department has managed to pursue and promote a future urban vision for the city, a task that is often left to planning and redevelopment authorities.[22] In Philadelphia, water drives the agenda. And advocacy efforts surrounding water target both the underground network—the sewered streamsheds—and the open surface lands.

Neukrug began his PWD career in drinking water treatment in 1978. He followed as the agency's first director of the PWD Office of Watersheds and then served as commissioner of the department from 2011 to 2016. Through his work in the Office of Watersheds, and subsequently as the head of the department, Neukrug was at the forefront of developing an actionable plan to transform the city. His approach was progressive yet pragmatically incremental, by both methodically and ambitiously tackling its stormwater mandate. As part of the clean water regulations, cities are required to manage the stormwater output and to prevent polluted runoff from overflowing into waterways.

In Philadelphia, the stormwater management plan, *Green City, Clean Waters,* is part of the larger *GreenPlan Philadelphia,* initiated by former mayor Michael Nutter and prepared by Wallace Roberts & Todd, a collaborative practice of city and regional planners, urban designers, landscape architects, and architects, and successor to Wallace, McHarg, Roberts, and Todd.[23] The strategy behind the work is this: "many modest undertakings are combined to produce a large-scale transformation."[24] The result is a scatter, a distributed system that, when scale is achieved, will read across the city as a

Figure 11. Contemporary water management superimposed on a McHarg overlay map, Philadelphia.

common network, common both as commonplace and mundane and as a collective effort to manage the shared resources of storm, surface, and groundwater. The interventions are modest and standard. The potential lies in the aggregation. The efforts are top-down, using federal dollars and city administrators, but they rely on constituent participation. The desire is to foster activity as a measurement of success, and no activity is too small to register. An early annual report boasted the engagement of 9,300 Philadelphians in the hydrological crusade, a fact listed aside a picture of a knitted PWD tree sleeve, a clear sign that agency is fostering all types of publicity and activity. The department also supports what is known as "drainspotting"—the act of celebrating drains with an art or graffiti act. The message from the water department is that this project is current, visual, and, most importantly, open to all.

Green City, Clean Waters has proved itself feasible in various different ways. It has funding mechanisms in place, implementation underway, and a strategy of insertion with little to no demolition beyond the selected sites. The twenty-five-year, $2 billion stormwater management plan was officially signed in June 2011. Since then the "Big Green Map" of projects is being continually updated.[25] By early 2015, the map showed 362 stormwater tree trenches, 72 stormwater planters, 42 stormwater bump outs, 98 rain gardens, 10 stormwater basins, 141 infiltration/storage trenches, 35 porous paving projects, 21 swales, 2 stormwater wetlands, 33 downspout planters (too small for the map), and 31 other projects. Six months later, the map showed over 120 additional projects, with a dramatic increase in tree trenches. By 2019, the projects were so numerous that they were solely delineated by realm: public projects on streets, private regulation projects, private retrofit projects, and stormwater grants. At the scale of the city, the cartographic icons are large enough to cover the entire map. This is, of course, deceptive. For example, tree trench has a large icon but is a very small entity in a giant city, on the order of 100 square feet (or approximately 9 square meters)[26] in 140 square miles (or approximately 360 square kilometers). But the ethos is clear: the effort does not rest on any individual effort, *and* no effort is too small to be noted (see figure 12 for a project types and distribution).

The system is what matters. An aggregation of common land has the capacity to address excess water. Again, no square footage is considered too small to consider. If water can be collected, it should be. The tiny footprint has value, and the collective constellation marks a turning point for the city, one where water surfaces and marks the civic realm. Thus, the projects tend toward the mundane, with a few exceptions, including Penn Park and the Pennsylvania Energy Company green roof. These projects have design presence, pointing to the need for aesthetic concerns to enter the technological mindset.[27] Overwhelmingly, the everyday is celebrated, with an exciting momentum. A green roof on a bus shelter is remarkable, both for the goal to seize an opportunity on any type of space and for the scalar implications.[28] There are over three hundred bus shelters in the city.[29] Barrels attach to houses, trenches to trees, swales to streets. It is

Figure 12. Stormwater infrastructure, Philadelphia, 2015: a snapshot of the Philadelphia Water Department installations by type and location.

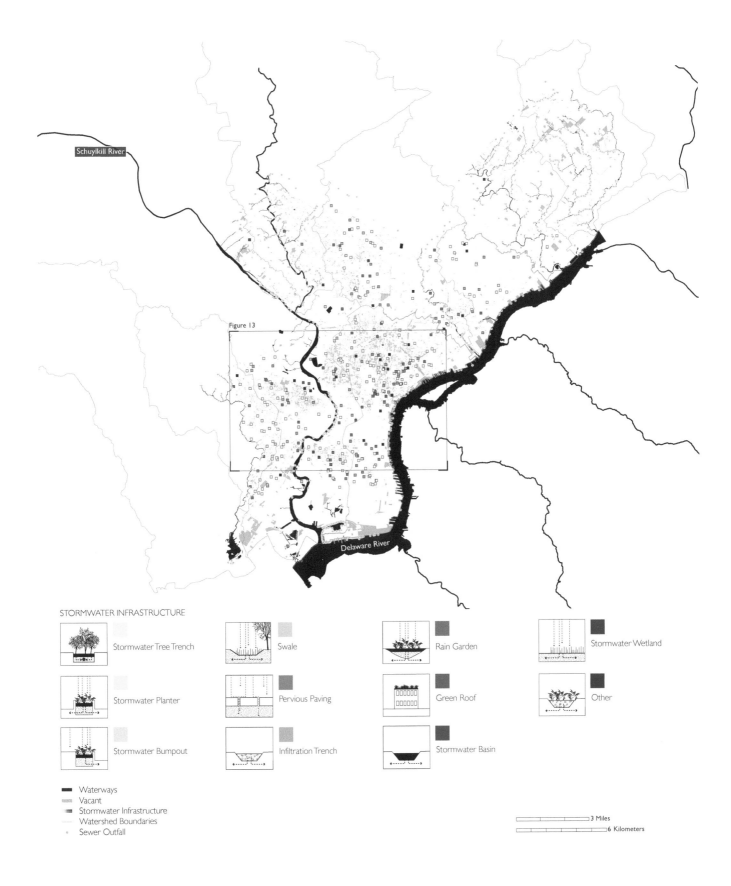

Schuylkill River

Figure 13

Delaware River

STORMWATER INFRASTRUCTURE

Stormwater Tree Trench

Swale

Rain Garden

Stormwater Wetland

Stormwater Planter

Pervious Paving

Green Roof

Other

Stormwater Bumpout

Infiltration Trench

Stormwater Basin

▬ Waterways
▨ Vacant
▬ Stormwater Infrastructure
— Watershed Boundaries
• Sewer Outfall

3 Miles

6 Kilometers

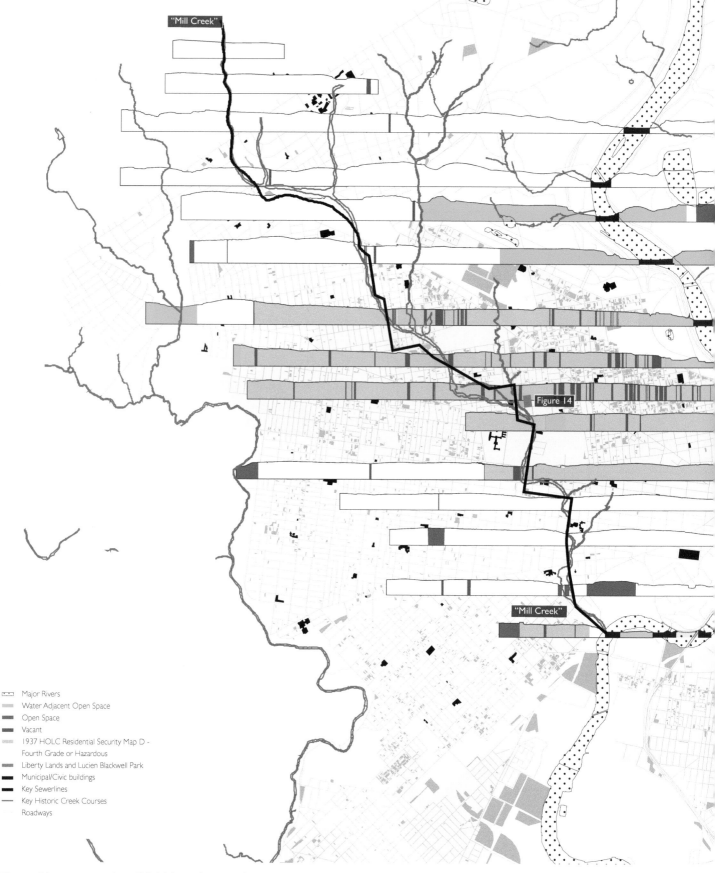

"Mill Creek"

Figure 14

"Mill Creek"

"Mill Creek"

Major Rivers
Water Adjacent Open Space
Open Space
Vacant
1937 HOLC Residential Security Map D -
Fourth Grade or Hazardous
Liberty Lands and Lucien Blackwell Park
Municipal/Civic buildings
Key Sewerlines
Key Historic Creek Courses
Roadways

Figure 13. Itinerant cross-sections, Philadelphia, with topography, redlining, sewers, and infiltration shown.

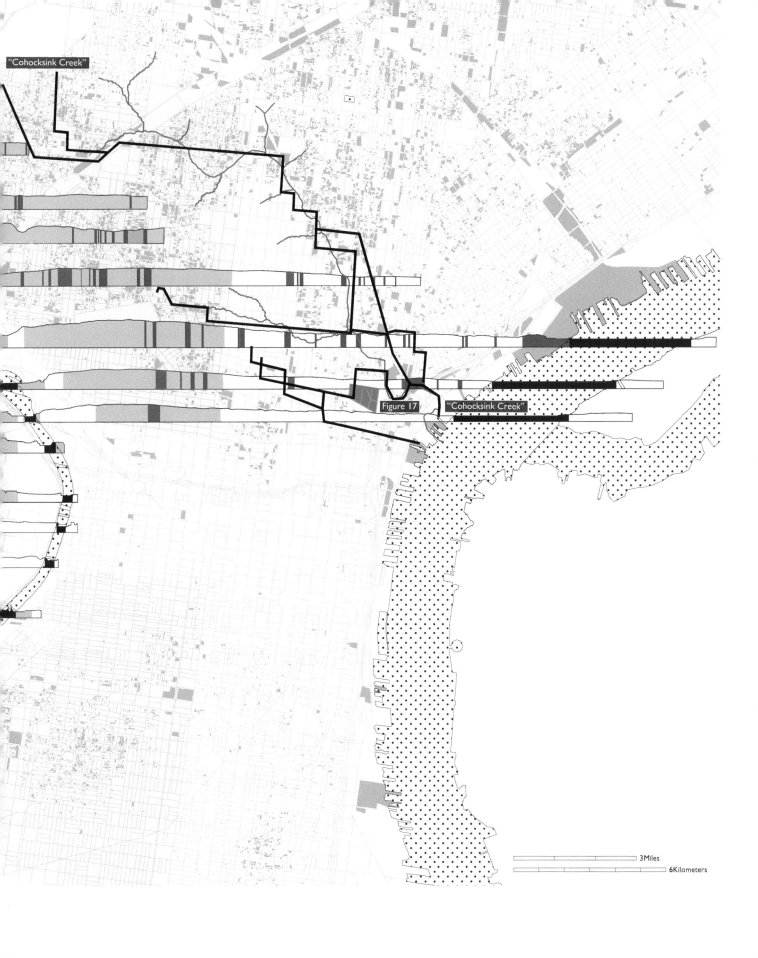

"Cohocksink Creek"

Figure 17   "Cohocksink Creek"

3 Miles
6 Kilometers

the opportunistic, even parasitic quality and the sheer number that become impressive: nearly a thousand installations in four years, and counting.

Philadelphia's stormwater ambition, if it can be called that, is remarkable. The city is committed to meeting mandated storage levels through a creative combination of modest interventions. In 2011, the National Resources Defense Council gave Philadelphia the highest emerald rating for its green stormwater initiatives, praising its long-term planning, its retention standards, and its impervious surface reduction, among other qualities.[30] Philadelphia has become a leader in the transition from gray to green infrastructure, leveraging its position through rich publicity campaigns and political momentum. (Sustainability was central to former Mayor Nutter's 2007 campaign platform, and his deputy mayor for economic development was an architect.) The program works because the city's leadership is invested in all ways, including politically. All eyes are on Philadelphia placing greater pressure on the quality of the projects to be exemplary—both as hydrological infrastructure and as designed civic space.

This is the same cry Spirn issued over thirty years ago in the *Granite Garden*:

> *In the next decade [1990s], the dilapidated, outmoded water supply, wastewater treatment, and storm drainage systems in many older American cities will have to be overhauled. This will entail the expenditure of billions of dollars and considerable upheaval in dense urban centers. Short-term expediency must not prevail; the opportunities for redesign must be seized.*[31]

To some extent, this is happening in places like Philadelphia, where a conscious decision is made to foreground rather than bury the hydrological agenda, where the co-benefits of water projects are being considered, and where a social agenda is being levied.[32] The projects are often coupled with educational and cultural institutions. In other places, the coupling of systems is slower, and pavement is removed and replaced readily as underground tunnel construction wages onward.[33] But in comparison to infrastructural projects of recent years, the conversation is reopening as a frugal reincarnation of past infrastructural promise, when parks and sanitary improvements align, when civic space and water storage collide. Past efforts were grandiose, as expressions of human engineering capacity, while present efforts rely on the incremental, the opportunistic, and the crowd-sourced to tackle the large-scale hydrological issues. Proliferation becomes a means to adapt to a given urban condition while reshaping its hydrological footprint. And the opportunistic, proliferated green and blue lands form what is, in essence, a distributed common ground for the city.

The Philadelphia water story can be writ large. Water begins as foundational resource, shifts to being a presumed utility, and winds up a shared concern. It has been tamed, buried, polluted, unearthed, cleaned, stored, and, most recently, released. In terms of the urban cycles, it has registration—that is, the infrastructural changes are responsive to economic and environmental exigencies and vice versa. The system has been modified incrementally. Policy has shaped it. The results have geographic ramifications. The watercourses have been contained and squeezed to fit within the urban fabric. The pipes have followed the lowlands, as an efficient engineering response to directing water. The filtration plants have been built on cheap lands that meet elevation and location requirements—at high points and close to outlets. Watersheds and water supplies have been protected, when not superseded by industry, encased in parklands like the expansive Fairmount Park.

While these water-related decisions have been incremental, and driven by the requirements of the water systems, the physical footprint of these changes points toward both ecological potential and social impoverishment. Somehow, in each story of institutional disenfranchisement, there is always a stream. Take the recent, if extreme, example of Ferguson, Missouri,[34] and a trip on Google maps to the major landmarks: starting from the Ferguson convenience store, where Michael Brown is said to have shoplifted, across from Dollar Store, near rent-to-own cars and furniture for less, and then take a right before the fenced-off creek, a right at the boarded-up restaurant, down Canfield Road to where Brown was shot.[35] Hydrology is there, through the topographic low points and the fenced-off creek, a hidden potential character in the story. The hills and valleys still exist, and the social occupation plays out in this rolling terrain. Draw sections across the map, and the intersections become clear. This is the urban circumstance.

Constructed Lines of Water: Poverty and Promise

Philadelphia is still known as a city between two rivers—the Delaware and the Schuylkill—but the myriad of small streams and basins in between those big rivers have faded from the collective memory. What happened to them? The answers vary. Some were modified with dams and races to power early industry. Some were collectors of industrial effluent. Some were graded and converted to sewer to meet the needs of the growing city. In general, the hydrological profile of both the visible rivers and the hidden streams is controlled and hardened, polluted and degraded. Areas of the greatest violations often correspond to areas of greatest political, economic, and ecological vulnerability, places where rich resources meet poor populations, an example of how the sociological and the environmental cities overlap.

Back again to Mill Creek—that underground piped and sewered stream that is indirectly evident on the surface *and* in its eponymous neighborhood—which is a good example of overlapping ecological and economic conditions. The water may be buried, but its presence is reflected in the market value of land, the aggregation of unoccupied parcels, the propensity for flooding, or even the catastrophic opening of the ground. Spirn and her colleagues pursue these relationships, describing the rich narrative of the creek and its neighborhood as ecological and social bottomlands where low-lying properties are marked by flooded basements, subsidence, and disinvestment.[36]

The Mill Creek neighborhood was developed largely in the late nineteenth century as an early streetcar suburb for the expanding city, located along the extension of Market Street, one of Penn's original grid lines and the divider between the northern and southern halves of Philadelphia. Two of Philadelphia's eighteen diagonal streets cross the neighborhood.[37] Formerly trails along ridge and valley lines and turnpikes connecting cities, the diagonal streets were incorporated into the city, creating triangular anomalies to the overarching urban grid. The grid is morphed three-dimensionally as well, reflecting the undulating topography and soggy ground beneath it.

Mill Creek is a classic example of a soggy and devalued urban landscape—one filled with substandard soils, one given substandard loan ratings, one deemed unsafe both physically and socially, one cleared, one renewed, one cleared again, and one, ultimately, full of available land where land speculators are aggressively targeting these parcels and the homes of long-time residents. Spirn notes the intersecting harmful flows of water and capital, past and present. In the 1930s, the US Congress created the Home Owners' Loan Corporation (HOLC), an entity capable of granting mortgages to promote home ownership as a means of generating economic stability. Armed with this powerful economic tool, the HOLC was capable of also inequitably distributing loans, engaging in racist and classist practices that privileged some neighborhoods (homogeneous, real estate "hot spots" with white, non-Italian, non-Jewish occupants) over others ("obsolescent" with barriers to real estate sales and an "infiltration of a lower grade population"). Instead of investing in the housing stock, services, and transportation, the HOLC and its subsidiaries restricted loans and made loan collection decisions based on their neighborhood assessments. They created residential security maps, coloring areas with "hazardous" real estate conditions red, in a practice known as "redlining." The 1936 and 1937 maps of Philadelphia are predominantly red, including the Mill Creek neighborhood. On the survey sheet, the local lender described the Mill Creek area as "rolling" terrain that, despite its high levels of occupancy and good transportation, was a poor sales market with high levels of property obsolescence and a substantial Italian and African American population.[38] Overall real estate market desirability was trending "downward."

The economic redlining and subsequent disinvestment are, of course, coupled with the poor soil and building conditions in the Mill Creek drainage basin. Forced abandonment in the lowlands was driven by the hydrological and edaphic characteristics of the ground, plus the economic market devaluation that plagued the entire terrain. The most dramatic evacuation occurred after a sewer cave-in on Funston Street in 1961, when four buildings were destroyed and 111 were condemned and demolished.[39] This followed other events in the 1940s and early 1950s that result in other demolitions.[40] The cave-ins, while alarming, did not deter the city from commencing a project to

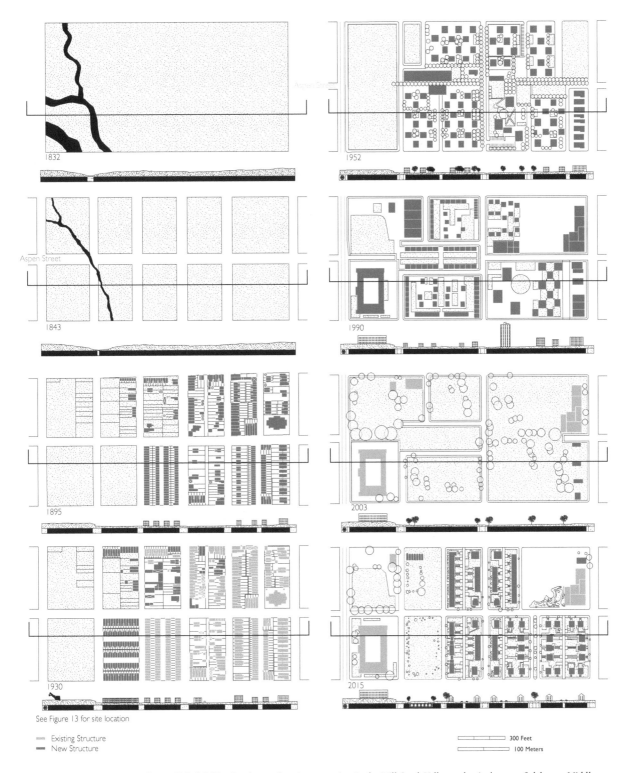

See Figure 13 for site location

1832

1843

1895

1930

Aspen Street

1952

1990

2003

2015

300 Feet
100 Meters

Figure 14. 4400 to 4800 Aspen Street, Philadelphia: site plans and sections over time in the Mill Creek Valley, at the site between Sulzberger Middle School and the Lucien Blackwell Homes and Park.

build public housing adjacent to the buried creek.[41] After securing urban renewal funds, the Mill Creek site was selected in 1948, and the architect Louis Kahn hired to produce the design.[42]

Dan Kiley was the landscape architect, and Cornelia Hahn Oberlander, the well-respected Canadian landscape architect, worked on the project early in her career. Kiley did the overall planning, and Oberlander produced detailed designs for the first phase of the project. Deeply committed to social engagement and democratic ideals, Oberlander ensured that each courtyard had a well-balanced landscape: lawn, hedge, understory, and canopy trees. In the end, funds were not made available to execute the details, resulting in a banal landscape of lawn and tree, but the overall planning scheme was respected. The lands directly above the sewer were left free of buildings, but low- and high-rise structures occupied the floodplain. The urban renewal program was attracted to the same set of parameters that detract the private lenders: inexpensive, available land and disenfranchised residents. The buried creek carved a path for future projects, opening expanses in the city for building and unbuilding.

The Mill Creek Apartments from the 1950s and 1960s were demolished in 2002 and were replaced by the suburban-style, low-rise Lucien Blackwell Homes, named for an African American politician from West Philadelphia. The plan and section drawings in figure 14 chart the transformation on the blocks inclusive of and between Sulzberger Middle School and the Lucien Blackwell Homes. Some land has been freed and converted to parkland, but overall, the move to reconstruct housing was as if to say that the roots of abandonment were in name and style rather than endemic, despite evidence and publications to the contrary. Spirn's efforts to make the landscape legible and respected went largely unheeded—at least temporarily. More than a decade has passed, and the intense focus on stormwater management brings new attention to the landscapes like the Mill Creek bottomlands. These landscapes exist across the city as liberated grounds awaiting adoption: arrested swathes of green, potential tracts to be embedded within the city's larger water management plans.

Watery Commons

When Howard Neukrug moved into his role as PWD commissioner, he hired a landscape architect to be his chief of staff. Her name was Mami Hara, and in a largely engineer-dominated agency, Neukrug sent a clear message: design of the public realm is a fundamental component of the work of the water department.[43] To properly execute a plan to manage water on the surface of the city is to properly design urban civic space.

In the past forty years, the waters in the city have again surfaced, conceptually and literally, and this common resource is again manifest. The river that made the city, as McHarg puts it, is coming back. And it's not just the river; it's the streams and lakes, the ponds for retention and detention, the wet marshes, pools, fountains, barrels, and cisterns.[44] Water has always been at service to the city, but this service is becoming less hidden. This is true in Philadelphia and elsewhere. Rivers and streams are being unearthed, or even moved as in the case of Providence, Rhode Island, which reconfigured its downtown in the late 1980s and early 1990s with an ambitious river relocation project. The confluence of the Moshassuck and Woonasquatucket Rivers was moved out from under a post office, and the Providence River was uncovered downstream creating an uninspired yet visible and canoe-able water body for the deprived city, one celebrated with more than two hundred bonfires.[45] This is just one example. Old, polluted waters are being tackled and engaged. Discarded by industry, they return to civic duty. Rivers course through downtowns, lined with promenades and plazas; lakefronts attract recreation and wildlife; and plazas collect and convey stormwater—most convincingly in Rotterdam, where water squares are being designed to function both as dry and wet basins for people and water.[46] Cities and regions are transforming. Take the Lignite-mining region of Lusatia, Germany, where an International Building Exposition was leveraged to transform the scarred landscape into a place of marshes, marinas, and beaches. The lignite fields are filled to form an interconnected web of ten lakes, designed to promote tourism to the region. From the quotidian to the spectacular, the hydrological landscape is emerging on fallow lands.

It is curious to note that in the rights of the traditional British Commons—pasture, pannage, piscary, turbary, estovers—the rights related to the acquisition of clean water and the disposal of excess storm and dirty waters are missing.[47] Yet the management of water rights figures prominently in the story of the commons, especially as that story merges with issues of environmental stewardship of the basic, common resources of air, water, and land. Political economist Elinor Ostrum's *Governing the Commons* demonstrates the great potential for common property resources, rather than the great unpotential described by ecologist Garret Hardin.[48] Ostrum shows numerous historical examples of successful collective use of water. Cases include the huertas in Spain, the Zanjera irrigation communities in the Philippines, and the groundwater basins in California. These are places where water is a commonly managed resource rather than a distributed utility or a privatized good.

With hydrological resource and management systems in mind, the common can be understood in different ways—as a public good, for example, or as a shared physical space. These two readings come together in the surficial management of stormwater, where the collective efforts are visible within the city and where the infrastructural investments are structured around the shared management of resources and presented as an urban vision. It is true that this civic realm is governed by a set of hydrological efficiency parameters, and, too often, its potential is presented as a generic greenwash over the aging city. In the renderings of the future Philadelphia, a green roof panacea proliferates, entering the public realm, for example, as a proposed park-like system over the sunken Vine Street Expressway. The image vaguely recalls Boston's Back Bay

Fens, a landscape driven by the needs of hydrological infrastructure of an expanding nineteenth-century city, now hemmed in by a busy and complicated traffic pattern. The center city, too, as a vibrant and prosperous part of Philadelphia, is greenwashed, given a tone rather than a design, a tone that allegedly produces an improved lifestyle. Instead of flooding and pollution, there is fishing and ambling along the river against the skyline backdrop. These promotional images fall short of Spirn's decree, both for their lack of design aspiration and their societal reticence, but the sheer ambition of the project points to an expanded commons, a dispersed equivalent of Fairmount Park, an extensive and spongy public realm. The impetus may be technical, reduced to a contemporary engineering problem, but the specific form has flexibility both at the level of the individual type, the basin, and the level of the overall aggregation, or city of basins.

The initial stages of the *Green City, Clean Waters* plan operates like the city's thwarted commons. Here, it is not commonly held property but rather a cultural commons. Physically, the plan articulates a shared language of residual space through the deployment of barrels, trenches, swales, and basins throughout the city. It also has a collective component, where individual action is leveraged toward the common good of reducing runoff and flooding. While the actions are voluntary, such as the placement of a rain barrel at a downspout or the installation of a garden, they are incentive-driven actions through a stormwater fee structure based on impervious surface. If impervious surface is reduced, the fee is in turn reduced.

These individual actions, by residents and business owners, are reinforced and managed by government action. So, while the boundaries of the resource are clearly defined and monitored, the terms of use are locally specific. This means that the collective shares in the benefit of the resource but does not have power over the operational rules, or the specific plan of action. The individual is subject to fees, and their influence is limited by plot line. The larger agenda is managed centrally, with visions focused on the central city, and with projects enacted where there are the fewest barriers to implementation and the greatest impact available, both in terms of stormwater capture and political recognition. In the end, the transformation proves incremental and the urban design guidelines are minimal, resulting in a strong push for more absorptive surfaces regardless of their social, material, or formal impact.

One Lonely Basin at a Time

Recently, I took another self-guided tour of Philadelphia's hydrological landscape, this time as part of a citywide exploration of *Green City, Clean Waters* projects on formerly and currently vacant lands. At my urging, Mami Hara, then still the chief of staff at PWD, suggested sites, and I headed off to see five completed projects and four pending projects.[49] Three of the smaller projects are in the Mill Creek watershed, and one is just outside, in a traffic intersection on the west side of the Gray's Ferry bridge, the same bridge with a view to the Mill Creek outlet. This was where I started, curious to discover how the neighborhood had evolved in the past decades and keen to imagine it as central in the debate on abandoned properties and water management in Philadelphia. On one hand, it is central—with a relatively high number of projects planned and completed—and on the other, it still suffers shocking disinvestment. The distribution of projects is, again, political and opportunistic. It reflects hotspots of advocacy in neighborhoods such as Northern Liberties and Kensington, where the local notfor-profits are well organized. For example, the photograph in figure 15 is of the "Big Green Block" on the sites of the Shissler Recreation Center and the Kensington High School for the Creative and Performing Arts, a collaboration between the PWD and the New Kensington Community Development Corporation. The projects are attached to

Figure 15. Shissler Big Green Block, Kensington neighborhood, Philadelphia, 2015.

existing, often public, community structures such as schools, recreation centers, farms, gardens, and parks and are reflective of the intrinsic water storage capacity found in low-lying elevations and open landscapes.[50]

On the tour, the individual projects are small—isolated basins serving their micro-watersheds. But together the accumulated projects form a larger image, like a connect-the-dot game. The dots alone show the distribution of public amenities. And as the points are connected, the line of the creek is revealed, as well as new trajectories and patterns of social occupation. The basins are physically isolated but operate on multiple scales. They have their direct catchment areas—for water and populations—of one hundred square feet (nine square meters) to over an acre (half a square kilometer) or from a residential household to school community to a population of neighborhood park goers. They also have their associated networks—each basin belongs to a property, to a block, to a neighborhood, to a watershed. In fact, each project is listed by address classified by type, neighborhood, and major watershed—the largest being the Schuylkill and the Delaware and the smaller being Cobbs/Darby, Tookany-Tacony/Frankford, Pennypack, and others.[51] The delineations are both social and hydrological, and indeed the basin sits at this very intersection. It is designed to be a collector of water, of plant material, and, at times, of people.

Again, visually, the "Big Green Map" serves as a spatial database for the projects, which are assigned icons by typology and later ownership and structure. For example, the traffic island on Gray's Ferry is a "rain garden," whereas on the West Mill Creek Farm the interventions are "swales." Armed with addresses and typological classifications, I visited the site of a future "stormwater basin" in Overbrook, the "swales," "pervious paving," "infiltration trenches," and "stormwater tree trenches" in the Mill Creek bottomlands, the "storage trench" in Clark Park, and the "rain garden" near the Mill Creek outfall. The sites on my two tours—the one of the key moments along Mill Creek and the one of the *Green City, Clean Waters* projects—understandably correlate. But the icons and the addresses tell little about the landscape condition. The typologies, necessary for the system design, for explanation, and for evaluation, require expansion, blurring, and crossbreeding. The subtleties, for instance, between a stormwater basin (a vegetated depression to store, infiltrate, or hold runoff) and a rain garden (a moderately depressed garden designed to collect surface runoff) are hard to perceive, both in situ and in definition.

It is clear, from the "Big Green Map," that there are many more rain gardens than stormwater basins (ninety-six versus twelve, at the time of my second tour) and, by inference, that they are easier to implement and thus are more popular. It can also be said that in the past the basins are typically large and unadulterated, but the current trend is for smaller, planted depressions. The terminology and the classifications rest with the engineers and designers for whom the differences and applications are clear.

Figure 16. Awaiting Lucien Blackwell Park and Recreation Center, 4600 Aspen Street, Philadelphia, 2016: a view of the Mill Creek Valley before park and building construction.

But in the city, the circumstance of each project is more crucial: the scale, the adjacencies, and the social use. A garden or a basin in a traffic island is not the same as one in a schoolyard—and a basin tucked into a small corner of a park is not the same as one that creates a large and inhabitable topography with different uses in wet and dry conditions. To tally the points is impressive, but ninety-six rain gardens can only say so much about the transformation and occupation of the urban landscape. The stories are rich and ultimately tell of topographical experiences best appreciated by living in and moving through the city.

At the end of my second Mill Creek tour, fifteen years after the first, I am once again perched above the creek on 47th Street, and I see that the panoramic view from the schoolyard has changed, so that the topography is even more present. The prospect is quiet, nearly devoid of its haunted past, maturely serene from all angles. The abandoned Mill Creek Apartments are gone, and the open expanse commands the foreground, an arrested swath that, I later learn, unfortunately embodies the lost potential of a different scale for the city's stormwater management program. Sitting below all the adjacent property, it is a relatively giant basin—four acres or three football fields in area—as well as a powerful opening in the fabric, a visually arresting meadow punctuated by tree specimens from past plans.[52] Underneath is another basin, a detention basin—hidden—perched atop the line of the buried creek. On top is a frighteningly banal park that screams of its bureaucratic client's—the Philadelphia Housing Authority—lack of spatial and programmatic vision. The sewer runs underneath 47th Street to the west, and the oddly suburban Lucien Blackwell homes rise to the east. The elevation is felt, the street descends ever so slightly into the valley, but the feeling is merely symbolic. (Figure 16 is taken standing in the valley, almost on top of the sewer, with my back to the park, looking north at a part of the landscape described above, at a part that is now home to another building built atop the creek bed, the Lucian Blackwell Community Center. The water remains buried. The faith in engineering remains firm.)

Beneath the Surface

After taking in the prospect, I head down the hill and out of the Mill Creek watershed, driving north to Girard, crossing over the Schuylkill and through its Fairmount Park buffer, east across the city and into the Delaware River watershed. Forty (100 square kilometers) of the city's roughly 140 square miles (360 square kilometers) drain directly into the Delaware, while the entire watershed drains nearly 13,000 square miles (approximately 33,650 square kilometers), encompassing areas of 4 states, 42 counties, and all or parts of 838 municipalities in the Mid-Atlantic region. The Schuylkill is a tributary of the Delaware. The hydrology is connected, even if these connections are interrupted, manipulated, and not felt on the trip through the city. Northern Liberties—and Liberty Lands—my next stop, feels environmentally, culturally, and physically far from the Mill Creek basin. Yet, a closer look reveals some key similarities.

The buried Cohocksink Creek, like Mill Creek, is still prominent in the city fabric. The snaking line of Canal, Laurel, and Bodine Streets reflects it. Irregular blocks form a hydrologically inspired road network, a counterpoint to the rational grid that extends from the center city. The creek was first canalized to support proliferating industry and later was encapsulated as part of the sewer network.

Liberty Lands—a park that borrows its name from William Penn's liberties[53]—sits to the west of the creek line and occupies a two-acre pentagonal plot. The name is fitting. Much has happened to the land since it was set aside as part of the liberties, but somehow, through a series of direct and indirect actions, it has found its way back as a free-form neighborhood respite (figure 17 traces the site's transformation in plan and section, a drawn accompaniment to the following text). Before, the site on the banks

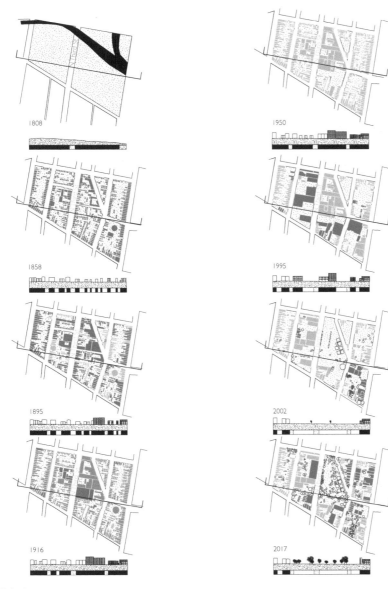

1808

1858

1895

1916

1950

1995

2002

2017

See Figure 13 for site location

See Figure 13 for site location

— Existing Structure
— New Structure

300 Feet
100 Meters

Figure 17. 900 to 1000 North Third Street, Philadelphia: site plans and sections over time around the Cohocksink Creek, at Liberty Lands Park.

of the Cohocksink Creek was a perfect candidate for industry. For over one hundred years, it was an integral part of the leather district and home to a key kid and Moroccan leather producer. After a period of vacancy, the cluster of industrial buildings was purchased in the 1980s by a speculative developer. The property accrued back taxes, was subject to multiple fires, and was ultimately seized by the city. The site was then given to the Northern Liberties Neighborhood Association (NLNA). As a condition of this transfer, the buildings were demolished for safety reasons, leaving a cleared and toxic ground. The NLNA, with superfund cleanup dollars, citizen vision, and volunteer labor, created a common of sorts—a liberties—for the neighborhood, with community garden plots, a play area, a stage, lawns, and groves. The NLNA owns and maintains the site, raising funds through annual parties. The format is relaxed, and the ownership structure allows for risk.

The NLNA paired with the Pennsylvania Horticultural Society and the PWD on a stormwater demonstration project at the north end of the site that transcends the definitions of the *Green City, Clean Waters* program. Labeled a "rain garden" on the "Big Green Map," the runoff management system draws water off the adjacent street and collects water in the park through surficial rivulets into a basin and cistern system. From here, the gray water is cleansed and stored for lawn and garden irrigation. It works, from a stormwater perspective, reducing the volume running into the city's pipes and rivers. It performs as a water management tool, but the spatial consequences are underwhelming. Unlike the meandering brook filled with children across town at the Seven Sisters Park—a true family hot weather destination—or the alluring fountain at Dilworth Park outside City Hall Plaza, the water is not celebrated as a park feature. Even the planting is nondescript. So, while the grading and storage system exceeds its capacity goals, it underperforms spatially, failing to provide a strong daily anchor to the north end of the park. The activity is pulled south and east toward the active garden plots, play area, and picnic grove.

Thus, standing with my back to the basin and its attendant amphitheater and stage, my eye is drawn south to a mural that forms the backdrop to the park. Kids are swinging on the swings, and behind them is a series of vignettes painted on the wall. Philadelphia is a city known for its murals, so it is not unusual for an open space or even a fallow lot to have a painted scene, but this one highlights the very subject of my interest in the land on which I stand.[54] Painted by neighborhood artist Dennis Haugh, whose motto is "stand in the place where you live," it is a telescoping set of maps showing the hydrological underpinnings of Liberty Lands. There on the wall is the map that haunts me, of Philadelphia's streams (and sadly missing the other map that haunts me of the streams, culverts, and sewers superimposed in space and time). On the wall, the terrain appears watery like wet paper, with Cohocksink Creek singing its presence and a big red star saying, "you are here." On the ground, the landscape is lush, but dry, full of neighborhood children playing and people ambling through the sporadic trees (see the photograph of the mural in figure 18). Of course, there is a glaring disconnect between the 1852 map on the wall and the landscape under foot. Besides the obvious wet-dry distinction, the layers of fill, toxicity, and past use are hidden. One narrative is privileged, the hydrological one, but it is hard to understand the burial without the economic, political, and social backstory. It is exciting to see the old maps of the site

Figure 18. Liberty Lands Park, Philadelphia, 2018, showing the Dennis Haugh mural and play equipment.

and its creek but frustrating that the other social layers are obscured, leaving a cleaner but less contested history. Only the explicit is rendered.

From Resource to Utility to Commons

To return to the hydrological imperative, and the city's stormwater mandate, the directives are changing the surface of the city (figure 19 illustrates these topographic shifts on three of the sites mentioned in this chapter: Lucien Blackwell Park, the Shissler Big Green Block, and Liberty Lands). Overall, the Philadelphia model—as seen through the recent transformations on the individual sites—is a funded initiative to convert the city's water distribution with an implicit urban agenda—focused on distribution as a means for impact and implementation. It operates by evaluating available land (available physically, economically, socially, and politically) for potential and then matching lands with appropriate water management typologies. The initial implementation

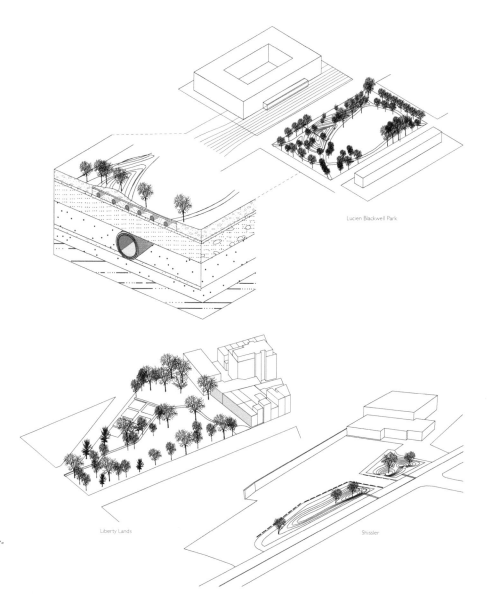

Figure 19. The making of a basin: axonometric drawings of the micro basins and places of stormwater capture at Lucien Blackwell Park, Liberty Lands Park, and the Shissler Big Green Block.

strategy focuses on several target areas, beginning with PWD-owned facilities, the development of Stormwater Management Enhancement districts, the greening of campuses, schools, and publicly owned parking facilities, the maximization of public parkland as green infrastructure, the conversion of street profiles, and finally the evaluation of vacant lands.[55] Together these lands balance ease of installment with available acreage. In other words, they are most available, large repositories of impervious surface across the city. They are the obvious place to start a program concerned with increasing drainage areas, water storage capacities, and greened acreage.[56]

To return to the idea of the commons, the Philadelphia system points to the potential for hydrological overhaul to shape a shared landscape. The commonality is defined by measures of aesthetics, scale, time, management, and ownership. The landscape operates as a commons on six levels: through its banal undertones; through its relational qualities; through its multiscalar potential; through its opportunistic decision-making structure; and through its impact on the public realm.

Banality

Water management is a necessity, an everyday reality that is managed through bureaucratic and property structures. Water must stay on-site or enter a public control system. It should be cleansed before being discharged slowly. Its celebration is a co-benefit to be considered only after water quantity and quality regulations are met. It is a mundane and universal concern, affecting both the public and private realm, where individual decisions have consequences for the collective. The course of stormwater is a form of a public good, and for many years its management on public lands has been governed by municipalities while its private management has been uncontrolled, regulated at the level of the system but individually left to good faith.

With the imposition of stormwater rates, rainwater water has been brought into the utility world. It is worth emphasizing the roots of the word "utility," which comes from the Latin *utilis,* meaning useful. On the one hand, rainwater has become more banal. It can have less to do with the perception of the body, the sensation of rainwater splashing on skin, and more to do with bureaucratic formulas, calculating storm events and surface area permeability. With the future pointing toward more frequent, intense, and erratic storms, and increasing instances of dangerous flooding, the imperative is felt. Although there are movements to combine these performance criteria with a greater aesthetic and cultural agenda,[57] the mere need to hold water is a prosaic necessity and thus a commonplace reality, a reality that affects all, one held in common. We are made of water, after all.

The material conditions of these micro-commons are also commonplace, engineered but mundane. Designed for infiltration, a collection of water-tolerant plants sits atop a base of aggregate (see figure 20). It is the juxtaposition that provides intrigue, the different material qualities of harshness expressed from a single vantage. The plants may seem fragile, but they are tough, willing to bear both the hydrological gradient from extreme wet to extreme dry as well as the harsh environments of pavement, traffic, pollution, and use. There is a compression of space and material, time and geography, speed and climate: car, road, basin, pavement, and gas station, in this instance. On what was formerly marshland sits a miniature marsh carved out of an industrial landscape. It can be considered as an ironic and, yes, once again, banal expression of the cyclical qualities of urban development.

Relations

The overall scale of the hydrological concern transcends the individual basin and its material composition, mirroring instead the scale of the watershed. It is a large and relational one. The watershed is everywhere. It infiltrates the urban environment, in ways that are real and in ways that are metaphorical. Cities flood, and cities hold river festivals. The process of implementing water infrastructure is complex, as the process of unencumbered land acquisition and accumulation in a developed North American city is perhaps more so. In other words, it is difficult to gain access to any land, much less land that can be transformed into a viable stormwater sponge. It is likewise difficult to maintain the implemented sponges without dedicated resources. Most funds are dedicated to construction rather than monitoring and maintenance.

And yet, while these constraints may sound dire, they can produce an interesting outcome. And in the end, any willing person and any available piece of land, no matter the size, are engaged. Here, it is relevant to reflect on the artist Gordon Matta-Clark's Fake Estates project, itself a critique of the arbitrary nature of property delineation. In the mid-1970s, the artist purchased tiny slivers of land in Queens—for example, a tiny alleyway between two structures that resulted from a property line adjustment. He then documented these spaces, with the deed from his purchase alongside a map and a photo.[58] On the one hand, the representation is deadpan—a subtle commentary on the absurdity of property. On the other, as our cities build up and unbuild up, these residual slivers have an increasing physical presence.[59] While perhaps not quite as narrow or irregular, many of the *Green City, Clean Waters* projects occupy similar slivers within the city, adding legibility to curbs, meridians, rights-of-way, and parking islands. They are indiscriminate and become a unifying field across a heterogeneous landscape. The background remnants transform into to a glorious humdrum, foregrounded.

Scales

With the *Green City, Clean Waters* program, the potential for multiple scales of project is well documented. It is at the core of the mission: no effort is too small, and yet, the more spaces for water capture, the better. The common materials and function marry the individual plots, while the typologies are called out separately on project maps and made up of different design ingredients. But the ingredients are similar—water storage and water absorptive devices that are repeatable and scalable. The plots are related both by their topographic positions (as low-lying) and material expressions (often soft and marshy). Together, they create a new layer across urban landscape and by their very number become something that can be read at multiple scales. The hydro-plots are embedded in the urban consciousness of the city, both physically and ideologically. They represent the expression of an obsession with performance, one to be quantified, seen, and touted.

At the core of this is the basin itself, as a material condition carved into the previously impervious urban ground. As mentioned above, it is an engineered form of a shallow profile, complete with several layers of highly specific soils and aggregates designed to hold and percolate water in a specific way. Atop the soils sit a suite of plants chosen for their hardiness and their ability to live with and without water. These species—black chokeberry, blue flag iris, swamp milkweed, to name a few—become ubiquitous (see figure 20 of the basin, depicted across the seasons). Commonplace plantings specified for our commonplace existence. And as our climatic conditions become increasingly varied, these extreme—and often polar conditions—are ones we all must endure.

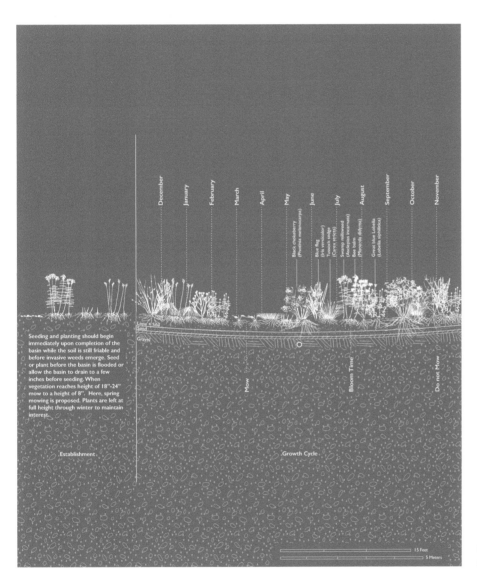

Figure 20. Stormwater meadow, illustrating plant material and cyclical care within a basin.

Even when the civic realm is being defined as a form of technology, the projects are changing the way the city looks, the way it is physically perceived by citizens, not just the way it works. The importance of this is slowly being recognized, allowing landscape scholars and landscape architects involvement in a territory recently dominated by engineers.[60] Designers are participating directly in the design, construction, and governance of the hydrological common ground. The surface of the city is being transformed. Given the relative pressures of space and budget, the projects are inherently multidimensional. Water infrastructure masquerades as urban design, and vice versa.

Opportunities

Budget and government capacity constraints also contribute to an expanded notion of the commons. The water storage landscape is a clearly defined and locally specific resource whose ultimate adoption rests with the citizen body.[61] Indirectly, the projects are accepted as part of the urban palimpsest. Directly, individuals and organizations are enlisted to maintain the newly implemented infrastructure. As with almost all public infrastructure constructed in the twenty-first century, there is little funding for maintenance. By bringing the guts of the city to the surface, cities are finding a way to allow for maintenance to remain in the public realm (as opposed to be taken on as private projects) without paying for it with government dollars. The ultimate maintenance of the sites has an impact on the implementation strategy. Through public process, both the land and the stewardship constituencies must be identified. The landscape of actors and governmental relationships is as important as the physical landscape of low-lying topographies. As a result, schools and long-standing institutions rise to the forefront as places for insertion. The roofs of the library and the energy company anchor the flying verdant carpet seen in the project imagery while the micro-wetland doubles as a capture and educational device for the local school and the abandoned parcel.

The Public Realm

Politicians are pragmatic. Projects arise where the fiscal and political landscape merge with the physical ground, especially in the early years of the project. The projects seek a balance between ease of implementation and maximum visibility. Signature projects in the center city area are featured in project literature, showcasing expansive green roofs and key waterfront park projects. New nonresidential construction is required to meet stormwater guidelines through infiltration, runoff volume reduction, and slow release of water. These projects are mandatory but represent only a small portion of the impervious urban environment.[62] Other projects must be carved out of existing hard surfaces and property structures. Here, the initiatives become more political, reflecting the nature of government cooption and cooperation, and through the emergence of absorptive materials, the political landscape begins to be legible. Schoolyard projects indicate general cooperation between the water and school departments. The less siloed the agencies, the more potentially far-reaching the work. Willing caregiver organizations are mapped through physical interventions in the surface of the city. Active individuals and groups successfully lobby for increased investment. In the end, this human-driven territory of initiative is matched with the land availability.

At times there is overlap, and at times the vast areas of abandonment and disinvestment remain untouched. This land has no clear adopters, and its subsurface condition is largely untested. While these properties continue to fall through the cracks in the early phases of implementation, the sheer ambition of a project to capture, clean, and slowly release its stormwater on the surface of the city means that the tentacles of investment will be forced to be far-reaching. The city will eventually be blanketed with this new form of commons. It is driven by federal and local initiative, but it is being sustained by a collective endeavor. Ultimately, limited resources are pushing the project toward an even more robust common one that includes collective management at its core. Each project has local terms and the potential for a stewardship model that allows for collective power of the operational rules—with means for monitoring, sanctioning, resolving conflict, and self-organizing. It could even be argued that the success of the program depends on these principals as proven ingredients of viable common pool resource management.[63]

Conclusions

Much has been written about the *Green City, Clean Waters* plan as an innovative stormwater proposal, yet it is rarely considered as a means to reinvent the abandoned urban landscape or define the future urban common; it is rarely examined through its implementation and maintenance mechanisms or set in relation to a longer history of water management in Philadelphia. A balance between the top-down deployment and regulation of a citywide initiative and the local management of its individual projects would inset a collective layer into the civic realm. Indeed, it would recast the stormwater, or watercourses more generally, as a dynamic social and hydrological expression of urban life. In so doing, in moving from resource to utility to commons, the banal and distributed hydrological infrastructure is leveraged once again—but this time as a means to transform the way the urban environment looks and works. It is a system built over time, as another chapter in the story of the interdependence of water and urban development (see figure 21 for an idea of relating the daily, yearly, decennial, and centurial cycles of history, economy, population, storms, and hydrology). It is a story that is rich and ongoing in the low-lying extant landscape of Philadelphia and beyond.

The traditions of the Lenni Lenape, of William Penn, of Ian McHarg, of Anne Whiston Spirn, of Howard Neukrug, of the future designers and their teams—they all

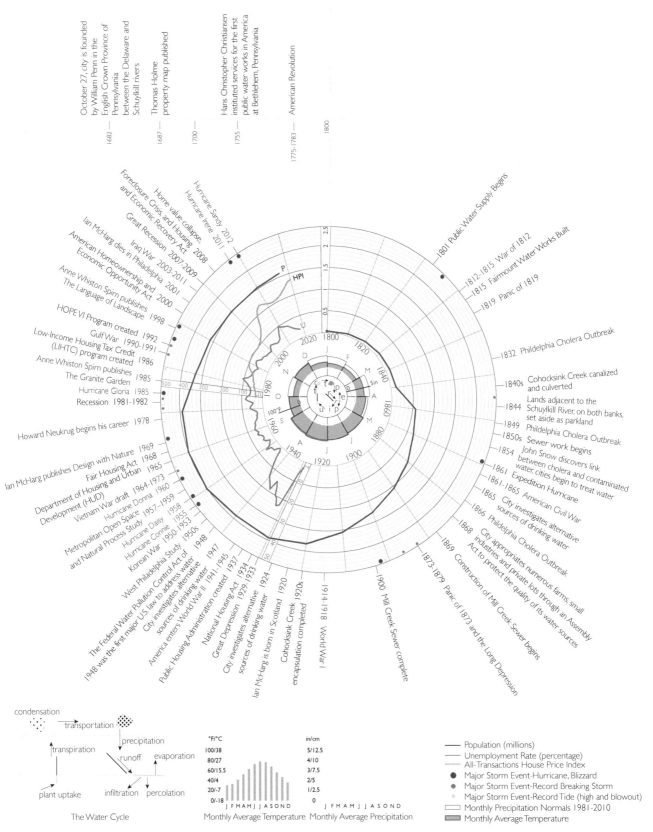

Figure 21. Hydrological time cycles: a diagram of housing, policy, economy, people, and water over time.

seem to become collaborators, taking the city forward. The trajectory has had its starts and stops, but it can be seen as a thick line. And along this line, which at times circles back, each protagonist has (serendipitously or intentionally) built on the previous one, investigating the environmental and social potential of nested scales from the regional watershed to the neighborhood stream-shed to the parceled site. The most recent distributed but aggregated system expands the view of the city. It affords the city a greater topographic, hydrological, and cultural legibility. More plainly, the city is reaching back to the river's edges. At the localized low points, on the urban campuses and schoolyards, in parks and along socially active corridors, another layer is being added to the civic palimpsest—this one contributing increasingly to the legibility of the others. The surface of the city is transforming slowly—slowly but dramatically. The trajectory is cyclical, as the marshes, once filled at the water's edge, reemerge inland, peppering the city with watery ground. And the water cycle itself is cyclical, precipitating through the city air, draining across its landscapes, evaporating again into the airspace. The hydrological section is running deeper, everywhere.

2

GLEISWILDNIS
200 Years of Ecology in Berlin

The Ideological Grounds

I do not know if the ecologist Herbert Sukopp and the architect Oswald Mathias Ungers ever met, but they both worked in a similar context—a divided Berlin full of unrealized potential, a place nearly unimaginable to anyone walking through the streets of the Berlin of today. Since then, Berlin has endured massive development. It is not the development put in place by these 1970s visionaries who worked in a context of slow transformation. It is development that happened in a relatively hurried fashion, beginning in the 1990s, when Berlin was in a rush to return to its role as German capital, and extending into the 2010s as the last of the inner-city voids were being developed. The ruderal vegetation that began to grow unfettered in the 1970s—the very ruderal vegetation that inspired Sukopp's theories and informed future city policies—was largely squashed under construction staging grounds in the 1990s and replaced by capital projects. The green sea with which Unger frames his architectural archipelagos has been filled in with gray pavements and constructions. But imagine for a moment that the 1990s never happened, that the ideas of Sukopp and Ungers are still operating in a former Berlin, a place of intrepid plants and radical planning. We imagine this other Berlin not for purposes of nostalgia but rather to place the contemporary landscape discussion that is happening in Berlin today—a debate about the careful balance between design and wildness—into a broader ideological context.

Sukopp, an urban botanist working out of the Institute for Ecology at the Technische Universität Berlin, closely observed and documented the biological succession occurring in the pause created between the widespread wartime destruction ending in 1945 and the post-unification reconstruction beginning in 1990. Starting in the late 1950s, Sukopp and his colleagues began observing the ecological conditions found in

Figure 22. Gleiswildnis, Gleisdreieck Park, Berlin, 2015.

the city's ruderal landscapes and wastelands.[1] They mapped the species (intensively),
focusing on particular sites and monitoring them over time. Through this rigorous
fieldwork, they recognized a correlation between species composition and the structure of the city, a relationship that Sukopp idealized in his emblematic cross-section
of Berlin. Sukopp and his team thought of the city as a pluralistic entity. The city is a
mosaic that can be understood through its biotopes, biotopes whose very classification
indicated the extent and types of human use. A biotope, formed from the Greek roots
for "life" and "space," is a habitat defined by the long-term associations between its
specific floral and faunal species. Ruderal compositions, now well established in urban
ecological study, are differentiated from other types of vegetal cover—forests, bogs,
and grasslands, for example.

Remarkably, the biotope classification system endures—spearheaded by a city that
is proudly nearly half vegetated (figure 23 highlights the vegetal masses in conjunction
with the city's rail infrastructure and fallow grounds, while the base map in figure 24
shows a broader set of biotopes). The distinctions indicate historical evolution and
the process of succession: vacant land is differentiated from places with immature soil,
from dry and neglected grassland, or from fallow vegetated land. Starting in the 1980s,
biotic potential becomes a way to evaluate urban land—and Sukopp and his team

argued that urban development types could be reframed as biotopes and that development decisions could be based on these biotopes. Their research supported a theory of urban ecology and as a basis for policy, explored through the development of the Species Protection Program.[2] Sukopp and his colleagues created biotope maps of the entire city, based on their early fieldwork, designed to promote a valuation system that considers the existing species in order to determine whether a site should be conserved, maintained, or developed. Biotope mapping continues today as a means to assess and conserve existing habitat and to drive habitat creation in heavily developed areas. The urban ecologists have discovered rare species (a French moth imported on war trains, for example) and exuberant nature living in the city's abandoned spaces. The stagnation of development creates exotic habitats, and these habitats warrant conservation in a heterogeneous city. What Sukopp did is change the thinking about what was growing in the city: he argued for the urban wild to be considered as a legitimate open space typology, one dependent on human influence to exist and human insight to remain.[3]

In 1977, Ungers, a former Technische Universität Berlin architecture professor and Berlin transplant who spent some time living and teaching in the United States, and his collaborators, working in the same West Berlin context, proposed the *City in the City: Berlin; A Green Archipelago.*[4] The speculation countered the concept of urban repair, or the historical reconstruction of the city desired by many at the time. Proponents of urban repair wanted to put the entire city back together, to restore it to its prewar condition by replacing buildings with buildings, ignoring the potential that the altered city might have for an alternative structure. Ungers and his team, on the other hand, proposed not to rebuild the whole city, but to concentrate development around existing strongholds, to enhance them and use them as a way to create a series of urban islands. They understood that Berlin had lost population, while its boundaries remained fixed, and yet saw a city needing to move forward in a way that did not compromise the quality of life for its remaining inhabitants.

This is, in fact, the first of five theses in the *City in the City* manifesto. Ungers and his collaborators saw an opportunity to transform the structure of the city. Their approach was a selective investment, contained and articulated within many islands. These floating agglomerations are set in an open grid, conceived to house all of the urban support systems for the archipelago. The support systems are described in clear words but are non-existent or murky when drawn. The ambition of the grid is extensive. The manifesto states this explicitly: "The green interspaces form a system of modified nature and contain a repertoire of types that range from suburban zones to parks and woodland to urban areas put to agricultural use."[5] The grid is described as a "nature-culture system" and is thought to have parkland in terms of both recreational and cultivated space and automotive infrastructure. The plan's connective tissue is fluid, a sea that could be conceived of as a designed urban wild set against the tightly constructed and idealized architectural islands.

Conservation Landscape
Grassland
Green Space
Forest
Vacant Neglected Areas
Vacant, not classified as a
type of green space
Water
Roadways
Rail Lines

3 Miles
6 Kilometers

Figure 23. Rails and landscapes, including vacant lands, Berlin: a reading of the city showing large reserves and rails as structuring elements.

Urban Islands, from Ungers et al.

01   07   13   19   25   31   36   41   46   50   53   55   59
02   08   14   20   26   32   37   42   47   51   56
03   09   15   21   27   33   38   43   48   52   54   57
04   10   16   22   28   34   39   44   49
05   11   17   23   29   35   40   45
06   12   18   24   30   58

Standing Water
Flowing Water

Vacant Areas
Dry + Neglected Grassland
Fallow Greenland
Dwarf Shrub and Heaths
Bog + Marshes

Bog Shrubberies
Bog Alluvial Forests
Bushes and Trees Groves
Fresh Meadows
Forests
Acres
Green + Open Space
Mixed-Use Housing

Small Businesses
House and Allotment Garden
Other
Ungers Plan

Forest 1984-89
Park 1984-89
Garden 1984-89

Key Plan of Urban Islands, from Ungers et al.

3 Miles
6 Kilometers

Figure 24. Biotope/island mash-up, Berlin: O. M. Ungers and team's islands from 1977 set atop the biotope classifications for the city.

To explore these two perspectives simultaneously, the work of the Sukopp and Ungers teams is overlaid, literally, producing a mash-up of biotopes and islands (see figure 24). Life, space, and imagination are collapsed. Two ideas of wildness are brought together, representing the merger of very different, but sympathetic, ideas on the future of Berlin at a time when future thinking was particularly fertile. The biotope-mapping project is a scaled, analytical land-use system designed to parcel the city into a habitat mosaic. The green archipelago, on the other hand, is a rhetorical investigation designed to develop a theory of city making through unmaking. In the overlay, the correspondence is obvious: the highlighted architectural islands sit amid the building-heavy fabric, colored red on the original biotope maps but shown in gray on the mash-up. It is easy to imagine the red crumbling away—with Berlin becoming greener and greener.[6] In fact, this process has happened a little bit, though development of the open spaces in inner Berlin is contentious as the city has little affordable housing, and development ambition is often misaligned with citizen need. Contemporary ecologists such as Ingo Kowarik, who trained with Sukopp, continue to develop ecological projects in Berlin. At the same time, contemporary designers including Ökoplan, Fugmann Janotta, Topotek 1, Büro Kiefer, Ateliet Loidl, and geskes.hack Landschaftsarchitekten, among others, articulate Berlin's landscapes through deliberate design intervention that highlight the gradients of biotopes through uncanny juxtapositions. The micro-seas around the architectural fragments remain micro-seas with little expansion since the 1970s. The open sea is certainly still a fragmented body—not really functioning like a singular sea but rather like a series of lakes fed by the same underground water system (even though this is a metaphor, Berlin does have a healthy if threatened aquifer). Still, the influences of Sukopp and Ungers, and their teams of thinkers, resonate. Berlin's landscape has grown over the past sixty years, and the future plans indicate further investment. While some wilds have been tamed, others have been integrated carefully, designed into the urban fabric to create a specific identity for the city. The ruderal is still very much present and alive in the design of the common spaces of the city.

Ruderal Identities

My first encounter with Berlin's ruderal landscapes was a trip precisely choreographed to see the wild landscape conditions which I, and many others, know from research to be a significant part of the city's identity. Yet, I was taken, and even surprised, by the prevalence of spontaneously occurring vegetation. I arrived by bus from the Tegel Airport, snaking through Charlottenburg-Nord and disembarking at Turmstraße near Alt-Moabit and Ottopark, about two and a half miles from my final destination near Anhalter Bahnhof and some of the well-known wild parks on the southwest side of the city. I expected the twisting stately Robinia and Betula stands set against a rippled and wavy ground of rubble and meadow, there in the southwest, to match the photos and reports of my colleagues and friends, but I did not expect the extent of volunteer plants colonizing open ground elsewhere. The median on Alt-Moabit was full of them; even the Ottopark had a welcomed scruffiness that seems to fit the culture perfectly. Later I would see planters with clusters of spontaneous herbaceous species, pure wild meadow parcels enclosed and protected, buildings built around preexisting trees, an entire defunct airport denied development through citizen action. To my North American eyes, the scene was unimaginable and thrilling.

Urban Wilds

I have been a long enthusiast of the urban wild, and my understanding of its potential draws from a specific relationship to it; as an American landscape architect, I was deeply interested in the tension between abandonment and development, between emergent and determined, between unruly and control, between clear and enigmatic. Here, I use this perspective to elaborate on the evolution of the ideas behind these landscapes and then explore the incorporation of the wild into design as a means to articulate layers and cycles evident in urban change.[7] I look at the relationship between abandonment and wilds, oscillating between North American and European examples, with a final focus on the Berlin-specific case studies. In doing so, I argue for the importance of wild vegetation as a cultural, ecological, and economic response to growing inventories of abandoned land, more generally, and then concentrate on how the Berlin projects have become the definitive expression of this practice. The ruderal and the spontaneous have invaded cities over the past sixty years, encouraged by the environmental zeitgeist of the 1970s, commandeered by the design acumen of the 2000s, and expanded upon by the climate conscience activism of the contemporary moment. These wilds—evolving, successional spaces formed by ecological and human factors—allow for longitudinal readings of the city.[8] Here, past and present uses create hybrid spaces, where the species composition, the spatial curiosities, and the inventive occupations point to past histories of human development and undevelopment followed by intensive floral and faunal establishment. They form a type of enduring common landscape, existing on sites of former infrastructure and building, where pause has allowed for the formation of different biotopes. As a collection, the wilds are inherently multiscalar, existing in small slivers of land, on individual parcels, and as parts of larger corridors. Together, as is evident in Berlin and elsewhere, they embody an aesthetic—a controlled unruliness—that establishes a strong civic identity while being sensitive to limited economic and environmental resources.

The "Uns" of the Urban Wild

In other words, the urban wild (in this case, as a specific classification of open space) epitomizes the polyvalent factors at play in city transformation. As both a misunderstood landscape and an elusive term, the urban wild is often described by what it is not—a park, a natural landscape, or a wilderness—rather than what it is—a successional piece of land, shaped by ecological drivers in response to human actions over time. In English, the word "wild" is explained most clearly by antonyms, defined by a series of "uns": uncultivated, untamed, uncontrolled, undomesticated, and uninhabited.[9] The wild is seen as other, and the urban wild is an oxymoron. The two words together—with "urban" relating to a city or inhabited place—are provocative but contradictory. For this reason, arriving at a succinct definition of the "urban wild" has been difficult, with numerous shifts over the past forty years. The spaces are obvious to visitors—they are viscerally felt but escape the same clarity in words.

Since gaining parlance in the 1970s, the American English language and perception surrounding the urban wild has changed to reflect a balance between human and environmental agency. Originally perceived as something pristine, something remaining untouched amid the human-led co-optation of land for city making, the (American English) "wild" is now seen as dependent on human action. It still stands apart from built and infrastructural landscapes but is understood as a creation and by-product of these urban conditions. Firmly ensconced in a reality where human influence on ecosystem functions is undeniable, the wild, too, has transferred its allegiance with nature alone to embrace its crossbreed status.[10] In order to delve into the ideological formation of the term, the urban wild is understood within this trajectory: from wilderness to novel ecosystem; from natural to adapted; from remnant to reemergent; from wasteland to valued land. In German ecological parlance, the term *heberomy* measures the scale of human disturbance on a site. It is a term used by Herbert Sukopp and fellow ecologists to describe urban biotypes, species distribution, and built-up zones.[11] The six-part scale classifies the cultural influences on a landscape relative to its soils and substrate and to its vegetal composition. The range extends from *metahemarobic* (or toxic with strong cultural influence destroying organisms to extreme physical effect and near complete denudation) to *ahemarobic* (or untouched by humans). It is the four intermittent gradations (*polyhemarobic, euhemarobic, mesohemarobic, oligohemarobic*) that are of the greatest interest. Polyhemarobic exhibits great cultural influence, albeit short term and nonperiodic, resulting in highly altered ground conditions with fewer, highly disturbance-tolerant species. Euhemarobic are sites of continuous cultivation with changed soils and conditioned or maintained flora. Mesohemarobic are less altered meadows, pastures, and woodlands that have periodic but present human involvement, whereas the oligohemarobic have nearly no changes to the soil or vegetal structure and appear nearly natural.[12] Over time, the conceptual understanding of the urban wild has shifted on this scale, from the ahemarobic and oligohemerobic toward the euhemarobic and polyhemarobic end, with human influence gaining greater recognition. Abandonment, instead of yielding what was considered in previous thinking an unproductive wasteland, becomes a driver of ecological succession, the disturbance factor behind an important cultural and ecological typology.

As a cultural entity, in Berlin historically and now potentially even in other countries, the wild can be described as a space that embodies history, where sets of actions over time yield specific spatial conditions.[13] It is a registration of political and economic climate, where complexities—pollution, social stigma, infrastructural change, political division—provide the seven- to forty-year developmental delay necessary for wild landscapes to establish.[14] The sites are actual palimpsests, with past signifiers—light poles, pavements, structures—interwoven with present growth—Rhus, Ailanthus, Robinia. They operate as oases, for reflection, for exploration, for passage. The wandering shortcut is a primary use.

As these sites become sites of designed public landscapes, much of the work is curatorial, subtractive rather than additive. Vegetation is cleared, framed, and altered more through on-going management rather than deliberate plantation. Succession can be arrested or fostered. Found material can be pruned or cleared, as needed, but what makes the wild a wild is that the vegetation is not deliberately planted or aggressively cultivated. The evolution is continuous, enabling transformations of composition, use, and configuration. Maintenance is a land management and safety strategy. Mowing and thinning are necessary but infrequent. The loose spaces provide animal and human habitat, allowing for greater freedom of expression, interpretation, and invention.[15]

The urban wild is complicated, in the best sense, and as such is challenging to describe clearly. Its uses, its functions, and its genre-bending existence understandably make officials, who rely on clarity, uneasy. Even among wilds supporters, there is a divide between those camps that see the urban wild as an opportunity for insertions and improvements and those who value it only as is, as uninhibited as possible. To date, alteration and conservation are the main proactive strategies to emerge from these debates. Both alternatives often suppress the dynamism of the wild—by stopping change, limiting the possibility of alternative futures and varied ecological outcomes. Both these negate the power of the wild: its surprising emergence, its unruly development, and its essential precariousness. The wild should be seen as a material condition to be nurtured but not mummified. Arguments for flexibility in open space have been circulating for over two decades,[16] and the urban wild is arguably the perfect venue for articulating a middle ground between conservation and park, between neglect and control, between ecology and design. The "ambivalence and ambiguity" of the urban wild should not be seen as a failure but as an opportunity for further exploration, elaboration, and invention.[17]

From Wilderness to Novel Ecosystem

Early definitions of the urban wild are situated within past readings of wilderness, either within its earliest incarnations as a wasteland or deserted and savage landscape, an antithesis of the orderly and good; or its later readings as a sublime, bastion of frontier ruggedness, fraught with moral and cultural interpretation.[18] The wild is equated with the natural, its human influences largely underplayed. There is a desire to force appreciation by emphasizing its otherness rather than its domesticity.

The idea of the wild as being something found within the city rather than apart from it — the urban wild — emerges in the 1950s, 1960s, and 1970s as planners, designers, and ecologists tackle the intersection of environment and development, slowly uncovering means for a productive coexistence. But the urban wild, here, is still thought to be pristine, aligned with the good "nature" over the bad "culture." This wild exists despite the development surrounding it and not because of it. Early writings align the urban wild with the un-urban wilderness as a means to garner support for nature conservation in the city. For example, Time-Life Books published a volume written by nature writer Ogden Tanner, *Urban Wilds,* in 1975, as part of the American Wilderness series. Other titles in the twenty-seven-book series include *The Northeast Coast, The Grand Canyon, The High Sierra, The Great Divide,* and *Sagebrush Country.* The inclusion of a book on urban wilds is remarkable; the implication is to place these landscapes among the nation's most wondrous. Through the books, wilderness is defined as wild and uncultivated, manifested in sites designated for their spectacular beauty. The books are of the coffee table variety, full of color plates and descriptive texts. The *Urban Wilds* edition is no exception. Apart from the cover, which shows the classic urban wild shot of marshlands in the foreground and city skyline on the horizon, the photographs inside display nature, devoid of human presence, with beautifully rendered macro-shots of insects, birds, and flowers. The author, Tanner, seeks to reveal the presence of this seemingly pristine condition found within the metropolis, arguing that a long drive is not necessary to find wild beauty. Cities everywhere, including the book's prime subject, New York, have "unorganized scraps of nature" found among their "hilltops, woods, reservoirs, swamps, streams, abandoned canals and railroad rights of way."[19] There is no distinction made between this nature and that of Yosemite, both nearly equally constructed and valued. This idea is to show that cities, too, have created and preserved their wildernesses, with San Francisco cited as the North American exemplar. The book is a nature guide to such places as Jamaica Bay, the Meadowlands, and even the avian diversity of Central Park, a highly constructed and maintained landscape often mistaken for indigenous. Imported landscapes and species are couched in this language of nature. Notably, the chapter on the Cosmopolitan Crew of species with "adaptive vigor" treats the now-reviled tree of heaven (*Ailanthus altissima*), starling, and opossum with the same reverence. Tanner visits the "disturbance communities" along an abandoned railway in Van Cortlandt Park, finding a "lovely collection" of diverse plant species. He even suggests that the Ailanthus, a resilient immigrant, both "beautiful" and adapted to the condition of the urban wild, might be a replacement for the struggling American chestnut.[20] Tanner's view is remarkably contemporary, couched in antiquated language of pristine wilderness and unfettered nature. Yet, his failure to see the hybridity of the spaces neglects the importance of a grounded and layered cultural and ecological approach.

Historian, planner, and landscape advocate Elizabeth Barlow Rogers also champions geo-biophysical New York City in her early work, uncovering the wild flora and fauna that stubbornly survive urban life.[21] In *The Forests and Wetlands of New York City* from 1969, she expresses the dueling dynamic of environmental and political forces shaping the open space future of the city. There is a keen recognition of the complex production of urban space. For Barlow (and for me), the wild embodies this production. In her contribution to the Cooper Hewitt Design Museum Urban Open Spaces project in 1979, an effort to expand traditional definitions of open space to reflect a broader range of activities and typologies, Barlow specifically describes the role of the urban wild:

> The seemingly artless kind of landscape planning is in fact a highly sophisticated and scientific ecological reordering to produce landscapes which, unlike traditional gardens, appear to be happenstance, fortuitous, and spontaneous rather than works of horticulture and landscape architecture.[22]

The entry is illustrated by drawings of plant species—rye grass, switchgrass, angelica, parsley, comfrey, bayberry—reminiscent of a nature guidebook. Her focus is on the influence of the social and political climate on the ecological, but it is still somehow couched in a one-sided championing of the environment. The urban wild is a "native ecological plant community" intensively cultivated and managed on disturbed urban sites. She presents the wild as a response to heightened environmental awareness and the impact it has on landscape preference. Given widespread degradation, the desire shifts from constructing controlled landscapes to replicating wilds:

> Now in a technocratic age we have come full circle and want to create landscapes that are no longer a vision of paradise but rather that "rude" and "horrid" nature itself. Out of some deep-seated psychological necessity we have begun to domesticate wildness in our cities rather than lose it from our lives.[23]

The urban wild, here, is a simulacrum of nature, created with species thought to be native to North America on sites deeply transformed by a long history of human occupation. The human agency rests with overt political decision-making and economic development trends. The unintended consequences of these actions are ignored, both at the site level and the scale of the globe. The idea that the wild needs direct human sponsorship to take hold is contemporary, but the reversion to a past nature is reflective of the early concepts of the urban wild as a natural rather than a hybrid space.

The urban wild became a catch phrase to support land conservation against development and to advocate for a stop to environmental degradation in the United States in the 1970s. After the boom of the 1960s, the subsequent recession in the 1970s gave the term some traction. Recessions are good times for urban wilds; they are, in this sense, economically elastic. Notably, the term "urban wilds" was ascribed to a governmental grant–funded "natural conservation program" in Boston designed to preserve the wealth of "unprotected natural areas of remarkable beauty."[24] The Boston Urban Wilds is an inventory-turned-land-protection program aimed at thwarting development of parcels of woodlands, meadows, and wetlands throughout the city. The language is heavy on the description of ecological character. There are only minor asides to the idea that these sites—along railroads and industrial shorelines, as parts of abandoned estates and institutional buildings, marooned in seas of asphalt—might have past histories of abuse, neglect, or alteration. The word "reestablished" appears as well as the phrase "may not be completely undisturbed."[25] The language has political undertones, as if admitting to past infrastructural intruders, devious dumping, and promiscuous paving might diminish the appreciation of the site as found. If allied with the natural rather than the degraded, the wild has a better chance for survival, even though its existence despite centuries of urban growth points to a shrewd and admirable, if unspoken, resilience.

It has taken decades for this unsavory reputation to diminish—and for the urban wild to be understood as one valued outcome of abandonment and degradation. Throughout the 1980s and 1990s it remained associated with nature areas and even, at times, "native plant communities."[26] Only recently, with a rise in literature on succession and abandonment, is the urban wild identified with evolving, hybrid landscapes marked by ecological and cultural agency and value. New language has emerged, especially coming from Germany by Sabine Hofmeister, Hein Konigen, Ingo Kowarik, Norbert Kühn, and others, to express the cohabitation of the wild and the urban: "fourth nature,"[27] "third wilderness,"[28] "novel ecosystem."[29] Through these concepts, there are ways to express and celebrate unpristine qualities rather than to hide and deny human influences. The past wilderness becomes the wildness, or William Cronon's "right nature," the kind found anywhere that humans have forgotten to see, recognize, and appreciate.[30]

From Natural to Adapted

In this hybrid reading, the urban wild is still driven by succession, only this time with overt mention of past human occupation and direct reference to its human-dominated surroundings. The "urban wildscape" as written about by landscape scholars Anna Jorgensen and Richard Keenan represents "urban spaces where natural as opposed to human agency appears to be shaping the land, especially where there is spontaneous growth of vegetation through natural succession."[31] While the term "natural" is perhaps misleading, the idea is that the "urban wildscape" is a highly manipulated landscape where plant growth is extensive yet subjected to human impact. Photographs of the "urban wildscape," in this case, show images with evidence of human use—tents and shopping carts, for example—nestled within the wild vegetation. It is clear that the vegetation is dominant, but that the landscape is layered. This hierarchy fits with the definition of "fourth nature" as a "new wilderness" supported by "succession on urban-industrial sites."[32] The "third wilderness" is also described as a "nature-culture hybrid" where land has been set aside to evolve "without human interference."[33] The reference, while not explicitly urban, does connote wildness on previously inhabited land.

A distinction is made between "wilderness" and "wildscapes" where multiple management objectives lead to choreographed spaces. With the latter definition, the hybridity is pronounced. The vegetation is loosely managed to allow for architectural relics, rubble piles, recreational activities, and cultural events to exist. The reading points to a balanced socioecological understanding, a reading more consistent with the actual found conditions of the urban wild. By comparison, "novel ecosystem" is a biological term defining an ecosystem that has been "heavily influenced by humans but is not under human management."[34] Cartographically, it is defined as "unused lands embedded within agricultural and urban landscapes" by the ecologist of the anthropogenic era Earl Ellis.[35] In fact, an urban wild can only be partially considered a "novel ecosystem." As a cultural landscape, it does not exist without management, even if intervention is both intentionally and unintentionally subdued.

In all the contemporary definitions and associated terms, the urban wild is linked with ecological succession as moderated by a human-altered landscape. The spaces have a cyclical temporal structure with multiple agents; the urban wild is not just time and human impact in a mixing bowl but the mixing bowl as well. More emphasis is still given to the natural colonizers, but the definition does not mask past history. The wilds are not truly natural spaces but ones that have adapted with time. There is an obvious underlay of human abandonment. These are the landscapes that have gone largely untended, the human leftovers, no longer controlled or exploited. Formerly abandoned, they have been given value as productive urban sites. They are, as well, the bio-reserves of the future, evolutionary landscapes that offer alternative perspectives on vegetation, time, maintenance, and use.[36]

From Remnant to Reemergent

While a few urban wilds do fall into the remnant category, the majority spring from abandoned and distressed lands. On the whole, urban wilds are no longer aligned with the pristine landscape, as a relic that has resisted development. Instead, they are second-, third-, and fourth-generation landscapes, places where plants have colonized disturbed sites during developmental pauses. The vegetation of the urban wild is not native but spontaneous—occurring by chance and migration—adapting well to the soils and climate of the given conditions.[37] The reputation is that of a weed or an invasive, heavily rebuked in the past, though reactions have calmed considerably since the early studies of the 1950s.[38] A weed is a cultural construct, used to describe a plant out of place, and is a metaphor architecturally for an alien encounter.[39]

"Invasive species" is a controversial term, championed by the ecological restoration community, and used to classify non-indigenous or alien, widespread species perceived as a threat to native ecosystems.[40] The term is the main ammunition used to vilify the novel ecosystem, both culturally and ecologically. For decades, where resources permitted, aggressive eradication has been promoted, arguing that the invasive species cause harm to economic, environmental, and human health systems. While some are extremely harmful, others are not. Some have clear aesthetic, medicinal, and ecological value. Currently, wholesale removal is becoming less prevalent, and arguments are emerging for the intentional and designed use of some wild species for cultural, ecological, and economic reasons.[41] The species are more reflective of the past histories of site; they offer biomass, nutrient cycling, and shade while requiring fewer resources to maintain.

The barrier to encouraging wild species continues to be perceptual, influenced by context. For example, a wild meadow in an expansive campus or country-like setting is desirable—even as a replacement of past agricultural use—whereas one spontaneously occurring on an urban parcel is jarring, a foreign reminder of past prosperity and present neglect. Yet out of context, the value differences are arguably less discernible to the unbotanical eye. Both are rich and vibrant, visually and functionally. The key is to frame the wildness, to render its otherness enviable. Through juxtapositions and curated interventions, perception can be changed. The urban wild can be emancipated as a resurrected landscape, freed from its cultural baggage of human failure, allowing multiple species to flourish in a resource-restrained manner.

From Wasteland to Valued Land

Wilds are minimal-maintenance landscapes that fall outside the conventional treatment of a civic landscape. Typical regimes include mowing, damage and safety control, selective pruning, and occasional insertions of planting and built structure. There is a split between three schools of thinking: advocates for leaving the urban wild as untouched as possible; land conservation supporters who espouse a natural areas maintenance strategy; and proponents of seizing the opportunity for further site improvements. Again, the balance is delicate between opportunistic appropriations of the loose space where unprogrammed, unmediated, unregulated, flexible use is accommodated,[42] and the encapsulation of the use into a fixed amenity that undermines the very experience it once afforded. The wild is a space that does not conform to typical urban mores. It is allowed to look unkempt and be used with few restrictions. But it is precisely through the urban wild that the potential range of city experiences is expanded.

The urban wild, with its hybrid qualities, has the ability to occupy an important ecological and social niche in the urban environment. It fits within a larger mosaic of dynamic land use, constantly evolving to support diversity of species and experience. But in leaving it untouched and allowing unfettered succession, biodiversity and social engagement are diminished with time. By considering it natural and arguing for long-term conservation, with aggressive management tactics to preserve existing or impose desired qualities, the process is stagnated and the urban wild lost. By allowing development to subsume the wilds, the ecological and social identity they provide disappears. It is crucial to see the wild as a hybrid space capable of accommodating the "range of productive processes that underlie urban transformations" rather than a perpetual holding ground.[43] The wild requires specific management and design to promote both ecological succession and cultural engagement. The layering is continuous and dynamic. Indeterminacy is the point. Diversity is the goal.

Sukopp and his colleagues articulated the urban wild as a typology in the urban matrix, as a kind of material to be deployed, as well as a landscape to value for its intrinsic contributions to greater fabric. The city has a range of complex spatio-temporal conditions that represent different habitat types and different cultural uses.[44] These landscapes represent a gradient of management from the overtly horticultural to the entirely neglected. They exist in different stages of succession from cracking pavement to established woodland. They support diverse floral, faunal, and human uses from sustaining to leisurely. The urban wild is a crucial part of this mosaic, contributing to the cultural and habitat diversity of the city. It must be understood for what it is individually and systemically. To reiterate, it is a constantly evolving, successional landscape, influenced by both ecological and human agents. It is a highly layered cultural space with a rich history of past use too often veiled by an emphasis on environmental systems. It is spontaneously vegetated, low-maintenance, and welcoming of unconstrained social uses. It is multiscalar, ranging in size from a small parcel to an entire coastal marsh system. As a remnant of undeveloped land or a site of past destruction, the urban wild has a cultural identity, an ecological robustness, and an inchoate future to be further defined, embraced, and managed.

Berlin Wilds: The Ruderal and the Rail

Berlin is the city where the urban wild is truly at home. The so-called wasteland—or vegetated, abandoned property—is considered a productive landscape by the city government, included with agricultural and educational landscapes.[45] Ruderal vegetation is understood, culturally, as viable habitat to be respected, again due to the extensive work of Sukopp and the Berlin School of Urban Ecology.[46] Wild landscapes do not carry the same unsavory socioeconomic connotations of danger and neglect. As a result, spontaneously growing vegetation is abundant, along rails and canals, in medians and tree trenches, and in parks and gardens. There are names for parks that merge spontaneous vegetation and human access (*natur-park*) as well as wild urban woodlands that emerge on rail infrastructure (*Gleiswildnis*). Berlin's landscapes form a wide gradient from defined wasteland to managed wild to manicured border. In fact, the strict species protection laws and extreme advocacy in the city make some wastelands and species practically sacred, altering projects and, at times, barring any type of development.[47]

Much is written about the role of a species-driven urban ecology in postwar Berlin and its influence on the design development of the city. The sociologist and environmental historian Jens Lachmund, who writes a comprehensive account of urban ecology in West Berlin, likens the relationship between Berlin and species-driven urban ecology to that of the Galapagos and evolutionary biology.[48] Theoretical innovations are linked to specific places—and the wide embrace of wild vegetation is particular to Berlin. The landscape architectural historian Sonja Dümpelmann describes it as "a Berlin-specific ecological awareness," in her accounting of the design projects taking place at the city's abandoned airports.[49] Berlin is a city that has adopted the urban wild as a culturally important and ecologically productive landscape, as the poster child of its specific breed of urban ecology. It is a place where the wild is a revered ecological habitat and a landscape with particular social characteristics. Paths are inserted, clearings are designed, views are constructed, and exploration is welcomed. The Berlin wild is a material condition adopted extensively by both ecology and design. It is for this very reason, for the particular and exciting marriage of ecology and design, that the following projects are exemplary and worthy of closer investigation.

Wilds in Practice: Grünanlage Hallesche Straße and Anhalter Bahnhof

To happen upon Grünanlage Hallesche Straße is to experience the evolution of the dry and sunny ruderal wild.[50] The black locust (*Robinia pseudoacacia)* woods are maturing since designated a protected landscape back in December 1987 to ensure the conservation of wild habitat in the urban core. The site is small, bounded, and discrete. It is a 0.7 hectare (1.73 acre) intact patch of woodland set amid a larger block of commercial and institutional buildings: a hotel, a courthouse, a school. It is also adjacent to the Anhalter Bahnhof site, a former train station destroyed during World War II and abandoned thereafter. Despite a strange amalgamation of tent performance space, architectural ruin, museum outposts, and protected woodland, the Anhalter Bahnhof site allows for a wonderful connection between the Grünanlage Hallesche Straße and larger wild park sites to the north and the south (for the connection refer to figures 30 and 32; for a drawing of the Grünanlage Hallesche Straße site itself see figure 25).

Grünanlage Hallesche Straße is unique within its immediate context and in the city at large. It stands as a small island amid other developments. It also holds a special place

Figure 25. Grünanlage Hallesche Straße structure, Berlin: axonometric view showing the distribution of black locusts, paths, and other amenities, as well as the location relative to the school and the District Court.

DSL Bank Berlin

Amtsgericht Berlin-Tempelhof-Kreuzberg

Clara-Grunwald-
Grundschule
Primary School

Möckernstraße

Hallesche Straße

in the history of ruderal vegetation in Berlin, as likely the first spontaneously vegetated landscape in Europe, and worldwide, to be deliberately conserved and left largely untouched. Its designation as protected green space occurred in the small window between the 1984 presentation of the working report of the biotope mapping project, its conversion into the West Berlin Species Protection Program in 1988, and the fall of the Berlin Wall in 1989.[51] The landscape architect and environmental planner Martin Schaumann, who was responsible for the Hallesche Straße project in the district of Kreuzberg, remembered this span as a great time to be working in West Berlin. The city had resources—time and money—and the area had vibrant, verdant wastelands. The site at Hallesche Straße, with its multilayered vegetative structure and manageable size, stood out as a clear choice for early protection. Though its designation as a protected landscape happened in 1987, the design work to open the site to the public was completed several years earlier, in the spring and summer of 1983. Following a change in the local administration (and the creation of a local nature division in the district government), there was impetus to test new ideas about building green spaces in the city. The Hallesche Straße site was full of rubble piles—a terrain of small hillocks of debris and trash—and emergent vegetation. Previously this type of landscape would likely be cleared, but instead the ruderal habitat was integrated into the project, as an experiment. As a result, the project is a rare instance where a small urban wild has persisted and adapted amid development pressure.

The current space is bound by Hallesche Straße to the north, Möckernstraße to the west, Kleinbeerenstraße to the south, and a primary school to the east. Prior to its destruction during World War II, the same block was predominately residential. The tight row of stately buildings, prewar, was sandwiched between the Nazi-era letter-sorting center, Postamt SW 11—the largest of its kind when it was built in the early 1930s, complete with a tunnel connection to the impressive Anhalter Bahnhof train station across Möckernstraße—and the large institutional complex of the district court for Tempelhof-Kreuzberg. Heavily damaged by aerial bombing during World War II, the residential buildings were demolished, and the site became home to a series of rubble piles in the decade after the war. Over time, vegetation well suited to the dry, poor soil conditions colonized the landscape, beginning a thirty-year procession of succession from fallow ground to herbaceous meadow to dry woodland (see figure 26 for plans and sections of this evolution). Grünanlage Hallesche Straße is a wonderful example of black locust woodland, with its exquisite, craggily and idiosyncratic tree forms creating an extensive canopied space of dappled light.

The black locust (*Robinia pseudoacacia*) is native to eastern North America, and while it tolerates numerous soil and climatic conditions, it excels on dry and sunny sites with nutrient-poor soils. It is a fast-growing (see figure 27), nitrogen-fixing tree with rot resistant wood.[52] It is a pioneer species that has become adapted to urban sites throughout North America and Europe. It was introduced to Europe in the mid-1600s by the

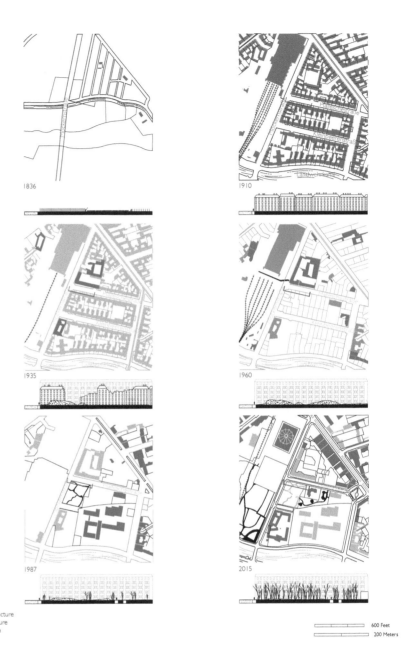

1836

1910

1935

1960

1987

2015

— Existing Structure
— New Structure
☐ Existing Path
■ New Path

600 Feet
200 Meters

Figure 26. Grünanlage Hallesche Straße plans and sections over time, Berlin.

French as a reforestation species and quickly dispersed throughout Europe, given its suitability for this application, likely arriving in Berlin in 1672. Black locust was planted heavily in central Europe during the late eighteenth and early nineteenth centuries as firewood, lumber, and erosion control on deforested sites. It continues to be planted for economic uses as well as recognized as providing benefits as an integral part of

Figure 27. *Robinia pseudoacacia* (black locust): a drawing of the material nature and growth patterns of the species.

novel ecosystems on abandoned urban and industrial sites.[53] At Grünanlage Hallesche Straße, the black locust is celebrated. It is understood as part of the urban story.

Fitting with its elusive definition, the urban wild is more often a reactive classification: a designation placed on an existing space whose existence is often a matter of human neglect. Crucially, it is a term used to describe a condition of human abandonment rather than a condition of desired open space. Somehow the wild happens de facto, and the decision is whether to keep it moving forward rather than whether to create conditions to foster its initial existence. This is still the case with the Grünanlage

Hallesche Straße, a space fostered by war destruction, development stagnation, and conservation during a briefly ripe political climate for such conservation. It is a historically significant site, a place to imagine a past Berlin, a living homage to an almost lost cultural condition. Its position in the greater wild urban woodlands' discussion is underplayed, and its appreciation limited.[54] It is perhaps too understated for general consumption. But then it is desired for its intentional lack of overt design, thus encouraging less calculated uses. Unlike other designed open spaces that resulted from the faunal and floral studies, it was not conceived of as a park or part of a larger park landscape. It remains woodland, a place for children's play, a place for dogs to rush free and catch sticks, a place to amble and sit among the black locust trees.

As we have seen, this does not mean that the space lacks design, or that it only considers its tree population. The first design decision, in fact, is to keep the site, without significant demolition or construction. The project's aim is to demonstrate the potential of using existing, uncultivated vegetation—of maintaining a disregarded habitat—while opening the site to play and occupation. The original design is simple and remains. Its hallmark is the thirty-year-old clearing in the forest. Until 2014, the site functioned as an open pass-through, a brief woodland experience embedded within the city. Now, it is enclosed, cutting off circulation, to create a *naturerfahrungsraum,* meaning "nature experience room for children."[55] The site is adjacent to a school, and its evolution is fitting. The locust trees, whose wavy, idiosyncratic silhouettes are unlike any found in nursery cultivation, remain, with selective thinning to allow in light. The rubble piles persist, their gentle erosion and subsidence recalling their age. The place is haunting yet alive with the free play of dogs and children (see figure 28). The interruption in the built fabric recalls a sordid history. Its quietness calls to the memory of its former inhabitants brutally displaced.[56]

On the parcels adjacent to the south, O. M. Ungers worked as the architect hired to rebuild the District Court building. The courthouse was also significantly damaged during the war, leaving only a small part standing. With Berlin's reunification, the decision was made to rebuild the District Court. Ungers worked on the project from 1989 through its completion in 1994. He and his team inserted a narrow building, integrating the preexisting structure and mature plant life into the final project. Governed by the policies and regulations that have been put in place because of Sukopp and others' work, he respected the tree canopy that resulted from years of postwar vacancy. The outcome is a tree grove that extends from the Grünanlage Hallesche Straße to the Landwehrkanal, a canal from the mid-nineteenth century. The urban wild structures the urban design of the larger area, creating a calm that offsets the busy streetscapes that circumscribes it. In a miniature sense, the District Court is an island within the wild fabric, a fabric that extends to the east and south, through a series of open spaces atop the defunct rail infrastructure of the city. It is possible to leave the nearest U-Bahn stop at Möckernbrücke and wander beneath the black locusts, moving between sites

Figure 28. Grünanlage Hallesche Straße, Berlin, 2015.

without following traditional roads and sidewalks, analogous to the freedom of moving off-grid through a series abandoned urban parcels.

Across Hallesche Straße are the wilds of the former Anhalter Bahnhof train station and yards. The site is immense, bracketed by the extant facade of the former station to the north and stretching over the Landwehrkanal to the south. Here, the ruderal vegetation envelopes the Deutsches Technikmuseum where the building architecture bends around preexisting wild vegetation. The sites ultimately connect to the Park am Gleisdreieck (see below) and beyond, following the lines of the old rail system. The result is a beautiful route through the city where woodlands weave between transit stops, where old relics yield arresting views, and where new construction is integrated to leave patches of *Gleiswildnis* amid the necessary infrastructure of a global city. It is possible to be immersed in woodlands and reemerge in technology, bringing a bike with you all the way.

Wilds in Practice: Natur-Park Schöneberger Südgelände

If Grünanlage Hallesche Straße is the hidden example of wild urban woodland, Natur-Park Schöneberger Südgelände is perhaps the most celebrated.[57] The park, which opened to the public in 2000, embodies the political realities of integrating existing spontaneous vegetation into a recreational landscape. It is both a compensation project for central rail construction that occurred elsewhere and a result of strong advocacy from ecologists, environmental activists, and visitors who grew to love the site during its so-called dormancy. Proposals for rekindling rail activity on the site were defeated, and the 18-hectare (44.5-acre) tract became a place to foster wild habitat and increase recreational ground in the city. The Südgelände site represents a negotiation between opening public access and conserving the ecological function of the place, as well as an experiment in fostering biodiversity through differential management of the

Figure 29. Natur-Park Schöneberger Südgelände, Berlin, 2011.

successional landscape. To this end, the site is designed to have protected meadows and woodlands, as well as larger places for gatherings and events, through circulation, remnant rail elements, and art installations.

The park planners, ÖkoCon & Planland, provided a variety of vantage points and experiences, while largely preserving the vegetation intact and maintaining the qualities of exploration, discovery, and surprise inherent to the site, at least in the eyes of the site newbie. These include viewing towers, alcoves and platforms, elevated walks, at-grade paths, trestle paths, swings, climbable sculptures by the Odious Group, and graffiti walls. In addition to these insertions, the ecologists consulting on the project helped orchestrate a three-pronged site management strategy. The approach arrests succession in places to promote rare species and diversity, maintains tree groves in locations, and allows other parts of the site to continue to develop into woodland with as little management and intervention as possible—more in line with the initial approach at the Grünanlage Hallesche Straße site. The result is an experience that transitions between clearing, tree stand, and forest; between light, dappled, and dark; between distant, proximal, and immersive.

Having never visited the site in its pre-park condition and having limited ability to predict alternative futures for the site, I am unable to know the effect the park designation has had on the preexisting vegetation. Could the site have been conserved as a wild open to the public with a set of governing rules—as could be said of the Grünanlage Hallesche Straße? Or was the political condition post-unification too different from the one just before? Does the compromise meet the greater objectives of the idea of the city as a collection of urban biotopes? In the face of development pressure, can all nine levels of heberomy exist in the urban environment? These are questions to ponder on the itinerant routes through Berlin's wilds.

To a visitor, it is clear that the Südgelände site has been designed. For me, this is a wonderful instance where the design enhances rather than detracts from the site's allure and wild identity. On a purely ecological level, the walkways may be intruders, but their presence is perceptually light. This is, of course, not by accident but the result of a long set of negotiations between the designers, ecologists, artists, and citizens. The elevated walkways were important to the ecologists as a means to maintain certain biotope types that required humans to stay above while letting light filter through the perforations to the flora below. The design is an effective registration of the many interests in the park—and perhaps this is why it is an example for many of how to achieve a balance between human intervention and ecological will. The industrial aesthetic does not overpower. The site remains about the character of the plant form and the choreography of the experience of the vegetation. The best art pieces frame through-portals, elevate perspectives, and privilege vantage points. The guided elevated transect provides a strong contrast between the two conserved extremes. On one hand you see the open meadow and the dense forest, and then the branched circulation through the groves traces the former rail lines and trestles in a way that evokes the feeling of a trodden desire path, allowing one to imagine as if they were moving through the pre-park site, following the remnant lines as guides.

The path system is a means of tying together the various spaces in the Südgelände site—and the walks on-site connect to walks through the adjacent landscapes as part of a regional planning initiative to link diverse spaces across greater Berlin. In addition to guiding the development of the various park projects, the Berlin Senate Department for Urban Development and the Environment has developed a system of twenty green walks—ranging in length from the seven-kilometer Bullengraben Walk along a small watercourse to the fifty-nine-kilometer (thirty-seven-mile) River Spree / Berlin Glacial Valley Walk across the entire territory—to connect the city's remaining corridors and recreational spaces.[58] The system, like the conserved green spaces and nature parks, stems from the landscape conservation program. The connections are thin filigrees that still allow for some of the cut-throughs and off-road experiences of lushness that was a signature of Berlin of the 1980s. Way-finding devices guide the contemporary walker through a diverse set of spaces and experiences, a macro-scale version of some of the scripted walks and trails found in the individual parks along the way. The signs are needed, as the routes are long and complex with many jogs, a reflection of the fragmented nature of the open space system. When experienced in totality, the long walks give an understanding of the ecological parameters of the city—its hydrology, geology, and physical morphology—while the fragments offer local snippets that highlight individual landscapes. The Natur-Park Schöneberger Südgelände is on the forty-five-kilometer (twenty-eight-mile) *North–South Walk* that follows a Spree tributary to the north and the parks that have developed on the former rail and airport infrastructure to the south.[59] The route provides a physical link between a series of sites with celebrated spontaneous vegetation providing a thread between Südgelände and two other sites, Templehofer Freiheit and Park am Gleisdreieck, with the former Anhalter Bahnhof site and Grünanlage Hallesche Straße just to the east of the path (see figure 30 for sections through the city and sites, along the routes of walk and rail).

Wilds in Practice: Park am Gleisdreieck

If Grünanlage Hallesche Straße is a conserved wild, and Natur-Park Schöneberger Südgelände is a conserved wild operating as a park, then Park am Gleisdreieck is a park with patches of conserved wild. Located at the confluence of two major rail lines (*Gleisdreieck* means "triangle of rails"), the twenty-six-hectare (sixty-four-acre) park represents the largest and most ambitious of the rail wasteland conservation and conversion projects undertaken by the city. The project resulted from decades of protest, notably of a major ring road project planned for the site in 1965 and ultimately defeated by citizen action. This halt created the possibility of an open space plan for the area.

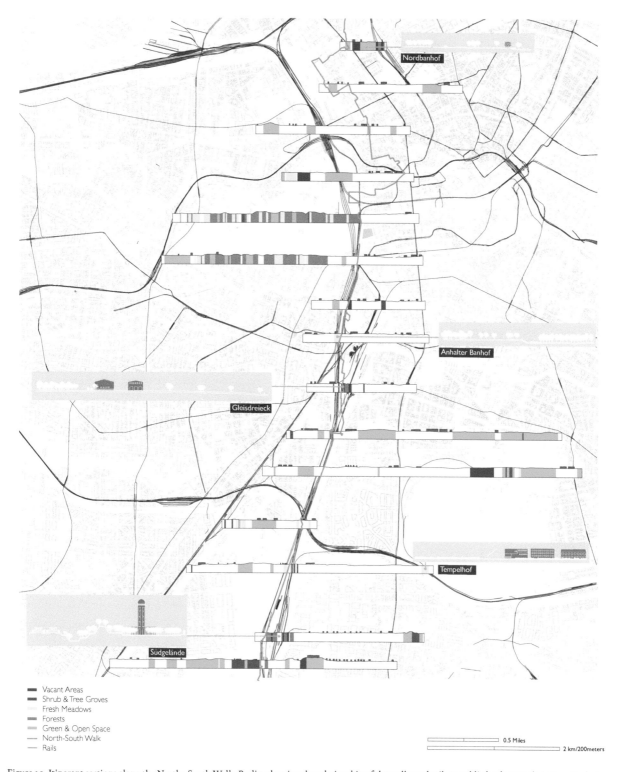

Vacant Areas
Shrub & Tree Groves
Fresh Meadows
Forests
Green & Open Space
North-South Walk
Rails

Nordbanhof

Anhalter Banhof

Gleisdreieck

Tempelhof

Südgelände

0.5 Miles

2 km/200meters

Figure 30. Itinerant sections along the North–South Walk, Berlin, showing the relationship of the walks and rails to public landscapes that integrate design and wild vegetation.

However, the character of this open space was widely debated for decades, with one vocal group calling for a nature park, like Schöneberger Südgelände, where the *Gleiswildnis* would be left relatively intact and public use would be heavily confined. The ultimate site design followed another trajectory, responding to multiple pressures on the developing city. Some *Gleiswildnis* remains, but the site also functions to open up urban connections once sealed off by the inaccessible site and provide numerous recreational and programmatic amenities for the surrounding communities.

The rail infrastructure on the Gleisdreieck site was heavily damaged during World War II and all rail activity ceased with the construction of the Berlin Wall in 1961. While development plans—such as the ring road—were being considered, vegetation grew—the botanist Ulrich Asmus identified 417 different species in the first site survey conducted in 1980—and people fell in love with the wild woodlands.[60] The first demands for a nature park came before reunification and were quickly dismissed as the site was used as the temporary construction staging ground for the extensive building at Potsdamer Platz, with long-term plans for a permanent park. Park discussions resumed in the late 1990s and early 2000s.

Today the vegetation structure in Park am Gleisdreieck is heavily altered, but there are still significant stands of wilds, especially in the Flaschenhalspark, or Bottleneck Park, area to the south. Again, a group of nature park advocates dominated the early discussions, forcing the city to invest in a comprehensive citizen's participation initiative to extend the discussion to a larger constituency. Part of the outreach included an image survey conducted with park abutters with four park types represented: nature park, landscape park, modern park, and sports park. The nature and the landscape parks were the most desired—and in the end, the design is a hybrid between these typologies: with a heavily programmed exterior of playgrounds, skate parks, gardens, and cafés; an open center with manicured lawns and small, less maintained wild stands of preexisting vegetation; and linear swaths of heavily conserved and largely off-limits *Gleiswildnis*. The one location where the wilds are more accessible and where the paths weave in and out of vegetated stands is in the Flaschenhalspark (the left side of figure 31 is in this area).

The Park am Gleisdreieck, designed by the Berlin-based landscape architects Atelier Loidl, exemplifies the fruitful struggle required to articulate a middle ground between conservation and park, between neglect and control, between ecology and design. The urban wild becomes a material to deploy, not through an additive operation like a traditional planting scheme but through allowance and maintenance. While there is certainly nostalgia for the Gleisdreieck site of the 1980s, there is also a recognition that it is through compromise that the wilds still exist in the park, and through the park that they will continue to exist here and elsewhere in the city.

The park represents its multiple histories—trains still pass through the middle albeit museum trains making their journey from museum to museum; ruins still sit in stands

Figure 31. Park am Gleisdreieck, Berlin, 2015.

of locust and birch; kids of all ages play vigorously on the swings, slides, and trampolines; residents appreciate the straight connection between neighborhoods; citizens enjoy events on the large, central open space in the city; rare flora are protected in the wilderness areas. Here, the two legacies of provocative design and urban ecology coalesce. The balance is, overall, commendable, but the old wilds cannot help but feel contained—not so much because of the spatial distribution but because opening the site to a large population meant closing the wilds off to human use. They are most engaging as immersive experiments rather than as mature landscapes that have achieved conservation status. In the transition between the east and west parts of the park, squeezed in-between heavy infrastructure, itself a kind of wild, you find a moment like this, where a perched meadow surprises, extending the horizon and meeting the rail soaring above in an unlikely but arresting marriage.

I had the pleasure of being guided to this point by Almut Jirku, from the Senatsverwaltung für Stadtentwicklung und Umwelt (Senate Department for Urban Development and Housing), who played a key role in the inception of this project—and many other key landscape projects—as part of the competitions team for the municipality. On her tour of the recently completed park, she paused here, as if to understand it as the key view of the park, where the many layers collide spatially to reveal the park's intent in action. Jirku, and her team, demand an open process for the evolution and design of Berlin's landscapes. In this process, they strive for diversity—for parks to be open to everyone—and to be places where people feel good. (Jirku also stopped to photograph the "Refugees Welcome" marker on the right side of figure 31 as if to embrace the park as a site for open political dialogue.)[61] Back on the perched meadow, these aspirations resonate as the wild landscape cascades downward, to a sea of passive and active recreation beyond. The park is full of conversations, negotiations, fruitful compromises, and recognitions of the future challenges of affordability that its very existence provokes.

Wilds Connected: Berlin Landscape Planning and the North–South Landscape Corridor

Grünanlage Hallesche Straße, Natur-Park Schöneberger Südgelände, and Park am Gleisdreieck represent three time points in landscape planning in Berlin, three uses of the urban wild, and three parts of near-continuous landscape of distinct public parklands (see figure 32 for a map of their locations). This is not coincidence, of course, but rather because they are located at sites of abandoned infrastructure, connected and united by a desire and mandate to compensate for other infrastructure and building projects elsewhere in the city. A lot of the conserved wilds, especially those owned by the Deutsche Bahn, achieve conservation through compensation. For example, the Grünanlage Elise Tilse on the Anhalter Bahnhof site was created as compensation for the destruction of another natural area in the construction of the Hanover-Berlin high-speed rail. Slowly, the sites of postwar rubble piles, former transportation infrastructure, defunct rail yards, and airports are being defined and designed. While the landscapes share similarities with other landscape design projects built on defunct industrial and infrastructural sites, they are also clear products of a Berlin-specific approach.

As established, Berlin is paradigmatic of a species-driven ecological approach in the creation of urban open space.[62] The preservation of individual sites, species, and specimens as natural monuments began in the early 1900s, followed by a federal policy to protect larger nature reserves in 1935, and areas that can be integrated into and conceived of as public landscapes.[63] This tradition is furthered through the fieldwork of the botanists and "what earlier had been a kind of unintentional experiment—the spontaneous development of vegetation in the destroyed city—became a model on which the governance and shaping of urban space was intentionally based."[64] Fieldwork

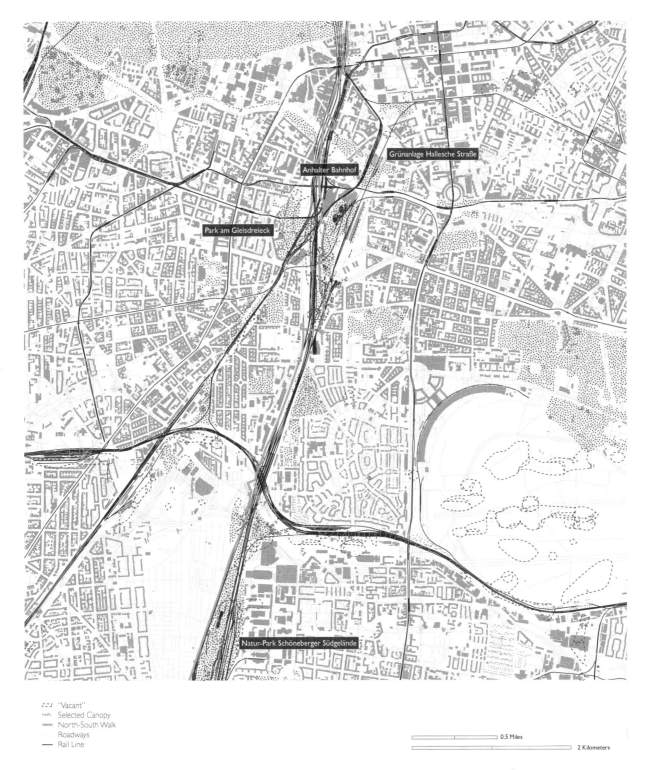

Grünanlage Hallesche Straße

Anhalter Bahnhof

Park am Gleisdreieck

Natur-Park Schöneberger Südgelände

"Vacant"
Selected Canopy
North-South Walk
Roadways
Rail Line

0.5 Miles

2 Kilometers

Figure 32. Plan from Anhalter Banhof to Natur-Park Schöneberger Südgelände, Berlin.

becomes a political project with spatial outcome. Ostensibly, this is true: the work of the ecologists drives policy decisions and results in a series of public landscapes that consider their biotopes and, to varying degrees, preserve the preexisting spontaneous vegetation in their designs. The urban open spaces, conserved and constructed from 1987 on, embody the aforementioned fourth nature—a term taken from Ingo Kowarik and the Berlin School of Urban Ecology that carries through to signify a cyclical trend of habitat establishment.

The designs and maintenance regimes embrace the remaining spontaneous vegetation fully, without wanting to eradicate dominant species; they have an aesthetic that includes industrial and informal materials; and they aim for a controlled freedom that is forbidden in other public parkland. For example, graffiti is allowed in Natur-Park Schöneberger Südgelände, except on Sunday. Sheep graze as a form of maintenance. Dogs are allowed to roam in Grünanlage Hallesche Straße. People transgress. However, the projects also represent a compromise between ecology and recreation that can render an inherently wild and dynamic landscape static. There is an irreconcilable conflict between species protection and heavy human use, as well as between biodiversity and ecological succession.[65] The results, in a struggle for balance, create a formal and forced separation between ecologically protected areas and places of human use. It is equally exciting and frustrating that biotope evaluation has entered the realm of urban development and park design. The efforts to integrate human and nonhuman habitat in the urban mosaic are laudable. Yet the limitations of pure conservation, expressed differently on each of the sites, has the potential to undermine the dynamic quality of the wild. A harsh dichotomy exists between spaces for plants and spaces for people, affecting the spatial design. The three sites highlighted—Grünanlage Hallesche Straße, Natur-Park Schöneberger Südgelände, and Park am Gleisdreieck—are nimble in these regards. They present a more dynamic approach to conservation, allowing for the co-evolution of habitat and human experience in a developed metropolis.

The ecologists in Berlin created a cultural value that did not previously exist. Through their documentation, they revealed a functioning ecosystem that is not a pristine or an undeveloped remnant but rather a reemergent landscape on highly disturbed sites. They found a high level of biodiversity as well as viable social uses that change with time. The ecologists visited the sites over decades, using them as research areas, where their ecological succession is part of their value as study parcels. The studies were driven by circumstance (the ecologists had no access to sites outside the city and great access to rubble piles in the city) rather than hypothesis. The level of ecological function found was surprising and rich.

In many ways, it is the measurement and articulation of this new value that is the greatest contribution of the work, rather than the red lists of species they seek to protect. The ability to study the sites over time—and to watch them change—gave substance to the project, laying the groundwork for future scientific pursuit and speculation. The work was well known throughout Europe. For example, Sukopp contributed to the landscape planner and architect Ian Laurie's *Nature in Cities: The Natural Environment in the Design and Development of Urban Green Space* from 1979, a text referenced by Anne Whiston Spirn and Elizabeth Barlow Rogers, among others. Gonçalo Ribeiro Telles, the landscape architect, planner, and politician, referenced Sukopp extensively in his *Plano Verde de Lisboa*.[66] Sukopp attended major conferences on urban ecology and urban design, and he read, channeled, and reinterpreted the work of Ian McHarg.

Wilds as a Network: Green Grid Redux

Still, there may never be a condition of urban abandonment so great, over a time span long enough to allow for a radical departure from the past—to see the scale of Unger's Green Grid in practice. Perhaps, in reality, the pluralist city is more suited to the responsive mosaic of the Berlin urban ecologist than the speculative islands in a green tissue envisioned by Ungers and his collaborators. There is no question that the condition of West Berlin in the 1970s was a unique moment, constructed by very specific social and political conditions, where wild landscapes could proliferate on abandoned sites—and where a green sea could live, at least on paper. It is unclear how extensive the conserved wild lands might have extended had the momentum not shifted with the reunification of the city and its designation as capital. It is, however, clear that for a system as thick and rich as Unger's Green Grid to evolve, either major demolition must occur, or a longer-term view must be taken.

To date, the power of the urban wilds rests with the individual sites, and the systemic linkages have been weak (see figure 33). In Berlin, there are spectacular sites and fragments, but the relationships between them have yet to become structural. This is similar to the conditions in Boston and New York, where ecologically robust sites have emerged—and in the case of Boston fifty-four urban wilds are protected—but they remain isolated tracts of land, both physically and conceptually. The potential exists for the sites to be connected in both geographical and thematic clusters. In Berlin, the wilds cluster around defunct rail infrastructure as well as the locations near the former wall. They seem to relate in plan, but on the ground it is still hard to link them. In Boston and other North American cities, the extant constellation is a remarkable indication of geological condition and development practice over time. A shoreline system could unify the city's largest marshes; inland streams, like the previously mentioned Bussey Brook, could highlight the wilds that populate their watersheds; while the outcroppings of puddingstone, a sedimentary formation specific to the region, could be a network of dispersed but related monuments. The initial wilds surveys, in Boston, New York, and Berlin, arose out of identifiable conditions: thin soils, rock and rubble outcroppings, hardened streams, abandoned rails, and stormwater impoundment areas, to name a few. They have developed individually as sites, removed from their shared

Walks
01 River Spree/Berlin Glacial Valley
02 Spandau
03 Heiligenseer
04 Lübars
05 North-South Walk
06 Lindenberg Corridor
07 Hönow
08 Kaulsdorf
09 River Dahme
10 Britz-Buckow
11 Wannsee
12 Havel Lakes
13 Barnim Villages
14 Wuhle Valley
15 Teltow Villages
16 Humboldt
17 Teltow Canal
18 Inner Park Ring
19 Tiergarten
20 Bullengraben

Figures 30 and 32

A. Nordbahnof   B. Tilla Durieux   C. Gleisdreieck   D. Südgelände   E. Görlitzer   F. Anhalter Bahnhof

Conservation Landscape
Grassland
Green Space
Forest
Vacant Neglected Areas

Fallow Railway
Ruderal Forb
Vacant, not classified as a type of green space
Roadways
Rail Line
Walks

3 Miles
6 Kilometers

Figure 33. Wilds, parks, and walks, Berlin: map showing the distribution of sites and routes across the city.

origins. The beauty of Unger's proposal is the thickness of the sea, its form, its size, and its widespread purpose.

The urban wilds have not been planned from their onset, but rather observed and then included in a policy and planning effort. They represent the anti-planned that is, at times, grandfathered into the plan. The idea of the network is post facto, as a means of connection only.[67] In a way, the wilds are more like Unger's architectural islands, but without the matrix that contains them. As isolated fragments, they sometimes become lost. They are individual tiles detached from the larger continuous mosaic. As a result, there is no relationship between site and context. This is a function of the reactive conservation of a spontaneously developed space. The decision-making process is not about where wild spaces should occur and how best to cultivate them socially and ecologically, but rather a triage-type system to determine whether or not existing wilds should be kept.

Wilds as a Preemptive Idea for Future Abandonment

The urban wild is a name ascribed to a space that exists physically in the city, a default that can either be accepted or changed. But the urban wild has the potential to be a preemptive insertion, a landscape deliberately designed into the cycles of urban development. As such, the urban wild would be integrated into the city, physically related to its context. In West Berlin, the urban wilds in the 1970s, by their sheer number and extent, were a part of the fabric—places to walk dogs, shortcuts to move between destinations, planted retreats for shade and discovery. They functioned within their context, as a shared landscape reflective of the city's culture and status. The amount of wild and wasteland has, of course, diminished with development pressure—and some key study sites have been lost or built upon[68]—but the wildness is still imprinted in the city's civic identity.

When solely conserved, the wilds stand as relics to a past time, largely frozen, isolated, and anachronistic. But when they adapt to the changing needs of the residents, as seen in the three case studies, they can evolve without ceding their wild characteristics. The integration of wastelands into Berlin's developing landscape has fostered a larger conversation about the value of the wild in the city. This is played out through a set of experiments and initiatives that—through individual projects—aim to foster this wildness in a proactive way, by making and catering the wilds to meet a cultural agenda. In other words, by allowing encroachment and other uses (recreation, cultivation, education, exploration), more of the wilds can persist.

The urban wild does not have to be relegated to a description of a found condition. Given its range of size, structure, and meaning, it has an incredible potential to be responsive to socioeconomic and political conditions. The extents of wilds can expand and contract organically with economic fluctuation, but the extents can also be controlled deliberately. By preparing the ground and guiding development with maintenance, the wilds can be made and used to promote biodiversity and social flexibility. It may very well be that the spontaneous wilds created through abandonment do not all make sense in the longer-term evolution of the city and that keeping them might result in odd fragments that suffer from disintegration and poor connection, for the flora, the fauna, and the people. If the wild does not make sense in one location, it could still be fostered elsewhere, where the social and ecological conditions are more appropriate.

The spaces have different meanings and appropriateness depending on the socioeconomic and physical context. But as we face a changing climate, we must turn to the wilds and understand their cultural and ecological relevance. An area of great need might need a more intensive investment to sustain the health and welfare of a community. An area of great density might benefit from a connective retreat as an alternative way to move within the urban fabric. A place of great environmental degradation might welcome a resilient ecosystem to offset the toxicity. A hot place might benefit from cool. A wet place might benefit from absorption. A barren place might benefit from exuberance. The key is not to freeze the wilds that remain or be nostalgic about those lost. Instead, the idea is to retain the dynamism of the wild sites and to appreciate them as a design material for inclusion in the city as part of the overall floral, faunal, and human diversity.

Wilds as Commons: Cycles

Ultimately, the wilds, too, function as commons, as shared resource and utility for the city. They may now be claimed—or even owned—but their previously unclaimed status allowed for their evolution. In fact, their very existence is a reflection of certain spatial conditions in the city, for example, as discussed here, the defunct rail lines in Berlin. The wilds reveal an intrinsic quality in the city, and in Berlin's case, the sites have been reinforced through additional landscape initiatives to strengthen their presence in the city. Their very evolution requires a long pause in active ownership and use; an abandonment that opens them up to collective experience. The Berliners who wander onto the ruderal sites share their resources with each other, with the floral and faunal colonizers, and with the city. The collective excitement over the spaces leads to their continued evolution into defined and more lasting resources within the city (see figure 34 for an idea of relating the daily, yearly, decennial, and centurial cycles of history, economy, population, ecology, succession, and wildness).

The most successful transformations are the longer lasting ones where the design respects the need for discovery, informality, and incongruous juxtaposition to remain and grow. These wilds exist within the larger landscape of the city and operate well only in opposition to places of heavy construction and manipulation. A gradient is needed, and the wilds sites perform, as biological machines for the city. And while sheep graze

Figure 34. Wild time cycles: a diagram of plant growth, housing, population, and climate over time.

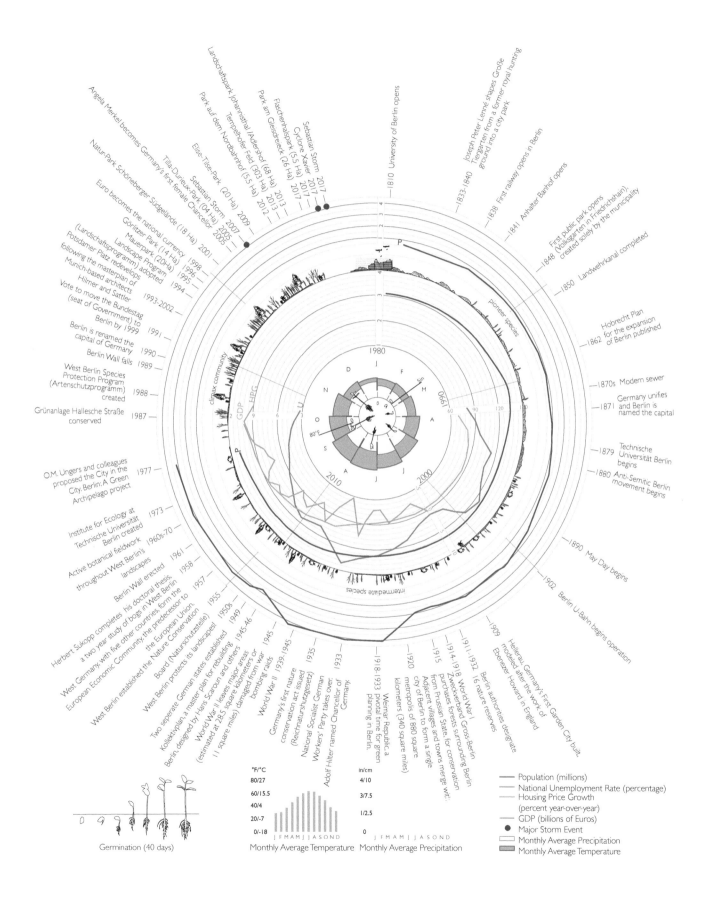

Angela Merkel becomes Germany's first female Chancellor 2005
Natur-Park Schöneberger Südgelände (18 Ha) 2000
Euro becomes the national currency 2001
Görlitzer Park (14 Ha) 1998
Mauerpark (20 Ha) 1996
Potsdamer Platz redevelops following the masterplan of Munich-based architects Hilmer and Sattler 1993-2002
Vote to move the Bundestag (seat of Government) to Berlin by 1999 1991
Berlin is renamed the capital of Germany 1990
Berlin Wall falls 1989
West Berlin Species Protection Program (Artenschutzprogramm) created 1988
Grünanlage Hallesche Straße conserved 1987
O.M. Ungers and colleagues proposed the City in the City, Berlin: A Green Archipelago project 1977
Institute for Ecology at Technische Universität Berlin created 1973
Active botanical fieldwork throughout West Berlin's landscapes 1960s-70
Berlin Wall erected 1961
Herbert Sukopp completes his doctoral thesis, a two year study of bogs in West Berlin 1958
West Germany, with five other countries, form the European Economic Community, the predecessor to the European Union. 1957
West Berlin established the Nature Conservation Board (Naturschutzstelle) 1955
Two seperate German states established 1949
West Berlin protects its landscapes 1950s
Kollektivplan, a master plan for rebuilding Berlin, designed by Hans Scaroun and others 1945-46
World War II leaves major areas (estimated at 28.5 square kilometers or 11 square miles) damaged from war bombing raids 1945
World War II 1939-1945
Germany's first nature conservation act issued (Reichnaturschutzgesetz) 1935
National Socialist German Workers' Party takes over. 1933
Adolf Hitler named Chancellor of Germany.

Landschaftspark Johannisthal / Adlershof 2009
Tempelhofer Feld (303 Ha) 2013
Park am Gleisdreieck (26 Ha) 2013
Flaschenhalspark (5.5 Ha) 2017
Cyclone Xavier 2017
Sebastian Storm 2017
Park auf dem Nordbahnhof (5.5 Ha) 2012
Elise-Tilse-Park (20 Ha) 2005
Tilla-Durieux-Park (04 Ha) 2005
Sebastian Storm 2007
(Landschaftsprogramm) Landscape Program adopted 1994

University of Berlin opens 1810
Joseph Peter Lenné shapes Große Tiergarten from a former royal hunting ground into a city park 1833-1840
First railway opens in Berlin 1838
Anhalter Bahnhof opens 1841
First public park opens (Volksgarten in Friedrichshain) created solely by the municipality 1848
Landwehrkanal completed 1850
Hobrecht Plan for the expansion of Berlin published 1862
Modern sewer 1870s
Germany unifies and Berlin is named the capital 1871
Technische Universität Berlin begins 1879
Anti-Semitic Berlin movement begins 1880
May Day begins 1890
Berlin U-Bahn begins operation 1902
Berlin authorities designate 16 nature reserves 1909
Hellerau, Germany's First Garden City built, modeled after the work of Ebenezer Howard in England 1911-1932
World War I 1914-1918
Zweckverband Gross-Berlin purchases forests surrounding Berlin from Prussian State, for conservation 1915
Adjacent villages and towns merge with city of Berlin to form a single metropolis of 880 square kilometers (340 square miles) 1920
Weimar Republic, a pivotal time for green planning in Berlin. 1918-1933

pioneer species
climax community
intermediate species
GDP   HPG

1980
1990
2000
2010

D J F N M O A S J A J

80°E

5 in
P

Germination (40 days)

°F/°C
80/27
60/15.5
40/4
20/-7
0/-18
J F M A M J J A S O N D
Monthly Average Temperature

in/cm
4/10
3/7.5
1/2.5
0
J F M A M J J A S O N D
Monthly Average Precipitation

—— Population (millions)
—— National Unemployment Rate (percentage)
—— Housing Price Growth (percent year-over-year)
—— GDP (billions of Euros)
● Major Storm Event
☐ Monthly Average Precipitation
☐ Monthly Average Temperature

once again, literally, there is room conceptually for greater definition of the shared utility of the spaces, greater alliance with the common over the park. There are certainly still questions as to what the wilds are and what they can best offer. Until this is fully investigated, through the design and management of related sites, the full plurality of the city is in jeopardy, the exigent love child of ecology and design developmentally delayed.

3

HORTAS

500 Years of Agronomy and Landscape Planning in Lisbon

It is somewhat rare—even now—that a landscape architect is interviewed on television during the coverage of a major storm event, but the Portuguese landscape architect Gonçalo Ribeiro Telles was not a typical landscape architect. He was a designer, academic, politician, coordinator of the definitive ecological plan for Lisbon, and consummate advocate for the responsible development of the environment. In his television interview following the 1967 metropolitan Lisbon floods, his message was clear and resounding. Urban design, and more specifically the decision to build in the floodplain, was to blame for the disaster that killed over five hundred people.[1] The Portuguese philosopher and environmentalist Viriato Soromenho Marques remembers Telles's straightforward declaration forty years later.[2] For Marques and others, Telles words were extremely direct and noteworthy in a political climate that dissuaded public criticism.[3]

While Ribeiro Telles was referring to the situation in Odivelas and other small settlements in a vast drainage basin northwest of the city's airport, he could have been referring to the contested valleys within the city of Lisbon. An image search of *cheias* (floods) and *Lisboa* (Lisbon) reveals countless images of waters rushing past stately buildings and city cars floating above inundated streets. Some of these streets follow the lines of the city's major valleys, which include, moving from east to west, Olivais, Chelas, San Antonio, Valverde, Anjo, and Alcantara (see figure 37 for the valleys, with the impermeable surfaces within filled in black). These finger-like valleys extend up from the Tagus River (Rio Tejo) and into the city, figuring prominently in the urban form and agricultural legacy of Lisbon. Geological lines surface as the street grid and civic spaces in places such as the Campo Grande.[4] Steep embankments are vegetated and even farmed. The upper plateaus and lower floodplains are populated with

Figure 35. Micro-furrows,
Lisbon, 2014.

buildings, with hard and impermeable surfaces that tax the watershed. Pavements in
the floodplains are ubiquitous.

The largest valley, the Alcantara, which drains half of the city's surface waters, is a
major transportation corridor with rail lines and highways running down the middle. It
is an environmental planner's nightmare. Significant structural overhaul is required to
address the flooding issues caused by the development of the valley. In recent years, the
city has focused its stewardship efforts on more readily achievable initiatives in other
valleys, including the Chelas valley, a smaller ravine that parallels the Alcantara on the
city's eastern edge. In Chelas, unlike the more central and more developed valleys, significant parts of the valley remain unpaved. In the open lands, agronomy finds its place.

The farming of the interstices is a citywide practice in Lisbon, where many of the
city's immigrants have deep ties to agriculture and bring their expertise to the municipal landscape (see figure 36 for the distribution of open lands, horticultural parks,
and vacant land across the prominent topography). The farmers occupy city-owned
lands spontaneously, capturing both the physical and temporal gaps in the urban development. They seize opportunities in areas where building lags, and in the past they
have been quickly evicted when land values rise, and speculation takes over. They find
other plots, often on steep slopes, determined to carry on key cultural practices. Their

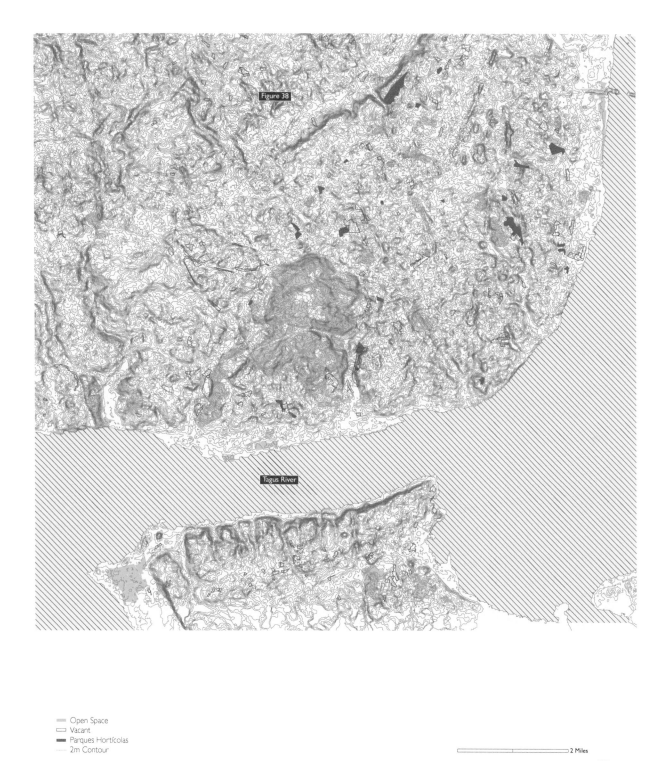

Open Space
Vacant
Parques Hortícolas
2m Contour

Figure 38

Tagus River

2 Miles
4 Kilometers

Figure 36. Valleys and vacancy, Lisbon: a reading of the city through its topography.

persistence is beginning to resonate with city officials. The city is engaging existing allotments and planning future ones, as part of a greater focus on the role of urban agriculture in the environmental planning process.

In this chapter, the symbiotic relationship between the valley landscape and agronomic tradition is explored in several sites across the city where the histories of development and cultivation are intertwined. The protection of the soil is a political, socioeconomic, and ecological project, one that underlies the city's green planning and agricultural initiatives. Cultivation is a long-standing practice in the city—one representing both cultural patrimony and contemporary struggle.

Soil and Water

In fact, to understand Lisbon's relationship to soil and water is to understand the city. Located in one of the three major basins in the country, Lisbon's estuarine soils are good for cultivation—a fact recognized by the prehistorical and ancient Roman occupiers as well as the current purveyors of the remarkable landscape. Rich soil is hard to come by and, once disturbed, is difficult to regenerate.[5] While fertile soil takes thousands of years to form, it can fallow remarkably quickly.

The center of Lisbon, on its riverine edge, is built atop alluvial soils, while detrital sedimentary rocks with limestone of Miocene age underlie much of rest of the city. The geology is varied, with marine and continental sands, clays, and carbonates, and a volcanic complex to the east.[6] It is the quasi-rural areas[7]—both within the city and in the valleys to the north and east—that are the most suitable for agriculture. Here the water drains from the mountains, through and around the city, into the rich and navigable estuary of the Tagus River (see figure 37 for the distribution of valleys, soils, and building in the lowlands).

The rich soil of the floodplains creates a bed for agriculture—a place for crops, and later development, as the availability of food and water bring settlement. This mixture of agriculture and development remains central to the fabric of Lisbon, where parts of the city have stayed agricultural, marking a continued investment in the soil as an integral part of the cultural heritage. This is not to say that the soil has not suffered. Compaction, contamination, and infrastructural investment contribute to a hardening and deadening of many of the fertile valleys. The remaining parcels—the residues—leave thinner and at times discontinuous fingers tenuously stretching through the urban fabric.

Lisbon is a water city, and its outlook has been toward its maritime connections and exploitations. The city develops and redevelops from the water's edge, extending outward into the nearby mountains. It is also climatically connected to the ocean, allowing for mild winters that contribute to its agricultural viability. Crops proliferate year-round. Water is an issue in the dry summers, and Lisbon has the classic urban dilemma of too little water at times and too much at others. The careful manipulation

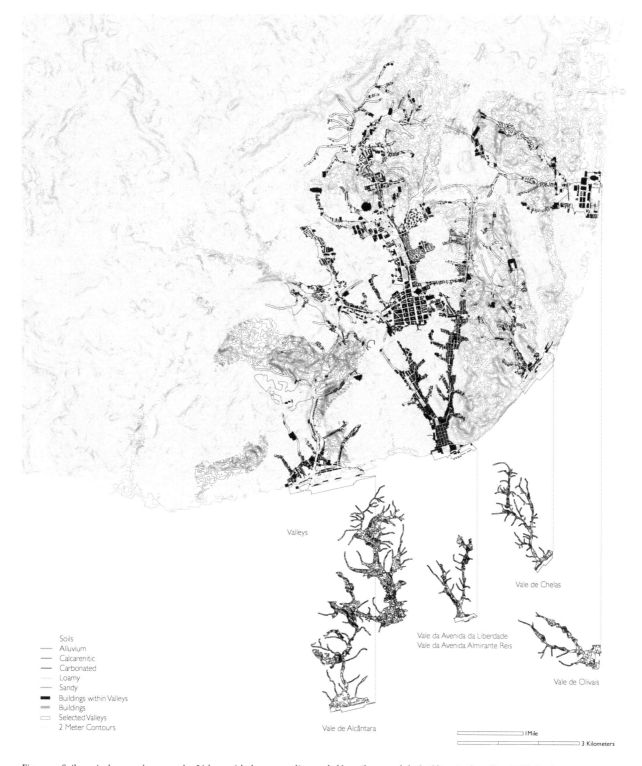

Soils
— Alluvium
— Calcarenitic
— Carbonated
— Loamy
— Sandy
■ Buildings within Valleys
■ Buildings
▭ Selected Valleys
2 Meter Contours

Valleys

Vale de Chelas

Vale da Avenida da Liberdade
Vale da Avenida Almirante Reis

Vale de Olivais

Vale de Alcântara

1 Mile

3 Kilometers

Figure 37. Soils, agriculture, and topography, Lisbon, with the contour lines coded by soil type and the buildings in the valleys highlighted.

of the soil—the micro-topographies—allow for the crops to weather the hot, dry summers, but irrigation continues to be a concern, one in fact that has contributed to the political reorganization of some of the city's agricultural plots (see the micro-furrows in figure 35, for example).[8]

Earthquake and Flood

The city's soil and water resources are unstable, literally, prone to earthquakes, floods, and landslides. The ground is seismic, with a major earthquake destroying a large portion of the city in 1755. The story of Lisbon's development, in fact, cannot be told without mention of the 1755 earthquake. The 8.7 magnitude All Saints Day (November 1) event killed an estimated sixty thousand people and generated tsunamis that destroyed all the major ports along the Iberian Peninsula. It halted Lisbon's economic and colonial prowess, forever shifting the European power dynamics. The capital city required rebuilding and, thus, a plan. Prior to the earthquake, development had largely been unregulated and unguided. With the extensive destruction, Lisbon decided on a morphological shift. Instead of rebuilding what was, the city opted for a new urban organization, based on the plans of military engineers Carlos Mardel and Eugenio dos Santos. This is the first of several plans for Lisbon executed under forceful political leadership. This time the driver of the urban plan was Marquês de Pombal, a military leader and minister for foreign affairs at the time of the earthquake. He was appointed by King Jose I to oversee the reconstruction efforts. The Mardel and dos Santos plan for the realignment of the Baixa (downtown area) from medieval warren to modern grid was chosen from among six alternatives as the basis for reconstruction. The roughly sixty-block area, in a flattened plane—or valley—between two hills, forms one of the few succinct grids of the city. It is a place where military engineering and enlightenment ideals trump the geological substrate.

This rational valley is a site of episodic flooding. The low-lying, hardened ground cannot absorb heavy rainfall or water surges that happen periodically, most notably in the flash floods of 1967, 1983, and 2008, among others.[9] Waters flow from multiple directions: rainfall travels overland, through the city, into its valleys while rising waters from the Tagus River seep into the city via the low-lying valleys. The Baixa neighborhood sits in the most central of these linear tentacles, a square basin fed in one direction by the river and in the other by the city's two grand avenues—Liberdade and Almirante Reis.[10] These monumental avenues trace two streams that once flowed through the city, meeting at the Rossio plaza north of the Baixa, before emptying into the Tagus River. The urban form of Lisbon, while driven by idealistic planning efforts, still reflects its underlying geomorphology (again see figure 37).

The ground has been relatively quiet in the last 250 years since the 1755 earthquake, but the city still prepares for a foreseeable, if unpredictable, earthquake in the future.[11]

The subduction zone remains active. Lisbon is built on a volatile and undulating ground. Development contends with this topography, and the attractiveness of flat land has led to building on the level hilltops and in the expansive floodplains. As a result, the city floods, and managing floodwaters is a major focus of Lisbon's twenty-first-century urban planning initiatives.

Opposing Sides of the City

As mentioned, the Baixa neighborhood occupies the center of the city of Lisbon. From here, the city expands to the west and east. This expansion has not been uniform, and the characteristics of the two sides of the city largely reflect this uneven development.

The two sides of the city have geographical similarities, but because of the direction of development over time, have distinct constructed footprints (see figure 38). These distinctions, which can be traced to the post-1755 earthquake reconstruction efforts, were reinforced by subsequent planning efforts. Beginning in 1938, shortly after Portugal's authoritarian regime was installed in 1933, Duarte Pacheco, the Portuguese secretary of state for public works and the mayor of Lisbon, commenced a major planning initiative. Instead of focusing on a street and grid infrastructure that reinforced the general topography of the city, Duarte Pacheco and his main contracted planner, the French-trained, Polish-born, Russian garden city enthusiast Étienne de Groër, set aside large tracts of land for ecological reserves and housing estates. And while agriculture was not a major player in these planning efforts, the citizens of Lisbon have always farmed. It is precisely at the intersection of the ecological reserves and the housing estates that this farming takes place.

To the west, the city is shaped by the strong form of the Parque Florestal de Monsanto (Monsanto Forest Park), the result of the city appropriation of agricultural lands and a Duarte Pacheco reforestation project undertaken by prison labor in the 1930s. The project was designed to both bracket development and address soil erosion on the bare Monsanto hill. On the other side of the city, to the east and north, the open space system envisioned by de Groër and Pacheco is more fragmented. The plans were compromised, forced to contend with the large footprint of the airport, which opened in 1942, and subsequent development projects. The resulting system, the Parque Orientale, is defined by a series of interrelated large parks, woods, and informally developed agricultural valleys.

The initial Pacheco and de Groër initiatives were synthesized into the 1948 Plano Director de Urbanizacao de Lisboa (PDUL), the official master plan for the city. The PDUL structures the growth of the city largely by defining a peripheral green belt and thereby shifting the focus from a radial north–south organizational system to one of concentric rings designed to protect the countryside from urban pollution. In this project, the west becomes clearly defined, executed in a manner consistent with the

Parques Hortícolas
① Quinta da Granja
② Quinta das Carmelitas
③ Telheiras Nascente
④ Parque Bensaude
⑤ Jardins de Campolide/
   Amnistia Internacional
⑥ Quinta de Bela Flor
⑦ Boavista
⑧ Rio Seco
⑨ Parque Vinicola
⑩ Vale de Chelas
⑪ Vale Fundão
⑫ Quinta das Flores
⑬ Graça

•··•. Selected Canopy
▬ Parques Hortícolas
   Chelas Project (see Figure 43)
— Roadways
— 2m Contour

0.5 Miles

2 Kilometers

Figure 38. Two sides of the city, Lisbon: map of the urban fabric between Monsanto Forest Park and the Chelas neighborhood.

garden city ideals of de Groër.[12] The east lags behind, becoming a post-1948 project of the subsequent technocratic regime of planners. The different treatments between east and west are reflected in the design and execution of their signature open spaces: again, Parque Florestal de Monsanto and the aforementioned agglomeration of landscapes collectively known Parque Orientale, as well as the appropriation of land for agricultural pursuit.

Big Reserves

The Parque Florestal de Monsanto is the largest protected green space in the city, measuring nearly 1,000 hectares (roughly 2,500 acres). It was created with a single, authoritative move. In fact, land was expropriated and planted in military fashion: seized and marked quickly with an ambitious reforestation plan. The planting regime creates an overall armature for a diverse set of spaces that include an ecological park, agricultural plots, a series of recreational clubs, municipal offices, a defunct raceway, a large highway and viaduct, and a prison—the same one that provided much of the labor for the park construction—occupying a clearing at the top of the hill. Built as a fort in the nineteenth century and used as a military prison, the building continues to function as a maximum-security civilian prison. The prison is not far from the Miradouro Panorâmico de Monsanto, an abandoned and defunct restaurant from the 1960s that serves as a graffiti platform and lookout point over the park and the city. The top of the hill is denuded, allowing for views across the forested bands and the neighboring developments. The park, largely designed for the automobile experience, is strange—and programmatically diverse—but its strong figure is visible across Lisbon's urban landscape, and the Lisbon landscape is visible from the park's top elevations. At one time, the park was also home to the municipal agencies that oversee the construction of some of Lisbon's newer landscapes, including the soon-to-be discussed Parque Hortícola (horticultural park) projects.[13]

By comparison, the Parque Orientale is hard to find. It is sometimes referred to as one of the large peripheral reserves—the eastern equivalent to the Parque Florestal de Monsanto—and a key part of the Estrutura Verde Principal, or ecological structure of the city. In reality, it is a series of tenuously connected valleys and parks: Vale da Montanha, Vale de Chelas, Parque José Gomes Ferreira (Mata de Alvalade), Parque da Bela Vista, and Parque Urbano do Vale Fundão (Mata de Chelas or Mata de Don Dinis).[14] On the ground, the project of creating a large eastern park for the city is incomplete. The existing parks operate independently from each other and the interstitial landscapes. Yet, the potential is vast, as open lands proliferate in the eastern valleys where the topography, soils, and politics have slowed urban development. Here the fallow landscape is an extensive and dominant terrain, like a broad river flowing around extant buildings.

The park designs are simple but effective. They contend with significant topographical change, and their designs reflect the diverse elevations. The Mata de Alvalade (1950 to 1951), designed by Ribeiro Telles, was the first eastern park built after the adoption of the 1948 PDUL. The design is an early manifestation of Ribeiro Telles's ecological principles. Simply, it is woodland where the selected tree species are adapted to the park's microclimates. The trees line the adjacent Avenida do Brasil and descend along the southern slopes, stopping shy of a valley clearing. Here, the meadow is punctuated by small groupings of riparian tree species. The design, only partially realized, mimics the clarity of Ribeiro Telles's words on ecology and the city. The landscape is quiet and poignant, embodying its topographical and hydrological condition while providing a place for reflection, relaxation, and sport in the city. The wooded Parque Urbano do Vale Fundão, anchoring the other end of the system of valleys, parks, and agricultural plots, designed by the landscape architect Álvaro Dentinho in the 1970s, also reflects its topographic section. There are dry pines in the uplands, poplars in the lowlands, with a dry riverbed at the bottom. The section is clear, reflecting the shape of the land and working with the terrain rather than against it. The eighty-five-hectare (210-acre) Parque de Bela Vista, located in between the two woodlands, is one of the largest parklands in the city. It retains the bones of its history as a farmland estate and is notable both for its high prospect with views of the city and the river and its valley clearing with places for picnicking. Paths and roads bisect the park as well as the broader terrain in which the parkland sits.

The three parks are part of the post-1948 expansion of the city of Lisbon. They sit at the fringes of a district profoundly marked—socioeconomically and physically—by inadequate technocratic municipals plans, including the 1960s Chelas Urbanization Plan.[15] This plan is part of a series of developments to increase Lisbon's housing stock and is discussed in detail later in the chapter. The eastern parks cling to the edge of its territory, an area expropriated by the city to create a new district. The topographic parti of the Chelas district is clear: massive residential complexes occupy the hilltops, while the valleys are maintained without buildings. Giant roads—sometimes three lanes in each direction—move up and down the terrain clumsily connecting the housing developments to the broader city. The resolution between the buildings, the large roadways, the designed parks (which, it should be noted, sit outside the plan itself), and the residual landscape—of which there is a considerable amount—is coarse. The rural character of the predevelopment site is present. The parks bleed into tightly packed mazes of allotment gardens, established and tended by residents of the housing estates. The allotments, despite limited water in certain seasons, are lush and fruitful. The valleys are alive, and the city is working both to better support current agronomic practices in the district and to bolster the ecological network of valleys throughout the city through the design of landscapes that accommodate agriculture, ecology, and recreation.

The *Plano Verde de Lisboa*

The *Plano Verde de Lisboa* is a plan and publication from 1996 coordinated by Ribeiro Telles with his colleagues, landscape architects Maria Teresa Alfaiate, Inês Norton de Matos, João Gomes da Silva, Manuela Raposo Magalhaes, and Luis Paulo Ribeiro, among others.[16] This document developed a strategy to convert the basic structure of the city, as initiated by the de Groër plan, into an ecological system for the metropolitan area (see figure 39 for the initial esquisse as well as the adopted plan and the subsequent implemented projects). The scheme, generally adopted into the official city master plan in 2007, includes three east–west bands of differing character connected by valley radials. The first band includes the peripheral areas of Parque Florestal de Monsanto, the eastern parks, the airport, and the remnant agricultural estates. The second band includes the state-owned properties and the public housing developments. The third band is the area along the Tagus River. Radial spokes along the city's main valleys—the Alcantara, the Avenida de Liberdade, and Chelas—run transversely through the swathes. In this scheme, the valleys do not just connect the bands. Instead, they are fundamental to improving the ecological and social qualities of life in the city. They are conceived of as means to encourage urban ventilation, channeling air currents moving up from the water into the congested areas of development. They are also recognized as the most conducive sites for planting. The valleys, as sites of former tributaries and drainage basins for the adjacent hills, have reserves of deep, moist soil. The protection of this soil is an environmental and cultural project. The valleys retain traces of the city's rich agricultural history and still serve as the reserves for the farming practices of the current inhabitants.

The system derives inspiration from the "continuum naturale," a concept introduced in Portugal by the landscape architect Francisco Caldeira Cabral, which called for a continuous system of landscapes to support wild habitats and ensure a territorial equilibrium between man and environment.[17] To Cabral's "continuum natural," Ribeiro Telles added the "continuum culturale" and the "genius loci," arguing for the importance of both preexisting architectural spaces and the expression of geology, hydrology, and climate in the city. The *Plano Verde de Lisboa,* as a component of the city's overall planning document (Plano Director Municipal or PDM), calls for attention to the ecological and cultural landscapes of the city. It is designed to facilitate air and water flow, to replenish soils, and to enhance access to wild space within the metropolis. The plan clarifies previous planning efforts, building them into a guiding plan for future development. In doing so, the ecological structure proposed balances a discontinuous landscape system in the central part of the city—encapsulating the articulated open spaces of the Mardel, dos Santos, and Ressano Garcia plans—while reinforcing a continuous periphery that makes sense of the large reserves set aside by de Groër and Pacheco.

1996 Green structure of Lisbon Schema

- Continuous peripheral system
- Semi-continuous system interspersed with collective equipment
- Continuous radial system
- Discontinuous traditional city system
- Riberinho system

Municipal Ecological Structure 2012

System structural corridors
- Hydrologic system
- Estuarine system
- Green Space
- Green framework built spaces
- Permeable green street to preserve
- Parques Hortícolas
- Wooded areas
- Retention / stormwater basins

Projects

- Completed
- Completed bridge
- Existing
- Existing - Monsanto
- Existing bridge
- Preserved
- Preserved bridge
- Construction areas
- Covered areas
- Planned areas

0.5 Miles
2 Kilometers

Figure 39. *Plano Verde de Lisboa:* initial sketch, adopted plan, and implemented projects.

The *Plano Verde* strengthens the landscape systems already at play in Lisbon, balancing cultural and ecological agendas. The strategy is exemplified by the visions for the continuous radial valleys, as partially implemented in the area leading to and around Parque Florestal de Monsanto and in the projected initiatives in the Chelas region.

Structural Corridors

The Corredor Verde de Monsanto (Green Corridor of Monsanto), one of the first implemented moves of the ecological plan, is a series of landscapes in the north of the city, connecting the center of the city to its peripheral green belt. It extends from the Avenida de Liberdade, again the key nineteenth-century valley boulevard, and the Praca dos Restauradores, a civic square at the boulevard's southern end, to the forested reserve.[18] Again designed by Ribeiro Telles and his team, the project links historic landscapes with contemporary ones—the last stretch was completed by late 2012. The Parque Edward VII, a late nineteenth-century formal expanse at the top of the Avenida de Liberdade, forms a knuckle in the Green Corridor, where the axial city with its extensive views to the river meets the winding pedestrian route that carves its way through the interstices, connecting recreation grounds, orchards, and agricultural landscapes, to arrive at the Parque Florestal de Monsanto and the former estates of the area, such as the Quinta da Granja beyond. The connection has been made tenuously, without the supporting experiential qualities of the route in place. The route is developing, still strong in idea but weak in execution. It is the beginning of a cycling and pedestrian infrastructure, with key bridges in place, but the landscapes along the way—the places of thickness in the plan—are immature. The route is polite, a politically achievable gesture that uses available lands while avoiding those of the greatest contention—the connection to the Alcantara valley, for example. Descending the hill from the newly minted Jardim Amnista Internacional, the corridor lands flat, literally and figuratively, on the Rua de Campolide. The corridor hugs the sidewalk; the figure of the forest of Monsanto is present but obscured by the intense web of roads and rails in the foreground. There is still a half-kilometer to go, over rails, and under highways, alongside the types of neglected landscapes usually associated with the infrastructural right-of-way. There is room to expand, but the complexity of the territory has left it untouched temporarily. It is easy to encompass the residual green on the planning map—to color it as part of the corridor—but the designed reality is sometimes a struggle when compared with the potential. It is obvious, in situ, to the pedestrian, left unguided in the final stretch to uncomfortably move along a busy thoroughfare while a vast valley system sits in purgatory.[19] The juxtaposition of the landscape and the orientation map says it all. The red line continues, on paper and on the literal ground, as a line to follow, but the experience of moving along that line, by and through the emerald green–colored masses, is not verdant. The lone pedestrians have opted to wait for the bus.[20]

Incremental Projects

Since adopting the *Plano Verde de Lisboa* as the aspirational ecological structure for the city, the municipal government has been planning, designing, and building small projects to incrementally address the overall performance of the city. In other words, the city's strategy is a mosaic one, where small parcels eventually come together to create larger patches, corridors, and reserves. This approach is evidenced by the prolonged construction of the Corredor Verde de Monsanto, where the city added properties and projects over time, eventually completing the connection between Parque Edward VII and Parque Florestal de Monsanto. The method is understandably incremental and piecemeal, but not unsubstantial, especially given the recent economic and political climate.[21] In the office of the director of Direção Municipal de Estrutura Verde, Ambiente e Energia within the Gabinete de Projecto de Estrutura Verde (Municipal Division of Green Structure, Environment and Energy within the Green Structure Project Office) sit over seven hundred white project binders and a pinkish-red map of the city documenting the work to date on the *Plano Verde*.[22] The map shows the ecological infrastructure projects carefully inlaid into the city. The small fragments aggregate to form interconnected territories within the built fabric. The darkest red-pink marks the completed work, the mauve shows the next projects in the pipeline, and the diagonal hatch overlay indicates places where there is a future plan. The intensity of the drawn marks reflects the level of physical resolution: the deep pinks are precise and executed; the lighter pinks have form, and their opacity masks the city underneath; the hatches are loose and ambitious and are drawn overtop larger swaths of the city. The latter have yet to be negotiated and embedded (this information is overlaid on the large map in figure 39 and called out in the third small diagram). The *Plano Verde* emerged out of a tracing of the city, from the aerial perspective, where the pockets of green were connected and reinforced, idealistically, without direct reverence to property, politics, and people. Now, the plan is being ground-truthed, resulting in a chipping away at its larger terrain to address the environmental (flooding and earthquakes) and socioeconomical (food security, immigration, and poverty) concerns of the city. The two-pronged ambition is important and deliberate. The city's planners, over time, have come to understand that the future needs to address both the unstable and impermeable urban terrain and its mobile and fluctuating populations.

Parques Hortícolas

These two agendas—the environmental and social—meet beautifully in the Parque Hortícola (horticultural park) projects. Here, the core ecological work of the environmental plan pairs with the citizen-driven desires for an agronomic enterprise. Stemming from the *Plano Verde* work and in response to societal pressures, the Lisbon City

Council initiated the development of a citywide strategy for urban agriculture. Given the rich history of cultivation in the city and the needs of the active farming community, agriculture proves the most logical place to begin grounding the green planning efforts. Prior to 2007, in its official plans, the city had overlooked the hundreds of allotment gardens that pepper the city's hillsides and valleys. These informal land appropriations were seen as a peripheral practice rather than one to integrate into the urban design process. This changed with the adoption of the *Plano Verde de Lisboa*. A three-person commission—project coordinator Maria João Sobral, Rita Folgosa, and Maria José Fundevila—was dedicated exclusively to the study of the urban gardens. The team addresses the biological, managerial, and design aspects of the gardens.[23] Through their efforts, the city developed a new park prototype for the city, one that is structured around food gardens but is anchored by bike and pedestrian pathways and includes other recreational amenities. The intention is to provide a conceptual and material framework for the food gardens, to integrate existing farmers into the planning and design process, and to become a leader in the practice of urban agriculture. When considered over a longer period, agriculture—a means to colonize the Lisbon territory, superseded once population and trade are established—is again an ingredient of city making. This is an indication of shifting values as well as an example of an urban cycle. Old ideas are introduced again and are transformed to meet current cultural considerations.

These Parque Hortícola projects represent some of the most inspiring municipal work related to the *Plano Verde*. Here, the underlying aim to protect and enhance the soil conditions of the city is infused with a social necessity for subsistence. The planning efforts organize an informal reality in Lisbon. The abandoned hill and valley landscapes are being used for cultivation—to produce food for consumption, distribution, and sales. At one time Lisbon's topography was maximized for agriculture—and Sunday visits to the gardens were a ubiquitous pastime across classes. Now, it is a practice left to the fertile corridors, for the largely disenfranchised. But, again, this is changing to foreground agriculture in order to valorize current cultivation practices and extend the cultural lineage of production landscapes. While providing for safe and healthy growing practices for newer residents, the city has developed a typological landscape to merge agricultural, recreation, and mobility. Skate parks and playgrounds are placed within tracts devoted to gardening. Bike and pedestrian pathways move through the allotment landscapes. And most importantly, freshwater access is provided for crop irrigation.

To a visitor, it is disarming in its clear-sightedness. The rural landscape of production, once subsumed by the city, is being given new life. The cycle is direct and evident, especially at Quinta da Granja near the Parque Florestal de Monsanto and in the areas surrounding the Parque Orientale and the neighborhood of Chelas. In these locations, despite the long history of technocratic planning, the distant and near agricultural pasts have not been fully erased. On the ground, time is eloquently condensed, and the remnants of ancient *quintas,* or farm estates, can be seen alongside contemporary *hortas,* or food gardens.[24] This occurs in close proximity, on a single site such as the Quinta da Granja, or across a territory where parks such as Bela Viste have retained traces of their past agricultural organization and parks such as the Parque Hortícola do Vale de Chelas, a half kilometer away, present an agricultural future.[25] In an era of social and economic disjunction, these landscapes provide social, environmental, and economic continuity to the city without relying on the category of the nation for direction.

On the Ground

I am a visitor to Lisbon. I am not the typical tourist. Instead, I have come to see the agricultural projects that occupy the fallow urban landscape—aggregations of tiny gardens, tended largely by Cape Verdean immigrants, on forgotten lands nested along highways, rails, valleys, and other corridors throughout the city. As a visitor, my understanding of the Portuguese Estado Novo (New State) is learned rather than lived. I know that António de Oliveira Salazar ruled Portugal for over thirty years, an authoritarian regime that curtailed political freedoms, but of course I do not have a visceral sense of the impact on the social and material urban constructs. Nearly a half century after his death, the physical and economic presence of the past regime, and its colonies, is everywhere in Lisbon, the capital city. Some of my tour guides have remarked that it was easy to build things during the Salazar era, and the many looming buildings from the period reflect this. Their scale and monumentality are a sort of geologic testament to old fascist power; their aging facades and unkempt entrances reflect subsequent unease and economic hardship.

I am struck by the massive weight of the physical constructions on the landscape. Yet, it is not the heaviness of the actual architecture that haunts but rather the way in which that architecture sits on Lisbon's hilly terrain. The story of modernist planning and its disregard for local conditions is an old one, but here the clarity is remarkable. The steep topography amplifies the miscalculations. The plans—even in their best forms—relied on flatness. In fact, I am used to seeing this type of clunky architecture against rational and relatively flat grids. But the landscape in Lisbon is the opposite. The extreme topography leaves the massive modernist towers sitting disconnected on the high ground. The valleys between them are rifts, physically and socially. I perceive them, then, as double-deep chasms (figure 40 shows a series of sections through two valleys, a drawn itinerary of topography, infrastructure, building, and cultivation).

The buildings appear both immovable and tenuous, heavy weights on land that falls away beneath their foundations. They are cold and stern, of varying architectural quality, while the valleys are warm, cultivated, and animated by the evidence of active human care. The physical juxtaposition of these two poles—the planned, technocratic building

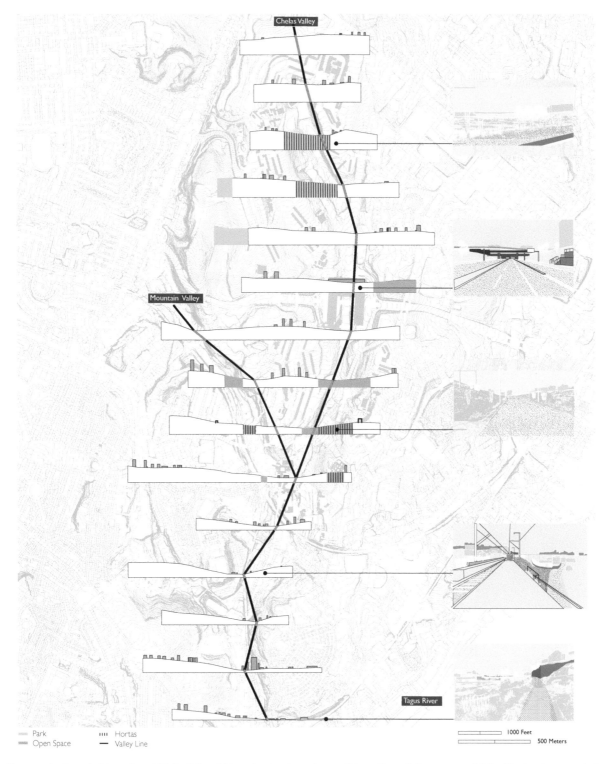

Park   Hortas
Open Space   Valley Line

1000 Feet
500 Meters

Figure 40. A trip up the Mountain and Chelas Valleys, Lisbon, showing alternating conditions of heavy infrastructure and deft cultivation; hortas are indicated by the black lines in the green fills.

and the spontaneous, incremental use—sparks an unhealthy dialectic. The immobile encounters the mobile. The historical circumstance abuts the contemporary flux. The government plan is set against adaptations made by people who are categorically excluded from the planning process yet are responsible for the outcome of the planning. Government agency—and the abuse of this power—abuts local circumstance.

The history is a mini-urban cycle: from agronomic colonization, through designed habitations with unintended allotment gardens, back to designed agronomic inhabitation. In the end, the fertile soil—and its use—cannot be denied. The landscape itself has agency, an agency brought to life by immigrant cultures deeply dedicated to the cultivation of land. Again, the planning is sloppy, at times, neglecting nonconforming landscapes, leaving residual slivers that result from unresolved geometries. But ironically, it is thanks to this neglect that the residues lie open for appropriation. In the past few years, these appropriations are being recognized, by the city and through design, as the basis for the new ecological parks that reinforce local practice while bolstering environmental systems at the regional scale. On one hand, the planning process has shifted: the government, which, fifty years ago, produced and executed inadequate megaplans for its underserved constituency, today looks to members of that disenfranchised community—the allotment farmers who have appropriated the unclaimed city land—for new micro-plans to execute within the gaps left by the previous megaplan. On the other hand, the farmers become agents of government planning. The plan is both theirs and someone else's, given to them, again, to carry out.

It occurs to the visitor that the local residents are tenders of an appropriated landscape, and that their care is oddly powered by the vacuum of alternative forms of care. In many instances, once this temporary landscape is reclaimed by a city for development, the local care is ignored and obliterated. In other words, local power, or agency, only exists when there is no other course of action. When a government bends to sanction volunteer and spontaneous use, it is remarkable. Validation and compensation are the next steps.

But it is also remarkable, in a territory planned and designed precisely to exert control over informal occupations of the land, that subsequent informal occupations are driving the future planning and design of the territory. In the space left behind by grand planning gestures—the bold and shortsighted urbanism of previous decades—incremental land practices have found agency. The architecture has largely failed, its big feet clobbering the terrain. Instead, cultivation offers a means to build on the ingrained richness, rather than the perceived poverty, of the slivers and ravines of the city.

East and West Redux

Of the numerous projects I visited, two stand out for their deft negotiation of terrain, investment in soil, and transformation through multiple timescales: the Parque

Urbano da Quinta da Granja, located on the eastern edge of the city, on the north side of the Parque Florestal de Monsanto in the Benfica parish, and the Parque Hortícola do Vale de Chelas, in the western parish of Marvila, bracketing the city and its agricultural planning projects. Again, the development of the two sides of the city is distinct, as reflected in the landscape structure to which the two projects belong and read at the scale of the project. It is true that both sit in fertile valleys, on former farmlands, with large institutional neighbors. They share a close proximity to the Segunda Circular roadway, or second ring road that circumnavigates the outer portions of inner Lisbon, located approximately 6 kilometers (3.7 miles) from the Baixa (see figure 38). They both exist at the nexus of the topographic and concentric planning movements, and yet the resolution of the urban fabric near Quinta da Granja is much tighter than near Vale de Chelas. Quinta da Granja reads like an ancient hill and estate, framed by ever encroaching development while the Vale de Chelas sits independently, sunken from the city, sidled on the slopes above its urban ravine.[26]

Benfica

Benfica, the civil parish where Quinta da Granja is located, has been continuously occupied since prehistory with archaeological remains from the Paleolithic, Neolithic, and Chalcolithic periods.[27] The area is ideal farming terrain—a fertile valley with an active watercourse—and agronomy plays a central role in the development history of this northeastern corner of Lisbon. Numerous agricultural estates from the sixteenth, seventeenth, and eighteenth centuries mark the territory. The parish grew from these farming roots, with populations spikes in the 1730s to accommodate the laborers working on the nearby Aqueducto de Aguas Livres, in the 1750s as people relocated after the 1755 earthquake, and in the 1940s and 1950s, following the major planning efforts of the 1930s and 1940s and the development of the nearby Parque Florestal de Monsanto. In the mid-nineteenth century the area was still dotted with farms, country estates, rich gardens, orchards, and allotments. Today this structure reads, as the agricultural grid has given way to the urban grid. The *azinhagas,* or small lanes, that once formed passageways between property lines are still a part of the city's infrastructure. And the farm properties themselves form a type of patchwork, framing the insertion of other types of use. Some large estates remain in private hands, while others have been converted to park and development projects. For example, Parque Bensaúde sits on the site of Quinta de Santo António das Frechas. Estádio da Luz, home of the Benfica football club, has the footprint of an agricultural estate, as does the giant Centro Colombo commercial mall, across the giant Segunda Circular roadway from the stadium.[28] Just beyond, the Quinta da Luz housing estate fills another former property. In fact, the term *quinta* itself shifts from describing a large agricultural estate to describing a housing estate, which might, itself, have occupied the same ground as the prior agricultural one. The grain and terminology of farmsteads is retained as the city grows. In Benfica, sites were subsumed as the population increased, until the 1990s, when building stagnated with population decreases that mirrored the citywide trend of outmigration and economic crisis. Development pressure returned with the economic recovery after the 2011 bailout, heightening the importance for policies guiding urban agriculture and ecological planning efforts on the municipal level.

Quinta da Granja: From Quinta to Horta to Parque Hortícola

The Quinta da Granja, a pre-Roman site and seventeenth-century agricultural estate, is a remarkable topographic purity set amid a sea of large-scale, peri-urban development.[29] Its sculpted hillside rises above the spaghetti of elevated roadways that hem it in. It sits across Avenida Lusíada from the Centro commercial Colombo mall, where pedestrians can pass under the roadway that separates the two sides, effectively passing through a type of time machine from a testament to twenty-first-century retail to one of Roman agriculture and planning (see figure 41). The cardinal directions—the *cardo* and *decumanus*—are still clearly inscribed on the smoothly graded slopes of the Quinta site. At the top, the eighteenth-century farmstead also remains, as an institutional building.[30] At the base is the site of the Parque Urbano da Quinta da Granja with the city's first designed, constructed, and sponsored *hortas urbanas* (horticultural plots).

The Parque Urbano da Quinta da Granja occupies a small portion of the site of the overall Quinta da Granja site. The Camara Municipal de Lisboa retained just over three hectares for the construction of the urban park, which opened in 2009. The park, designed by the landscape architect Maria José Fundevila, in collaboration with the architect Rui Pires, under the coordination of the architect João Rocha e Castro, includes the hortas urbanas, a kiosk with terrace, a playground, fitness equipment, a garden, and a bike and walking path.[31] The city's hortas urbanas are small, 160 meter by 160 meter (525 feet by 525 feet), food-producing allotment gardens, provided by the city and rented at nominal fee to local farmers for use. This type of gardening existed on-site prior to the park's inception—and, in fact, the provision of safe and respected gardens was the prime motivation behind the park project. In other words, the project is to create a park that centers on allotment gardening, to elevate and sanction a practice occurring across the city. Farmers—in need of sustenance and committed to the cultural project of cultivation—tend to the unclaimed interstices of the city. They occupy unwanted terrains, in the physical and temporal gaps in the built fabric. At Quinta da Granja, the city creates its first project validating urban agriculture, recovering a long-standing cultural practice for Lisbon and its immigrant populations. In the park, the city consolidated and organized the gardens that predate the park project, strung along the road and nestled at the bank of the slope. The city replaced the former warren of gardens—richly organic but without larger community buy-in or supporting

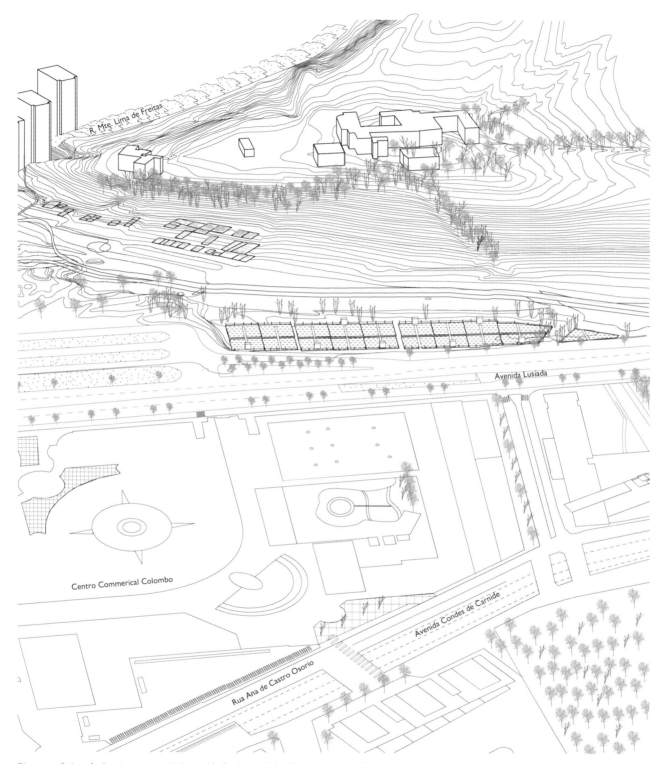

Figure 41. Quinta da Granja structure, Lisbon, with the Centro Colombo commercial mall in the foreground and the Quinta da Granja hortas and hillside beyond.

irrigation—with thirty-eight clearly defined plots. The definition is spatial and operational. Each plot comes with a patch of new organic soil, delineated by a path, enclosed by a gate, and served by secure storage, water access, and a contract. The fundamental shift is not aesthetic but rather a change in investment. The idea is not to impose order but rather to promote, to jointly manage, and to provide the guarantee of clean soil, water, and tenure.

Perhaps it is obvious, but to arrive at Quinta da Granja from central Lisbon and the Baixa by car is circuitous, disorienting in route, yet the sequence of landscapes, abstracted, provides a succinct capture of the Lisbon territory. It is a perfect transect for a visitor seeking to gain an on the ground sense of the landscape. And I have the perfect guide, landscape architect João Gomes da Silva.[32] We drive along the Tagus River and snake through the Parque Florestal de Monsanto, onto the busy highway of the Segunda Circular. From here, our car exits and curves around onto the elevated Avenida Lusíada, past the stadium and mall and the Quinta itself, circling down and back to reach the ground to drive along the site and park. In other words, the disorienting trajectory includes city, river, forest, highway, city, monument, and road. Against this, at times, illogical trajectory, the rational layout, of both the larger Quinta property and the agricultural plots within it, is affirming: gravity, the direction of the sun's movement, and quality of the soils are its defining properties.

Leaving the parking, crossing the threshold into the park, and heading toward the group of hortas along the park's edge, the grade slips downward, distancing the streets and traffic and amplifying the garden calm. From the sidewalk, the view is over top of the gardens, with their red shed roofs dotting the foreground against the plane of the hillside and its olive trees. The project is a testing ground for the future Parque Hortícola projects, meant to be simple and, above all, accommodating for the farmers who have tended to the property and will continue to invest in its soils. All of the projects are infrastructural, laid out like mini-cities, with lines delineating the plots and shared services supporting them. The commitment is not to displace any urban farming but rather to sanction the practice and anchor it to larger park projects. The plots are uniform and gridded, framed by planting, accessed by a communal pathway, and fenced in groups of four, with a gate, water access, and a shared shed for each group of four plots.[33]

At the Quinta da Granja, the hortas urbanas form a vibrant community within the park for the farmers and the general park-goers—a respite from the busy streets, commerce, and sports activities of the surrounding neighborhood. The articulated sidewalk along the edge and the internal path system allow for the passerby to slip into and through the gardens and park, to bear witness to clear and committed practices of cultivation. Here, the city's rich and changing agricultural landscapes are on prominent display. The hortas compliment the patrimonial conceit of the estate while

challenging its social status. The singular, grand gesture frays into a collective and hopeful enterprise.

Figure 42. Quinta da Granja, Lisbon, 2014.

Plano de Urbanização de Chelas

Leaving the sun-stroked hillside of the Quinta da Granja, we head west on the Segunda Circular toward the largest Parque Hortícola project. Again, the two sites share a similar distance from the city center and are similarly surrounded by mega-roadways that make the pedestrian feel diminutive. They both occupy fertile valleys, former locations of both historical agricultural estates and contemporary informal farm plots. Agriculture is ingrained in their DNA. Yet, the layers of history are treated quite differently. Arguably, in Benfica, the occupied past is present, incorporated in the organization of the neighborhood. In Chelas, which takes its name from a sixteenth-century convent, the geological presence of the valley is far more pronounced than the logics of former occupation. The ground is steep and at times messy, with traces left seemingly inadvertently, to be discovered by the intrepid rather than revealed with intention. This disjuncture speaks to the history of planning. While the development of Benfica was a relatively slow and incremental process, with periodic pulses, the development of Chelas, located in the Marvila parish on the city's west side, was traumatic, halting, and poorly executed. The entire area stayed predominately agricultural for longer, in a relative stasis, until government planning efforts of the 1950s targeted the area for major housing projects.

The aforementioned Plano de Urbanização de Chelas (Chelas Urbanization Plan) was a direct response to a public housing program, Habitações de Renda Económica (Affordable Housing), launched in 1959 by the Portuguese Estado Novo for 128,000 new inhabitants in Lisbon.[34] Designed to eradicate informal settlements cropping up in the city, the program gave the newly created Gabinete Técnico de Habitação (Technical Housing Office), or GTH, the authority to plan and build social housing to meet the identified housing crisis facing the city.[35] Coming at a time of increased urbanization in Lisbon, the project was a last attempt of the Estado Novo to exert control over the physical territory.

Chelas and the surrounding district of Olivais, areas just south and east of the Lisbon's Airport, was a loosely occupied agricultural area in 1959. Technically part of the city, this area was considered rural and therefore underutilized. Previously the difficult topographic conditions prevented major building, but the GTH, armed with the discoveries of modernism and its new political power, was unfazed, and this eastern front of the city was deemed the perfect place for its new housing experiments. On over 737 hectares (1,821 acres), or 10 percent of the city's total area, the municipality planned three contiguous developments: Olivais Sul, Olivais Norte, and Chelas.

At 510 hectares (1,260 acres) and designed for 55,300 inhabitants, Chelas was by far the largest, most complicated topographically, and, to this day, the least resolved of these three developments. Anticipating growth, the municipality began seizing private land in the eastern part of the city for expansion in the 1930s.[36] This included land adjacent to the Chelas project but did not include the majority of the land within the area of the urbanization plan. Instead, the city's slow expropriation of the nearly 250 private estates within the area of the Chelas plan continued into the 1970s.[37] So slow was this expropriation that the execution of the Chelas plan lasted nearly fifty years.[38] During this time, the political, economic, and social climate changed dramatically. The Estado Novo was ousted with the 1974 revolution. Portugal joined the European Economic Community in 1986. Immigration continued to increase, and social traditions shifted.[39] The Chelas project was conceived at the tail end of the functionalist city movement, when faith in the modernist project was waning but no subsequent ideals were yet in place.[40] The project represents a huge government investment with great social implications executed without clear or lasting guidance.

The Chelas plan is dominated by the housing-centric, technical concerns of the GTH. It is divided primarily into housing zones (I, J, L, M, and N) with a central commercial zone (O) designed to link the housing clusters together into a larger district (see the top plan in figure 43). The plan resembles lungs, both in its plan configuration and its intended function. The activity in the trachea-like central zone oxygenates the bronchi-like housing clusters, relying on its mega-roads for movement. But the Chelas plan fails to circulate activity through its tissue. Part of this failure is due to the poorly phased implementation of the plan—again executed over decades[41]—part is due to the lack of connectivity, and part is due to the lack of communal spaces. Taken together, these oversights represent a paucity of investment in the public realm and a gross misunderstanding of the topographic conditions in the area (see the bottom plan in figure 43).

The project provided housing units, and housing units alone. The buildings, aptly, were constructed on the ridges and away from the valley drainage system—but the valleys sit between them with no direct connections across. To move between the zones on the provided routes as a pedestrian, transit rider, or motorist is nearly impossible. The planners seemed not to have fully understood the difficulties that the steep valley sides pose for connection. Instead of adapting the previous zigzagging grain of development, which provided clues as to how to navigate the topographic conditions, they imposed a cellular system, comprising linear and disconnected developments.

Zona O, the intended nexus, was not realized until 2008. As a self-contained mall with housing towers rather than a neighborhood center, it feels borne out of an even more antiquated ideology that an enclosed shopping center could generate economic and urban stability. Again, instead of providing the life the area needed, it only furthers the social and physical isolation. The public transit network is equally meager, forcing people to walk great distances to have access to the rest of the city of Lisbon. Without these lifelines, the developments are island-like. The unarticulated, dead spaces around the buildings complete the sense of isolation. They are park-less towers-in-a-park, sitting like stale éclairs on a cake plate. The physical development screams of the housing-centric approach of its planners. They say: only housing units are needed to solve a shortage of housing units.

Yet, the developments have plenty of raw open space, which, while city-owned, has no clear assertions of civic ownership and identity. In this absence, the local population is resourceful in using the spaces for gardening and food production. In the large valley below Zona J, for instance, hundreds of small allotments have emerged in the past decade, interspersed with remnants of centuries-old structures. Intrepid gardeners have discovered the dry but farmable soils here and all along the valleys in the area (see figure 44 for the expansion of the valley hortas from 2001 to 2012).

Housing
Green Zone
Expressways
Embankments
Industrial Zone
Planned Roads
Developed Roads
Zones

1959

2010

Plan: 2000 Feet
1000 Meters
Section: 3000 Feet
1500 Meters

Figure 43. Chelas over time, Lisbon, showing the Chelas Urbanization Plan on top and the built condition on the bottom.

2001

2007

2012

Existing
New

1000 Feet

500 Meters

Figure 44. Hortas below Zona J, Lisbon: three plans showing the incredible proliferation between 2001 and 2010.

In these spaces, the unplanned movement from housing unit into valley landscape is excitingly alive. It is precisely where the plan left undefined green that resident-driven ecological and social investment has taken hold. If you stand with Zona N2 to your back, for example, you see a narrow path deftly negotiating the steep terrain in a way that the four-lane highways traversing the neighborhood cannot. This is the route from house to garden required for economic subsistence. It is a route that was once taken by squatters, by people who illegally farmed city-owned land. Now it is the route taken by tenant farmers to sanctioned hortas banded together into the municipally funded, designed, and operated Parque Hortícola do Vale de Chelas.

Parque Hortícola do Vale de Chelas: From Quinta to Horta to Parque Hortícola

The present-day agricultural activities fit within a long history of landscape cultivation in Chelas. Past land colonizers were lured into the valley for its amenable soils just like current inhabitants. They incrementally built up garden estates that capitalized on the favorable growing conditions as well as the topographically enabled views to the Tagus River. Again, these relatively small, enclosed agricultural estates, some with elaborate gardens and houses, are known as quintas. While particularly abundant in Chelas, quintas are a quintessential Lisbon landscape typology.[42] They have existed in the city for centuries; some, like the Quinta da Granja, have Roman and Visigoth origin, while many others were built between the sixteenth and eighteenth centuries. They are part of the rural legacy of the place and are fundamental to understanding the way in which the city's valley territories have been claimed, colonized, and cultivated.

In 1959, the Chelas area was covered with quintas. Over twenty-five were called out by name on the Plano de Urbanização de Chelas base map.[43] In fact, this was the area with the greatest concentration of extant quintas in Lisbon. The urbanization efforts were not sensitive to this cultural history. The plan did identify key views and buildings to preserve, but the seven clusters were all located to the periphery of the main developments and not integrated well with the new constructions. Instead, the urban design, starting with the analysis and continuing through the execution, fragmented a continuous terrain and replaced it with essentially nothing. The spaces between the buildings were left unarticulated, either intentionally through a wise decision to maintain the valleys free of buildings, or unintentionally through a lack of design of the open spaces within the zones, or both.

Most of the quintas have been demolished, and only in the Parque da Bela Vista is the rural structure deliberately maintained. The other quinta remnants are on the valley slopes and remain, not because they are deemed of cultural value, but rather because their location in areas found to be unsuitable for building somehow spared them. Today, on the sides of the valleys, the organic organization of the terrain — occurring over centuries and at the hands of individuals and small groups of people—presents a stark contrast to the stiff, ahistorical, planned layouts of the housing developments. Here, in the richness of the soil and the deep-seeded cultural practices of cultivation, the legacy of the quintas is alive. The actual structures may have disappeared or been degraded, but the human activities persist and evolve.

If the quinta represents "a deeply humanized landscape" where different systems of land ownership and exploitation are expressed over a long history,[44] then the horta is its postcolonial successor. A horta is an allotment plot, a small garden farmed for subsistence or pleasure. The valleys of Chelas, and to a lesser extent the city at large, are covered with hortas, where residents either squat on unregulated municipal lands to grow food or, more recently, rent plots, sheds, and spigots from the city for personal use.

In the past decade, the city of Lisbon has finally recognized the cultural importance of urban agriculture and has initiated the citywide strategy to organize and facilitate local agronomic endeavors within city-designed, -built, and -managed horticultural parks. The first Parques Hortícolas including Quinta da Granja opened in 2011, with the Parque Hortícola do Vale de Chelas following two years later. The parks build, conceptually and literally, on the historical quintas and the contemporary hortas, to provide an armature that promotes the agricultural practices of the city.

The Parque Hortícola do Vale de Chelas is one of the city's largest to date with over two hundred active plots on nearly six and half hectares (sixteen acres). The project, built on the hillside below the Igreja Santa Clara (Saint Clare Church) and above the Chelas valley floor, organized a preexisting community of hortas into an expanded park. The site is an obvious one for the municipal promotion of agricultural activity: it is municipally owned land in one of the important ecological corridors identified by the *Plano Verde de Lisboa* with a rich history of agricultural use and a preexisting farming community that depends on the land for food production and economic viability. Further, it sits within the contentious Chelas development, where the government failure to provide humane affordable housing to a largely African immigrant population has been well publicized over time.[45] Finally, prior to city involvement, the subsistence farmers had been allegedly tapping into a nearby school's sewer waters as a means of irrigation during periods of drought, giving an immediate health-driven impetus to restructure the land.[46]

The project is one of reorganization rather than reconception (see figure 45 for before and after photographs of the site). The transformation is subtle but complete and instrumental. The reinstallation of the hortas improves access, public perception, and irrigation quality. It is a strategy for land improvement and cooperation, aimed to provide social and physical stability. The moves are simple. The plots have been equalized and arrayed along the hillside in linear terraces descending to the valley floor.[47] Intermittent, evenly spaced paths cut directly from the top of the hillside to the bottom. As at Quinta da Granja, for every four gardens, there is a windowless wooden shed.

Figure 45. Parque Hortícola do Vale do Chelas, Lisbon, 2007 and 2015: the two photographs show the before (*top*) and after (*bottom*) park conditions.

The shed's warm hue glows in the incredible Lisbon light while its red corrugated roof compliments the earthy tones of the dry valley. Adjacent to this shared shed—its use negotiated among the individuals[48]—are rain barrels to collect water from the roof and the water spigot through which clean water flows in times of need, mostly from June through August. The material palette is restrained and controlled: wood and metal sheds; wood and wire fences; small wood retaining elements for the terraces and paths. The same materials are used around the city, and this is a deliberate aesthetic choice, a means to mark the territory as unified and intentionally designed, both on individual sites and across the multiple Parques Hortícolas projects in the city.

To cultivate the site is to enter into an agreement with the city. For a nominal yearly fee, the water and shed are provided.[49] In turn, the gardeners agree to respect the property and its material palette, maintain their cultivation practice, use water prudently, complete garden training, and garden organically.[50] The rules are clear and intended to

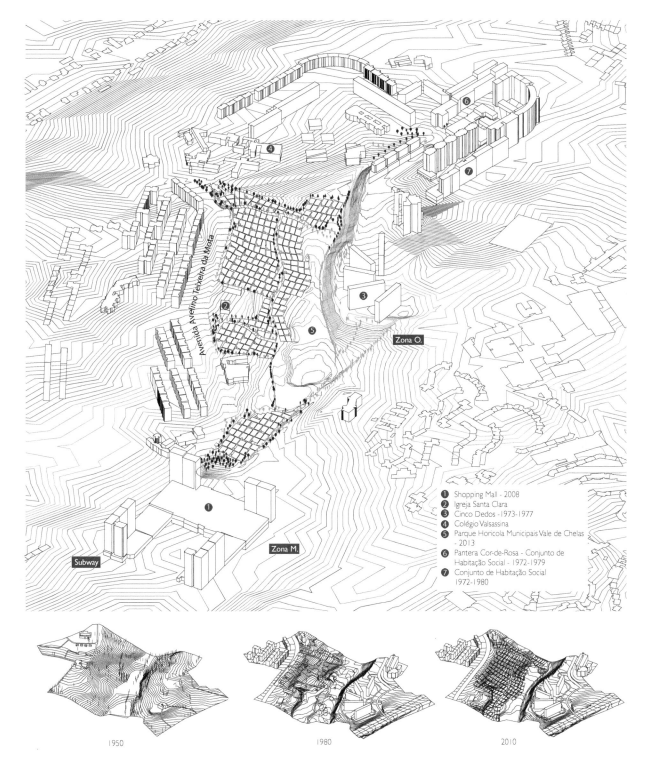

Subway

Zona M.

Zona O.

Avenida Avelino Teixeira da Mota

1 Shopping Mall - 2008
2 Igreja Santa Clara
3 Cinco Dedos -1973-1977
4 Colégio Valsassina
5 Parque Horícola Municipais Vale de Chelas - 2013
6 Pantera Cor-de-Rosa - Conjunto de Habitação Social - 1972-1979
7 Conjunto de Habitação Social 1972-1980

1950

1980

2010

Figure 46. Parque Hortícola do Vale do Chelas, Lisbon: an axonometric view of the valley topography and horta layout.

maintain the communal atmosphere of the hortas and to elevate their status within the Lisbon landscape vernacular. The hortas, rather than reviled and falling victim to racial and cultural biases in the city, are instead invested in and celebrated as an organized community embedded within a larger park structure.

The conversion is not perfect. For example, oddly, there is now a paved path at the bottom of the valley impeding drainage; and other amenities, including the lighting and the playground, have come slowly and are not fully integrated with the gardens. The city has invested in the agricultural agenda but lagged with the other park amenities. But overall, the Parque Hortícola do Vale do Chelas is full of good intentions, supported by physical design interventions and social agreements.

These interventions work on multiple scales: from the individual 160-square-meter (1,720-square-foot) plot to the clusters of four plots that share a shed; to the larger park that includes skating, play, and other forms of recreation; and finally to the municipal system of green valleys that form the cross grain of the city's ecological plan, the *Plano Verde de Lisboa*. Through the valuation of subsistence farming and the inclusion of immigrant cultural practices, valleys are rendered integral to the lifecycles and sustained vitality of the city (see figure 46 for the spatial transformation and physical integration of horta and valley).

Conclusions: Common Landscapes and Toolkits for Mediation

The Parques Hortícolas Municipais become a contemporary form of landscape commons, one where land is collectively cultivated through understated means.[51] The cultivation is achieved through the careful organization of key quotidian design elements: shed, spigot, fence, path, and terrace. These additions, plus a facilitated negotiation process of plot assignment and a simple contract, yield a shared ecological and cultural amenity. The city owns the land but transfers the right of use to local farmers and citizens, including many recent immigrants from Africa.[52] The design of the terrain becomes a form of mediation of both the social and physical landscapes. The allotments are clustered around shared sheds, water, and access points. The rows of allotment clusters form terraces to best occupy edge conditions and steep terrains. Water is managed collectively, as it circulates through the gardens and descends down the grade. The public can move through the sites, freely, in the spaces between and around the gardens. Occupation is promoted, managed, and regulated. Commons have rules— and this contemporary reinterpretation is no exception. It is a right to use the land, but that right comes with responsibilities for both the city and its farmers.

In a near-tragic architectural turn, the project's banality is what makes it remarkable. The design is beautiful without trying to do too much. It is analogous to an introvert whose quiet, listening presence is welcome in a room of loud extroverts jockeying for attention. The design embodies the rough elegance of its terrain. It adapts the intrinsic structure of the previous allotments while respecting the grain of the various site conditions. It generates a symbolic lushness that celebrates the collaboration between city government and city dweller. There was skepticism on different sides of the project—from the preexisting farmers who feared displacement to the general the public who dislike the disorderly hortas—but so far the parks are working, as respected social enterprises.[53] As one walks through them, there is a sense of optimism. The farmers are actively tending the plots, the soil manipulated with great expertise. The spaces are lush, as the clean water allows for the crops to flourish in a way they cannot in the plots without municipal spigots. The materials and distribution of the gardens give a sense of harmony to the landscape, a legibility that links back to the images of the valley in its pre-urbanization plan state and forward to an aspirational state of social and environmental justice.

In Chelas, the juxtaposition of design and tradition is exemplified in the moments where the local cane structures, constructed by farmers to support legume crops, meet the city's red-roofed sheds (see figure 47 for side-by-side drawings of shed and cane teepee). The cane, *Arundo donax,* considered an "invasive" species in Portugal, is widely used in agricultural practice as a material for building fences and plant support mechanisms. Likely an ancient introduction from India into the Mediterranean basin, the cane has been around a long time, dividing land and supporting climbing plants. In the Chelas valley, the farmers form teepee like lattices to support beans, a necessary ingredient for the Cape Verdean specialty Cachupa. The beanstalks wind themselves around the cane, overflowing at maturity, signaling bounty, sustenance, life. The cane structures, a similar height and girth as the shed structures, are light, ephemeral, and seemingly transitory. By contrast, the sheds represent a more durable stamp on the terrain. On the one hand, they could be critiqued as too fancy for a garden shed. On the other, they signify a proud investment in the land and its farmers, designed to be relatively lasting beacons of a sustained agricultural and social promise. The cane is flexible and accommodating while the wood is a firm anchor. Both constructions signal an incremental investment in human capital that stands in stark contrast to the looming architectural leviathans on the hillside above.

As I stand with my back to the buildings and peer over the steep edge and into the valley below, I am stuck by this marvelously dexterous negotiation of multiple terrains. The bank is so steep that it appears impassable to the nonresident's eye, but the well-worn footpath indicates the contrary. The soil looks dry and infertile, but the lush bean and cabbage stalks indicate the contrary. The social environment looks inhospitable, but the human activity indicates the contrary. The valley is about the perseverance of the landscape, and of its inhabitants, of its crops, and even of its governing body. All have an inherited agency here. What began as a single-minded endeavor has evolved into a place where—out of neglect—many agents take hold.

In facing the valley, it is possible to momentarily forget the past political and

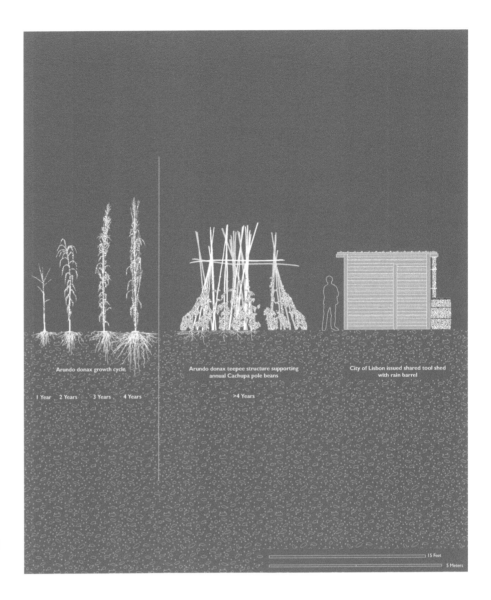

Figure 47. Shed and tepee, with *Arundo donax* and Cachupa beans; material condition and growth cycles are highlighted.

Figure 48. Agricultural cycles: a diagram of plant growth, housing, labor, migration, and climate over time.

architectural failures of the buildings in the background and see the value of this common project for the city now and in Lisbon's future.

In *Evocações do Passado* (Evocations of the Past), a set of recollections of key cultural practices, written by the playwright José Pedro do Carmo in 1943, hortas, is a chapter. The tone is of lament, for past times lost to development. He makes a plea "to remember with care what tradition has bequeathed to us from a past that gradually disappears."[54] He writes sadly of a lost landscape, erased in favor of urban growth and development, and with it "one characteristic, perhaps the most beloved by the people, was lost, which was known by this designation—the gardens."[55] When I walk through

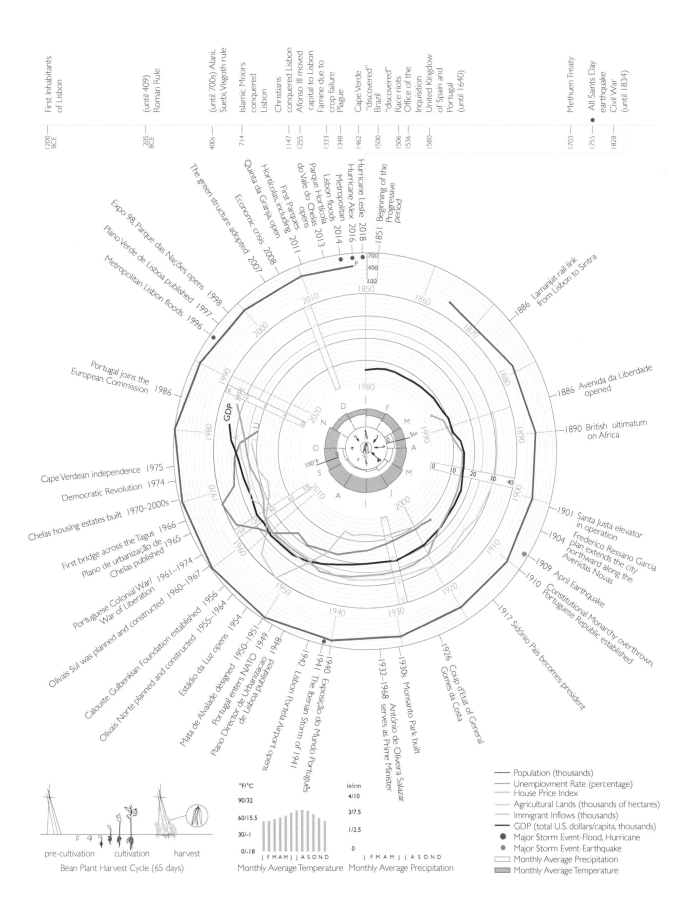

First Inhabitants of Lisbon — 1200 BCE
(until 409) Roman Rule — 205 BCE
(until '700s) Alani, Suebi, Visgoth rule — 400s
Islamic Moors conquered Lisbon — 714
Christians conquered Lisbon — 1147
Afonso III moved capital to Lisbon — 1255
Famine due to crop failure — 1333
Plague — 1348
Cape Verde "discovered" — 1462
Brazil "discovered" — 1500
Race riots — 1506
Office of the Inquisition — 1536
United Kingdow of Spain and Portugal (until 1640) — 1580
Methuen Treaty — 1703
All Saints Day earthquake — 1755
Civil War (until 1834) — 1828

The green structure adopted 2007
Quinta da Granja open
Economic crisis 2008
Horticolas, including First Parques
Horticolas 2011
Parque Horticola do Vale do Chelas 2013
Lisbon floods
Metropolitan 2014
Hurricane Alex 2016
Hurricane Leslie 2018
Beginning of the Progresso period
1851

Expo 98, Parque das Nações opens 1998
Plano Verde de Lisboa published 1998
Metropolitan Lisbon floods 1997
Metropolitan Lisbon floods 1996

1886 Lamanjat rail link from Lisbon to Sintra
1886 Avenida da Liberdade opened
1890 British ultimatum on Africa

Portugal joins the European Commission 1986

1901 Santa Justa elevator in operation
1904 Frederico Ressano Garcia plan extends the city northward along the Avenidas Novas
1909 April Earthquake
1910 Constitutional Monarchy overthrown. Portuguese Republic established
1917 Sidónio Pais becomes president

Cape Verdean independence 1975
Democratic Revolution 1974
Chelas housing estates built 1970–2000s
First bridge across the Tagus 1966
Plano de urbanização de Chelas published 1965
Portuguese Colonial War/ War of Liberation 1961–1974
Olivais Sul was planned and constructed 1960–1967
Calouste Gulbenkian Foundation established 1956
Olivais Norte planned and constructed 1955–1964
Estádio da Luz opens 1954
Mata de Alvalade designed 1950–1951
Portugal enters NATO 1949
Plano Director de Urbanização de Lisboa published 1948
1942 Lisbon Portela Airport opens
1941 The Iberian Storm of 1941
1940 Exposição do Mundo Português
1932–1968 António de Oliveira Salazar serves as Prime Minister
1930s Monsanto Park built
1926 Coup d'Etat of General Gomes da Costa

Population (thousands)
Unemployment Rate (percentage)
House Price Index
Agricultural Lands (thousands of hectares)
Immigrant Inflows (thousands)
GDP (total U.S. dollars/capita, thousands)
● Major Storm Event-Flood, Hurricane
● Major Storm Event-Earthquake
☐ Monthly Average Precipitation
☐ Monthly Average Temperature

pre-cultivation   cultivation   harvest
Bean Plant Harvest Cycle (65 days)

°F/°C
90/32
60/15.5
30/-1
0/-18
J F M A M J J A S O N D
Monthly Average Temperature

in/cm
4/10
3/7.5
1/2.5
0
J F M A M J J A S O N D
Monthly Average Precipitation

the gardens, with optimism, I think of these passages—and of the growth cycles of the city—to, yes, understand the loss, but also to see the birth of new gardens. In evoking the present, I put aside lament and nostalgia, for transformation and mutation. As hortas are part of Lisbon's centuries-old DNA, not to be forgotten, not to rest only in grainy photographs and crumbly pages of text, but to be lived through new generations and their evolving practices. The city, here, cycles through its geology, its soils, its crops, and its tenders (for more, see figure 48 for a cyclical cross fertilization of climate, politics, migration, and harvest).

4

SPEELPLAATSEN

100 Years of Play in Amsterdam

The story goes that Jakoba Mulder, a landscape architect for the city of Amsterdam Public Works Department, passed a young girl digging in a tree pit on her way to work one day. Mulder was struck by this image—and her subsequent realization that the city severely lacked proper spaces for children's play. The year was 1947, and Mulder decided to do something about it. At the time, nearly all playgrounds in Amsterdam were private and thus required membership or payment. As a result, they were not accessible to all children in the city. Mulder immediately called for a playground to be built at Bertelmanplein, a public square in the south of Amsterdam. While this initiative built on her work at Beatrixpark, a large park also in the south of Amsterdam where she designed a large, sandy play area, which opened to great success in 1936;[1] it is Bertelmanplein that was a catalyst for a substantial playground movement in the city driven by Mulder and her colleagues at the Public Works Department. In the years from 1947 to 1978, the city famously built over seven hundred *Speelplaatsen* or playgrounds in the city.[2]

Up to this point, the specific city responses to fallow and abandoned land in this book have focused on strategies that largely incorporate live matter. These strategies have taken many forms, and some have included paved areas, but as a secondary element. As we have explored, some are intentional: for example, place sod and mow; transition it to a land bank; use it to collect storm water, as in Philadelphia, or grow crops, as in Lisbon. Others, out of lack of resources, do nothing and allow spontaneous vegetation or activity to self-organize—only to later build on these efforts to conserve land, as in Berlin, and design space to invite further use. In the case of Amsterdam, the dominant response to urban abandonment was, and has been, to pave (and sometimes wall to bar access). This was a particularly true of the post–World War II period when the city was responding to its war damage and its more extensive housing crisis. Here

Figure 49. Sandbox, Amsterdam, 2015.

the pavement strategy also became a strategy to bring play and children into the public life of the city. So, while Amsterdam and its well-known playground system may seem like an outlier in a treatise on how to approach and design with abandonment, it represents both a rudimentary response, to introduce play space, and a rudimentary material, pavements, including aggregates and sand. Further, it is a chance to understand a municipal program within its political and social context and to see how the program and the spaces it engendered have evolved with time (and changing political and social contexts).

In the post–World War II period, the city coupled a few interests (greater need for housing and density; increasing numbers of children; new housing estates without open space plans) and utilized every space (abandoned parcels; lots created by wartime demolitions; oversized roadways; available interstitial spaces within new developments) to create an impressive web of play spaces. It was a land-use strategy that worked incredibly well. The deployment was incremental, coupling a palette of pavements, play elements, benches, and trees with small available pockets of space. Again, the city designed and installed the first of these playgrounds at Bertelmanplein in 1947. Again, Bertelmanplein was near where Jakoba Mulder lived, and the work was completed under the guidance of Mulder; her superior, the Public Works director Cornelis van Eesteren; and the architect Aldo van Eyck. Van Eyck, who went on to become one of Amsterdam's most well-known architects, was a young employee of the department who volunteered to design the playgrounds. This choice was, perhaps, driven by his distaste for the massive building projects taking most of the department's time and energy.[3] After the success at Bertelmanplein, the next playgrounds were planned and designed both through city initiative and in response to citizen demand. The Public Works Department received hundreds of letters requesting playgrounds for specific sites. For example, one woman in the Raamgracht area in Amsterdam Centrum wrote in October 1958: "On behalf of the children from the old inner city of the Jewish quarter, I would like to ask you whether it might at last be possible now to turn the disused area in the Zandstraat–Moddermolensteeg into a playground or something similar."[4] The corresponding Moddermolensteeg playground opened in 1960, and in 1971 it was redesigned. The neighborhood, greatly affected by demolition, slum clearance, and rebuilding—has since been rebuilt. A giant scar—most evident through the age of the buildings, with a predominant diagonal of 1960s and 1970s construction—cuts through the area. A small square remains between the Zuiderkerk, a seventeenth-century church, and a mixed-use building from the 1980s, but play is no longer the focus. This is the type of mini-cycle indicative both of the need to consider the city as an evolving entity and to voice alarm over densification of buildings and displacement of people, landscape, and use. Landscape is neither sacred nor a dispensable holding ground for market-rate building construction.[5] It lives in-between, as an urban fabric responsive to the social and environmental needs of its citizenry.

The playgrounds are well documented for their iconic design and their place within the architectural works of Aldo van Eyck.[6] They are also admired for their sheer number, both by cities that try to replicate the program and by historians who understand them as a polycentric web dotted across the urban landscape.[7] The individual play elements unify the spaces and became signature designs in their own right. The metal climbing dome is synonymous with the Amsterdam playgrounds of van Eyck and his colleagues. But it is the organization of the elements and the careful thought given to the view lines and movements, both essential for playgrounds, that make the spaces work. The common yet simple elements and the limited budgets allowed for many play spaces to be built across the city. The playgrounds were an essential part of the Amsterdam landscape from the late 1940s through the 1970s, and even today, the city—by comparison—has a wealth of play spaces.[8]

Here I focus on play and on pavement, sand included, as a means to activate the urban landscape and to create a common social infrastructure for the city. Yes, the play climbing domes and concrete stone and mountains are ingenious, but so, too, are the immense sandboxes that command a central role in the organization of the spaces. The ground surface defines the use and provides a structure for the sites—an economical means to transition a rubble pile, an undefined ground, or an intersection into a mini play plaza. The before and after plans and photographs of the sites indicate that the changes in the ground plane were by far the most radical transformations of the sites. In addition to understanding the role pavement has in defining the urban ground, I would like to place the Amsterdam project in its specific context—a thirty-year urban cycle—and also understand it within a larger idea of play as a means to inhabit the abandoned landscape and address the well-being of an urban citizenry.

Sand

Defined by its particle size, .05 to 20 millimeters, its siliceous qualities, and its warm yellowish-red hue, sand is a texture, a color, and a material.[9] It is used as a measure for soil texture, as all soils are classified by their percentages of sand, clay, and silt. Thus sand is nearly synonymous with the ground, a common ingredient in core samples, and is used to represent material flows in the city.[10] Sand is a heavy metaphor, from dust unto dust, materially representing the lifecycle of an organism, a person, or a city.

Sand is also the representative material of the first public playgrounds, both in Amsterdam and elsewhere (see figure 50 for a material exploration of sand and play). The sandbox (or sand bath), a device for sensory play, was a staple of the noted educator Friedrich Froebel's kindergarten. Responding to a suggestion from his former student and friend Hermann von Arnswald in a letter dated 1847, he included a sand bath in the kindergarten as a way to introduce topography to young children.[11] Sand is readily available or easily procured in most places and makes for an inviting texture for play. The sand bath is seen as a kindergarten in miniature, and this idea, of the sandbox as garden, quickly makes its way outside into large and luxurious sand piles in public parks and gardens, as seen at Beatrixpark. Empress Frederick, the English-Prussian monarch, working with Froebel's niece and fellow educator Frau Schrader, set aside space in Prussian parks for children's play and provided sand mountains as the main attraction.[12] Modeled after these sand piles in Berlin's parks, the first public playgrounds in the United States were essentially giant sandboxes constructed in 1885 in Boston's North End. The Boston sand gardens opened for three hours a day and were so popular that the city passed legislation to fund ten more playgrounds in 1898.[13] The model proliferated, spreading across the country, with playgrounds opening at rapid rates from the 1880s onward. These playgrounds were built on a foundation of sand and, with time, became more and more elaborate domains of play and recreation.

Public Play: Chicago

The provision of civic space for play is a fundamental municipal concern, and while the design of these spaces has changed, the underlying desire for a safe and accessible place for children to be outside in the city has remained constant. The health

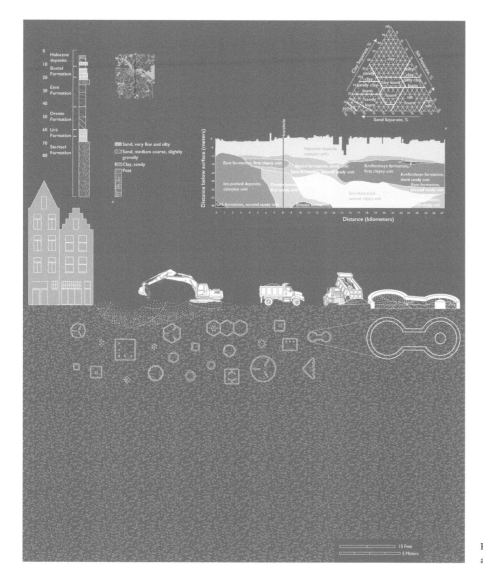

Figure 50. Sand: a drawing of material conditions and sandbox configurations.

and development of the child is a core societal interest. The idea that the public playground is essential for this well-being is one that has been pushed by public officials, social reformers, and designers at various times, in specific geopolitical contexts. In other words, there have been particular cities, programs, and eras that have served as models for the playground movements. Amsterdam, between 1947 and 1978, is one of these and should be understood in the context of other movements for design and civic play.

Borrowing from the European example, American cities started investing heavily in public playgrounds during the Progressive Era, as part of a larger social reform movement to improve working and living conditions in cities.[14] The investment was quick and significant: in 1890, there was only one public playground in the United States, and by 1917, there were close to four thousand.[15] While Boston and New York provided park funding earlier, Chicago became the model city for the progressive playgrounds. The city built nearly fifty playgrounds between 1900 and 1925.[16] The first playgrounds were associated with settlement houses, but soon the city expanded the sites, placing them in accessible and available plots throughout the city, especially on the South Side, where park leadership was particularly strong.[17]

The playgrounds, from their inception, were seen as a means of "urban blight" eradication.[18] The well-known social reformer Jacob Riis gave a speech in Chicago in 1899 on the way playgrounds could improve living conditions in the slums, using examples from his work in New York. The audience was convinced—and sought economical means to activate unoccupied properties in the city. Mary McDowell, a social worker, used twenty-five dollars from her local alderman to put a sandbox and swing set on an abandoned lot near her settlement house. The simple playground was deemed an instant success.[19] From here, the Chicago Playground Association, a voluntary organization of playground devotees, pushed park officials to develop a strategic approach to the introduction of play spaces in the city.[20] The eighteen directors, including an architect and the landscape architect Jens Jensen, reacted to the haphazard deployment of the first playgrounds. Instead, they proposed a three-part agenda: investigate the current conditions and needs; form local committees to generate interest; and, most notably, secure the use of vacant lots for playgrounds.[21] Unlike the large parks systems that often precede residential development, these small parks were designed to fit within residential neighborhoods, to occupy the interstices and be in close proximity to people's homes.

The playground itself becomes a type of metaphor, a place to experiment, to literally play with the ground and to create using the liveliness of play rather than using the inertness of the plan. It is a ludic idea, one where the "playground" is used to communicate a new intention for the city. The park districts worked with contracted designers to create the small park facilities. While the idea of providing for children's play in the city came from a European precedent, the American designers aggrandized this precedent. The Chicago parks had swimming pools, bathing houses, gymnasiums, recreational courts, and elaborate climbing structures. The well-known Olmsted firm, responsible for the larger Washington and Jackson parks in Chicago's South Park District, was hired to design the district's playgrounds as well. The fourteen parks—which ranged dramatically in size from 10 to 322 acres (4 to 130 hectares)—were not places of pastoral beauty but rather were social centers for the growing immigrant populations. South Park District commissioner J. Frank Foster visited Germany during his tenure and was underwhelmed by the design of his park's distant primogenitor. For Foster, the German sand gardens were nothing but "bare patches of ground," allowing him to declare in 1908 the "play park . . . an American product of the present decade."[22]

Chicago's population doubled between 1880 and 1890, with more immigrants arriving at rapid rates until the 1930s. The need for more parks and recreation was linked to the population growth; while at the same time, the small parks were being inserted into leftover spaces within the city in an effort to embed resources within the expanding residential fabric. They were tied at once to void and to activity—and became a way to move resource closer to beneficiary. The playgrounds were linked to housing—directly to settlement houses in the beginning and indirectly through the need's assessment analysis that led to their later placement.[23] The network had to be robust immediately to meet the needs of the growing city. Once the first playgrounds were successful, the city leaders mobilized quickly to build others. Many of the first playgrounds still remain, though their form has been altered significantly with changing trends in safety and recreational needs. Further, the playgrounds still stand amid a larger field of abandoned properties especially on the South Side of the city, an area that faced significant racism and structural disinvestment from the 1940s onward. The idea of activating the abandoned urban landscape with play remains current, but the mechanisms are even more locally determined, absent the same possibility of government investment.[24] With a faint public network already in place, the play spaces are largely singular initiatives for specific lots and communities. Health continues to be a driving factor as childhood obesity, asthma, and type 2 diabetes are of significant concern, especially in places with high levels of disinvestment and land abandonment. While the networks of play are linked to growth and prosperity, the pinpointed insertions can bring a play area closer to an extant population when investment diminishes and patchworks emerge. Cities with large inventories of abandoned land often have large acreages of parkland, but these lands, designed for another era, are far from the needs and residences of the local constituents. With the prospect of greater health crises, including pandemics with associated quarantines, and with the known correlation between structural disinvestment and racism and health outcome, the opportunities to make reparations, restore justice, and embed a public health and play infrastructure within neighborhoods only stand to increase.

Public Play: Amsterdam

If Chicago led the playground charge in the Progressive Era, Amsterdam took over after World War II. As part of the massive restructuring of the city, led by the Office of Public Works and its functionalist director, Cornelius van Eesteren, the playgrounds were humble insertions in the city fabric, finding their way into the old city as well as the new districts.[25] Again Jakoba Mulder's sand creation at Beatrixpark was a precursor to a large network of sandboxes deployed across the city.[26] These sand areas anchored small pocket plazas with innovative pavement patterns, climbing elements, and planting plans. The playgrounds were incrementally deployed, occupying the interstices of the city, just as the small parks had done decades earlier in Chicago. Only here, in Amsterdam, over seven hundred *Speelplaatsen* or playgrounds were constructed in a thirty-year period. They became part of the collective consciousness of the city, as spatial representations of a child-centered era, where play becomes deliberately visible in the public realm.

As in Chicago, the Amsterdam playgrounds were both the first public play spaces in the city and a means to activate vacant parcels and underutilized spaces. The architect Aldo van Eyck, then a municipal employee working with van Eesteren and Mulder, designed some of the first playgrounds in the Amsterdam system. He adapted and executed an idea about leisure present in the architectural discussion of postwar reconstruction, notably written about by Le Corbusier in the Athens Charter.[27] For Le Corbusier, this essential leisure program was mainly to be found in large parks and then possibly was supported by the reclamation and use of the interstitial vacant lot. For van Eyck, it was the reverse: the playgrounds were both a means to bring children into the urban public realm and a way to capture the small, leftover, and forgotten spaces for architectural projects. The move deliberately represented a counter-idea to the comprehensive urban extension plans that dominated the architectural consciousness of the era. Van Eyck explained, "The sites thus adapted were for the most part there, waiting (as many similar sites are waiting in every city of the world), forsaken, useless and dead: innumerable islands and plots left over by road engineers and demolition workers; often better suited for the use by children than for development as ornamental public gardens."[28] The playgrounds were the antithesis of ornamental: created by demand, for active use, using local and ordinary materials in extraordinary ways.

Van Eyck and his colleagues developed a kit of playground parts that could be adapted to the particularities of the nonconforming sites. The design challenge lay in the odd shapes of the lots—for example, the long and narrow strips or the triangles carved from roadways—which required ingenuity to make them safe and inviting play spaces. Van Eyck used pavements of materials found nearby to structure the spaces, concrete sandboxes of various shapes and dimensions as anchors, and climbing structures to animate and direct movement.[29] Benches placed in locations that provided clear sightlines for caregivers watching the children and trees, when possible, complement the play elements. It is the balance between the unique qualities of each playground and the uniformity of the materials across the entire system that makes the project exemplary as a common strategy for both abandoned parcels and leftover slivers of the new housing estates. They are banal yet clever. While usually named solely after their location, the titles for the playgrounds in Alfred Ledermann and Swiss playground designer Alfred Traschel's seminal 1959 text *Creative Playgrounds and Recreational Centers* reflect both location and the site conditions. For example, the titles read: "Play-space on a traffic island, Jacob Thijseplein, Amsterdam, Holland," "Play-space in a green strip, Zaanhug,

Amsterdam, Holland," and "Temporary playground on a building plot, Dijkstraat, Amsterdam, Holland. The names reflect the ideas behind the project: namely that small play spaces can and should be easily inserted anywhere.

From Bertelmanplein to 700 *Speelplaatsen*

During World War II, the municipal planners had already begun to discuss the need for playgrounds in the city and the potential to place them on small, empty sites throughout the old city. They even made a radical suggestion that these sites could be created, through demolition, in areas without small open pockets. The city would acquire the land, short and long term, for the construction. Almost immediately after the war, this project came to fruition. In the end, demolition was not required (see figure 51 for the distribution of playgrounds relative to the city's defining structural elements).

The playground initiative—intended to build one new playground in each of Amsterdam's neighborhoods—began at Bertelmanplein, with a play-space on a traffic island.[30] Mulder demanded the insertion, and van Eyck worked on the assignment with great enthusiasm. Even though the playgrounds were not his idea and the locations were given, he welcomed the challenge. He designed all of the elements—including the central sand pit. It was a rounded rectangle with a thirty-five-centimeter (fourteen-inch) lip around it for sitting, cut in two places for access, with three extruded cylindrical concrete play tables for play sand baking and an aluminum climbing frame set inside. At three feet deep, the sand pit provided room for digging and tunneling without being too deep and dangerous. In the surrounding area, van Eyck designed wood benches and incorporated the existing plane trees to form a light enclosure for the dominant sand feature.

At Bertelmanplein, the site was without a long history. In fact, the square was at the northern end of the city's first wave of expansion projects. It is part of the architect H. P. Berlage's Plan Zuid, accepted in 1917, for the construction of new neighborhoods to the south of the central core. Since the playground was located on fairly new city ground, the transformation was less extreme than in some of the subsequent playgrounds. Prior to the project, it was already a small, if banal, square, wrapped on all sides by roads, including the busy connector street, Bernard Kochstraat. The site had ten existing street trees and was bounded by Amsterdam School housing designed by Johannes C. van Epen.[31] The designers further articulated the site by circumscribing it with a low curb and paving it in a fashion similar to the surrounding streets. The result was a small play plaza that belongs both to the larger city and to the adjacent buildings, full of children waiting for a space to play.

Aldo van Eyck designed Bertelmanplein as a singular playground, creating each of the elements specifically for that site. At this point, it would have been hard to predict that this playground would be the first of over seven hundred created in Amsterdam

Figure 51. Canals, interstices, and vacancy, Amsterdam: playgrounds are shown in relationship to the city's overall ringed structure.

Green Structure
City Parks
Green Urban Areas
Centruum
Vacant
Playgrounds
A10 Motorway
Roadways

2 Miles
4 Kilometers

over the next thirty years. Van Eyck worked on these playgrounds as a city employee until 1951, when he left the city post, but he continued his involvement, completing many more designs as a contract employee. The early designs were more elaborate and idiosyncratic, occupying the open slivers found in the older parts of the city. As the city expanded, the playgrounds were installed in the new developments. These become a means of occupying the underconceived ground plane rather than resulting from an act of carving away the ever-evolving city. In the periphery, the sand pits were smaller and more plentiful, with each housing group having its own play area.[32]

Planning Amsterdam

To plan Amsterdam is to control water, as the city famously sits several meters below sea level. The buildings rest on piles driven deep into the sand, and an elaborately engineered system of dams, dykes, and canals manage the watery terrain. In fact, the damming of the Amstel River was the first act of city making, and the over 100 kilometers (or 62 miles) of canals define the concentrically expanding urban form. With over 165 constructed waterways and 1,200 bridges, the moving over, under, and by water defines the urban experience. Originally a moat-like defense system, the canals supported trade in the golden age of the seventeenth century and now are largely an infrastructure for touring, social boating, and living. The city expansion is marked by the canals, especially the Grachtengordel or canal ring of Amsterdam Centruum—which generally refers to the four grand canals of Herengracht, Keizergracht, Prinsengracht, and the Singel that ring the Dam Square and the old city. The Jordaan neighborhood sits just across the Prinsengracht from this historic core, created with the Third Expansion of the city. The Fourth Expansion completed this famous ring. The historic periods of growth are marked by the construction of canals, some of which have since been filled to grow the city from the inside rather than constantly expanding outward (see figure 52 for a map coded by dates of building construction). Thus, the development of the city is a negotiation between wet and dry, both at the larger citywide scale, as land reclamation allows the city to extend in all directions, and at the scale of the plot, street, and block, as former waterways are filled and opened. With rising sea levels and increasing storm events and surges, more water is slowly being let back into the Dutch cities. The balancing act continues—and contemporary squares, while still highly paved, include provisions for storm water to fill and percolate as well as for play to happen.[33]

In 1947, Amsterdam was a growing city.[34] Its physical footprint was extending outward. Its population was increasing, especially its young population, due to the postwar baby boom, and the city was struggling to house all of its residents.[35] Unlike other cities in the Netherlands, Amsterdam did not suffer major war damage[36]—only a small amount of housing was destroyed for fuel needs—and therefore, the major building

Dates of
Construction

— <1800
— 1801-1850
— 1851-1900
— 1901-1930
— 1931-1945
— 1946-1960
— 1961-1975
— 1976-1985
— 1986-1995
— 1996-2005
— 2006-2014

▨ Open Space
▬ Waterways
▭ Centruum
▱ Vacant
▪ Playgrounds
— A10 Motorway
--- Centruum

Ⓐ Jordann

Ⓑ Zeedijk-Centrum

Ⓒ Laagte Kadijk

2 Miles

4 Kilometers

Figure 52. Building construction over time, Amsterdam, including playground locations and callouts for the Jordaan, Zeedijk, and Laagte Kadijk.

efforts were taking place as part of the city's expansion plan. Land was reclaimed from the sea and prepared for massive, publicly financed housing developments. The Netherlands, Amsterdam included, addressed its postwar housing crisis through national organization with large, prefabricated social housing estates, exploiting construction advances to generate blocks and blocks of similar flats.[37] The buildings were modern and rational. They were aggregated into complete neighborhood units, modeled after garden cities such as Radburn, New Jersey, and Letchworth, England, but with a mix of row houses, mid-rise, and high-rise apartments, schools, commerce, and administration. The neighborhood development was a collaboration between municipal planners, building architects, and national funders. This building boom—from 1945 to 1970—paralleled the period of the playground construction, and the two cannot be considered separately. While the playgrounds were sometimes positioned as a minor but significant humanist response to the functionalist building craze happening within the housing sector, they also were a part of the same social housing complexes.[38] The first playgrounds—and the ones most documented—were often central gap-fillers, occupying the small voids found in the denser, old fabric within the A10 ring, abutting the historic canals. Others were built in parks and traffic islands. But many—over half of the seven hundred—were built on new ground, for the families in the new housing estates (see figure 52).

The Dutch Housing Act of 1901 (Woningwet) encouraged the creation of housing corporations and cooperatives to build social housing complexes. They required municipalities to make these housing projects part of the formal plans for the city and its expansion. The housing act was considered the beginning of the Dutch welfare state, as well as the framework within which urban expansion happened. The well-known and respected architect H. P. Berlage drafted the first plans for expansion. His famous Plan Zuid of 1917, referenced above, added four neighborhoods to the south of the city to accommodate the growing urban population moving from the countryside to the city for industrial work. The western expansion was built loosely on Berlage's precedent in the south, constructing another four neighborhoods on recently annexed land.[39] To help with the significant growth in the urban fabric, the city created a division dedicated to urban planning within the Department of Public Work in 1928. This group, led by three urban designers, architects, and modernists—L. S. P. Scheffer, Theo K. van Lohuizen, and Cornelis van Eesteren—was responsible for the creating of the General Extension Plan of Amsterdam (AUP).[40] This plan, created in 1934 and adopted in 1939, created a framework for the growth of the city, laying out land uses and target densities for the many neighborhoods designed to accommodate the ongoing and anticipated population surge. Van Eesteren, a functionalist, went on to become director of public works, overseeing the enactment of the expansion plan, beginning with the garden suburbs to the west and, ultimately, continuing with more growth to the south and north of the city.[41] As previously mentioned, his department was also responsible for the playground construction. And while the expansion plan was executed in plan, with austere bird's-eye perspectives showing uniform blocks devoid of the messiness of the city, the first playgrounds were created through an idiosyncratic, on-the-ground method of locating small slivers within a layered urban condition. Van Eesteren, known as a top-down planner, however, embraced the playgrounds—often becoming concerned with small details—as a means to both clean up older parts of the city and to animate the neighborhoods constructed as part of the AUP (figure 53 shows the playground distribution atop the AUP as well as broken down by construction period).[42]

Nearly a decade into the program, the year 1954 marked a shift in the playground deployment. Aldo van Eyck resigned from the city in 1951, and although he continued to design and oversee the designs of the playgrounds, others became involved as well. In 1954, nearly all of the playgrounds had been built within the preexisting fabric of the city, located within the A10 highway ring. In the years after, more playgrounds were associated with the new garden cities, and by 1978, full constellations appeared in Amsterdam's expansion neighborhoods. Thirty-six of these belong to Van Eesteren's garden city, Slotermeer. These designs, on the whole, while never reduced to "types," were more standardized, in response to the more uniform character of the sites and the geometries of the clean strips in front of the new housing structures.

The playground project continued steadily for thirty years, with one playground built in the 1940s, and roughly 155 in the 1950s, 390 in the 1960s, and 155 in the 1970s.[43] In addition to spreading outward with time, the playgrounds were also aggregated in clusters. Described as a polycentric net, the distribution was wide but with pulses of numerous playgrounds in a single neighborhood. On the one hand, citizens saw a playground and requested one for an open space nearer to their house, yielding multiple projects in close proximity. On the other, available land was often bunched in particular areas of the city—war demolition sites were near other war demolition sites; vacant parcels near other vacant parcels; large road rights-of-way were near other large road rights-of-way; and open space next to open space in the new territories being colonized by the city. The designs took advantage of both small, discontinuous parcels and the increasing number of children in the city, giving meaning to the proliferation of play lots in close proximities. In the beginning, the sandboxes were large, and they got smaller as time progressed and the playgrounds became more abundant. The playground construction was truly a process without an overarching plan, whereby the sites were developed through desire, need, and demand. The project is scalable and elastic, important qualities for strategies contending with a perforated ground condition. The department did not set out to build seven hundred playgrounds, but rather just kept building them through the Dutch housing boom of 1945–75. It seemed that any place that wanted a playground, and any site that met minimum criteria, got one. As a result, several generations grew up with this common and shared experience. They have

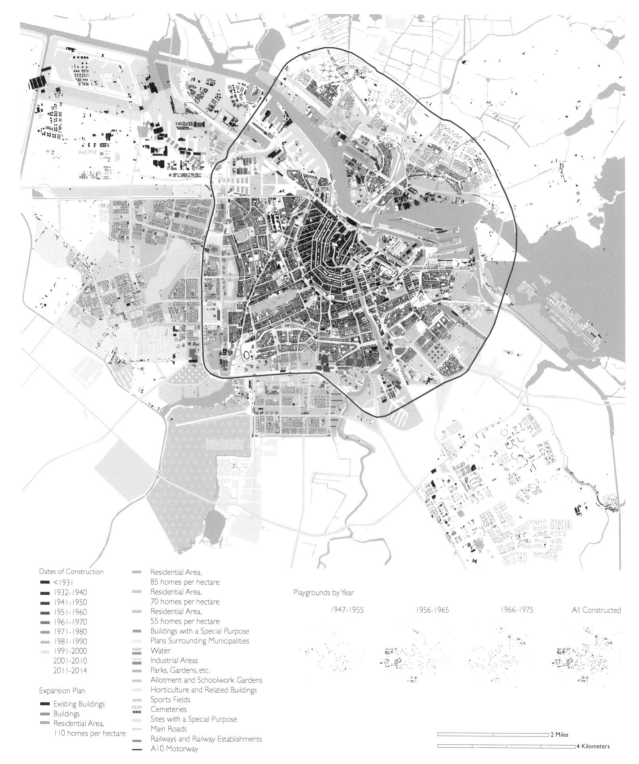

Dates of Construction
- ■ <1931
- ■ 1932-1940
- ■ 1941-1950
- ■ 1951-1960
- ■ 1961-1970
- ■ 1971-1980
- ■ 1981-1990
- 1991-2000
- 2001-2010
- 2011-2014

Expansion Plan
- ■ Existing Buildings
- ■ Buildings
- ■ Residential Area,
  110 homes per hectare

- Residential Area,
  85 homes per hectare
- Residential Area,
  70 homes per hectare
- Residential Area,
  55 homes per hectare
- Buildings with a Special Purpose
- Plans Surrounding Municipalities
- Water
- Industrial Areas
- Parks, Gardens, etc.
- Allotment and Schoolwork Gardens
- Horticulture and Related Buildings
- Sports Fields
- Cemeteries
- Sites with a Special Purpose
- Main Roads
- Railways and Railway Establishments
- A10 Motorway

Playgrounds by Year

| 1947-1955 | 1956-1965 | 1966-1975 | All Constructed |

2 Miles

4 Kilometers

Figure 53. Playground and the General Extension Plan of Amsterdam, Amsterdam.

all played in the sandboxes, jumped across the jumping stones, climbed the climbing mountains, and hung from the aluminum structures. This could be said of any era of playgrounds in a city, but it is particularly strong in the Amsterdam case.

Temporality

The fluidity of the construction process can be contributed, at least in part, to the fact that the playgrounds were designed to be temporary. This is not to say that they had a particular life expectancy or were built with nondurable materials—sand, concrete, aluminum, wood, and trees are all quite lasting—but that their designers envisioned them as meeting a particular need at a particular time. There was an astute recognition that city building is a process, and that all elements of the built environment are to some degree temporary. The temporariness here did not represent a short-term investment, a lack of commitment to maintenance, or a cheapening of the design. Rather, it was an idea of experimentation and of meeting a present need without having to predict longevity or assess the future. Van Eesteren, who's AUP was very much designed to last, saw the playgrounds, instead, as mutable and evolving, included in the reconstruction of the city "in a way that is not more than temporary."[44] This is true of the playgrounds occupying the sites of former buildings—again Dijkstraat is called a temporary playground on a building plot—and of the playgrounds added to the reconstruction sites. As the city has evolved in the nearly seventy years since the first playground was built, many of the sites have transformed—either into new forms of playgrounds that conform better to contemporary conventions or into parking areas that respond to the great shortage of parking in the city, or into other types of open space. Many have also been built over, as neighborhoods change and demands for real estate increase across the city. Dijkstraat is in fact now a building, as its early name suggested. The playground was transformed in 1972.

While many harbor a nostalgic feeling about the playgrounds and their loss, it is, instead, important to see them as a specific and logical strategy for the building and baby boom period in Amsterdam, to understand how the means of design and implementation might continue to be powerful and relevant even if the particular style and use is no longer the most relevant for the contemporary city. The city changes, through long, short, and continuous cycles, a notion intrinsic to the very existence and arguably the very success of the program in Amsterdam.

Amsterdam is a city of rings, most generally defined by the canal ring and Amsterdam Centrum, by the area between the Centrum and the highway A10, and finally by the area outside of the A10. This is both a geographic distinction and a temporal one. The city expands outward, and the time of the building construction indicates the rings. The central ring is largely full of pre-1800 buildings, the next a confetti from many eras, and the buildings outside the A10 are post-1950 (see figure 52). The following section focuses on a few specific playgrounds built on abandoned plots in the Amsterdam Centrum, rather than those inserted into the newer developments at the city's edges. The sites were without specific building plans at the time of the playground construction but have since evolved. The cases explore the playgrounds within urban design histories of the sites and their specific cultural contexts. Rather than lamenting the loss of the remarkable individual designs, the playgrounds are understood as an effective strategy for urban abandonment at the moment of their construction and seen as a collective investment in the necessarily adaptable social infrastructure of the city. They work at both the scale of the individual parcel and the entire urban agglomeration. This is a rare and exciting achievement.

Individual Case: Zeedijk

The two most powerful representations of the playgrounds—both at the time of their construction and in the many subsequent articles and books published on their significance—are, again, the before and after construction birds'-eye photographs that show the radical transformation of the sites and the detail photographs of joyous children midplay. These are particularly relevant to the playgrounds built into the existing interstices of the city. They demonstrate the way in which each space is altered, from a site of rubble and dumping to one of play; exemplifying how difficult sites can be revivified and enlivened through local design ingenuity. It is not a matter of applying set types to different places but rather approaching each site with a clear understanding of its geometries and physical and social contexts. And yet, the sites are not overthought nor rendered complicated. Instead, the designs are conceived of for easy execution, with appropriate budgets, and available materials.

Zeedijk, meaning seawall and referring to the street name where the playground is located, is in the Nieuwmarkt district of central Amsterdam, on a site where a medieval monastery once stood, and a Chinese temple now stands. In 1955, when the playground was designed, the site was a large and irregularly shaped abandoned lot created through the forceful erasure of a number of structures. Numbers 108 to 112 Zeedijk, a part of the monastery subsequently repurposed for commercial use, was demolished in 1944 after the deportation of their Jewish owners.[45] After additional buildings at 114 to 118, collapsed, numbers 106 to 118 Zeedijk Street were left as an opening in the city. In order to prohibit access to the debris-strewn sites, the city constructed a high wall along the street, hiding the expanse beyond. At this time, there were three other open parcels in the same block of the Zeedijk, creating another large space, between 92 and 102. This was a uniquely porous condition for the street, with the adjacent blocks having continuous facades of buildings.

With the first acts of the playground design, van Eyck and his colleagues removed the high wall, revealing the openness beyond. They remarked the edge of the site with a low, sixty- centimeter (roughly twenty-four-inch) wall across half of the opening to the sidewalk, and balanced this with another low angled wall, offset from a building wall at the rear of the playground. This essentially unified the space by pulling geometry from its complex edge, while creating a small exterior and large interior space. The pavement choices—with gray materials to match the sidewalk in the outer room—and white tiles and brown bricks in the interior room—reinforced the separation. The site had two clear thresholds: the street and an anteroom off the street that led into the main play space. The exterior space was calm, with somersault frames and a turnabout; while the interior space was dynamic, with the circular form of the sandpit and the circular arrangement of climbing frames overlapping the different types of pavement.[46] A line of jumping posts occupied the space between the two large plan-view circles. A bench along the rear wall further focused the attention inward. The perimeter of the space was formed by an eclectic array of buildings, of varied heights, and van Eyck addressed this potentially cacophonous edge by commissioning the artist Joost van Roojen to create a mural to encompass the playground.[47] The vivid geometrical forms on the walls— lines, rectangles, square and circular swatches of color—reinforced the language of the space.[48]

The before and after photographs demonstrate the immediate transformation of the space, despite the fact that the after photograph predated the mural completion.[49] The site remained active as a playground for many years, with modifications conducted in 1970. However, at some point, its use transitioned, and the site became known more as a hangout for alleged drug users rather than children. By 1978, the playground was no longer in existence. This was three years after the famous riots in the Nieuwmarkt district and a moment when the city planners started to look back to the historic core, after decades of intense building on undeveloped land at the edges.[50] In fact, the late 1970s marked a turn away from the big, modern plan and toward a reinvestment in the historic core. The temporary playgrounds lasted as holding grounds for new construction to come. In 1994, the planning process began for a Chinese temple on the Zeedijk sites, and the building opened in 2000. The site returned to its early roots as a place of religious worship, with a pronounced change in culture and style. The neighborhood, once part of the medieval city, is now home to Amsterdam's Chinatown.[51]

Individual Case: Laagte Kadijk

Laagte (lower) and Hoogte (higher) Kadijk are the two main east–west streets of the small Kadijken neighborhood. The roughly 170 by 900 meter (550 by 3,000 foot) area is encompassed by waterways—the Nieuwe Vaart and the Entrepotdok—and named for the hydrological infrastructure that makes the ground dry and the built environment atop it possible. The Kadijken Island was constructed in the late seventeenth century and was transformed into an active shipping and warehouse district in the nineteenth century. From 1900 to 1930, a considerable number of social housing projects were constructed—especially on the south side of the neighborhood—to accommodate the city's housing demand. The area has slowly transitioned from industrial to residential use, with only a few water-based businesses remaining off of the Nieuwe Vaart.

At the time of the playground design and construction, from 1953 to 1954, pre-1800 residential fabric surrounded the site. The void itself, the width of six narrow Amsterdam row houses, was again hidden from street view by a high wall. Behind this barrier lay an expanse full of abandoned cars, tires, and debris. Across the street, in an area that will become continuous residential fabric was another walled-off area full of discarded materials. Thus, the playground was inserted into a transitioning neighborhood, one where the influx of residents ultimately necessitated a play space for children. The before photograph of the site shows a pair of children peering into the open gate at the enticing landscape of tires and cars beyond while the after photograph shows the newly constructed site full of children climbing, with their caregivers watching nearby.

The site is a clean rectangle, and in order to unify the edge condition, a high wall was constructed on two sides as a means of separation between the play area and the adjacent buildings. The street edge is marked with an open climbing structure that was later turned into a low fence with a gate. The first composition was simple, with a large circular sand pit and benches on one side and jumping stones and climbing arch on the other. Benches along the back wall faced the street, allowing for a layered view of the playground in the foreground and the street beyond (see figure 54 for drawings of the site transformation).

Unlike the Zeedijk example, the playground on Laagte Kadijk has remained a playground, a small pocket still open as the residential fabric has filled in around it. The design is no longer the same—first the climbing arch was rotated, then removed along with the sand pit, and only three jumping stones remain as vestiges. The design has changed, even been compromised, but the respite of the site has lasted. Like the populations of the shrinking cities where the emphasis is poorly placed on those who have left, much is made of the disappearing playgrounds—of the forty-four in Central Amsterdam, only a handful remain, all with total design alteration. But in a program designed to build one playground in each neighborhood, the fact that some remain, after over fifty years, seems remarkable. And though the Laagte Kadijk site is heavily critiqued as having no resemblance to a van Eyck playground, it is still an appealing enclave with perfect shade for an afternoon of play (see figure 55 for the view into the space).[52]

In the Laagte Kadijk block, the rest of the voids have been filled with housing, built with time over the last century. Some of the buildings directly adjacent were constructed as recently as the 1990s. In a place where landscapes perish quickly, and where

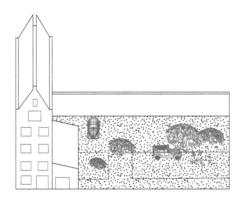

1930

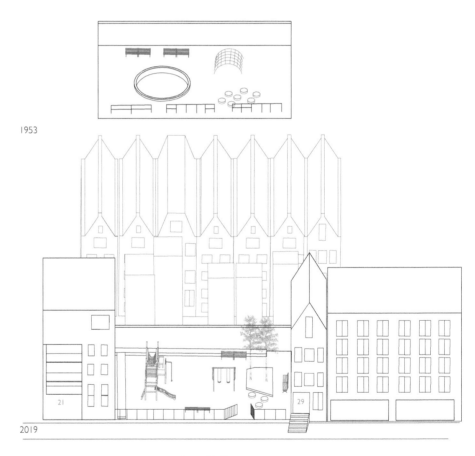

1953

2019

Laagte Kadijk

Figure 54. Laagte Kadijk, Amsterdam: axonometric view showing the evolution of the playground with time.

Figure 55. Laagte Kadijk, Amsterdam, 2015.

resident demands govern, the playground still has a key place. On a warm September afternoon, children flock to the slide and swings and even the jumping stones. Nearby residents have set up a table for an outdoor meal, with friends stopping by as their schedule permits. The shady space may have lost its original elements but not its charm and intent. With time, the playground system has been sized and adapted to the contemporary city, with each site collecting layers, and uses, aptly reflecting a greater preoccupation with stuff and short-term gratification than existed in previous decades.

Neighborhood Case: The Jordaan

The two playgrounds on Zeedijk and Laagte Kadijk both sit amid a varied urban fabric of buildings built in different eras. It is understandable that a program designed to temporarily occupy open building sites would be best suited for places with such openings, and that these places, with time, would reflect these voids through buildings and open spaces designed and built at different times. The Zeedijk and Laagte Kadijk streets are eclectic collections of small insertions, a condition exemplified across the entire Jordaan neighborhood (see figure 56 for a set of sections through the space, coded for dates of building construction, forming an itinerant experience of the eclectic qualities).

In Amsterdam Centrum, the Jordaan neighborhood had the most playgrounds constructed by the city during the 1940s to 1970s (figure 56 also marks the playground sites). This also means that the Jordaan had the most puzzling postwar gaps. In 1954, Cornelis van Eesteren, in a memo to his department, linked the playground insertions in the neighborhood with an urban restructuring agenda, seeing them as a means for "cleaning up" the Jordaan.[53] The subsequent maps produced by the department showed this effort, with gaps being filled red for potential playground locations. In all, fourteen projects were installed, of which few remain. Yet, there are still a number of playgrounds in the neighborhood. It is a short walk from the charming two-sided micro-lot on Mouthaansteeg to the restored and reinserted van Eyck style playground in the traffic medium on Palmgracht to a large wood-filled playlot at the end of Lindenstraat, to the cluttered interior lot on Slootstraat with its live chickens and extensive inventory of plastic riding toys.

The Jordaan is a storied neighborhood—a classic tale of displacement, on par with London's East End or New York City's Village, and only barely escaping the fate of Boston's West End.[54] Constructed in the seventeenth century to house the laborers working on the expanding city, the Jordaan was heavily populated by the nineteenth century. By the mid-twentieth century, the perception was one of deteriorated living conditions, leading to the desire for "cleaning up" that van Eesteren alluded to in his playground memo. By the postwar reconstruction period, there was an urban renewal type proposal for the slum clearance in the neighborhood, pushing demolition as a means of rectifying living conditions.[55] The residents, a vocal and left-leaning group, protested, and with a changing tide in planning by the late 1960s and 1970s, preservation ensued. The idea of neighborhood clearance gaining traction is unimaginable in the present-day Jordaan, an enchanting neighborhood with high real estate value where renovated historic buildings house residences, galleries, shops, and cafés. The working class has relocated. The playgrounds have filled in, but the inner courtyards remain as horticultural sanctuaries. There are a few places where the public can penetrate—one at the hidden playground on Slootstraat and others in select locations where the landscapes meet and occupy the street edge.

Another one of these moments is at Palmgracht, a long linear space surrounded by streets and slender buildings from the seventeenth, eighteenth, and nineteenth centuries. The strip, originally one of the eleven canals in the Jordaan, runs between the Brouwersgracht (Brewer's canal) and the Lijnbaansgracht, which continue to bracket

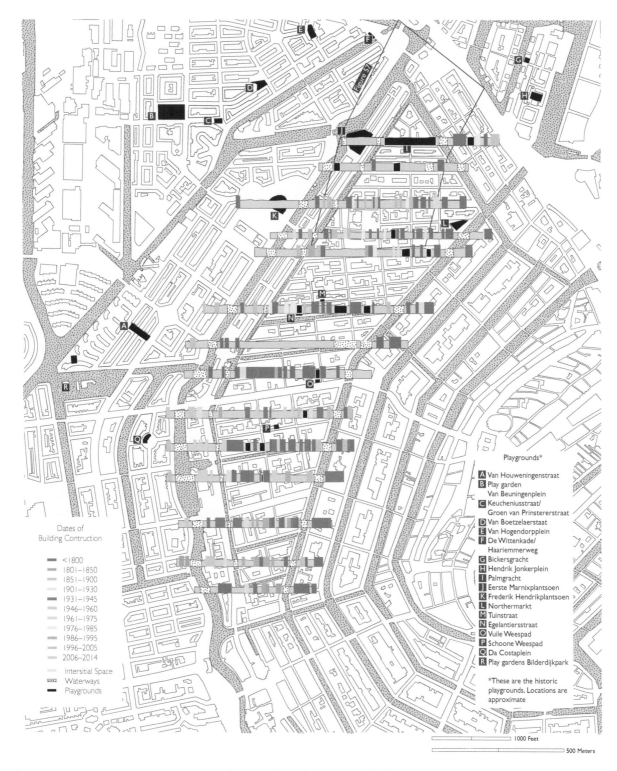

Figure 56. Itinerant sections across the Jordaan, Amsterdam; color fills highlight the dates of building construction, and labels indicate the approximate locations of the historic playgrounds.

Dates of
Building Contruction

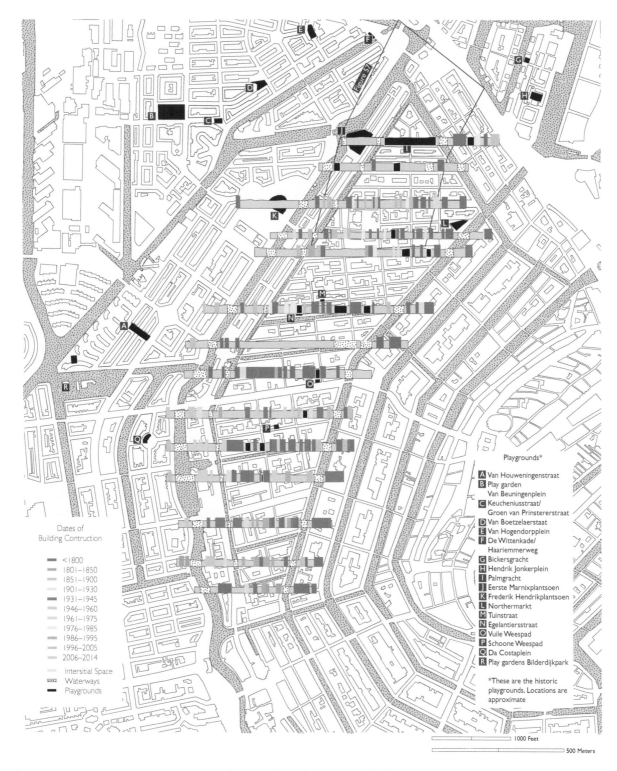
<= 1800
1801–1850
1851–1900
1901–1930
1931–1945
1946–1960
1961–1975
1976–1985
1986–1995
1996–2005
2006–2014
Intersitial Space
Waterways
Playgrounds

Playgrounds*

A Van Houweningenstraat
B Play garden
   Van Beuningenplein
C Keucheniusstraat/
   Groen van Prinstererstraat
D Van Boetzelaerstaat
E Van Hogendorpplein
F De Wittenkade/
   Haariemmerweg
G Bickersgracht
H Hendrik Jonkerplein
I Palmgracht
J Eerste Marnixplantsoen
K Frederik Hendrikplantsoen
L Northermarkt
M Tuinstraat
N Egelantiersstraat
O Vuile Weespad
P Schoone Weespad
Q Da Costaplein
R Play gardens Bilderdijkpark

*These are the historic
playgrounds. Locations are
approximate

1000 Feet

500 Meters

the space (the site and context is shown in figure 57). Due to poor water quality and the need to accommodate surface traffic, the Palmgracht was filled in the late nineteenth century. Originally, supplanted with an allée and promenade, it was selected as a playground site in 1950, with construction completed by 1952. Through the design, the trees were curated, with play elements inserted beneath. Because of its history, as a part of the hydrological and civic infrastructure, Palmgracht remains an interstitial landscape, even as the city fills in around it. As an open space, it cycles (see figure 58 for the transformation of the site with time).

First, it was part of the elaborate canal system to drain the landscape for urban activity and to provide mobility across the territory. As this system reached obsolescence, the space transformed, becoming a boulevard like public space at a time when cities were opening, to allow sunlight and air to penetrate in response to health concerns.[56] Then, with the baby boom and increased residential occupation, the site became part of the playground network, evolving to include a roller rink in the 1980s, and then, with changing cultural practice, fell into disrepair. Finally, with renewed interest in the playground program from the 1950s to the 1970s, the site was renovated in the 2010s—to reference its original aesthetic.[57] A new climbing frame, with updated joinery, allows children to once again hang upside down and look into the nineteenth-century canopy, while older residents watch and talk on the perimeter benches. They are also a few, albeit restrained, new structures: swings, hanging bars, trampolines, a merry-go-round, and a bridge (see figure 59). The site, despite remaining a playground, captures the trajectory of the neighborhood: from wet to dry; from porous to filled; from utilitarian to affluent, all while remaining culturally relevant and full of fascination.

While the Jordaan was never even close to as porous of an urban condition as some of the abandoned contemporary residential fabrics discussed herein, it was a place with slots for playground insertion.[58] The first playground in the neighborhood was the one at Palmgracht, followed by the one at Anjeliersstraat/Madelievenstraat implemented in 1953, and the rest came quickly thereafter. The sites were selected by working over a map of the city, using red pencil to mark the potential locations. There was more than one version of this map. A working copy shows many shades of red, worked over, with more intensely colored squares being the final sites selected. A refined version omitted the process, narrowing the sites to a reasonable number for the nearby child population. These were perhaps documentations of the first neighborhood tours, the ones used to choose the sites, to design the sites, and to construct the sites. Subsequently, there have been many more such tours of the playgrounds in the Jordaan and beyond, taken by families and architecture enthusiasts alike. As the Amsterdam playground program has received much attention, the remnants have been well researched and traced. The first study tour was in 1980 by the architectural historian and Aldo van Eyck expert Francis Strauven, who assessed the sites, with the assistance of the Site Preparation Division, the same agency responsible for the site selection and implementation of

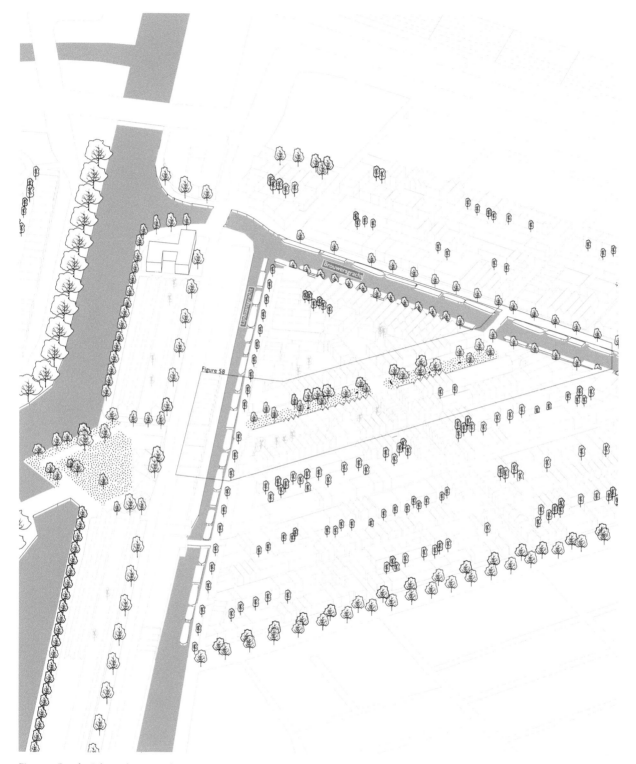

Figure 57. Broader Palmgracht, Amsterdam: axonometric view of the Palmgracht site within the northern portion of the Jordaan.

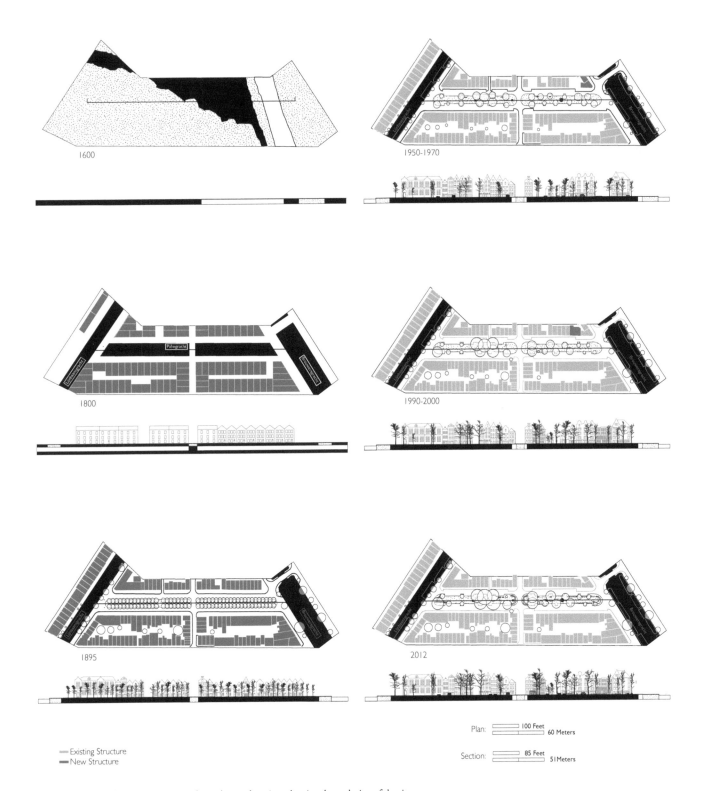

Figure 58. Palmgracht over time, Amsterdam: plans and sections showing the evolution of the site.

the playgrounds in the first place. Strauven, also oversaw an in-situ survey of the sites done in 2001 by students at the University of Ghent. Through this work, he laments the great loss of sites: 36 of 44 in the Centrum, with significant alterations among the remaining 8; 100 of 150 in the next ring, with only 15 of the remaining 50 in reasonable condition; and 140 of 360 in the expansion areas, although here 60 have retained their original form. The urban historian Liane Lefaivre, who has written extensively on the playgrounds, with Marlies Boterman, Suzanne Loen, and Merel Miedema published a bike tour of some of the remaining sites inside the A10 in 2002.[59] They found around a dozen of the playgrounds to be in favorable condition. Two young architects, Jonathan Hanahan and Rory Hyde, revisited Lefaivre and her colleagues' tour in 2009, reporting another 6 casualties in the seven-year lapse.[60] Finally, a pair of graphic designers, Anna van Lingen and Denisa Kollarova, put together the latest survey on the 17 playgrounds within the A10 that still exist in some form or another. The Laagte Kadijk playground

Figure 59. Palmgracht, Amsterdam, 2015.

is included in all three of the latest tours, but the Jordaan is conspicuously absent in the last—a white space on the guide map. The van Eyck playgrounds are gone. All accounts begin with the beginning—the Bertelmanplein playground—and all consider it one of the best examples of preservation, a small gem among what Strauven calls "wasted pearls."[61]

On the Ground

I take great inspiration and pause from these accounts. Somehow it is irresistible to look into the playgrounds, to admire their pervasiveness and sheer number, and to tally how many remain. I too, like my predecessors, embarked on a tour to see how the spaces have transitioned and how the city has grown up around them or absorbed them completely. Armed with the texts and guides, and a child, I visited over a dozen sites. It was not a comprehensive tour but gave a contemporary feel for playgrounds in the Centrum. Afterward I am left wondering why the original Bertelmanplein, Herenmrkt, and Jonas Daniel Meyerplein are largely intact, if with new equipment, while Dijkstraat and Zeedijk have disappeared, Laagte Kadijk has been transformed, and Palmgracht is being rebuilt. I do not know enough about the city to fully answer these questions, but my instinct is that it has to do with the planning of the neighborhood, the homogeneity of the building age surrounding the site, and the relative strength of the form and planting of the original parcel. Bertelmanplein and Herenmrkt are clearly inscribed in designed plazas rather than deftly inserted into openings and pocket parks woven into the interstices of the city. It is the plaza that holds them, while active local populations, who still need and use the slivers of open space, sustain the few small pocket play spaces that endure, such as Laagte Kadijk and the playgrounds reinserted in the Jordaan.

In fact, from even a quick visit, it is clear that Amsterdam still has beautiful and plentiful play spaces. It is a child's paradise. Now they are more varied, both through design and use. There are still classics, largely embedded in parks, such as at Beatrixpark, where the curves of the sandbox and the pool are exquisite, and at Sarphatipark, where the three sand circles frame understated, yet diverse equipment that appeals to all ages, even in the rain. There are vibrant squares, like Jonas Daniel Meyerplein, with actively used play equipment that collects incredible diversity, at least on a sunny September Sunday when a giant wheel, a pop-up clothing shop in a cart, exercisers, local musicians, and roller-blading children all do loops around the space. There are big playgrounds with new equipment, such as the Speeltuin UJ Klaren, where kids can ride their bikes down ramps and in big circles, and tiny, quiet playgrounds nestled into the dense residential fabric, suitable for a quick swing, climb, or jump. The playgrounds—and their child constituents—are alive in the city. And while I admire the compositional genius of the original playgrounds and the simple elegance of the structures, I do not think that the loss of the designs negates, in any way, the success of the program. In fact, I would argue the opposite, that the loss of the designs indicates aspects of their success, their ability to meet the needs of a generation and to provide the groundwork for future transformations. When the gaps persist, when the design lacks traction, then the city stagnates. Play spaces, of any landscapes, are susceptible to trends, to regulations, and to aging populations. But for thirty years, the playgrounds anchor their neighborhoods, delight their audiences, and create a collective experience across the city. They are designed, physical spaces that bring underserved urban populations and forgotten landscapes together, making them visible as a valuable part of the city. The program offers valuable lessons in the potential of spontaneity in municipal planning to take advantage of a lapse in development plans and to be responsive to citizen requests; the success of both local design specificity and citywide deployment; the elegant use of simple, rough, and readily available materials; and the embedded frugality across the system. These are principles to extract from the program that can inform the ongoing debate on abandoned urban landscapes, that can be used to address problematic social and environmental situations in the city, and that can be applied to similar flat, small, and porous residential fabrics.

Flatness

In thinking about how the playgrounds might inform other strategies for abandoned land, it is important to recognize the flatness of the city, the sites, and the designs. This is a strategy for a relatively flat landscape, both physically and ontologically. The abandonment here cannot be contributed to difficult terrain—steep slopes, subsidence, contamination—but rather to other types of political and social situations. In Amsterdam, some demolition was war-related. Other clearing occurred because building conditions were deemed to be substandard and populations were subjected to discriminatory practices. Roadway widening and infrastructural insertion leads to other urban cuts, though in Amsterdam these projects are also achieved through a filling operation due to the many canals throughout the city. It is a circumstance whereby gaps are made through both cutting and filling the existing conditions. The gaps are in areas that are highly urbanized or in others where the land was recently platted for housing development. The ground under consideration is flat and has been made dry through intensive engineering, and thus pavements—both permeable and impermeable—resonate. The open spaces of the city are regular—with a few large parks—and many, many small squares or "pleins" scattered throughout. The playgrounds are built on this existing condition, adding a fine grain to the city. The project understands the intrinsic characteristics of the local condition—design parameter number one—and introduces a bold, different, but complimentary vocabulary into the evolving language of city making.

Short Cycles

Amsterdam has always been a prosperous city. Its periods of population loss and abandonment have been extremely short. Here we are considering a flicker of porosity followed by thirty years of construction, really just over a generation. Still, the playground project manages to exist in this window and to take advantage of sites where once there was or will be development. In both instances, there exists an opening both physically and temporally. The city is leveled in select locations, and yet there are no known future plans for this ground plane. This occurs in older parts of the city as well as new ones where, much like the Chelas plan in Lisbon, only the buildings are considered and designed, but the interstitial spaces remain unarticulated. As mentioned, this is a temporary condition—as it is in all cities—but one more bracketed than in places of sustained disinvestment. For this reason, it is easy to understand the cyclical qualities of the sites, from built to open to occupied to built again, and then to extrapolate and envision them open again, only to invite another type of occupation. The play was relevant for the baby boom of the 1950s and beyond, whereas contemporary designs stress human and nonhuman uses to meet climate concerns. The thirty-year period also allows for an understanding of the cyclical reception of the play spaces themselves, from welcomed, heavily used, and demanded to underappreciated and unmaintained, to nostalgically missed, and finally to reinvested as a celebration of an iconic design that allowed for creative play and imagination (see figure 60 for a composite of development, migratory, demographic, and material timelines).

Small Stars, Big Constellations

Scale matters. Amsterdam is not a very big city, and again, its level of porosity and abandonment is nonexistent today.[62] Even in 1947, it was relatively low. Thus, the insertion of over 700 playgrounds makes a big difference at the citywide scale, while the small sites make a big difference on their individual streets. In this condition, 700 projects are impactful. In a condition of 40,000 vacant properties—the number often cited for Philadelphia, for example—700 projects is a relatively small number, representing fewer than 2 percent of the total. This comparison is not meant to diminish the Amsterdam playgrounds, but rather to indicate that their effectiveness and legibility is related to the size and porosity of the original condition. A considerate response needs to be scaled for both the individual lots and the aggregation of all potential sites. The Amsterdam example works on this level. Both scales are felt. The argument here, however, is not that a singular strategy can simply be scaled up or down to meet the needs of any given city. The number of play spaces that might be required to make the same impact in Philadelphia today does not make sense given the distribution of families in the city. It is nonscalable. Rather the idea is that the scale of the interventions

Figure 60. Sand cycles, play cycles, Amsterdam: a diagram of housing, migration, demographics, and playgrounds over time.

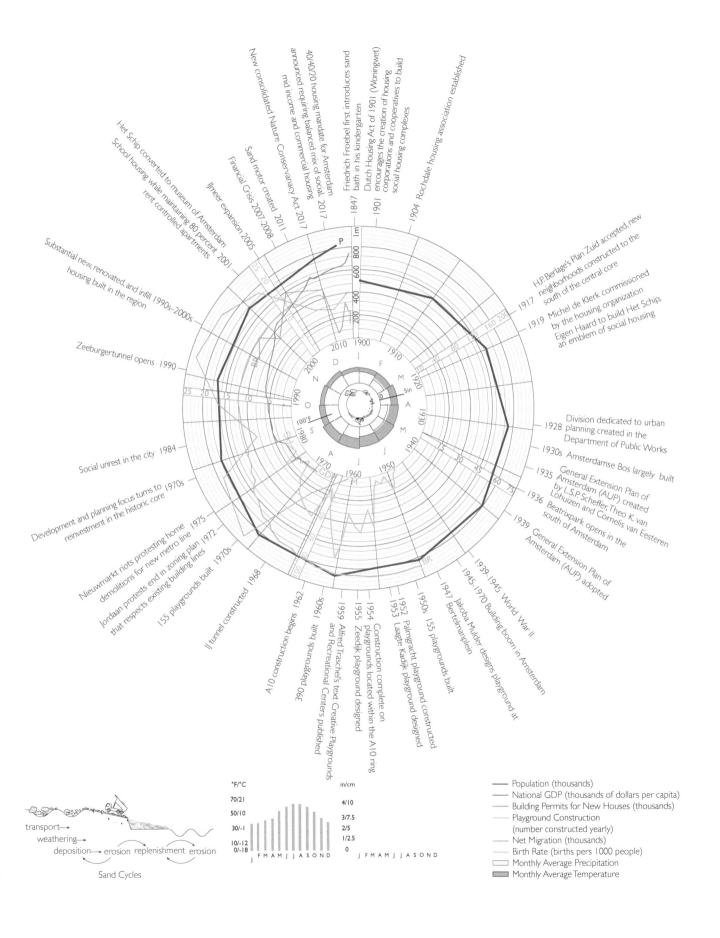

Friedrich Froebel first introduces sand bath in his kindergarten 1847
Dutch Housing Act of 1901 (Woningwet) encourages the creation of housing corporations and cooperatives to build social housing complexes 1901
Rochdale housing association established 1904

H.P. Berlage's Plan Zuid accepted, new neighborhoods constructed to the south of the central core 1917
Michel de Klerk commissioned by the housing organization Eigen Haard to build Het Schip, an emblem of social housing 1919

Division dedicated to urban planning created in the Department of Public Works 1928
1930s Amsterdamse Bos largely built
General Extension Plan of Amsterdam (AUP) created by L.S.P. Scheffer, Theo K. van Lohuizen and Cornelis van Eesteren 1935
Beatrixpark opens in the south of Amsterdam 1936
General Extension Plan of Amsterdam (AUP) adopted 1939
1939-1945 World War II
1945-1970 Building boom in Amsterdam
Jakoba Mulder designs playground at 1947 Bertelmanplein
1950s 155 playgrounds built
Palmgracht playground constructed 1952
Zeedijk Laagte Kadijk playground designed 1955
Construction complete on playgrounds located within the A10 ring 1954
1953
Alfred Traschel's text Creative Playgrounds and Recreational Centers published 1959
390 playgrounds built 1960s
A10 construction begins 1962
IJ tunnel constructed 1968
155 playgrounds built 1970s
Jordaan protests end in zoning plan 1972 that respects existing building lines
Nieuwmarkt riots protesting home 1975 demolitions for new metro line
Development and planning focus turns to 1970s reinvestment in the historic core
Social unrest in the city 1984
Zeeburgertunnel opens 1990
Substantial new, renovated, and infill 1990s–2000s housing built in the region
Het Schip converted to museum of Amsterdam
School housing while maintaining 80 percent rent controlled apartments 2001
IJmeer expansion 2005
Financial Crisis 2007-2008
Sand motor created 2011
New consolidated Nature Conservancy Act 2017
40/40/20 housing mandate for Amsterdam announced requiring balanced mix of social, mid income and commercial housing, 2017

transport→
weathering→
deposition→ erosion replenishment erosion
Sand Cycles

°F/°C
70/21
50/10
30/-1
10/-12
0/-18
J F M A M J J A S O N D

in/cm
4/10
3/7.5
2/5
1/2.5
0
J F M A M J J A S O N D

—— Population (thousands)
—— National GDP (thousands of dollars per capita)
—— Building Permits for New Houses (thousands)
—— Playground Construction (number constructed yearly)
—— Net Migration (thousands)
—— Birth Rate (births per 1000 people)
☐ Monthly Average Precipitation
▨ Monthly Average Temperature

must consider the scale of territory that requires addressing and adapt accordingly. The Amsterdam playgrounds did this effectively.

Ordinary Materials

The playgrounds used unsophisticated materials, found nearby but organized succinctly, to create an alternate vision for the lots. Through the use of sand, concrete, brick, tile, aluminum, wood, and trees, each site was transformed. The costs of construction were low, which allowed for the many projects across the city. In fact, when compared with the housing and infrastructure construction of the same era, the playground budget did not even register. Economically speaking, the stakes were relatively low. The projects embodied the rough elegance of a common landscape, and their use as play spaces was a common one. These are truly everyday, ordinary spaces, designed to be utilitarian and to provoke imagination. The materials reflect the everydayness while the abstraction—pure geometric and nonrepresentational forms—allows for creative interpretation. Elements are used for multiple purposes: climbing frames function as fences; sandboxes provide seating; domes provide exposure and enclosure. Their forms are universal, allowing for many combinations on many types of sites. The basic units are adaptable: the elements are both individually expressive and variable, and yet they form a cohesive family. The sandboxes are formed concrete containers filled with fine aggregate. The metal structures are aluminum bars cleverly fitted together. The benches are standard but elegant wood benches, with a slight curvature to enhance the profile. Cost and aesthetics are balanced. The budget is met without compromising design intent, intrigue, aesthetics, or durability. The playgrounds have a common material language—both ordinary and shared.

Ideas as Commons: In the Public Mind

In fact, it is this shared language that is embedded in the physical structure of the city and the memory of the generations of families who use the spaces. Time has allowed assessment of the playground landscapes as common cultural experiences. The physical urban landscape here operates like media. Just like everyone might remember a radio or television program, a video game or a movie, they remember a shared play experience, one that happened in the in-between spaces of the city, on cleared building sites, in traffic islands, in between monolithic new housing constructions. The districts of the city do not express their individuality but instead their collectivity. This may be mundane, or even monotonous and unrelenting, but it is effective. In other words, in lieu of each sector expressing its specific identity, the desire is to unify the city. The postwar building efforts in Amsterdam emphasized the collective experience, perhaps as a response to the isolation of the war period, planning comprehensive neighborhoods in order to foster a sense of continuity and community. The playgrounds are an integral part of the neighborhood structure.

They are a part of the communal experience. Before, without public play spaces in the city, the child is largely absent from the landscape. After, the children become a visible and active part of the city. They share common spaces and experiences, loudly and visibly, to the delight and dismay of the Amsterdam citizenry. Aldo van Eyck describes his playgrounds as making every day the phenomenon of the snowstorm: a moment when the city stops and the residents, especially the children, emerge together to play outside. The snow blankets the city to create a common landscape. The playgrounds—with their frequency and visual unity—achieve a similar collective, nonhierarchical network. And in turn, through editing and evolution, there are remnants from this time that allow for this collective memory to endure while giving space for urban experiences to grow and adapt.

Conclusions

Aldo van Eyck writes in his essay *The Child, the City and the Artist:* "Cities and here and everywhere, repulsive and magnetic. If decay and disintegration were proportionally counteracted by constructive effort, if common sense to imagination's hand, cities would perhaps still represent a positive mirror of society's aspirations and needs."[63] What is this constructive enterprise? It has definitely changed since this passage was written in 1962. We have moved away from the idea of treating cities as objects to be repaired when broken. We have recognized that there are alternatives to replacing buildings with buildings. We understand that being constructive does not always mean physically constructing something—that care is something to be designed as a constructive enterprise. We understand that our current building practices contribute heavily to environmental degradation and climate crises. We have also embraced the ideas behind van Eyck and his colleague's playgrounds, that construction can be a simple and frugal expression—one that opens spaces without prescribing uses; one that recognizes the given as an asset to be sculpted rather than replaced; one that is both temporary and durable. It could be said that the constructive enterprise is an enterprise that does not give up on landscapes that are maligned or have temporarily lost valuation. A constructive enterprise is one that understands the tedious process of city making and embarks on a project for the immediacy without compromising a longer-term vision. The constructive enterprise is not a constant but something that evolves across scales and times, adapting with the changing city rather that standing fixed, only to be left behind. Evolution is something to be embraced. Some playgrounds are lost, some endure, and some transform to address the contemporary concerns of the physical, economic, political, and social environment. The fear is not the loss of the designs themselves, but the loss of designs that achieve spatial quality while conserving resources and promoting inclusive systems and uses.

5

FALLOW LAND
150 Years of Disinvestment in St. Louis

St. Louis is located in the floodplain of the Mississippi River, a fluctuating riparian zone, largely underlain by porous karst topography. Floodwalls, levees, and canals attempt to control the hydrological impulse. Most if not all of the land has been drained and fortified to make human habitation somewhat less risky. The marsh and prairie lands are overlooked by bluffs and mounds, which in many cases have been flattened and shaped to accommodate urban development. A series of constructions, over time, has altered all the topographical highs and lows, and the terms of control get played out in a muddy and tenuous terrain that make it difficult to separate the physical conditions from the territory's cultural definitions. The biophysical characteristics of the bottomlands overlay with socioeconomic issues of race and poverty—all entangled in a cruel history of forced labor and serial forced displacement.[1] Deeper insight into these issues makes the fragility of the terrain more apparent—the floodplain is fragile socially, economically, politically, and ecologically. The rivers, the creeks, the karst terrain, the mud, the clay, the bricks, the labor, the industries, the construction, the destruction, the included and the excluded, the invested in and the disinvested, the occupied: the fallow are intertwined in the cyclical making and unmaking of the region.

St. Louis is a city where the contested issues of North American urban development and disinvestment unfold in concise alignment—making it a near-perfect landscape in which to explore the circumstances surrounding urban abandonment and the fallow conditions that result. Since the 1950s, the city has depopulated. It has seen a simultaneous increase in the inventory of city-owned abandoned property. The civic and public health nightmare that has resulted make it a place where people are working desperately to test new solutions to what are by now old and stubborn problems. St. Louis occupies a central place in U.S. physical, cultural, economic, and environmental geography. Its charged history, its present struggles, and its future potential make it an ideal place to

Figure 61. Demolition,
St. Louis, 2011.

uncover contested issues surrounding planning, design, and disinvestment. As St. Louis
historian and geographer Colin Gordon writes: "the American urban crisis has been
defined by a common set of conditions or circumstances. Those conditions and circumstances, in turn, were (and in some respects remain) more pronounced in St. Louis
than almost anywhere else." "St. Louis is not a typical City," noted one observer in the
late 1970s, "but, like a Eugene O'Neill play, it shows a general condition in a stark and
dramatic form."[2] No city is typical, but the stark clarity that comes from looking closely
at St. Louis makes it an example whose lessons can be applied far and wide.

Budding Bridges

Most of my recent trips to St. Louis have been by car, driving east to west. This means
that I have crossed the Mississippi River by bridge each time, as all visitors driving
west into the city must. In fact, ten bridges span the river and touch St. Louis city
and St. Louis county; from the Chain of Rocks Bridge in the north near mile 190 of
the Mississippi River to the Jefferson Barracks Bridge near mile 169 just south of the
city limits. Four of these bridges carry federal interstate highways, emphasizing both
the city's past embrace of technical planning and its central location, at a crossroads

of America's north–south and east–west routes. As mentioned, St. Louis is roughly in the geographic middle of the country, but it is at the eastern extent of the state of Missouri. The city is hemmed in politically, surrounded on the north, south, and west by the county, with which it severed ties in 1876, and on the east by a different state, with its own governance and legislation.[3] The bridges soar high above the river, and the road decks land blocks inland from the river's shoreline, which creates a vast distance between the city and its river. Bridges connect clearly, here allowing Illinois to join to Missouri over the Mississippi River, but they also divide, separating two sides of the bottomlands' physically continuous terrain.[4]

St. Louis is a part of many overlapping and intersecting agricultural, economic and cultural regions: from the much-maligned and not very usefully named Rust Belt with its implications of social and industrial decline, to the Breadbasket or Corn Belt with its rich soils, advantageous climate, and political support that allow for agricultural dominance. It is part of the Great Karst region, the Ozark Plateau province, and the Mississippi River Corridor. St. Louis is firmly in the Midwest but is also sometimes considered on the northern fringes of the South, or eastern fringes of the West. It is one of a number of "Gateways to the West," but the only one with a giant arch.

Given St. Louis's membership in all of these regions, I have begun to think of capturing the identity of the city, not as a gateway, but through this sequence of bridges. In addition to invoking the two notions of connection and division, the bridge becomes an interesting metaphorical lens through which to read the St. Louis landscape. The city, again, sits between two major rivers—the Mississippi to the east and the Missouri to the north and west. Thus, it is literally connected to its greater region through the physical bridges (see figure 62 for the physical bridges atop an altered landscape). But the bridge also operates as a conceptual tool to reveal the geographical, topographical, temporal, cultural, and conceptual underpinnings of the city. Here, the horizontal expanse of the terrain is understood through its historical divides but also through its potential for future connections: the bridge might navigate between disparate conditions. The bridge is a means to tell a story that extends from past to future. It's a story that builds on numerous legacies in the hopes of finding strongholds within the fragile urban environment.

Bridge Geographies

The movement from east to west is a disturbing and historic one. It is the direction of brutal colonization, whereby the first French settlers crossed from the Cahokia settlements, forcibly displacing inhabitants to construct their own buildings, establish their own quarries, and lay out their own infrastructure.[5] The French left behind the eastern settlements, crossing over the marshy river flats with nutrient-rich soil ideal for cultivation, past forested bluffs, to land on a clay and karst bed and build a city. Once they

	Waterways		Clark Bridge
	Vacant		New Chain of Rocks Bridge
	Open Space		Chain of Rocks Bridge
	Urban Renewal		Merchants Bridge
	Levee Areas		McKinley Bridge
	St. Louis City Boundary		Stan Musial Veterans Memorial Bridge
	Highways		Dr. Martin Luther King Jr. Bridge
	Dams		Eads Bridge
	Bissel Point Watershed		Poplar Bridge
	Historic Quarries		MacArthur Bridge
	Sinkholes		

3 Miles

6 Kilometers

Figure 62. Fallow lands, St. Louis, with bridges, highways, waterways, and sinkholes.

were established, the eastern edge of the river marked a gateway, an eastern frontier, and a place of departure to move further west. But this notion of St. Louis as a gateway, or at least an open gateway, is flawed. Now the city is both deliberately and inadvertently gated. It is circumscribed by its closed definition, caught between a county to which it does not belong and a river that it has not embraced. Again, the river is wide and separates two cities (St. Louis in the west and East St. Louis in the east) and two states (Missouri in the west and Illinois in the east). It is a fluctuating border, a jurisdictional divide that fragments the landscape and its management. The cities face inward, away from the water. The gap between the east and west resonates in the differential treatment of the banks, where each side, in its unique way, has turned its back on the river—either with a high flood wall or with land-use decisions that push people away from the river's edge. It seems nearly impossible to see the water in either city, much less to feel it, smell it, or have a view across to the other side. The east–west bridge is one in need of significant repair.

In the north–south direction, St. Louis again occupies a middle ground. Geographically, it is much closer to the center point of the country on the north–south axis than the east–west one. It has both strong northern and southern ties. After the establishment of the Missouri Territory in 1812, early colonial settlement arrived from Kentucky, Tennessee, and Virginia, resulting in an influx of southern agricultural practices. At the same time, by the middle of the nineteenth century, industry and immigration—including railroads—came from the eastern United States as well as Europe. Increasingly, just before and after the Civil War, the city became home to German settlers. By the time Abraham Lincoln was elected president and South Carolina succeeded from the Union, politics were racialized and complicated in Missouri. The state delegates elected to remain a part of the Union but were also staunchly opposed to federal control. While Missouri never joined the South, Confederates established a legislature there, and troops organized for both sides of the war. Guerrilla fighting was rampant in the state. It could be argued that the state legislature acted as though secession had in fact occurred.

Further, from the time of colonization through the moment of emancipation at the end of the American Civil War in 1865, Missouri was not a free state. Slavery was legal, and the state has occupied a critical place in the historical legislation surrounding human trafficking, racism, and freedom.[6] In 1819, Missouri requested admission to join the Union as a slave state and was granted this admission under the terms of the Missouri Compromise of 1820. Given that Missouri's pure admission would jeopardize the balance of equal slave and free states, Maine was admitted as a free state to maintain this equality. In addition, the Missouri Compromise stipulated that all states north of the parallel 36°30' would join as free states. This addressed the western territories but did not include the existing slave states of Missouri (the 36°30' marks its southern border with Arkansas), Kentucky, West Virginia, Virginia, Maryland, and Delaware, all of which lie north of the line.

After the compromise, slavery remained contested. It was in Missouri, in 1847, that Dred Scott, an African American male, sued for his freedom, having lived in a free state before returning to Missouri. Missouri precedent of the time indicated that slaves who had lived in freedom outside of Missouri retained their freedom upon return to the state. However, the court denied Scott's freedom, and through appeals, the case—*Dred Scott v. Sandford*—was heard before the Supreme Court in 1857, where again Scott and his family were denied freedom and citizenship. The decision is often referred to as one of the worst and most racist in history, inciting widespread dissent among the populace.

Next, the Missouri Compromise was further compromised and even ignored with the slavery debates during the formation of the states of Kansas and Nebraska. Fueled by railroad and other commercial interests, the Kansas-Nebraska Act of 1854 called for the organization of territories into states and made a concession to ignore the Missouri Compromise—both states lie north of the parallel 36°30'—and placed the decision of slavery's legality in the hands of a state populace vote. Again, this outraged Abolitionists and led to a series of violent border disputes from 1854 to 1861.[7] These served as precursors to the American Civil War of 1861 to 1865.

In each of these cases, Missouri at large, with St. Louis as its largest city, served as a territory caught between north and south—a metaphorical battleground for the debate of racist policies.[8] This status continues today, where contentious race relations are expressed through local politics and citizen action. In 2014, in Ferguson, Missouri, a town just north of St. Louis, Michael Brown, an unarmed eighteen-year-old black male, was fatally shot by a white police officer. Significant organizing and protests ensued, gaining tremendous national exposure. For months, activists and organizations from St. Louis and various cities around the country (DeRay Mckesson, Tef Poe, De Nichols, and eventually Black Lives Matter and Hands Up United) used their skills to take over the public realm—in this case, the streets—to fight for change. It was no accident that this happened in and around St. Louis, a place that has been at the forefront of protests against racist government policies for over 150 years.[9]

In the city proper, the north–south divide is pronounced—demonstrated through statistics, reinforced through cultural perceptions and structural inequities, and felt physically in the landscape.[10] While much of the city has suffered disinvestment, the north section of the city, located north of Delmar Avenue (colloquially known as the Delmar Divide) has endured more. It is a culturally reinforced boundary that underlines the structural racism so endemic in the city's history. The street is known as a racial and socioeconomic dividing line, where the population to the north is predominately black versus more mixed or even white to the south. Homes to the north of the line sell for significantly less than their southern counterparts. The hard line is becoming increasingly porous, with investment flowing across, but it still sits as an indelible marker in the city's culture geography. It is hard to have a conversation about the city without a reference to Delmar.

The bridge metaphor goes deeper than surface geography, into the soils and waters, the geology and vegetation. Cities, in general, in all their asphalt and concrete imperviousness, experience hydrological extremes, and in the American Bottomlands, despite efforts at flood control, the syncopations of storm events are irregular, with the occurrences tightening with climate stress. The historic crest data indicates more and more frequent surges, with several 40-foot crests in the past few years. Today, there are month-long stretches when the Mississippi River is above flood levels. The historic high-water mark of 49.6 feet is from the Great Flood of 1993, a flood that lasted for 104 days.

Most of the floodwater comes from the Upper Mississippi, a river section that is heavily managed by the United States Army Corps of Engineers. St. Louis sits on the divide between the northern river, where locks control navigation, and the open southern river, where engineered steps are not required for passage. Past emphasis on the northern river has been on maintaining and controlling navigation, while efforts to the south have focused more on flood control. In recent decades, since the 1993 floods, the St. Louis region has invested over $100 million in fortification. This is of some relief to a city on the banks of an ever-flooding river, but also of great concern as flood infrastructure often leads to greater flooding in an escalating war against erratic and extreme wetness.[11] The flood reports are a mainstay, with extreme levels measured in almost each of the past few years. When I began to develop this idea of the bridge as a means to understand St. Louis's urban landscape, the Mississippi River was flooding in St. Louis, and as I write this, the Mississippi River is flooding again. In addition to the intense flash floods of 2020, in 2019 the river passed the second highest crest mark of the 1973 floods.[12]

Rain and flood events are named by their likely frequency—for example, a one-hundred-year flood has a one percent chance of happening in any given year. Yet, lately, this size of storm happens several times a year. The famed Great Flood of 1993 is technically a three-hundred-year flood, but when calculating for what we can call flood inflation, it is more like a fifty-year flood. All this hydrological pressure then is an increasingly defining factor of St. Louis's fragile terrain—and a reason to rethink the management of its riverine and urban landscapes. The city is largely impervious to stormwater infiltration, and its fallow lands provide an opportunity to increase absorption and mitigate some local flooding in the non-karst areas of the city.

Geologically speaking, St. Louis is on mineral-rich land, ripe for extraction and construction, destruction and subsidence. It is underlain by carbonate bedrock with a karst topography of subterranean caves, springs, and sinkholes. Water seeps into the ground and slowly dissolves the layers of limestone and dolomite to produce fissures, cracks, and voids. Some of these are tiny while others can be occupied, and still others cover significant acreage. The beautiful Compton and Dry *Pictorial St. Louis* atlas from 1876 shows a pockmarked landscape, especially on the southern half of the city, and the Missouri Geological Survey Program has verified 15,919 sinkholes across the state with 106 within St. Louis itself.[13] On Utah and Wyoming Streets, for example, houses tilt—evidence of a vaulted and undulating underground.

This dynamic geological landscape proves both a challenge for the physical stability of the city and—simultaneously—a source of building material. The city mines its roots; it builds up with what's underground. Practically all the common building stone, as well as the material for the concrete and macadam roads, comes from the St. Louis Limestone, a formation belonging to the Mississippi or Lower Carboniferous that underlies the city. St. Louis is both a market and a producer for material. The city is quarry-rich, with over 150 years of mining history.[14] A few quarries still actively cut limestone just south of the city. Within the city, many of the parks are filled quarries, including Handy and Windsor Parks. The city has caves, too (and the requisite cave tours) and overall has a need to manage these subterranean cavities—and the water that filters in and out of them. The city is built on a tenuous ground.[15]

Because the subsurface is complex and geologically rich, St. Louis's extraction economies are diversified. In addition to limestone, the city mines its clays. To the south and the west of the city, the Cheltenham syncline contains seams of shale, coal, and fire clay from the Pennsylvanian period, buried beneath the layers of limestone.[16] Herein are the sources of the city's brick industry. St. Louis is a city built on a limestone foundation that is clad in brick. The environmental historian, landscape architect, and educator Jane Wolff explains that the use of brick increased after a huge fire on the Mississippi in 1849; a subsequent law stipulated that every building within a defined "fire line" had to be made of masonry, and a new economy emerged.[17] Along the River des Peres, extraction and manufacturing both supply the physical material for city making and support an exploitative labor economy of immigrants from Europe and the South. The city is growing. Resources are pulled from the ground, formed and hardened, moved near and far, stacked and cemented, and built up. Then, as the city contracts, brick structures are torn down; bricks are mined again or left pulverized in piles sitting atop the earth (see figure 63 for drawings of the mineral material conditions and markets). The brick story is a cyclical one: as the city builds and unbuilds, its material landscape transforms. Extracted and hardened fire clays form the units of construction and then disintegrate into a new ground material.[18] Brick miners mine soft mud for compressing and firing into brick, and they salvage bricks plucked from abandoned structures for resale. Old brick buildings become new brick buildings and landscapes. Wolff describes this as a metabolic process that extends to its limestone bases. St. Louis, a Brick City, is deep and mineral.

Figure 63. Brick, macadam, and sunflower, St. Louis: a drawing of material processes.

Interpreting the city's fragile terrain involves understanding how its various economic, social, and cultural policies inform the physical profile, from far below to far above the horizon. Even if the city seems flat at first glance, it has a rich topography, and although some of this topography has been leveled to create the city's infrastructural armament, there are topographic traces that appear through sinkholes and subsidence. To call it the former topography is a misnomer. It is still topography, and it hasn't gone anywhere. On these visible apexes and valleys, scholars have shown links between investment and elevation: investment on high ground and disinvestment on low ground.[19] The disparity is only growing as the country is more economically polarized and the climate risk more profound. As seen in Philadelphia, the underground can dictate patterns of vacancy as well as inform suitable land uses and opportunities on the surface.

One of these opportunities is for water infiltration, and another is for plant growth—and St. Louis has a rich history of horticultural experimentation. It is home to one of the country's oldest and most preeminent botanical gardens—a gift of business magnate and lover of the St. Louis landscape Henry Shaw.[20] The Shaw property includes the botanical garden and Tower Grove Park, his country estate, which to this day, is a well-funded and maintained public landscape in the city. The botanical garden opened to the public in 1859, and the Shaw legacy continues through the initial work of botanist Dr. George Engelmann, who pushed the public mission of the institution. It is further sustained by the scientific acumen of botanist Dr. Peter Raven, who directed the gardens from 1971 to 2011 and put the institution's contemporary contributions on par with its historical ones.

But here the idea is to open up a dialogue between the botanical garden, which is a highly managed and contained horticultural gem, and the spontaneous gardens and woodlands that form in places of abandonment across the city as testaments to the resilience of the dynamic social and ecological terrain (figure 64 shows a now defunct wild urban woodland from a distance). As seen in cities such as Lisbon and Berlin, periods of relative fallowness and pauses in traditional development give time and space for floral and faunal establishment. This growth is overlooked in myriad ways: the plants are overlooked, as are the resulting animals and crops and even farmers, all of which appear amid and even despite the dominant and often overwhelming narratives of decline. In fact, many things are actually happening now and have happened in the past forty, fifty, and sixty years that St. Louis has seen net human outmigration. For one thing, a forest can grow (and can be cut down) in that time.[21] And for another, evidence is mounting that we need to think differently about our investment in landscape—so if we built big parks at the turn of the last century, how will we address the many acres of fallow and vacant lands following this century's turn? How will we think about the spontaneous? Will it always be subservient to the cultivated? How will we move from past to present to future? These are important questions to consider in St. Louis, and beyond.

All of the bridges invoke these temporal shifts and demand a long view of the territory and its evolution. Thus, I want to emphasize the cycles of time—and come back to the gateway again, this time literally with the recently completed landscape project on the grounds of the Gateway Arch. The Gateway Arch is a national park, formerly known as the Jefferson National Expansion Memorial or JNEM. Set on the St. Louis waterfront, it is dedicated to the history of westward expansion.[22] The site is famously marked by Eero Saarinen's famous arch—to this day a remarkable steel-clad feat of engineering. It sits on a site of so-called slum clearance: beginning in the late 1930s, its forty blocks

Figure 64. Homage to the wild urban woodland, St. Louis, 2011: aerial view of the former woodland on the site of the former Pruitt-Igoe homes.

(91 acres or 37 hectares) of buildings were destroyed using federal New Deal public funding.[23] The clearance opened space for the memorial but created a significant disruption in the urban fabric that contributes to some of the current geographical divides previously discussed (see the small diagrams on figure 66 for the evolution).

The arch eventually became a bold statement, as an iconic, competition-winning piece of civic sculpture, but also, in a less intentional manner, as a mark of erasure visible down nearly every street in the city.[24] On Saarinen's competition team were Daniel Urban Kiley, landscape architect; Jay Henderson Barr, associate designer; and Lily Swain Saarinen and Alexander Girard, artists.[25] The early drawings showed an urban forest beneath the arch, but in the end, the signature design element was the arching allées of nine hundred *Liriodendron tulipifera* (tulip poplar) trees, three deep. The *Liriodendron tulipifera* is an extremely tall and stately tree with a pyramidal form. The potential scenographic effect complements that of the arch itself. Yet, budget cuts and delays prolonged the landscape installation. The site opened in 1965, but the landscape was not fully executed until 1981, and the *Liriodendron tulipifera* were replaced with *Fraxinus spp.* (ash) trees, with a remarkably different and less dramatic form.[26] They are shorter, rounder, and more irregular. They also became susceptible to the emerald ash borer, a deadly insect that can kill a tree within three to five years of infestation. Tiny root boxes and poor maintenance led to the decline of the canopy with time, and the imminent threat of the borer convinced the National Park Service to replace the trees. Coincidentally, the landscape architecture firm Michael Van Valkenburgh Associates won a competition to redesign the arch grounds with a more suitable management strategy and better connections to the city and the river.[27] The new team of landscape architects respected Kiley's ambitions—grounding their redesign with deep monocultural allées, this time of *Platanus × acerifolia* (London plane).

The $380 million project, which opened in July 2018, was a collaboration between the design team and a partnership of public and private funders, including the National Park Service, Gateway Arch Park Foundation, Bi-State Development Agency, Jefferson National Parks Association, and Great Rivers Greenway.[28] With it, there are parallels between the way we introduce canopy into the urban condition, past and present, with an effective robustness. Eight hundred plane trees—from the east—acclimatized themselves in the outer reaches of the region before making their mark on the river's edge. There is a significant cultural and geographic story here, but it is one that demands expansion and inclusion moving forward. The new project emphasizes connection. It reinforces the idea that the gateway cannot be a symbol or a gateway to somewhere else, and the investment cannot have a limited footprint. Instead, we have to move beyond the gates we have created to the past and to focus instead on the antidote to the symbolic and monumental, the closed and territorial. This requires a reach toward the means of connection, toward bridges that support the fragile terrain on which they land, with the particular hydrological, geological, and vegetal legacies—and even more so, support the people who rely on this land and its stability to endure. The investment must move beyond its limited footprint in areas with the greatest potential to attract market capital. In the past, the city has concentrated on big and often singular projects, where resources of any kind fail to infiltrate the city, horizontally across its expanse, or vertically into is geological and hydrological coffers. The contemporary arch project, like its predecessor, is still big and still singular. The prospect for bridging lies in its potential reverberations. The measured effectiveness of these waves is still to be determined.

Big Plans

The structure supporting many of the dividing bridges is tied to the role of transportation and comprehensive planning. St. Louis has a tradition of big plans, from the 1907

A City Plan for St. Louis, deemed the nation's first comprehensive plan, to Harland Bartholomew's work from 1916 through 1953, to the work done under the Interstate Highway Act of 1956, to the ambitions of contemporary greenway planning efforts designed to address the city's fragile terrains.[29]

A City Plan for St. Louis marked a turn in American urban planning, from the piecemeal to the holistic, from the individual topic (streets, parks, housing) to the communal enterprise (the whole political entity). The St. Louis Civic League, a Progressive Era institution, prepared the plan under the direction of six committees.[30] The document was rich with contributions from prominent civic leaders, including substantial work from leading landscape architects. The General Committee oversaw the plan and was chaired by William Trelease, the director of the Missouri Botanical Garden. Landscape architect George Kessler, well known for his park systems throughout the Midwest, was on the Inner and Outer Parks Committee, while landscape architect Henry Wright, a planner, urban designer, and social advocate, was part of the Civic Centers Committee.[31] At the time of the 1907 plan, St. Louis was the fourth largest city in the United States, and the plan was seen as a call to action to manage this growth—and to compete for more anticipated economic and population growth.[32] A prosperous city should be ordered and beautiful, the thinking went, and St. Louis could not continue in an unplanned fashion, with disregard for its river and landscape. Its propaganda argued that the plan was produced by the citizen designers for the citizenry at large—in this case the more than forty authors who represented the professional disciplines of city making. Their goal was to demand a better living environment. The plan was, of course, political, made by people in power to protect their interests, but to do so by improving the physical, environmental, cultural, and economic context of the entire territory. It was a strategic plan, meant to guide future resource allocation and build community. It was also groundbreaking in the sense that there was a contested set of arguments within the plan; that the city could act to protect its interests; and that planning should include both public and private property. Design-wise, the planners preferred radials, with axial vistas, to a straight grid. They sought to connect assets— through the aggregation of civic buildings and the development of over sixty miles of boulevards, parkways, and reserves designed to tie together the preexisting large parks, such as Forest, Carondelet, and O'Fallon. This included a focus on Kingshighway, a major north–south artery that touches all six of the city's large parks and cemeteries. An early road connecting the city to the common agricultural fields that radiated out to the west, the route was widened, paved, and dotted with smaller civic spaces. Like any plan, only portions were implemented, and subsequent actions, such as the large clearings and mega-highways inserted in later years, undermined the cohesion of the vision. There was an idea in 1907 that the resources exist—the river's bend, the rolling topography, the large open spaces—but are underutilized and disconnected.[33] The identified resources will change with time, but this argument comes back again and again, as access continues to be an issue for this city and others.

While the 1907 plan stressed community and connection, by 1947 the focus shifted. This change can be largely attributed to the efforts of Harland Bartholomew. In many ways, St. Louis defines the work of engineer-turned-planner Bartholomew and his frustrations with the dangerous realities of trying to implement a rational method of population distribution.[34] Bartholomew and his team assumed that the city would house one million people by 1980 — but that St. Louis County would not gain a significant population. He based his ideas around lessening traffic congestion as well as housing and land-use planning around static goals of population maintenance rather than anticipating a varied, uneven, and dynamic process. For Bartholomew, the issue was an imperfect execution of his rational ideal; but for the citizens, the issue was the incredible damage caused by the imperfect execution and the ensuing structural racism that persists in St. Louis specifically and in the development of US cities more broadly.

Harland Bartholomew was recruited to St. Louis from his job as the country's first municipal city planner in Newark, New Jersey. His role was to focus on the implementation of the 1907 plan. When Bartholomew arrived in 1916, progress on the plan was stagnant. But once landing the job, Bartholomew had another agenda: to develop, test, and prove his nascent rational, data-driven, and comprehensive method of planning. After the pauses caused by the Great Depression and the world wars, Bartholomew and his remarkably small staff launched the 1947 *Comprehensive City Plan*.[35] This document fundamentally reshaped the St. Louis landscape by driving future freeway investments, housing policies, urban renewal measures, and land-use regulations (see figures 65 and 66). It was a big, visionary growth plan for a city already bleeding westward to the suburbs. At its core were a few key ideas. First, and most reasonable but hardest to achieve, the city and the region must be planned together as a system.[36] Second, zoning was deemed fundamental, and uses were to be grouped rather than dispersed. (This was an idea shared with the 1907 plan.) Third, updated housing stock was required, as families were moving in search of newer and better homes outside the city. Fourth, and related, old areas should not be abandoned but reinvested in, even if this reinvestment took the form of large-scale clearing. And last, but not at all least, transport was a major component of the plan.[37] It is here where Bartholomew and his team made the greatest impact. He saw the street as a major opportunity and identified street traffic congestion as one of the major problems in the city. His response was a four-tiered system of roads. The existing four- to six-lane arterials were to be enhanced with six- to eight-lane at-grade urban distributing routes and eight- to ten-lane separated-grade interstate routes. Plate 20 in the plan shows a super-grid of four roughly east–west and four roughly north–south routes moving traffic into and across the city (see figure 65). They were a precursor for the four interstate highways that clumsily

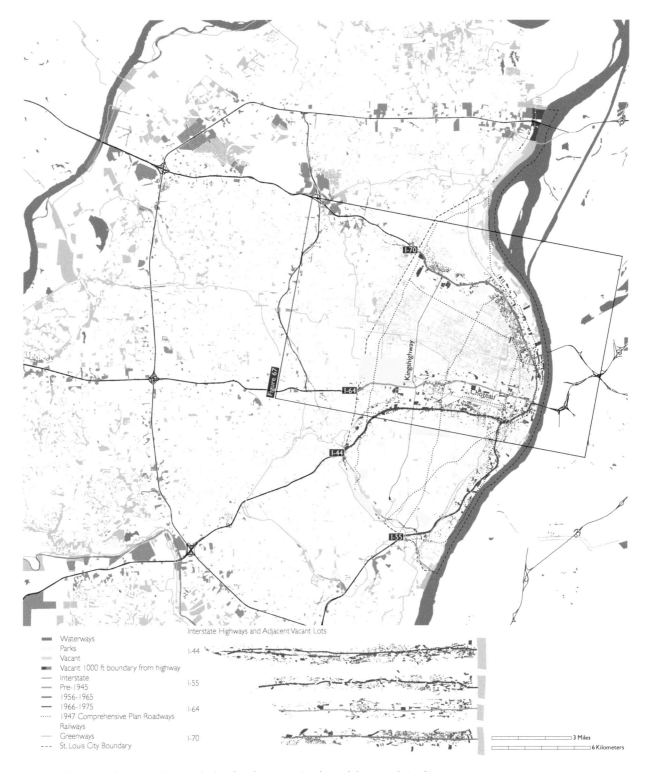

Interstate Highways and Adjacent Vacant Lots

Waterways
Parks
Vacant
Vacant 1000 ft boundary from highway
Interstate
Pre-1945
1956-1965
1966-1975
1947 Comprehensive Plan Roadways
Railways
Greenways
St. Louis City Boundary

I-44

I-55

I-64

I-70

3 Miles

6 Kilometers

Figure 65. Highways and greenways, St. Louis, broken down by construction date and shown in relationship to vacancy.

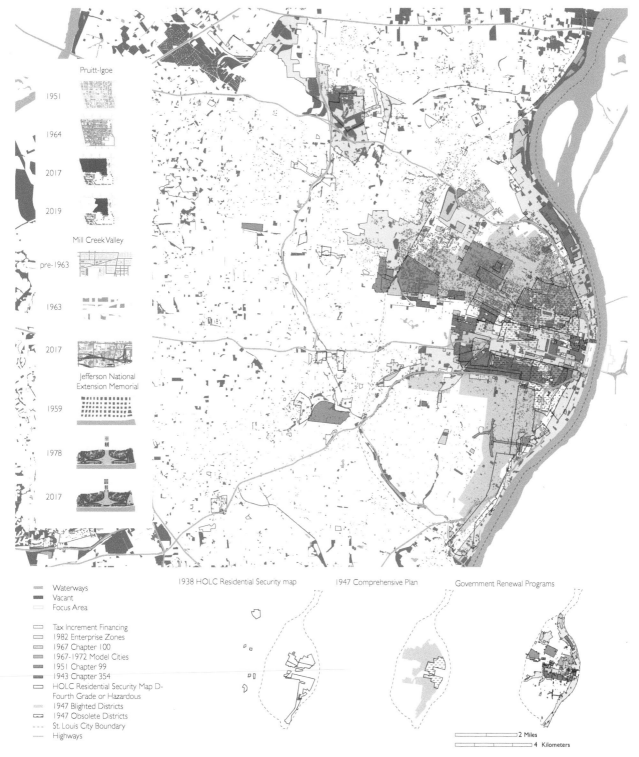

Pruitt-Igoe

1951

1964

2017

2019

Mill Creek Valley

pre-1963

1963

2017

Jefferson National
Extension Memorial

1959

1978

2017

1938 HOLC Residential Security map

1947 Comprehensive Plan

Government Renewal Programs

Waterways
Vacant
Focus Area

Tax Increment Financing
1982 Enterprise Zones
1967 Chapter 100
1967-1972 Model Cities
1951 Chapter 99
1943 Chapter 354
HOLC Residential Security Map D-
Fourth Grade or Hazardous
1947 Blighted Districts
1947 Obsolete Districts
St. Louis City Boundary
Highways

2 Miles
4 Kilometers

Figure 66. Urban renewal, St. Louis: map and callouts showing various programs and the impact on the Pruitt-Igoe, the Mill Creek Valley, and the Jefferson
National Expansion Memorial sites.

cross the terrain, whose final alignments were driven by land value (the least barrier to acquisition that targets most the poor, black, powerless, and disenfranchised) and route efficiency. What little sensitivity Bartholomew employed in locating this mega-infrastructure was lost in execution.[38]

At the time of the 1947 plan, there was little vacancy in St. Louis. Thus, the planners, in their aim to create housing opportunity and lure development, sought to open ground in the city for building. This was billed as a way to reinvest in the existing city—rather than find new sites for development in the suburbs—but ironically it was through the identification of *obsolete* areas.[39] Bartholomew chose this word for the areas—all predominately poor and nonwhite—that he felt had no room for rehabilitation. These places need complete clearing and redesign. The *blighted* areas, included with the *obsolete* ones on Plate 13 (see figure 66), were places deemed to be in the process of showing distress.[40] Bartholomew's nomenclature and aggressive take on opening the city paves the way for the widespread practices of urban renewal in the city. St. Louis, perhaps more than other similar cities, embraced renewal, making legal (and illegal) provisions and attracting a mixture of government and private investment to support this abrupt process of transformation (see figure 66).[41] Zoning as an exclusionary practice is at the core of Bartholomew and St. Louis's toolkit. Through zoning, it is possible to regulate the occupation and use of land, to favor those with means—for example, owners—over those without—in this case, renters. Despite the deep scars, the cultures of preference, zoning, and demolition in St. Louis persist. Once urban renewal, highway construction, and the provision of public housing became federal programs, these biases were further reinforced through legislation and mandatory formulas dictating the distribution of funds, units, and types of use.

Big Gouges

The sites of major demolition, urban renewal, and highway clear-cutting in St. Louis are well known.[42] This includes the previously referenced Jefferson National Expansion Memorial and Pruitt-Igoe housing sites as well as Plaza Square near City Hall, the Mill Creek Valley, and the Busch Memorial Stadium site, which cleared thirty-one blocks, obliterating the city's Chinatown neighborhood. Later, chunky demolition and building projects, funded with different mechanisms, include the America's Center Convention Complex (a merging of the convention center and football stadium into a mega meeting space) and the construction of Interstate Highways 44, 55, 64, and 70, which seem to cut through every part of the city. In fact, they touch over half of the city's seventy-nine neighborhoods, creating odd slivers of fallow land in their shadows. Effectively, the city—at its shaky peak but sensing an imminent slip—had a vision to clear out its core and start anew, with a housing-heavy, separated zoning scheme fed by massively scaled roads. Armed with a planning document, state laws, and access to federal funds, these big plans took ruinous hold.[43] And yet even now, despite this history, even when megaplans and megastructures have not proven to have catalytic effect, the city continues to imagine that these projects can transform. This is true across cities in the United States but has a particular resonance in St. Louis.

In the 1950s, renewal began with Plaza Square, a downtown site heavily targeted in the 1907 plan. The sixteen-acre "dilapidated slum" incorporated the area surrounding the city hall, the central library, the civil courts building, and the railway.[44] By urban renewal standards, Plaza Square was a relatively small project that added just over one thousand units of housing in six mid-rise buildings on four blocks, with associated parkland to the south and east. Yet, this initial work from site selection in 1950 to completion in 1962 paved the way for the largest renewal project, Mill Creek Valley, which officially began in 1954.[45] Mill Creek Valley was also a part of a central corridor, a desired link between city and county. But instead of providing this bridge, the outcome was instead a poster child for displacement and disinvestment, a sixty-year story of failed idea and execution.

In 1950, Mill Creek Valley, an African American neighborhood, sat on over 450 acres just west of the downtown. Despite poor terrain and substandard living conditions, it was a bustling community of culture, commerce, and residence. From the point of view of the political structure, Mill Creek Valley was the quintessential slum, with its vibrancy overlooked, its history underappreciated, and its state of decay aggrandized. A technical report, on the history of renewal published in 1971 by the St. Louis Planning Commission, describes the site: "The sewage-laden health-menacing creek that gave the area its name had long ago been drained and filled but Mill Creek Valley by the 1940's had decayed into 100 blocks of hopeless, rat-infested, residential slums."[46] From the 1940s onward, clearing was on the city's agenda, and the city never looked back.

Given racial zoning, restrictive covenants, and redlining practices, the Mill Creek Valley was one of the few areas of the city that were open to black inhabitants.[47] For decades, people built homes and established businesses there. In fact, in the clearance process, over twenty thousand people and eight hundred businesses were displaced, effectively destroying a key black community in the city. Relocation was poorly handled. Development funds lagged, and the area—commonly referred to as Hiroshima flats— kept its flattened horizon. The land was reallocated to a highway (roughly a quarter), industrial development (roughly a quarter), and residential, commercial, institutional, and public use (roughly half). The highway was built, and large institutions, such as St. Louis and Harris-Stowe State Universities, slowly colonized the land. But still the fabric reads torn, a giant pause between Forest Park and the Gateway Arch, a deceivingly banal and almost nameless low point in the city, politically and topographically. Today, unlike in 1947, the area has plenty of fallow land at its disposal (see the small diagrams on figure 66 for the transformation).

Greenways and Vacancy Planning

"Disposal" is an operative word, as the city's main priority with abandoned property is to dispossess it. Today St. Louis has a long-standing land bank, the Land Reutilization Authority (LRA), which accrues land as the "owner of last resort."[48] This agency is effectively a holding ground for tax foreclosed and abandoned properties. The LRA controls roughly 11,500 parcels, or nearly half of the city's 25,000 fallow plots. The city is developing strategies to stabilize, maintain, and transfer this land—and consistent with the past, this includes an emphasis on demolition. This demolition is carried out parcel by parcel—the city aims for seven hundred parcels a year. The efforts are scattered throughout the city but trigger memories of slum clearance and later planning debacles such as the Team Four Plan, where neglect or demolition was falsely proposed as a potential driver of urban change, especially in predominately black neighborhoods.[49] At best, the mood is continually defensive, rather than optimistic. At worst, it aims to clear disinvested, primarily black neighborhoods without local input or support, while proposing investment for white neighborhoods that have historically received such funds. The blind erasure and the blind hope for future fulfillment come across as one and the same. Create clean holes for others to claim and fill. But without changing policies, fiscal structures, and cultural perceptions, it is hard to imagine real transformation, especially the kind that benefits existing residents.

At the same time as the demolitions march forward, the desire for regional connections continues, like a constant, irritating itch. Embedded within this aspiration is the idea of a central corridor, connecting river to park, city to county, needs to resource. The Great Rivers Greenway, a regional public agency established in 2000, is the most recent enabler. The mission is to connect parks and waterways into a regional network of assets. The agency is behind several major urban landscape initiatives. For example, as part of the six-pronged force behind the Gateway Arch project, the Great Rivers Greenway managed taxpayer investment toward more integrated parkland. More recently, the agency has embarked on the Choteau (now Brickline) Greenway project, extending the parklands through the city and tackling that illusive middle. Following the path of urban renewal, the Brickline project moves from the river, alongside the highway and rails, past Plaza Square, through the Mill Creek Valley, to Forest Park and the county beyond. It tackles the central corridor in a way that touches the open areas of the city with higher real estate value, while avoiding those deemed less desirable by the market.

In the winning competition proposal, the team led by the landscape architecture firm Stoss Landscape Urbanism envisions this central corridor to be more octopus-like than past plans, with tentacles stretching north to Fairground Park and south to Tower Grove Park.[50] These are two large parks, with great histories, whose present condition reflects the racially driven disparate investment of their surroundings. The Greenway project, while moving east–west, recognizes that there are bridges needed in all directions of this divided city. The aspirations seem laudable, as long as the implementation plan is robust, and the bridges are not too slight. Time will tell as to whether a rich landscape can strengthen a complex terrain and satisfy, in the face of a city's desire to fully rebuild. The skeptic in me says the project is too big, too central, too unwieldy, and too ambitious for a place scarred by overdreaming and underrealizing, whereas the optimist loves the reorganization of the urban ground, not for megabuildings and tourist traps, but for a different kind of city, one that recognizes the value in the north and that there land does not need to be cleansed, delaminated, and filled.

Bright Spots

In fact, within this seemingly bleak and racist landscape, there are distinctive bright spots, where the evolution has followed a different story. In these places, the layers of past history are evident, and even if demolition and abandonment are visible too, the fabric registers multiple timeframes. It is not as if the areas are immune to the bigger planning efforts driven by political and economic trends, but rather the long-term transformation has multiple viable chapters. Yes, there is outmigration, clearing, highway construction, federally funded housing, and urban development, but there is also local activism, commercial longevity, music and arts practice, preservation, and rehabilitation.

Beyond demolition and property transfer, St. Louis does not have a clear strategy for its coffers of abandoned land. Unlike the other cities described in previous chapters, a city-specific response—something beyond demolition—is hard to identify. This has much to do with the complexity of the fragile terrain, scarred by its legacy of injustice, and something to do with its present condition of pervasive population loss coupled with economic and environmental insecurity. The city suffers the legacies of its racist policies, and yet it seemingly embraces traditional real estate development models—which often unfortunately lead to speculation and a further production of decline—and clings to big economic investment regardless of where it lands on the ground. The physical conditions and population densities show extreme variation, and as of yet, the future is very uncertain. The city is at a different stage, a stage where all the rudiments are viable, and some of the projects are set up as mini-laboratories designed to absorb water, foster plant growth, cultivate crops, and provide spaces for games and play.

As noted, St. Louis is adjacent to the bottomlands. It is flood prone and is serviced by aging combined sewer and stormwater infrastructure that, in some instances, flows through old brick pipes. The Metropolitan St. Louis Sewer District, with the City of St. Louis, the Missouri Department of Conservation, and a coalition of local nonprofits, has begun some pilot programs constructing rain gardens on vacant LRA-owned parcels as a means to test infiltration potential. The aim of the $13.5 million Urban Greening Project is to replace a thousand buildings in the Bissell Point Watershed with green infrastructure to address the historic flooding in the area.[51] The projects feel banal and managerial to date, but there is potential for a more robust civic overlay.

The garden—as a spatial type highly adaptable to the fragmented and irregular footprints of abandoned properties—is a primary tool of experimentation. St Louis, like many places with large coffers of fallow land, runs mow-to-own and land lease programs to promote land adoption and cultivation. Since leases begin in 1994, thousands of agreements have been made, reducing some burden on the city while allowing gardens to proliferate. Not-for-profit organizations, including Gateway Greening, Urban Harvest STL, and the Sweet Potato Project, support community gardening and agricultural initiatives across the city.

More experimental projects include the Sustainable Land Lab project, a collaboration between the city of St. Louis and Washington University in St. Louis to create a living laboratory to test strategies for vacant lot management. In 2012, the program selected six blocks in the Old North St. Louis neighborhood as proving grounds. The Chess Pocket Park and the Sunflower+ Project: STL were fully installed the first year—and the Sunflower+ project continues to expand to address other sites and communities.[52] While the sunflowers are visual, they also have potential as agricultural crops, paying homage to St. Louis's location in the country's farm belt (see figure 63 for sunflowers and bricks).

Stormwater impoundment, community garden, mini-farm, chess park: these are all viable ideas for a place still struggling to find its own. When coupled with artist-driven building rehabilitations, a music venue, an old school candy shop, a hardware store, a plant nursery, a cooperative grocery store selling seeds and produce, and a well-organized community of citizens, homeowners and advocacy groups, a critical mass becomes noticeable.

Short Cycles

Eight years ago, armed with a map of activity, and a tricky itinerary connecting disparate art and garden sites, I embarked on a tour of St. Louis landscapes. On the scale of urban cycles, eight years is both long and short. In places of economic prosperity and bursts of investment, eight years can radically transform a place. At the same time, fallow lands can sit for decades in moments of pause. In eight years, a sapling fruit tree might bear fruit, an *Ailanthus altissima* might reach considerable stature, while a *Quercus spp.* will not produce acorns for another decade or so. Eight years is short, but also plenty of time to clear land and cultivate a garden, or purchase a building and begin rehabilitation.

On this tour, the Old North St. Louis neighborhood stood out as a bright spot on the city's north side, where the grain of industry meets the grain of historic fabric, where there is a gritty energy that is infectious. I happened upon a cluster of sites of

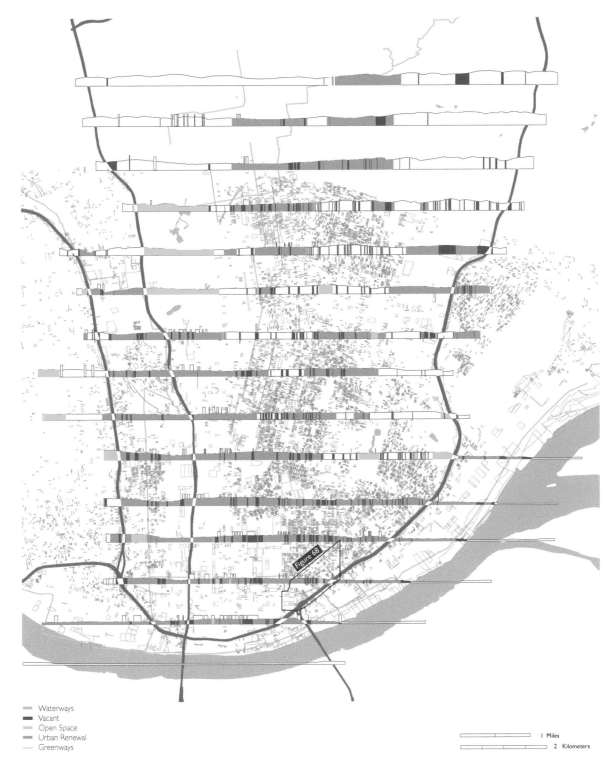

Waterways
Vacant
Open Space
Urban Renewal
Greenways

1 Miles

2 Kilometers

Figure 67. Itinerant sections along the highways, St. Louis.

interest—the Old North St. Louis Restoration Group was just finishing the restoration of a series of buildings in Crown Square; local artists such as Juan Chavez Williams were planning community arts buildings; a cooperative grocery store was the new tenant of a horseradish-bottle factory; and there was every type of garden scattered along the neighborhood blocks. You could even buy Baker Creek Heirloom Seeds from the Missouri Ozarks at the food co-op. These new businesses stood adjacent to two longstanding establishments, Marx Hardware and Crown Candy Kitchen, where locals have been buying tools since the late 1800s and drinking malts since 1913. The restoration work was forward-looking yet sensitive to historical legacy. Flyers sat in each window, alternating between describing the future commercial and residential potentials ("2 716–2719 N. 14th Street 2610 sf + Partial Basement, $9/sf," for example) and past uses and anecdotes ("the Hartman Shoe Company building at 2703–07 N. 14th Street first appears as a three-story brick store on a December 1922 building permit"). The neighborhood had a rare blend in St. Louis, of being on the north side and having a palpable combination of intact historical buildings and present activity and energy, albeit a quiet energy especially for a relatively dense urban environment.

Long Cycles

Old North St. Louis has a somewhat typical history, at least up until the 1970s. Located one mile north of downtown St. Louis, the area, like its neighbors up and down the Mississippi, was once part of a complex landscape of constructed mounds. It sat on the fringes of the Cahokian settlement, but had around twelve mounds, including "Big Mound," once located at the corner of Mound and Broadway. Once the ancient mound-building culture disappeared, the territory became a trading ground for other tribes, including the Osage, Sac-Fox, and Missouri. But, by the late eighteenth century, the area was covered with common fields and farmlands that supported the city of St. Louis. By 1816, with development pressure, the land was allegedly purchased by settlers from Kentucky and formed into the settlement of North St. Louis. The town was laid out with a grid, extending from the Mississippi River, with three circular exceptions: Clinton Place, Jackson Place, and Marion Place. These were designed to hold public functions for education, recreation, and religion. Jackson Place remains a circular park, despite radical transformation to the neighborhood. In addition, lands were left free at the riverfront, and today five acres remain as public access to the Riverfront Trail and river's edge beyond, a rare breathing space along the largely inaccessible waterway. The common landscape is part of the neighborhood's genetic code.

In 1841, the area was annexed by the city of St. Louis, and for the next hundred years, it became home to numerous groups of immigrants—German and Irish, then Italian, Polish, and Russian. There was also a growing but small community of African American residents, migrating from the South after the Civil War and settling on certain streets, enforced by racial segregation. The residential fabric of the neighborhood was composed largely of two- and three-story buildings from the mid- to late nineteenth century, dating from when it was a dense, low-rise residential neighborhood. In the 1950s, with fewer economic opportunities, housing bills promoting moves to the sub-urbs, and planned highways, outmigration began to dominate immigration. The per-centage of African American residents increased. Deliberate disinvestment ensued. Demolition began. Vacant buildings and fallow landscapes resulted.

On November 18, 1951, three new expressways were approved for St. Louis. One of these was the Mark Twain Expressway (Interstate 70), which connected St. Charles to the north and the Third Street Highway (eventually Interstates 44 and 64) to the south. It was planned to run through the center of Old North St. Louis. After some protest-induced adjustment to the routing from residents to the north of Old North, the final route runs above Tenth and Eleventh Streets, with on and off ramps at St. Louis Avenue. The construction displaced the African American community around Cass Avenue and affected local business and vitality. The three public circles in the original Old North St. Louis plan are now sitting against the bustle of the highway, separated from part of the neighborhood to which they once belonged.

When the next highway was proposed, the north–south connector from the 1947 plan, the neighborhood protested effectively. The plans were tabled in 1981, and the tide started to slowly turn to involve the neighborhood more in the planning and implementation process. On the housing side, this began with the Demonstration Cities and Metropolitan Development Act of 1966 (or Model Cities Program) that brought an influx of federal funding into the neighborhood through the early 1980s.[53] The program was administered by a local organization, the Grace Hill Settlement House.[54] While the ultimate recommendation was demolition and rebuilding, with the Murphy-Blair townhouses opening on nine blocks in the mid-1970s, the debate over demolition versus rehabilitation began. The project was controversial, with a number of residents blaming governmental investment for the loss of historic homes and the deterioration of the urban fabric.

In 1981, after a series of arsons, a number of local activists formed the Old North St. Louis Restoration Group (ONSLRG), the group largely behind the more recent land transformations and planning efforts in the neighborhood. The typical story began to change, with the listing of three districts on the National Register of Historic Places, bringing tax credits and momentum for building rehabilitations rather than the perpet-ual demolitions. The group moved into housing development, coalition building, for-mal planning processes, and land advocacy. A cycle was interrupted temporarily—and the neighborhood was now a magnet for the various citywide programs targeting the management of the fallow landscape. There are mow-to-own lots, community gardens on lands leased temporarily from the LRA, rainwater gardens constructed in partner-ship with the Metropolitan St. Louis Sewer District, and laboratory sites. Three of the gardens are part of a land trust that preserves the open spaces in the face of development (see figure 68 for plans and sections of the neighborhood over time).

Since my 2011 visit, things have slowed a bit in Old North St. Louis and also in fallow land experimentation. The economic and political tide turned with an economic downturn and a reduction in available federal funds. The ONSLRG still exists, but the board elected to let go of its permanent staff and has put on hold its ambitious plan for one hundred infill homes. As a volunteer-run organization, ONSLRG is still active in neighborhood development and is fulfilling its mission of creating a sustainable and welcoming community for all. The group has a relationship with the city and the LRA and provides oversight on land options to the roughly one hundred LRA-owned homes in the community. Through this relationship, the organization fights speculation. In the past couple of years, it has also been awarded bids and funds to develop a few infill, modular, energy-efficient homes—and has sold two to first-time homeowners. The group is feeling more financially stable and sensing another upcycle—with the potential to do more assets mapping, build organizational capacity, and push its infill work. Within the larger cycles, there are nested mini-cycles of local initiatives—from the daily senior's camp run on a lot outside of the Jackson Park Senior Center, to the weekly farmer's market at the 13th Street Community Garden, to the triennial infill development—sliding the neighborhood forward.

To open the ONSRLG website is to be confronted with sunflowers, or more specifically, the aforementioned Sunflower + Project: STL. The project is a field of sunflowers at 1318–24 Warren Street, developed under the leadership of cofounders Richard Reilly, of the Missouri Botanical Garden, and Don Koster, an architect and senior lecturer at Washington University. It was one of the winners of the Sustainable Land Lab Design Competition. The first growing season was 2013—and since then, the designers and some volunteers have been alternating crops of sunflowers and winter wheat. Gabion benches mark the locations of former buildings on-site, a scarecrow created by a local artist sits on a bench built into an old utility pole at the center, and colorful banners bring added life in the winter months. There is a berm off to the side, a resting mound for the tandem load of construction materials found on the site during the preparation work for the first planting.

Sunflowers are a trope—a joyful crop with mythic capacities for remediation and known abilities to attract pollinators and people. Nearly a decade ago, they covered every proposal for fallow land activation, but recently they have less of a presence. In St. Louis, they make sense. The *Helianthus annuus* has a long history in Missouri, where the Cahokian tribes are known to have cultivated the seeds. Soybeans have taken over as a commercial crop, but the sunflower is a fast-growing plant barely tolerant of poor soils and dry conditions. It starts small—either as seed or in greenhouses at the Missouri Botanical Garden—but quickly rises to a superhuman stature, its young flowers bending to the sun, all facing the same direction. Gratification is nearly instantaneous

1876   1909   1950   1974   2018

Parks and Gardens
Existing Structure
New Structure

1876

1909

1950

1974

2018

Plan: 100 Feet
          60 Meters

Section: 20 Feet
          12 Meters

Figure 68. Old North St. Louis over time, St. Louis: plans and sections of neighborhood change.

Figure 69. Sunflower + Project: STL, 2014.

yet short-lived, at once, a long cycle from ancient to contemporary cultivation, and a short one from seed to flower to seed.

While some have imagined sunflowers (or meadows or sweet potatoes or tree groves) to fill every vacant parcel, the reality demands a diversified approach. The genius of the Sunflower + Project: STL is in the simplicity and clarity of the idea—and the feasibility of its implementation. The notion is to test what minimum resource input could yield palpable impact—in this case seeds, seedlings, found materials, garden store rental equipment—and labor amounting to three- to ten-hour days and biweekly two-hour mowing and maintenance sessions. The project is temporary and low impact, with one crucial stipulation: no pesticides. The site has negligible contamination and poor soil that has only seen a one-time amendment of horse manure and mulch. The sunflowers struggle some years, and others they thrive. The *Cichorium intybus* (common chicory) always thrives.

Briefly the project expanded to include a large site on Delmar Avenue, in collaboration with alderwoman-turned-mayor Lyda Krewson, as well as a couple of smaller sites on the south side and north side. Then it contracted to a one-person operation with the focus back in the Old North St. Louis neighborhood. The pulses are both alluring, like an effervescent burst, and frustrating, like a broken promise. On Warren Street, the sunflowers are in a sixth cycle, complementing a suite of rudimentary approaches to vacancy in the neighborhood. Old North has invested in numerous cycles, and multiple increments of time, from the millennial to the generational to the diurnal register. Here the sunflowers feel like one of many ingredients, and the whole approach—art, music, protest, house, exchange, water, garden, and crop—feels particular and, even in a place as scarred as St. Louis, promising.

Momentum

The halting and positive momentum in Old North reminds me of other places: the area around Cherokee Street in St. Louis, the Idora neighborhood in Youngstown, Brightmoor and Corktown in Detroit, Ohio City in Cleveland. The questions remain: What is the longevity? What is replicable? These are places that have leveraged human capital to attract investment, where strong local leadership and a multipronged approach have created a network of common spaces for the neighborhood. With time, sweat, frustration, and continued optimism, the change is such that the city takes notice. The efforts are garnering support from the city through more traditional planning mechanisms, including inviting the Environmental Protection Agency and others to offer technical assistance. The neighborhood is playing out the rudimentary approaches: infiltrating water, cultivating plants, introducing play—through art and music—while diversifying land use, housing options, and economic opportunities. It could be a test case for other areas in the city, as well as a bridge to connect the north side to projects along the river and in the downtown area.[55]

The Old North strategy emphasizes preservation of the built fabric and transformation of the landscape. Demolition is not the answer here, but rather the recognition that a layered urban condition has value. There is also clustering, for example, around Crown Square and the Fourteenth Street Mall, where newer gallery spaces such as UrbArts sit adjacent to longtime businesses that have weathered the economic cycles (see figure 70). The enterprises tackle the physical built environment of the city—occupying urban space—while investing in community building and social equity. UrbArts promotes youth development through its poetry slam and artist shows. The founder, MK Stallings, writes of the organization's mission: "We must do through arts what others have not done through schools, public policy, and business in St. Louis. We've spent enough time surviving in their world of tolerated oppression, profitable exploitation, commercial art, muted voice, and limited opportunity structure. We must destroy their St. Louis and create ours."[56] "Destroy" might not be the operative word, given the desire to move beyond a clearing of the past, but replace "destroy" with

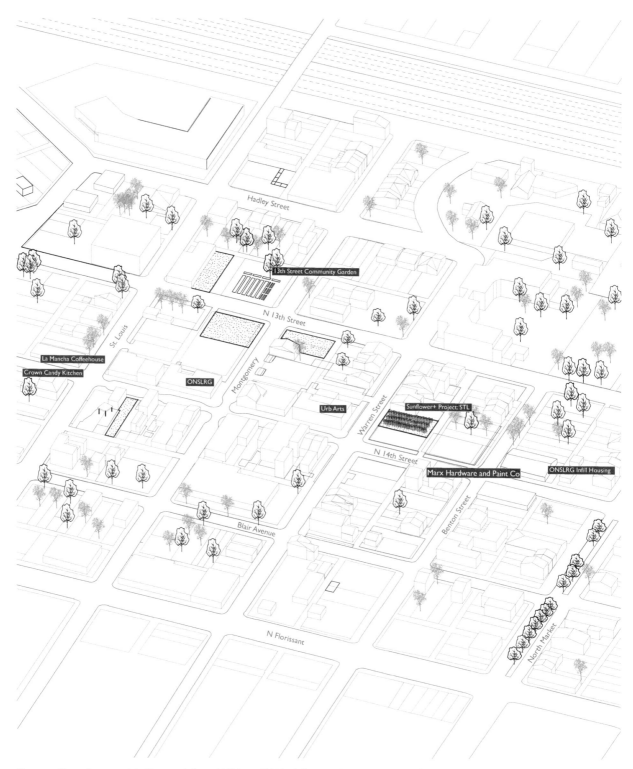

Figure 70. Crown Square and the Fourteenth Street Mall Area, Old North St. Louis, St. Louis, with specific sites referenced.

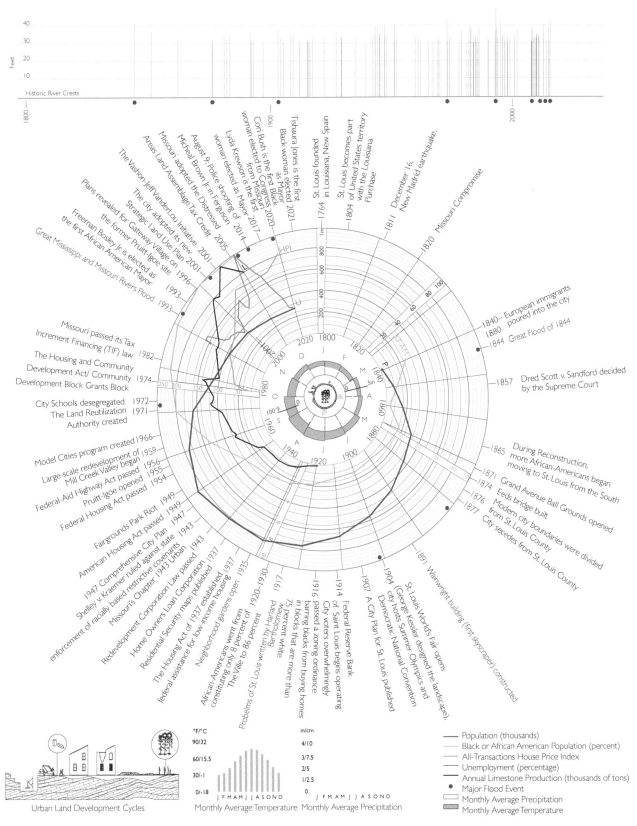

Figure 71. Fallow cycles, St. Louis: a diagram of climate, policy, economy, racism, and migration over time.

"transform," and the mission applies to all disciplines engaged in the project of city building. City building is a plural practice. The work in Old North St. Louis, while perhaps only engaging a self-selecting group of citizens at a small scale, points to this collective endeavor. Residents have formed not-for-profits, other organizations have provided funding, municipal agencies have become involved, federal tax credits give support, local universities offer technical expertise, and youth volunteer. The work is common, the landscapes are common, and the resources are common. Instead of falsely relying on the arch, the stadium, and other grand projects to save the city, focusing on local culture provides an avenue forward.

It is impossible to predict future directions, but St. Louis is midcycle, at a point when the activists in the city are striving to create projects and force policies to support transformation.[57] It is like Philadelphia with a few rain barrels and school stormwater gardens, or Berlin conceiving its first Natur-Park, or Lisbon with spontaneous hortas awaiting municipal validation, or Amsterdam building its first playground. Local activism is awaiting long overdue inclusive policy and positive investment—and at present, the predicted waiting time also seems long. In the meantime, the incremental is at work in patches. What is missing is the medium to support broader scales of time and space. There is still fixation on demolition, dreams of widespread infill, and big projects that land clumsily on the ground. In order to build lasting bridges, the bridges need to structure a terrain that simultaneously addresses head-on its volatile conditions (its social and economic inequities, structural racism, flooding, subsidence) and leverages all the local assets (committed people, open lands, ingrained materials, and temporal pauses).

CONCLUSION

The Common Project

The task of designing interventions for abandoned land and resource-strapped cities demands a new spatial and temporal approach. Traditional planning and design methods often embark on projects where the preconstruction phase is long. The methods are proven rather than experimental, and there is a clear title to clean, flat, and assembled land—in other words, legally and spatially the site is ready for building. Significant economic support is garnered in advance, in part because the potential for return on investment is nearly guaranteed, a self-fulfilling prophecy. Interventions for places of long-standing disinvestment, in contrast, happen incrementally and episodically, often periodically repeating themselves in altered forms. They occupy legally messy sites, often tax-delinquent and foreclosed-upon lands. They operate with greater associated risks while simultaneously embracing sensitive experimentation and innovation. They are incomplete, and they embrace this status and the potential for evolution and invention that this very incompleteness implies. If the city is dynamic and largely unpredictable, then this is especially true for places of disinvestment. Projects that can aggregate and mutate with time have greater resonance, and in this way, time, while a weakness in traditional planning and design, becomes an inherent parameter, a promising partner.

Spatial Strategies

The projects described herein point toward methods of land reform and to a critical reevaluation of colonial land grabs, capital markets, and the private ownership of property. They maneuver within these temporal and piecemeal conditions, where abandoned properties are scattered and noncontiguous, and where populations remain intermixed, to create common frameworks. To do this and to address these conditions,

Figure 72. City networks, showing dispersed, connected, and clustered systems.

three approaches are considered. I look at dispersed systems where many small installations, using similar materials and design language, are inserted across the city. Philadelphia and Amsterdam are examples here. By comparison, Berlin and Lisbon are the case studies for connected systems, where investments are concentrated and properties are proximal or joined to create impact through bands of related projects; and the clustered system, where many interventions aggregate in a particular location, driven by strong individuals, groups, and institutions, is examined in St. Louis. The approaches offer legibility (see figure 72) while providing some form of reparation for the ill-effects of social and physical fragmentation. They build on the intrinsic structure (or the non-structure) of abandonment in the city and the innate characteristics of the individual sites (low-lying topography, rich vegetation, fertile soils, even grade, neighboring populations). Designing landscapes from abandoned urban land begins by parsing opportunity and constructing a social, political, economic, environmental, and physical context for the project—a context that is derived from finding the inherent value in the existing urban condition and building capacity to enable communal care. The projects emerge from local practice, respecting previous occupations but departing radically as necessary. The projects overlay, consolidate, aggregate, proliferate, and adapt, all as a means to give form to a latent shared resource. In all this work—marked by the reallocation of the land, the physical design of the spaces, and the enabling of a common experience—what is most crucial is legibility, equity, care, and invention.

Temporal Approaches

These exemplary projects have developed over time, taking advantage of economic stagnation to gain measurable ecological and social traction. In each instance, challenging topographic and political conditions have allowed for an opening in the city. Unclaimed territory results from unstable ground conditions—steep slopes and subsiding lands, for example. But it also allows for unregulated use and unfettered vegetal growth. In some cases, the spontaneous uses can go largely untracked for decades, solidifying their hold on the terrain, and giving them footing in the subsequent redevelopment efforts. The wild landscapes of Berlin, the cultivated terraces of Lisbon—these are potent examples. Agronomic and vegetal landscapes require time to develop, reaching maturity years and decades after their initial establishment. Abandoned corridors can disappoint in their nascent phases, to some audiences, at least, appearing to be desolate or weedy. To their constituents—the urban farmers and urban ecologists—their value is understood immediately, but with time, education, and curation, they become more convincing to a broader public as viable urban resources. The longer holding patterns allow for significant structural change to occur. Individual parcels disintegrate. Connections are forged, and the larger figures form without forced displacement. With planning, property can be mutable. Time and organization yield legibility.

Although the landscapes emerge under the radar, they require long-term design input, management, and care to fully function and develop over time.[1] By and large, the projects analyzed in this book consolidate and adapt existing practices into a clearly defined, municipally supported design project: the collection of water, the growth of wild vegetation, the farming of open plots, the use of residual lots as playgrounds, and the development of surprising garden types. The emphasis, then, is not on wholesale invention, but on wholesale organization and guidance. It is important to note, however, that this does not imply a less ambitious transformation. The idea is not simply to take what exists and make it last. It is to learn from the local initiatives, to use staged means to strategically yet *significantly* change the landscape with time.

Gradations

Significant change necessitates different levels of design intervention and management, whether across sites or within individual projects. For example, in the Natur-Park Schöneberger Südgelände, a three-pronged approach has inserted a hard ground for recreational activities, maintained meadow landscapes through arrested succession, and left woodlands to develop without direct management. We see hybrid conditions establish, similar to the experiments in Lisbon where agricultural practices are consciously paired with recreational ones. At the same time, different agricultural sites—the spontaneous gardens and the amalgamated parks—have different levels of care and investment. In almost all cases, the intensely managed is paired with the less controlled, both within individual plots and across multiple sites. As planners and designers, we tend to think in binaries: public or private; cultivated or spontaneous; mown or not mown. But this has considerable limitations. The projects explored are conceived of as gradients, and along those gradients we see the resources deliberately allocated toward the maximum social and ecological impact. The goal can neither be a return to previous levels of management and development nor a filling of every fallow space. Instead, the strategy is to allocate different levels of resource, not based on land market value, demographics, or political will power, but rather as part of a multipronged effort with an equitable geographical distribution. In other words, there would be a range of spaces of high intensity and spaces of low intensity across sites, neighborhoods, cities, and regions.

Scalar Impact

The design and management of the sites also occurs across physical scales, from the small individual parcel to the entire regional system, from the storm trench to the watershed, from the individual specimen to the communal forest, from the crop to the agricultural belt, from the play mound to the urban health system, from the sunflower to the biosphere. The territory of abandonment is often too vast for a customized response to each instance. Instead, the toolkits are designed for proliferation and adaptability to individual site conditions. The designs work well at this level, with each deployment influencing the next, but the relationships, materials, and approaches are adaptable and repeatable. The distinct projects across the city are considered together and operate collectively in the planning and social conscious of the cities. In fact, as the programs grow, the spaces they create become part of a collective experience for the city. The rain gardens of Philadelphia, the ruderal spaces of Berlin, the allotment gardens of Lisbon, the play spaces of Amsterdam, and the art protests of St. Louis are part of the urban identity—visual manifestations of societal preoccupations at the moments of their conception. They are responses to insecurities and opportunities, including flooding and water quality, ecological resilience in the aftermath of ruination, food security and poverty, population changes and housing scarcity, and racial injustice. The physical spaces are markers of political, environmental, social, and economic trends.

The projects operate differentially across the physical scales of the terrain, occupying varied footprints, penetrating to distinctive depths, and reaching diverse heights. They can also be identified with different scales of time, both in terms of the eras in which they are best considered and the anticipated lifespan of the project itself. The temporal conditions of abandonment are unique. Each individual parcel seems volatile in the short term, and yet stagnant over somewhat longer time spans. They are dramatically transformed in an even longer time frame, and cyclically tied to the evolution of the land when considering its longest developmental history. I have seen this firsthand in visiting a particular neighborhood in Philadelphia biannually for the past fifteen years. In this time, the abandoned parcels vary considerably with season—naked in the winter yet teeming with vegetation in summer months. If the season is constant, the land appears unchanged—the condition in April of 2004 mirrors that of April 2019. Yet, archival research reveals that the parcels were full of connected row houses in the 1970s, only to face abandonment and demolition in the 1980s and 1990s, thus creating the rhythm of the fabric as it exists today: built, open, open, built, built, open, and on and on. The shift is dramatic and jarring, over the course of only a few decades. Further, archival research reveals an area covered with farmland, cleared from an area covered with forest, where indigenous routes cut across the landscape. This points to a potentially cyclical condition, emphasized throughout this investigation, where proposals for agricultural and silvicultural investment are considered for land where there was crop and tree cultivation a long time ago. Given the multiple time frames, multiple responses are necessary.

Often proposals for the neglected are temporary, and obviously the temporary has a place in conditions where the city is failing to meet the minimum requirements— clean water, clean air, food, utilities, education—for its citizens. At the same time, the temporary alone is shortsighted, especially in landscape terms where the material develops slowly. In these instances, a medium scale of several decades or a half-century is fundamental, given that even fifty years is too short when considering a transformation in the way a city is organized—given that changing the organization is an imperative in the face of failing economies, relations, and environments. In other words, small shifts cannot address the deep environmental, social, and racial injustices operating in our cities, today and for the past centuries.

Our collective failures—the unmitigated disaster of decades of local, state, and federal development projects—compel us as designers to embrace an evolution that begins with the well-being of the citizenry, that does not merely replace building with building, or replace one failed economy with another economy tied to the same unsustainable, time-sensitive property gains that once again jeopardize the citizenry's well-being. The challenge, of course, is to develop mutable guidelines that can transcend fiscal and political cycles and begin to inform and inspire cultural attitudes, behaviors, and memories. My goal here is to explore the hidden genetic codes of specific urban conditions in order to inspire robust projects elsewhere that can work both immediately and for generations to come. Admittedly, this is hard to do.

Design Principles

In case we forget: the physical elements of design are fundamental to these projects. We see it in the list of simple yet profound devices used to organize the sites: water retention and detention repositories in Philadelphia; vegetation, surface manipulation, circulatory and programmatic installations in Berlin; fences, sheds, terraces, water spigots, and community contracts in Lisbon; geometric surface materials, play equipment, and organized space in Amsterdam; almost all of the above, plus paint, and construction materials in St. Louis, if in an unresolved state (see figure 73). The projects embody a rough elegance that matches their restrained context. Expressive vegetation, careful delineations, bold surfaces, animated lines, and compact structures are the key materials. The components are nimbly deployed, providing ample contrast with their surroundings. They define and augment rather than stand in opposition to the terrain, removing the perception of raggedness without losing its textural grain. They take unassuming materials—vegetation, concrete, wood, mesh, metal, brick—and elevate them through astute configurations and uncanny juxtapositions. The designs are insertions that support the implicit and explicit codes of occupation. They are cohesive and discernable, respectful and imaginative. The aesthetics match the ecological fervor, the social freedom, and yes, even the fiscal constraints. With simple elements, the possibilities are immense.[2]

Responsible projects in the era of social and climatic crisis demand this constraint. They are nimble, symbiotic, at times attaching a civic realm to an infrastructural decree or using a public health outcry to reconfigure urban space. They are justly opportunistic, finding value in lowlands, on steep slopes, along rail lines, in disposed infrastructure, and in small, scattered parcels. They respect the wild urban woodland as a biological reserve. They use health concerns as a way to leverage public support and funding. They engage local practices to build project knowledge. They connect people with resources—the projects feed and grow and are fueled by participation; and they empower the people themselves, the users, to enliven the cityscape. They express the

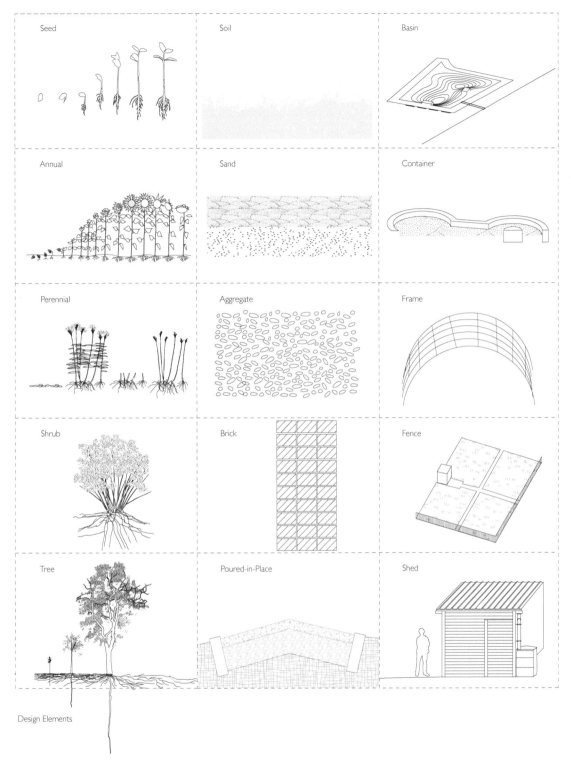

Seed

Soil

Basin

Annual

Sand

Container

Perennial

Aggregate

Frame

Shrub

Brick

Fence

Tree

Poured-in-Place

Shed

Design Elements

Figure 73. Design elements.

mundane. They do the obvious well. Above all, they understand that the creation of a responsive landscape structure is, in itself, a prudent proposition. Its construction is less costly, in the short term and more so in the longer term, its benefits measurable, and its occupation potentially free. And that very frugality leads to vast communal benefits.

In sum, there are several key principles that underlie all of the projects and together form initial design guidelines for abandoned land. The designs reject an aesthetic fascination with the void and move beyond narratives of only damage to ones of damage and desire.[3] They adapt intrinsic urban structures and practices. They take advantage of development delays. They reform property spatially and, at times, legally. They embrace care as a design strategy. They build trust and capacity. They operate telescopically across scales. They embody a rough elegance, and again they are frugal. Frugality, in fact, informs the entire project, a frugality that leads to communal dividends. But frugality does not mean a lack of investment or a compromised design. Instead, it points to a respect for resources. It is a frugality that leads to communal dividends, the community being the principal. Together, the strategies point to a restrained but effective approach to designing common landscapes out of abandonment.[4] These landscapes emerge through the establishment of shared resource value, reflected in physical design intervention and subsequent management practices on largely deprivatized sites.[5] The cases illustrate incomplete, immature, and imperfect forms of what are sometimes referred to as the commons, allowing for the extraction of principles, the implication of benefits, and the possibility to imagine a fuller incarnation. The promise rests in the shared utilities—hydrological, vegetal, agronomic, social—and their collective legibility designed over time.

These loose commons are by nature dynamic and unifying.[6] Their making is evolutionary. They represent a claimed landscape that resists concrete divisions—and indeed resists nearly all the divisions that are imposed upon it by the market economy. Thus, it is up to the citizens and the urbanists to point out the long-term communal cultural values that come with the effective care of these landscapes. It is through the model and operation of these shared spaces that the abandoned urban landscape is *un*abandoned, salvaged for the city and the region. While the strategies in this book point to public investment, the invocation of the commons points to something even more transformative: to co-governance and communal resources that transfer land from private ownership through public control into shared ownership. The co-governance model, as developed by law and policy professors Sheila Foster and Christian Iaione, investigates governing the city as a commons. They are developing projects using the *Co-City Methodology*—a way of working that sees the "city as a platform for sharing and collaboration, participatory decision-making and peer-to-peer production, supported by open data and guided by principles of distributive justice."[7]

The transformation of abandoned urban land is a logical place to start to assert greater power for citizens in shaping urban form. Again, instead of transferring property to the government and pushing it back into discriminatory capital markets, this co-city model promotes a co-governance scheme whereby "the community emerges as an actor and partners" with governmental agencies, knowledge institutions, civic organizations, and businesses "in a loosely coupled system." The work builds local capacity, underlying the importance of local inhabitants in the creation of the city and its landscapes. And while none of the examples discussed in the book are explicitly co-governed, they point to this as a potential next step—as a way to extend the physical, common landscapes into a model of collectively, into what might be considered a fuller commons.

Human Impact

Although there are many types of abandoned urban landscapes, with varied sizes, configurations, and locations, the projects uncovered in this book are closely linked with the residential areas, with the spaces of living within the city. They occupy small and large fragments that are embedded within neighborhoods. As common endeavors, they rely on this intimate relationship with the ways in which people inhabit their environment. They relate to cycles of housing, where the construction and destruction of homes runs parallel to the construction and destruction of landscape. The landscapes serve the houses, and the houses support the landscapes. The stories of each project and each city bring to life this relationship. In nearly every time-lapse sequence focused on the evolution of a landscape and its rudimentary elements, the cycles of housing are also evident. While some treatises on abandonment and design shy away from the entangled conditions of human occupation, housing, environmental injustice, and racial and ethnic discrimination, the intention here is to address directly inhabitation.

In Philadelphia, on the scale of the overall city, the basins collect the waters shed by development, in locations where occupation ebbs and flows. The creeks and sewer sheds underlie city blocks, registering at times in snaking street orientations that cut across the grain of the grid and in liberated swaths that collect new waters in cisterns and basins. The cycle extends from creek to house to sewer to house to basin to house. Along Brown and Aspen Streets, housing has impinged on the Mill Creek and its associated sewer, occupying a low and unstable ground to ill effect. Currently, some buildings have backed off, if slightly, to allow for water volume—and to welcome cultivation and recreation in the lowlands. Further east, on the Liberty Lands site, an industrial complex, embedded within a residential fabric, has burned, leaving a welcome hole in the neighborhood. It sits atop the banks of Cohocksink Creek, pulls water in off the street for self-irrigation, and anchors residential development at its edges. Run by a neighborhood organization that supports the local residents, the site, too, supports and is sustained by the adjacent residences.

In Berlin, the wilds emerge on sites of discontinued use and destruction, with the Grünanlage Hallesche Straße sitting atop row houses destroyed by war. Setting stones on the sidewalk or Stolpersteine mark the last residences of Jewish victims of the Holocaust, people and city senselessly obliterated. Photographs from the postwar period look desolate, with rubble piles foregrounding railroad ruins, and the Postamt SW11 postal building sitting like an awkward and horrifying expression of state power amid swathes of open land. Over time, vegetation and development have filled in—and the current block is caught between the wild landscape of the former Anhalter Bahnhof site to the west and the vibrant residential fabric of Kreuzberg beyond Ida-Wolff Platz to the east. Despite the transitory feeling outside the fences, the current wild serves as a refuge for the passerby—mainly children, dogs, and walkers—providing a shaded place to ramble. As new residences are being constructed, the neighborhood is gaining housing units—and the site, which owes its existence to the destruction of old homes, owes its continued relevance and vitality to the construction of new ones. The wilds, once ubiquitous and sprawling, are framed again by the infilling of city fabric. Abandonment is part of a past cycle, marked subtly in the characteristics of the trees. There is a temporal lapse between the housing cycle and the landscape cycle, an interdependency that pulses with destruction and construction, growth and decay.

In Lisbon, the hortas and the dwelling units have a direct relationship, where the evolution highlights codependency rather than displacement. Here, the inhabitants of the housing units are the purveyors of the landscape—the tenancies are synchronistic. This spontaneous symbiosis forms the basis of a project. The occupancies, once tenuous, find validation through the construction of city park infrastructure for the agricultural plots—the Parque Hortícola—and the development of housing cooperatives for the residences. The hold on the terrain is becoming stronger. The two activities—living and farming—are resynching with the forged relationship between housing zone and horticultural park. The past alignment, once reinforced by the quinta structure and subsequently severed by the quota-driven technocratic plans, returns. The growth of neighborhood and farm is not planned together but is supported through the subsistence farming practices of local residents. The proximity of home to garden plot activates the urban ground, literally incising furrows and pathways into the surface. The direct connections create a viable microcosm within the disconnected and cavernous valley where large roads and buildings sit heavy but remain rootless. The physical connections between building and ground plane are weak, but there is a deep tie that registers in the movement of people between home and garden, high ground and low ground, inside and outside.

In Amsterdam, as in Lisbon, the activation of the interstices follows the expansion of housing in the city, though in Amsterdam, the lag is not as pronounced. While the housing extension plan drives development, the articulation of the civic realm is considered as a part of the project. The first new developments proposed by the Amsterdam Expansion Plan are modeled after garden cities with function-driven housing units laid out around linear parks, inner grass courts, and agricultural wedges that extend into the neighborhoods. Areas such as Slotermeer are among the greenest in the city. The planning efforts, which focused on large green and blue infrastructures, are complimented by inhabitant-driven demands for recreational amenities, including the ubiquitous playgrounds. A combination of high birthrates and immigration following postwar decolonization led to increased housing and civic space demands. Between 1935 and 1969, the population grew by ninety thousand people, and the city built an impressive number of social housing units to address the housing shortage. Social housing was considered a solution to provide affordable residences while still suppressing wages to improve international competitiveness. To this day, Amsterdam has a high rate of rent control.[8]

The articulation of the gaps and slivers happened hand in hand with the collective projects of housing provision, city expansion, and population gain. As the city filled in, incrementally, new residents requested play spaces. The play landscapes, in fact, cannot be understood without the housing units—and like the development of urban play spaces elsewhere, the playground is a typology of the social state. As a city's human population shifts, and new gaps appear, play emerges as a communal response. While Amsterdam might be an outlier here as a city of seemingly perpetual growth, its playground project from the 1940s to the 1970s shares the same design tenets as other strategies for the abandoned and interstitial. Perhaps because the spaces were seen as temporary and because the program operated almost in opposition to the large planning efforts of the city, the strategy is pervasive, simple, adaptable, and economical. Play—like cultivation—is a coping strategy for fiscal down cycles—and it is the ambition that the inventions that operate outside the market have the potential to show alternative systems of value: health, well-being, joy, expression, the opportunity to be outside in close proximity to one's home. The interstitial open lands provide local opportunity for reclamation and reparation as more formal play spaces become farther from active populations. There are proximal places to play seemingly everywhere. Living and playing are definitively linked, and the linkage is heightened as other resources evaporate.

In St. Louis, wealth and opportunity are unevenly distributed. The city is an emblem for a divided city. The responses to vacancy, poverty, and injustice are piecemeal, anchored around personal, institutional, and organizational strongholds. These celebrate local culture and are often driven by the arts, music, youth, agriculture, and water. Although the government is sometimes involved in the transformation, many of the successful projects feature sustained individual efforts rather than central plans and subsidies. The two corridors often cited as examples of regeneration—Cherokee Street in the southern part of the city and North 14th Street in the Old North St. Louis neighborhood—follow this storyline. And the efforts, one enterprise at a time, often combine nontraditional living, working, and commercial spaces. The investment, albeit incremental, is totalizing. Residents drive it. And with time, the project becomes shared, expanding to include multiple protagonists and investors.

For example, in Old North St. Louis, some residents banded together to create the Old North St. Louis Restoration Group, "a community-based nonprofit organization" dedicated to revitalizing "the physical and social dimensions of the community in a manner that respects its historic, cultural, and urban character."[9] The group—and the neighborhood work—is still active over thirty-five years later. Again, the conversation has broadened to include the city, federal agencies such as the Environmental Protection Agency, community development corporations and local developers, architects, artists, and activists. With the proximity of Old North St. Louis to downtown, the river, and other planning initiatives, the city has taken an interest in the area—and has begun some investments in the physical fabric. The first projects, initiated by the Restoration Group and supported by community development corporation financing and technical assistance, targeted housing. Subsequent projects have broadened the scope and ambition to include housing, commercial properties, public space, and gardens. Again, solidifying housing opportunity has been a lynchpin in increasing lasting landscape interventions for disinvested properties. Without a parallel investment in housing and landscape, sustained impact is difficult to achieve.

The projects highlighted in this volume deliberately address the residential interstices and find themselves embedded within the city rather than at the edges and boundaries. The examples steer away from the idea of a landmark project toward multiple common and scalable strategies. Cities have transformed abandoned industrial and infrastructural landscapes, often along underutilized waterfronts into signature civic spaces. These spaces, which serve the populace at large, are often far from the places where the most underresourced populations live. They are designed to spur change, but the effects often underscore the uneven development of the city. The places of capital and cultural accumulation attract resources while the rest of the city does not. In fact, other parts of the city are actively disinvested in, as decision-makers use market strength assessment maps as a means to decide where and where not to invest. Further, city officials tend to ignore speculation, often by out-of-town investors, who purchase bulk properties with no intention of maintaining or occupying them. The past and current mechanisms of city making are designed to promote inequities, inequities that predominately effect Black, brown, immigrant, ethnic, and religious minority populations and others traditionally left out of the planning and design process. Stemming from the Black Lives Matter movement and a spatial-racial reckoning in the United States, advocates are exposing the complicity of design in the production of disinvestment and policy- and bank-fueled segregation.[10] And while the abandoned landscapes are not directly tied to this movement, they represent an opportunity for reparations, for the seeding of communal wealth in the form of civic landscapes. They have the potential to change the past patterns of resource allocation. It would be naive to think that the polyvalent and distributed strategies are evenly deployed. They are not. But they are more far-reaching, nimbler, and more capable of infiltrating the urban extents.

Plurality

In fact, the ties to human and cultural capital and the reality of limited fiscal resources drive original response. The projects described excel in design—but this is not the sort of design that emphasizes elaborate material uses. Instead, it is design that maximizes spatial transformation with minimal means. It is the type of design that operates on multiple levels—again, to absorb water and promote play, to increase habitat and provide mobility, to grow food and increase ventilation, to protest past inequities and to house future use. The responses, it might be argued, must do more than one thing to be defensible. In places with grave need and limited access, the plural is a necessity. The plural includes both the physical, spatial performance as well as the social engagement. The projects are tied to people and programming. For example, the first rain gardens are in schools in Philadelphia—and in St. Louis, neighborhood children receive credits cleaning debris from gardens. With a certain number of hours logged, they earn a bicycle. The education and care start early, as a means of investment in the urban terrain. The common project extends beyond the physical footprint.

Depth and Breadth

Thus, while these projects have planar dimensions—in fact, many of the figures herein are maps and plans representing the city as seen from above—a purely plan reading of the city masks conditions and opportunities. In places of disinvestment, it is standard practice to dwell on statistical and figure-ground comparisons from heyday to current situation. For example, St. Louis had just over 850,000 people in 1950 and just over 300,000 in 2019. Its blocks were intact in 1950, and now its more than over 20,000 vacant parcels yield streets with significant gaps between buildings. It is easy to dwell on these losses and gaps, among others, especially when counting people or drawing a figure-ground plan of the city over time. The visceral shock is palpable. But when the city is seen through a different lens, through the water moving through the watershed, say, or the plants emerging on fallow lands, or the stories of people adopting spaces, cultivating food, and building play areas in places where city parks do not exist—then the opportunity is palpable. With less emphasis on parcel boundary and building footprint, and without the binary fallacy of the figure-ground, it is possible to let go for a minute of the desire to rebuild what was and instead to imagine other collective city-making projects long enough for them to take hold. The urban section is deep, full of water, soil, geology, labor, and roots.

All of the projects herein aim to define the ordinary urban ground and its materials and constituents in multiple dimensions. They aim to mute the dominant narrative of loss long enough to forgo it. They embrace the many, the unknown, and the incomplete, not as points of weakness but as ways to project.[11] To do so is complicated, a conceptual Catch-22: to replace clear, straightforward narrative with something intentionally complicated, purposely lacking a singular and cohesive position. It is hard because there is always significant risk when we are considering people's lives and their future. It is hard because of the admission that this is only a small part of a large and complex situation. But it is necessary and vital, in order to overcome stagnation and unevenness and the associated injuries to the community.

By focusing on different cities, at different points in their historical, economic, and biological cycles, it becomes possible to imagine the ups as well as the downs and to see the evolution of a place as something that requires pause as well as fervor. The trajectory is deep, long, and multiheaded.[12] Almost counterintuitively, by seeing beyond the present, the surficial, and the singular, it becomes increasingly possible to make cities work again and work better, for the current populations, in the places adjacent to where they live, on the lands liberated by people who have migrated elsewhere. And it becomes possible to do so without forcing more displacement and disparity, more destruction and devastation.

EPILOGUE

The light in Lisbon is incredible, long, and warm. It casts a foggy glow over the city's well-polished stone and forces one's gaze upward, eyes tracing along and past the profiles of hills, moving deep soil to deep sky. Descending the hillside from the Jardim do Príncipe Real and Miradouro de São Pedro de Alcântara, through the Baixa and toward the trams at Praça do Comércio, the visitor gains a visceral appreciation for the city's topography, masonry, and afternoon sun (figure 74, section A). On one warm fall afternoon, I see people everywhere, despite the post-lunch lull and workday demands. In fact, the city can be experienced as a series of prospects, points that when positioned sit on sectional transects across the terrain. A city is never flat, physically or ontologically. It is we who flattened them and, by extension, homogenize our urban expectations. What if we took on the full topography, with all its messiness? What if we related the sectional qualities?

These thoughts run through my mind as I wait to meet Manuela Raposo Magalhães. She is a professor of landscape architecture emerita at the Instituto Superior de Agronomia (figure 74, section B), where, at the time, she was still touring incoming students and directing a research team devoted to national investigations of ecological structure. She is dedicated to studying the agricultural roots and ecological potential of the Iberian Peninsula while having a keen eye for design. She is not interested in works that make a small impact. She reads the territory with aplomb, and she reads it critically, toward a more reasonable future management. Trained in landscape architecture, with an agronomic emphasis—like many of the most accomplished Portuguese landscape architects—she has worked closely with Gonçalo Ribeiro Telles on Lisbon's Plano Verde.

On this September afternoon, she has graciously agreed to meet me, to show me some of her work, and to take me on a tour of the Chelas area. As we drive, she navigates the

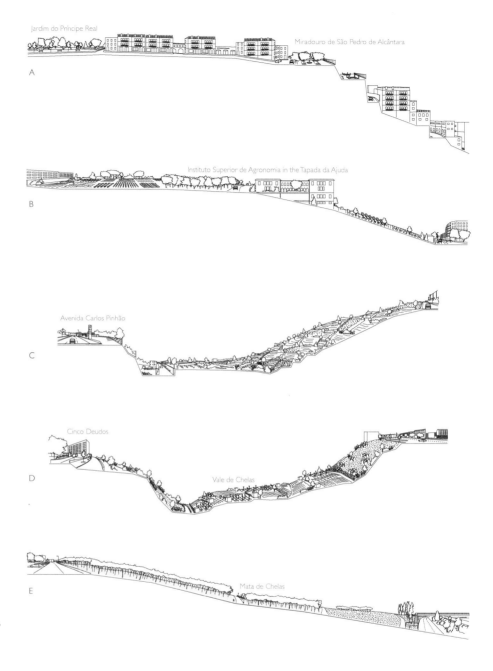

Figure 74. Deep sections through the city, Lisbon, 2014–19.

ups and downs of the city with great knowledge, passing both seamlessly and abruptly between the oversized and disconnected routes of the technocratic plan and the meandering remnants of the roman layout. We stop at a gas station along Avenida Carlos Pinhão, near where it blindly passes over the Azinhaga Maruja, to gaze over a valley that simultaneously shows the present cultivation practices and those of the near and distant past. The hillside is irregularly portioned into individual, Cachupa-rich gardens, showing the spontaneous plots assumed by contemporary residents intersecting with old Roman-era estates. It is, in a way, a glimpse of how the Vale do Chelas site—our next stop—might have looked a few years prior, before the construction of the municipal park. The view is hidden from the road and bridge above, sunken just out of sight, as if intuitively or even deliberately obscured in order to be preserved. Only by walking down into the gas station parking lot does the valley become evident. This is stop one. Perch one. Overlook one (also figure 74, section C).

Standing at our next stop, with the Cinco Deudos housing complex to our backs, Magalhães voiced her deep concerns over the relationship between housing and terrain: Can these estates somehow be demolished? Are there examples of this happening in the United States? And her ongoing concerns over the design of the park: How could the base of the hill, the line of the valley hold a paved path? How could the shed design be more mindful of the economic and cultural means of the farmers? In other words, how, even when we know more, do we continue to ignore the terrain with our designs?

I was listening but was also struck by the power of the valley and the moments, like the descending terraces of plots, where the design and the topography do so eloquently reinforce each other. This open prospect, like the previous, is alluring. The view of the horizon is dominated by sky; the warm earth descends across the foreground. The housing estates, while clumsy, have not closed the view. In a way, this project, about understanding the potential of abandonment, is about these lasting openings, where despite omission, destruction, and even abuse, an unrecognized calm exists. It is about seeing the wide prospect and imagining its present relevance as a place of awe and memory. This is stop two. Perch two. Overlook two (also figure 74, section D).

Magalhães, while navigating the difficult Chelas terrain, emphasized that landscapes are simple. The valley operates by shedding water from top to bottom. The micro and macro terracing arrests the water in its likely descent. Lush vegetation occupies the bottom and the perched wet points, while the dry species cling to the slopes. The condition is sectional—yet urban plans are usually drawn flat, from the bird's-eye view—and the design logic corresponds. Contour lines are often absent, as are slope and solar exposure. The ground material is missing. Its affordances and histories are overlooked. Yet there is incredible opportunity to be responsive through a careful interrogation of cultural and material conditions, to take in the deep, long view. We are driving in search of another project, a sectional one that derives its basic principles from the valley's wetness gradient. We stop to inquire directions to the Mata de Chelas, also called, we learn, the Mata de Don Denis or, as the map indicates, Parque do Vale Fundão. We drive mapless, a challenge given the topography and road configurations. No route is direct, a frustration that lends itself to keener observation. *Mata* means woods, and Magalhães has not been to this site for some years, but she knows it as one of the original Chelas landscapes, designed by Álvaro Dentinho, a talented if eccentric landscape architect who followed simple ecological principles. Again, the dry upland forest of pines gives way to stands of poplars, which cede to an open, dry riverbed. Here, the prospect is occluded; like so much of Lisbon's topography, the section is experienced rather than viewed. The paths move across the grade, curving from forest to forest to open, extending the section. The visitor is immersed as long as possible in each habitat.

The hillside is not as steep as the previous ones we have visited, so we walk straight, instead, along the section cut, our feet tracing the designer's sectional esquisse. It has taken me a few trips and many days to realize that the agency of the section here in a place of extreme topography is relevant regardless of terrain. The figure-ground may always have its allure when understanding urban abandonment: seeing the scattered buildings while the mind makes the connection that interstitial voids are places of demolition carries an immediate shock. But the section is a relief for the conscience. To read the city through its section is to see at once its structure, its thickness, its material, and its habitation. This is stop three. Perch three. Overlook three (also figure 74, section E).

Here, in the park, we finally make it to the bottom of the prospect, where we can look back to see where we have been and where we might be headed. Where we are headed in our immediate time frame is literally back up, completing the journey, the section, the cycle. Perhaps in the longer time frame, we are headed back up the hill as well, metaphorically to the top from the bottom and back again, over and over, collecting material, perspective, and difference as we go.

NOTES

PROLOGUE

1. This project is part of a national program; between 1957 and 1980, the United States constructed over forty thousand miles of highways.

INTRODUCTION

1. See Lopez-Pineiro, *Glossary of Urban Voids.*

2. See Desimini, *From Fallow;* Desimini, "From Fallow to Wild"; Desimini, "Limitations of the Temporary"; J. B. Jackson, *Necessity for Ruins.*

3. See Raganathan and Bratman, "From Urban Resilience."

4. These numbers are from 2014 from Lincoln Institute of Land Policy, *Land and Property Values.*

5. Anne Whiston Spirn's work focuses on the interplay of ecology and sociology, with a keen interest in the ability to read urban form as the unfolding of natural processes and human purposes over time.

6. Arnold Arboretum, "About Us."

7. In 1996, three tracts—one previously owned by the Arnold Arboretum, one owned by the Massachusetts Bay Transit Authority, and one owned by the city of Boston—were placed under the 1882 Arnold Arboretum Indenture.

8. The moniker "arboretum gone wild" is borrowed from former Arnold Arboretum senior scientist Peter del Tredici.

9. Benton MacKaye proposed an analogy between population shifts and river function, articulating a series of flows through words and diagrams. His outflow, reflow, inflow, and backflow attributed spatial properties to his friend and fellow planner Lewis Mumford's migrations. Mumford's seminal 1925 article described the fourth migration, or the "metropolitan invasion," as the beginning of sprawl in America. It followed, Mumford wrote, the first migration of westward expansion, the second migration of railroad and industry growth, and the third migration of urban densification. Urban historian and theorist Robert Fishman added a "fifth migration" to describe the re-urbanization of urban centers.

10. Both the economist Joseph Schumpeter and landscape historian J. B. Jackson argue that destruction and ruination are required for reinvention and progression.

11. Ignasi Solà-Morales Rubió published his seminal piece "Terrain Vague" two decades ago, adapting French film terminology to the urban environment and presenting an argument for the value of the void, an idea that has been widely repeated but not successfully transformed into architectural and urban design practice.

12. On the quantification side, Ann O'M. Bowman and Michael A. Pagano published *Terra Incognita* in 2004, following a survey sent to cities in the United States with populations greater than fifty thousand designed to quantify "vacant land." Their definition of "vacant land" is extremely broad, including abandoned properties, contaminated sites, and designed green spaces. And for the understanding the sensorial particularities, Solà-Morales Rubió began qualifying the Terrain Vague, and it has been continued by many, including landscape architects and urbanists Jacky Bowring, Luc Levesque, Gilles Clément, and Christophe Girot.

13. Gerald D. Suttles in "Cumulative Texture of Local Culture" argues that, through the media, the representation of urban culture is dominated by a narrative that sets the current city in relationship to its capitalist heyday, rather than treating the city as an accumulation of cultural expressions from multiple voices and even multiple pasts. Suttles's article appeared back in 1984, but popular culture still sensationalizes urban decline alone. In other words, the focus is always on the number of people who have left a city, rather than the number who have remained. In the case of Detroit, that remaining population still exceeds the population of Boston and other large U.S. cities.

14. Russell, "Late Ancient and Medieval Population," 1.

15. Ibid.

16. Oswalt, *Shrinking Cities,* vols. 1 and 2.

17. For more on predatory land practices see Akers and Seymour, "Instrumental Exploitation.

18. Oswalt, *Shrinking Cities,* vols. 1 and 2. Of the 250 entries in the two volumes (a number that speaks to the extensiveness of the project), only five of the contributors align themselves with the discipline of landscape. Two are included in volume 1 on research and three in volume 2 on interventions.

19. The "Feral City" is described thusly: Urban withdrawal creates vacant spaces. Wastelands, forests, and fields creep back into the city and increasingly determine its look and structure. Typical landscapes thereby undergo change and absorb urban elements and functions. Urban agriculture or community gardens can generate new social networks or the basis for local economies (ibid., 2: 143).

20. "Rurbanity" is a portmanteau of "rural" and "urban," evoking this creep of agriculture and landscape back into the city.

21. Ujijji Davis states: The Bottom reflects a colloquial term used to describe black communities within or surrounding larger—visibly segregated—urban areas. An eponym that either describes the presence of dark marshy soil or land of poor value, the term emerged in the twentieth century to illustrate both where black people lived and their social standing in American society. For more on the idea of the Black Bottom, see Davis, "The Bottom."

22. Hard surface materials technically fall outside of the realm of the "Feral City" section in the *Shrinking Cities,* vol. 2. Thus, I address topics from many of the other "cities" in Oswalt, *Shrinking Cities,* vol. 2, including demolition city, contraction city, and temporary city.

23. This is the walk described in the prologue.

24. The Bussey Brook Meadow, discussed above, is a good example of a wet meadow site used for stormwater impoundment. For more on stormwater management, see Spirn, *Granite Garden.*

25. For more novel habitat descriptions, see Tredici, *Wild Urban Plants.*

26. *Gleiswildnis* has no equivalent in English but means "rail wilderness," or the wild landscapes found along used and disused rail infrastructure.

27. Drake and Lawson, "Validating Verdancy or Vacancy?," 133–42.

28. The Richard D. Parker Memorial Victory Gardens, located in the Fens in Boston, is a good example of a place with longstanding participation. It is the only remaining continuously operating World War II Victory Gardens in the United States. The Victory Garden program was designed to address food shortages during the war, and many sites were used as places for cultivation. The practice was largely temporary, and the gardens disappeared with the end of the war and the associated food shortage.

29. A *horta* is an allotment garden or small agricultural plot.

30. Lisbon is a city with great topographic variation, including a number of hills and valleys. The character of the terrain figures prominently in the design of the city and is discussed further in the subsequent chapter.

31. *Speelplaatsen* translates as "playgrounds," though *speel* is "play" and *plaatsen* is "place." *Speeltuinen* also translates as "playgrounds" where *tuinen* means "gardens." Similarly, *Speelplakken* translates to "playground" where *plakken* is "spots" or "locations."

32. For a definition of "fallow," I include excerpts of my text "From Fallow to Wild." "Fallow, in many ways, is a fallacy. That is, defined as a period of inactivity. On any piece of land, there is always activity—and while resting might breed uncertainty in some contexts, the agricultural definition of fallow implies that dormancy is a requirement of sustained growth. Within this period of dormancy, there is action: plowing, tilling, and even the planting of cover crops. Fallow is a necessary pause. . . . In fact, describing abandoned property as fallow acknowledges its liminal state. . . . Fallow is both reversible and valuable, if indirectly so. By suspending immediate cultivation, future yield is greater. A time of fallowness increases fertility and is arguably necessary for longevity. With waiting comes reward. The condition of agricultural fallowness, however, is different from that of urban fallowness, because it is planned with a relatively predictable outcome. . . . By contrast, urban fallowness is unplanned and has an unknown future (Desimini, "From Fallow to Wild," 99).

1. STORMWATER

1. The Institute of Environmental Studies is the successor of the Institute for Urban Studies. Former director William L. C. Wheaton was one of the initiators of the research project and a former professor of Ian McHarg's during McHarg's studies at the Harvard University Graduate School of Design. Planning professor David A. Wallace was the project director and worked with Penn professors William G. Grigsby, William H. Roberts, Ann Louise Strong, Anthony R. Tomazinis, and planner Nohad A. Toulan on the project. The United States Department of Housing and Urban Development, the State of New Jersey Department of Community Affairs, and the Commonwealth of Pennsylvania State Planning Board sponsored the study. The study was conducted from 1957 to 1959, but the results were not published until 1970.

2. Steen Eiler Rasmussen, David Crane, and Robert Geddes were directly involved, and W. L. C. Wheaton, Martin Meyerson, Herbert Gans, Jack Dyckman, Chet Rapkin, Charlie Abrams, and others offered support courses.

3. McHarg, "Open Space from Natural Processes," 10–52.

4. The Merion Friends Meeting House is one of the oldest meetinghouses in the United States, dating from the late 1600s, and is included on the National Register of Historic Places.

5. A sign on the trail marks the view. The historical illustration can be seen in Lewis, *Redemption of the Lower Schuylkill,* which is compiled and posted on Levine, "Philly H$_2$O."

6. Anne Whiston Spirn is author of two important texts: *The Granite Garden* (1985) and *The Language of Landscape* (1998); the latter devotes a section to the Mill Creek landscape. She has written

extensively on the intersection of cultural and ecological systems and has taught courses at Harvard University, the University of Pennsylvania, and the Massachusetts Institute of Technology, where she is a full professor. She continues to work on the West Philadelphia Landscape Project, work that began in 1987.

7. Farr, "Mulch, Sinkholes."

8. I explore the different hydrological role in Desimini, "Blue Voids." It is also covered in Albro, Burkholder, and Koonce, "Mind the Gap."

9. "Stormwater" is defined as surface water, from rain events and snow melt, that runs over land into stream, creek, and river channels. It is also collected through storm drains and discharged or held in basins to mitigate overflow.

10. The city of Philadelphia began supplying water to its citizens in 1801.

11. At the same time as Philadelphia was considering and rejecting an expansive aqueduct and reservoir system to draw clean water from afar, Boston and New York were building elaborate systems. The Metropolitan Water District in Boston built the Wachusett Reservoir from 1897 to 1908 and the Quabbin Reservoir from 1930 to 1939, its two main contemporary drinking water supply systems. New York has three systems with nineteen reservoirs, the Croton constructed from 1842 to 1893, the Catskill built from 1905 to 1928, and the Delaware erected from 1927 to 1964. Its colossal tunnel project to create a third connection to these upstate sources is ongoing, a project that commenced in 1970 and is expected to be finished in 2035. For more, see Gandy, "Entropy by Design."

12. It could be said that prohibitive cost lies at the core of Philadelphia's water innovation—that the investment in the landscape was driven by a forced frugality. Both the early proposals for a supply aqueduct and the more contemporary proposals for an $8 billion stormwater storage tunnel were expensive, driving the city government to look for alternative measures.

13. The photograph is part of the historical collection of the Philadelphia Water Department and can be seen at "Mill Creek (Philadelphia)," https://en.wikipedia.org/wiki/Mill_Creek_(Philadelphia); Levine, "Philly H$_2$O"; among other places.

14. The most notable collapse occurred in 1961, when a section of the urban fabric in the 5000 block of Funston Street folded inward, destroying four houses and taking three human lives. The collapse was documented by the *Philadelphia Evening Bulletin* and the Department of Public Works. View images at the *Philadelphia Evening Bulletin,* "Fulton Street Collapse; Philadelphia Water Department, "Mill Creek Sewer Collapse."

15. Holme et al., *Map of the improved part of the Province of Pennsilvania.*

16. Milroy, *Grid and the River,* 56.

17. The Washington publisher and politician assembled what was probably the largest private collection of printed and manuscript sources on American history in the United States. It was purchased by the Library of Congress in 1867.

18. Ian McHarg became an assistant professor of city planning at the University of Pennsylvania in 1954 and reinstated the Department of Landscape Architecture at the school in 1956. Aldo van Eyck was an early invited critic (see chapter 4). By the 1960s, McHarg started inviting visitors whose specialties represented a broad range of intellectual disciplines (Spirn, "Reclaiming Common Ground").

19. McHarg, *Design with Nature,* 20–21.

20. Spirn, "Reclaiming Common Ground," 302.

21. Philadelphia was the first city in the country to provide drinking water to its citizens.

22. Through the Clean Water Act of 1972, the United States Environmental Protection Agency regulates pollutant discharge into open waters. The agency has developed pollutant control methods as well as "national water quality criteria recommendations for pollutants in surface waters."

23. Jim Kenney, who succeeds Michael Nutter as mayor, has proposed major investments to the city's parks and other civic infrastructure including recreational centers and libraries. There remains an emphasis on modest undertakings toward large gains for residents. He is also known for his sugary soda tax.

24. Wallace Roberts & Todd, *GreenPlan Philadelphia,* 11.

25. Philadelphia Water Department, "Green Stormwater Infrastructure Project Map."

26. This is an estimate based on site measurements.

27. In "Sustaining Beauty," landscape theorist Elizabeth Meyer argues that aesthetics are important for sustainability, that for a project to have lasting cultural relevance, it has to be designed to provoke a memorable experience, to create a lasting appreciation of its ecological function. In "From Stormwater Management to Artful Rainwater Design," Stuart Echols and Eliza Pennypacker curate and analyze twenty projects that leverage rainwater to enhance site character, quality, and value.

28. Here, I want to be cognizant of and recognize Anna Lowenhaupt Tsing's important work on nonscalability. The idea behind scale is not to equate the large with the small or to adopt the capitalistic stance that bigger and more is inherently better, but rather to point to a distributed, commonplace, and robust system to collect as much stormwater as possible with the ground onto which it falls. In other words, to treat the ground as thick, absorptive, flexible, and with hybrid social and environmental purpose.

29. There were 318 bus shelters in 2015, with implementation underway to add 280 more to the system. The city has recently rolled out a new design by the local architecture firm Digsau with the media technology firm Intersection. Philadelphia Transit Shelter Project, "New Transit Shelters."

30. Garrison and Hobbs, "Rooftops to Rivers II."

31. Spirn, *Granite Garden,* 168.

32. In a recent discussion triggered by the thirtieth anniversary of *The Granite Garden,* Anne Whiston Spirn lauds the progress made with regard to urban water systems and points to the need to further address social and income inequalities. Green, "Interview with Anne Whiston Spirn."

33. In the United States in 2011, there were 772 municipalities and 40 million people living with combined sewer and stormwater systems (CSSs), contributing 3.2 billion cubic meters of overflow annually from 43,000 combined sewer overflow events (CSOs) (Garrison and Hobbs, "Rooftops to Rivers II").

34. For more on the St. Louis landscape, see chapter 5.

35. I would like to thank Robert Sullivan for first describing this itinerary to me using my itinerary.

36. Spirn, "Identity," 160–63.

37. Finkel, *Philadelphia Almanac and Citizens Manual.*

38. On the site survey forms used to draft the 1937 Residential Security Map, it is interesting that the terrain is classified, even if the distinctions of *level, level to rolling,* and *rolling* (like Mill Creek) are quite coarse.

39. Spirn, "Restoring Mill Creek," 398.

40. See ibid. for a full accounting.

41. "Social housing" (see subsequent chapters) is a general term used to describe affordable housing, managed by multiple entities and designed to provide subsidized rents to tenants. Public housing specifically means that the government owns the property.

42. The Housing Act of 1949 gave cities the means to acquire and clear sections of the city deemed "slums" and offer the land for new development. For more on the program, see Ryan, *Design after Decline;* von Hoffman, "Study in Contradictions"; Zipp, "Roots and Routes."

43. Hara left the Philadelphia Water Department to become general manager/CEO of Seattle Public Utilities, continuing to work in a public realm often devoted to engineers.

44. Retention ponds are wet ponds that hold water continuously, and detention ponds are dry ponds that hold water in large storm events and slowly release it to the ground or another water body.

45. WaterFire, a sculpture by artist Barnaby Evans, is a series of braziers installed on the three rivers in Providence. Bonfires are ignited periodically, mostly through the summer months. The event is used as an urban strategy, underplaying the importance of quality urban design. The river's edge is desolate and ugly during the everyday daytime.

46. The water squares in Rotterdam are designed to combine water storage with public space amenity, creating large open plazas (not inaccessible marshy depressions) that function in both the dominant dry condition and the occasional wet one.

47. Or the rights: to send animals to graze in a pasture, to release domestic pigs to forage in the forest, to fish in unowned waters, to cut turf or peat for fuel, to cut timber, respectively.

48. Garrett Hardin's influential 1968 article in *Science*, "The Tragedy of the Commons," has become synonymous with the mainstream idea that there is a propensity to mismanage commonly held resources.

49. The barriers associated with incorporating vacant parcels—private land ownership, pressures to achieve the highest volume transfer for the least short-term cost, complicated multiagency coordination, less community involvement, and inconspicuousness—have left them largely out of the main planning and construction process to date. Four of the five completed projects were incorporated into larger initiatives—community facilities, community gardens, and parks—and did not actively convert vacant parcels to stormwater sponges.

50. This is the only parcel where the past vacancy was legible, where the stormwater trench and plantings were the sole improvements.

51. The watersheds reflect the surface hydrological systems—the visible water bodies. The buried ones remain unclassified.

52. The swath is now the 1.8-acre Lucien Blackwell Park, a minimally ambitious public landscape, with paths, benches, small tree groves, and a central lawn. It is part of the Philadelphia's Green 2015 Plan to introduce more park space in the city and its neighborhoods. The park implementation also addresses the underground debris from past demolitions, through smooth grading and soil amendments.

53. William Penn defines the "liberties" as the areas outside of the city center, as evidenced on his 1687 map with Thomas Holme. They were envisioned as a place of suburban retreat and figure prominently in Penn's methods of land distribution in the new colony. See Milroy, *Grid and the River*, 53–67.

54. Mural Arts Philadelphia, under the leadership of Jane Golden, has been actively creating art works across the city for over thirty years. The organization works with local groups to complete sixty to one hundred art projects a year. The murals have incredible range, both geographically and topically, covering nearly all neighborhoods and aspects of city life.

55. It should be noted vacant properties are given low priority ratings if they have a small drainage area, poorly suited topography, structures, severe dumping activity, a long distance to a Water Department stormwater inlet, mature trees on site, or potential soil contamination.

56. Philadelphia Water Department, "Green City, Clean Waters."

57. In "Public Works Practice," landscape architect Chris Reed argues that the discipline actively engages broad ecological and social agendas. In recent projects, the way the landscape works, or performs, is a criterion both for the impetus of a project and for its evaluation.

58. For project images and related text, see Kastner, Najafi, and Richard, *Odd Lots*.

59. Nicholas de Monchaux's *Local Code* project is a more recent example that builds on Gordan Matta-Clark's Fake Estates project to imagine alternative futures for residual urban slivers. See de Monchaux. *Local Code.*

60. In addition to Elizabeth Meyer and to Stuart Echols and Eliza Pennypacker, landscape theorist Pierre Bélanger argues that the landscape architecture discipline has ceded too much work to engineering practices. Landscape architects and theorists Anuradha Mathur and Dilip da Cunha recently organized a conference and book project, *Design in the Terrain of Water,* compiling a broad range of hydrologically driven design practices. Sea level rise initiatives including Rebuild by Design and Designing for Climate Change have engaged the design community for research and propositions. And, of course, at PWD, former chief of staff and deputy director Mami Hara is a landscape architect and was, at one time, the second highest-ranking official at the agency. This is rare for a contemporary municipal water authority.

61. These are parameters Elinor Ostrum identifies as necessary for effective governance of the commons.

62. It is interesting to note that one ecological definition of urban is based on the percentage of impervious cover, with greater than 20 percent considered urban.

63. Ostrum, *Governing the Commons.*

2. *GLEISWILDNIS*

1. Lachmund. *Greening Berlin.*

2. Ibid. See below for more on the Species Protection Program.

3. Sukopp did not classify sites as urban wilds, per se, but provided close descriptions of the vegetal characteristics of such landscapes and the relationships between historical event and floral outcome. He and his colleagues understood the city through its vegetal composition, linking species to land use histories and types of urban development. For example, the Oenothera coronifera or evening primrose could be linked to rail lines. Or a region of the city—the loosely built-up area he describes as zone 2—can be described through plant communities—Hordeetum murini, predominately Acer-Ulmus young growth transitioning to an Alno-Padion type of riparian forest.

4. *The City in the City* is a manifesto for the future of Berlin organized during the Cornell University Sommer Akademie of Berlin in 1977. Taking part in the project were O. M. Ungers, Rem Koolhaas, Peter Reimann, Hans Kollhaaf, and Arthur Osaka. The proposal tackles depopulation directly and proposes an urban plan of architectural islands within a landscape matrix. It is pluralistic and nonsingular. It highlights deconstruction and individuality. For more, see Ungers et al., *City in the City.*

5. Ibid., 106.

6. Berlin is only 52.8 percent built-up areas, traffic facilities, and special areas (biotype 12), or alternatively, it is 47.2 percent flowing waters, standing waters, anthropogenic regosol sites and ruderal fields, bogs and marshes, green spaces, herb fringe fields and grassland communities, dwarf shrub heaths, bushes, tree rows and groves, forests, fields, green and open spaces, and special biotopes (biotopes 1–11). With 47.2 percent water and vegetative cover, Berlin is quite blue and green. By comparison, New York is 42% blue and green, including tree, grass, shrub, bare soil, and water coverage (MacFaden, "High-Resolution Tree Canopy Mapping").

7. This builds on a previous text of mine; Desimini, "Deciphering the Urban Wild," 163–70.

8. The meaning of the wild evoked is further articulated in the subsequent paragraphs.

9. *Oxford English Dictionary.*

10. Crutzen, "Anthropocene," 1–5.

11. Sukopp, "City as a Subject," 281–98.

12. Ibid.

13. West Berlin, Great Britain, and the Netherlands have a longer history of recognizing the ruderal wilds, and there is greater understanding of these types of cultural spaces in North America, starting in the 1970s.

14. Clément. "Natural History of Forsaken Places," 40–43.

15. Franck and Stevens, *Loose Space.*

16. Corner, "Terra Fluxus," 21–33.

17. Jorgensen and Tylecote, "Ambivalent Landscapes," 443–62.

18. I am specifically only looking at the combination of urban and wild (and its variants, wilderness, wildness, etc.). For a larger discussion of wildernesses and wastelands in English, see Cronon, "Trouble with Wilderness"; Cronon, *Uncommon Ground;* Di Palma, *Wasteland;* Nash, *Wilderness and the American Mind.*

19. Tanner, *Urban Wilds,* 20.

20. It might be interesting to note here that the protagonist of the 1943 book *A Tree Grows in Brooklyn* by Betty Smith is also an Ailanthus altissima or tree of heaven.

21. Elizabeth Barlow Rogers is the president of the Foundation for Landscape Studies and a tireless advocate for American landscape architecture. She is instrumental in the revitalization of New York City's Central Park, through her work with the Central Park Conservancy and as park administrator. She is author of a well-regarded survey text on landscape design as well as several volumes on Central Park. In her early work cited here, *The Forests and Wetlands of New York City* (Barlow), and her recent book, *Green Metropolis: The Extraordinary Landscapes of New York City* (Rogers), she explores New York's other, and at times more wild, open spaces.

22. Barlow, "Urban Wilds," 118.

23. Ibid, 119.

24. Rhodeside, "Boston Urban Wilds," 10.

25. Ibid.

26. Spirn, *Granite Garden.*

27. Kowarik and Körner, *Wild Urban Woodlands.*

28. Hofmeister, "Natures Running Wild."

29. Kowarik, "Novel Urban Ecosystems"; Marris, "Ragamuffin Earth"; Hobbs et al., "Novel Ecosystems."

30. Here I refer to Cronon's text "The Trouble with Wilderness; or, Getting Back to the Wrong Nature," 69–90.

31. Jorgensen and Keenan, *Urban Wildscapes,* 1.

32. Kowarik and Körner, *Wild Urban Woodlands,* 9.

33. Diemer, Held, and Hofmeister, "Urban Wilderness in Central Europe," 7–11; Hofmeister, "Natures Running Wild," 293–315.

34. Marris, "Ragamuffin Earth," 450–53.

35. Ibid.

36. Clément and Jones, *Une Écologie Humaniste.*

37. Del Tredici, "Spontaneous Urban Vegetation," 299–315; Kühn, "Intentions for the Unintentional," 46–53.

38. Marris, "Ragamuffin Earth," 450–53.

39. Gissen, *Subnature.*

40. Coates, *American Perceptions.*

41. Kühn, "Intentions for the Unintentional," 46–53; Kowarik and Körner, *Wild Urban Woodlands.*

42. Franck and Stevens, *Loose Space.*

43. Brantz, "Natural Space of Modernity."

44. Kattwinkel, Biedermann, and Kleye, "Temporary Conservation for Urban Biodiversity," 2335–43.

45. This observation is based on a conversation with Almut Jirku, director of competitions at the Senate Department for Urban Development, Berlin, September 2015.

46. The Berlin School of Urban Ecology is an ecological movement promoted by Sukopp and supported by the work at the Technisches Universitat Berlin, now under the direction of Ingo Kowarik.

47. A key example of this is the canceled development project at the former Tempelhof airport site. After a public competition to introduce neighborhood development at the site's perimeter with park and wild lands in the center, citizen protest successfully halted the project. Through a referendum in 2014, Berliners voted not to allow the development of the edge. Instead, the entire site is conserved as open lands, left to spontaneous habitat creation and human uses. Tempelhofer Feld, as the park is called, with its long runways and sea of meadow, is open to the public for escape, exploration, and recreation (Tempelhofer Feld, https://gruen-berlin.de/en/tempelhofer-feld).

48. Lachmund, *Greening Berlin*, 221.

49. Dümpelmann, *Flights of Imagination*, 269.

50. *Grünanlage* literally means "green area" and in this case is a type of nature conservation area that forbids soil and habitat disturbance. (Verordnung zum Schutz des geschützten Landschaftsbestandteils Grünanlage Hallesche Straße/Möckernstraße im Bezirk Kreuzberg von Berlin).

51. Lachmund, "Making of an Urban Ecology," 204–28; Lachmund, *Greening Berlin*. The Species Protection Program was ultimately incorporated in the Landscape Programme including Nature Conservation (Landschaftsprogramm) adopted in 1994 as a legally binding strategic planning tool mandating precautionary environmental measures during the development process. Ecological concerns, including ecosystem services, biotope protection, and recreational amenities, are incorporated into development plans.

52. Del Tredici, "Spontaneous Urban Vegetation," 299–315.

53. Cierjacks et al., "Biological Flora of the British Isles," 1623–40.

54. In discussing the outcomes of the work of Herbert Sukopp and other Berlin ecologists and planners, the focus is on Schöneberger Südgelände Nature Park, Park am Gleisdreieck, Park am Nordbahnhof, Landschaftspark Johannisthal/Adlershof, and the ongoing Tempelhofer Feld project (see Lachmund, *Greening Berlin;* Dümpelmann, *Flights of Imagination*).

55. See Heimann, "Naturerfahrungsraum 'Robinienwäldchen.'"

56. Brass bricks known as Stolperstein, or "stumbling stones," can be found just outside of the site, on Möckernstraße. The stones, a project of the artist Guenther Demnig, can be found across Germany, slowly inserted to commemorate victims of the Nazi regime.

57. A Natur-Park is a typology governed by the Federal Nature Conservation Act whereby a landscape is protected through regulated use. The landscape is conserved but opened to limited public use.

58. See figure 33 for the walks within Berlin.

59. Berlin lies in the glacial valley of the Spree River, a major waterway that flows through northeastern Germany. The city formed on the banks of the Spree, and some of the city's most well-known sites still sit on its banks. The Spree is part of a network of constructed and unconstructed navigable waters that weave throughout the city.

60. Lichtenstein and Mameli. *Gleisdreieck,* 101.

61. Ibid., 121; Jirku, interview by Desimini.

62. Lachmund. *Greening Berlin;* Dümpelmann. *Flights of Imagination.*

63. Lachmund. *Greening Berlin*, 26–27; Dümpelmann. *Flights of Imagination,* 270.

64. Lachmund. "Exploring the City of Rubble."

65. Kowarik, "Novel Urban Ecosystems," 1974–83.

66. See chapter 4.

67. Here I refer to the recent planning regarding the wild spaces. However, in general, the idea to connect green spaces (in Berlin and elsewhere) goes back to the mid- to late 1800s, if not before. In other words, many contemporary green corridors are actually located on the grounds that were set aside for this purpose more than a hundred years ago.

68. Dörnbergdrieck is one of these. A site of significant field research near the Lützowplatz and not far from the Tiergarten, the site was cleared for a hotel project after Berlin's reunification. For more on this, see Desimini, "Limitations of the Temporary."

3. HORTAS

1. As we learn more about the role of building industries in accelerating climate change, and see more frequent and deadly disasters, this declaration seems even more prescient.

2. "Prémio Jellicoe para as 'utopias' de Gonçalo Ribeiro Telles."

3. In 1967, António de Oliveira Salazar was at the end of his tenure as Portuguese prime minister, and his Estado Novo authoritarian government suppressed public criticism, despite growing dissent.

4. *Campo Grande* translates to "large field" in English.

5. This is not just the case in Lisbon but is true everywhere.

6. Costa et al., "Assessing the Control," 1133–45.

7. I almost called this the hinterlands—but in reverence to John Dixon Hunt, I resisted and am in search of a complex vocabulary for the notion of the rural or countryside found within the city, a landscape that is different but still related to the urban. It is a place that has either a near continuous lineage of agricultural production or a place where agricultural use has returned after other types of land use.

8. This is covered more in depth in the Chelas case study described later in this chapter.

9. Leal, Ramos, and Pereira. "Different Types of Flooding," 735–58.

10. The city of Lisbon, under a 1904 plan produced by the French-trained engineer Frederico Ressano Garcia, extended the city northward along the Avenidas Novas. Ressano Garcia's approach to city planning focused both on the street as a trajectory of urban growth and as a means to organize civic space. Inspired by the Hausmann boulevards, Ressano Gracia inserted wide vectors into loose fabric, with roundabouts and associated malls, plazas, and parks. The Avenidas strengthened the central valley through the city, while ignoring the eastern and western peripheries.

11. Lisbon's plan for the Rockefeller Foundation's 100 Resilient Cities program identifies shocks and stresses, including flooding, seismic activity and landslides, and poverty, crime, and aging infrastructure.

12. Étienne de Groër was largely influenced by the work of Ebenezer Howard and the Garden City movement. He worked at multiple scales, from the city-region with its peripheral green belt containing urbanization down to the self-contained residential units.

13. The Municipal Division of Green Structure, Environment and Energy within the Green Structure Project Office has since moved elsewhere.

14. *Mata* means "woods," and the names in parentheses are the colloquial names for the parks.

15. This plan is further unpacked later in the chapter.

16. The entire team includes engineer Jose Manuel Mascarenhas, Dr. Filipe Themudo Barata, Dr. Cristina Gomes, Dr. Isabel Dias, Dr. Alexandra Pereira, and numerous landscape architects in training: Ana Clemente, Jorge Neves, Jose Veludo, Madalena Henriques, Victor Diniz, Sandra Felix, and Sofia Pires.

17. Cabral is largely credited with bringing the landscape architecture discipline to Portugal. He started the first course in landscape architecture at the Instituto Superior de Agronomia in Lisbon, and G. Ribeiro Telles was one of Cabral's first students.

18. The Avenida da Liberdade, or Avenue of Liberty, follows the alignment of an eighteenth-century public park, operated as a vector of urban expansion in the late nineteenth century, and is a recognized shopping address in the city. The square has an obelisk in the center, commemorating the Portuguese independence from Spanish rule gained during the Portuguese Restoration War of 1640–68.

19. In my conversation with Lisbon planner João Castro, he elaborated on the complexity of the Alcantara valley and the difficulty of addressing the longstanding abuse of potential landscape function. Castro, interview by Desimini.

20. The Corredor de Alcantara is in the process of being built, and the interventions have substantially improved the pedestrian circulation in this area. The improvements continue incrementally.

21. Lisbon entered a period of international economic bailout in 2011. After serving as the poster child of the European debt crisis, Lisbon's economy is now attracting foreign investment, with lower unemployment and an export economy.

22. The acronym DMEVAE/GPEV points to the complexity of the municipal organization. The staff of the DMEVAE/GPEV highlights bureaucratic divisions as a hindrance to project realization and comprehensive planning.

23. Fundevila, interview by Desimini; Delimbeuf, "Um pouco mais de verde."

24. The word *quinta* comes from the word for "one-fifth" and refers to the amount of produce, one-fifth of the total crop, paid in rent for the right to farm the land. The word now is used more generally to refer to an agricultural estate.

25. It is a 1.5-kilometer drive, given the circuitous, inefficient, and oversized road infrastructure.

26. See figure 38, this chapter.

27. The city of Lisbon is organized into twenty-four civil parishes (reduced from fifty-three in 2012 due to economic restructuring). The parishes are an administrative subdivision performing local public service functions. Consiglieri, *Pelas freguesias de Lisboa.*

28. The original Estádio da Luz was constructed in the 1950s, with the first match played in 1954. It was a monumental stadium that by the 1990s ceased to be viable. It was demolished, and a new stadium was built on the same site for the 2004 UEFA European Championship. The Centro commercial Colombo opened in 1997, with the controversial office towers opening in 2007 and 2011. There are plans to expand the shopping and build a third office tower.

29. Here, I use "peri-urban" to talk about a former edge of the city, where there are stadiums, malls, and large housing estates that you do not typically find in the center of a city due to the sequence of development and the vintage of these types.

30. It is a training and employment center for young people with Asperger's syndrome.

31. The architect João Castro has since left his position, and the political strength of the Municipal Division of Green Structure, Environment and Energy has palpably decreased.

32. João Gomes da Silva is a Lisbon native who is involved in the design and production of landscape in the city. He worked on the *Plano Verde de Lisboa* with Ribeiro Telles and others, was part of the Expo 98 project, and completed a beautiful project for the city's riverine edge along Avenida Ribeira das Naus with landscape architect João Ferreira Nunes.

33. Originally, the irrigation water was to be well fed by a system that tapped deep into the hillside, but the groundwater proved to be contaminated. In subsequent projects, the irrigation water is drawn from the main water supply system through pipes.

34. From 1932 to 1950, only 15,904 affordable housing units were constructed in all of Portugal. These units were single-family homes. The 1959 housing act dramatically increased the volume of units constructed, using a high-rise multi-unit housing typology (Tulumello, "Fear and Urban Planning," 1–20).

35. The GTH conducted a housing conditions survey and, based on the results, declared a housing crisis in Lisbon due to the high number of illegally occupied and overcrowded units. Gabinete Técnico da Habitação da Câmara Municipal de Lisboa (GTH), *Plano de urbanização de Chelas;* Nunes. "Le Gabinete Técnico de Habitação," 83–96.

36. Nunes, "Le Gabinete Técnico de Habitação," 83–96.

37. Heitor, "Olivais e Chelas.

38. By contrast, Olivais Norte was planned and constructed from 1955 to 1964 and Olivais Sul from 1960 to 1967 (Toussaint, D'Almeida, and Alcântara, *Guia de arquitetura de Lisboa*).

39. The democratic revolution of 1974 had unintended consequences for the settlement of Chelas, resulting in a highly segregated community of mostly African immigrants.

40. Here, the "functionalist city movement" refers to an analytical method, emerging from CIAM 4, "The Functional City" Congress, used by architects and planners to promote the functional separation of urban activity.

41. The housing was built from the 1970s through the first decade of the 2000s, with differing architectural styles and quality. The earlier developments, Zona I (1970s) and Zona N2 (late 1970s), have higher incidence of resident satisfaction than the later developments, Zona N1 (1980s), Zona J (1980s–1990s), Zona M (1990s) and Zona L (early 2000s) (Tulumello, "Fear and Urban Planning"). Zona J was once considered the most dangerous neighborhood in Lisbon.

42. Ribeiro Telles, *Plano Verde de Lisboa*.

43. Gabinete Técnico de Habitação da Câmara Municipal de Lisboa (GTH), *Plano de urbanização de Chelas;* Nunes, "Le Gabinete Técnico de Habitação," 83–96.

44. Ribeiro Telles. *Plano Verde de Lisboa,* 161.

45. This attention includes the popular film *Zona J,* directed by Leonel Vieira in 1998. The film is a fictional account of love and racism set in the Chelas neighborhood.

46. Matos and Batista, "Urban Agriculture."

47. Previously, the plot size varied widely, whereas the new plots are of equal dimensions.

48. At the onset of the garden plot allocation, preexisting farmers were involved in the formation of the clusters. Instead of being assigned, the farmers were asked to choose their shed partners.

49. The fee depends on the type of horta: for the horta urbana where production is either recreational or agricultural, the fee is higher than in the horta sociais, where use is restricted to meet the alimentary needs of the participant. The Chelas project is made up entirely of hortas sociais. The annual rent is roughly € 75.00.

50. Materials are limited to wood and cane, and gardeners are forbidden from constructing additional structures, including retaining ponds, within their plots.

51. The commons is admittedly a complex, loaded, and overwrought term, but one that nicely describes something shared and something mundane (Stilgoe, *Common Landscapes of America*). Its definition is tied to land use rights and property as well as spatial and aesthetic characteristics. It describes land with resource value but should not be considered a synonym for open lands. Commons are constructed and contested spaces, governed by rules with limited shared access. The term is used to describe rights of use on public or privately owned lands, on lands held in common ownership, or on unenclosed lands. The commons can also be a public good or a commonly held commodity, but here the term is being used to refer to the physical landscape.

52. Fonseca et al., "New Forms of Migration," 135–52.

53. The farmers' fears are not unfounded but are fueled by numerous past evictions, and the public dislike is likely driven by political bias and racism against the largely immigrant and African farming community.

54. In Portuguese: De todos o retiros e hortas que fiz referência neste artigo, poucos existem e dêstes movimento eé quási nulo; de outros new o local jaá se conhece e muitos apenas conservam as ruínas, a recordar com saüdade o que a tradiçaáo nos legou dum passado que a pouco e pouco se vai apagando (Carmo, "As hortas," 124–25).

55. Again in Portuguese: Por muios e diversos motivos, entre êles o arrasamento de quintas e outras propriedades em vários pontos, para efieto do alargamento da ciadade, perdeu-se uma característica, talvez a mais querida do povo, aquela que era conhecida por esta designação—as hortas (ibid., 117).

4. SPEELPLAATSEN

1. Lefaivre and Tzonis, *Aldo van Eyck,* 17; Lefaivre and Döll-Atelier voor Bouwkunst, *Ground-Up City,* 66–68.

2. The commonly referred-to total is 734. See Strauven, "List of Playgrounds," 132–42. Again, *speel-tuin* is another word for *speelplaats* or playground.

3. These projects are covered in the subsequent paragraphs.

4. Erik Schmitz, "Let our children have a playground. They need it very badly," letters to the Department of Public Works 1947–1958," in Lefaivre, De Roode, et al., *Aldo van Eyck,* 64.

5. We return to these ideas later in this text and in the conclusions.

6. The playgrounds are the subject of several publications by Liane Lefaivre and her collaborators and are included in books on Aldo van Eyck by Francis Strauven and Robert McCarter, among others.

7. For example, Hong Kong built a number of playgrounds associated with its public housing construction projects throughout the 1950s, inspired by the designs in Europe and in the United States. In Jerusalem, designers inserted Amsterdam-style playgrounds in the interstices of postwar housing developments. Again see Lefaivre, De Roode, et al., *Aldo van Eyck;* as well as Solomon, *American Playgrounds;* Kinchin et al., *Century of the Child;* Ledermann, *Creative Playgrounds and Recreation Centers;* and Rouard, *Children's Play Spaces.*

8. Amsterdam has 411 playgrounds within the A10 ring and south of IJ, representing an area of around 20 square miles or 50 square kilometers. By comparison, San Francisco, which is around 50 square miles or 120 square kilometers has 179 playgrounds. Berlin, which is over 340 square miles or 883 square kilometers has an unbelievable 1,850 public playgrounds.

9. U.S. Department of Agriculture, "National Resources Inventory Glossary." Sand, the material, comes in many hues, but sand, the color, is a tan-like shade.

10. At the 2014 Internationale Architectuur Biennale Rotterdam, the exhibition focused on urban metabolism with nine lines of inquiry including air, water, biota, food, energy, waste, humans, cargo, and sand, sediment, and construction materials.

11. Fröbel and Heinemann, *Froebel Letters.*

12. Wiggin and Smith, *Republic of Childhood.*

13. McArthur, "Chicago Playground Movement," 377–78.

14. The Progressive Era, generally considered to be between 1890 and 1920, marks a time of great social reform in the United States. Progressives believed that government was an agent for change and that human ills (poverty, racism, violence) could be addressed through educational, health, and workplace improvements.

15. McArthur, "Chicago Playground Movement," 377–78.

16. End sheet in Grand Army of the Republic Museum and the Chicago Public Library Cultural Center, "A Breath of Fresh Air: Chicago's Neighborhood Parks of the Progressive Era, 1900–1925," exhibit catalog, July 22, 1989, to November 11, 1989 (Chicago: Lake County Press, 1989).

17. J. Frank Foster was the general superintendent of the South Park District and was instrumental in the construction of the exemplary play facilities in his district.

18. "Blight" is commonly defined as decay, neglect, or economic destitute. It is imposed on urban areas as a means of justifying clearance and rebuilding, both with positive intention and, more often, with discriminatory motives. It is a term transferred from plant science, with negative connotations of disease and failure, and by consequence prejudice. As an urban term, it has its origins with the Chicago School and Progressive Era politics. For more, see Brentin Mock, "The Meaning of Blight," *CityLab,* February 14, 2017; Pritchett, "'Public Menace' of Blight," 1–52; Wilson, *Truly Disadvantaged.*

19. McArthur, "Chicago Playground Movement," 379.

20. Park officials included the directors of the individual park districts as well as the members of a special commission designated to investigate the introduction of small parks into the city and its wooded reserves.

21. McArthur, "Chicago Playground Movement," 385.

22. Ibid., 384.

23. Then, after the initial small parks program, play areas became linked to schools rather than housing. The schools were already distributed based on population density, and there was a clear logic to locating play areas with elementary education.

24. For example, the not-for-profit design group Public Workshop in Philadelphia (https://publicworkshop.us/) has been activating spaces with play structures and landscapes, while engaging local youth in the process of designing and making the appurtenances.

25. See below for more on van Eesteren. The playground is a publicly owned space, to be differentiated from a play garden, run by private associations. The playground is limited to static equipment for risk and liability reasons, while the play garden includes kinetic structures, such as swings, merry-go-rounds, and even slides. The play area is also called out separately, as a court for active recreation including basketball, volleyball, and roller-skating. Finally, the play pool is again separate and is rarely implemented due to the prohibitive costs of maintenance and construction. In contemporary examples, many of these types are merged, but the distinctions are important for understanding the design choices. See De Roode, "Play Objects," 93.

26. Another precursor was architect Piet Kramer's sand pits in the Zaanhof, from 1924, which he designed while an employee of the public works department.

27. The text was written in 1933 and published in 1942, as a provocation for post–World War II reconstruction in Europe.

28. Well documented and analyzed here as incremental, interstitial, ludic, participatory, ground up, polycentered systems (Lefaivre, "Space, Place and Play"; Lefaivre, "Ground-Up City").

29. For example, circular patterns broke up the monotony of larger sites (Jacob Thijseplein), whereas triangular paving patterns extended perspectives and visually broadened narrow sites (Dijkstraat and Saffierstraat). The basic rectangular, square, circular, and triangular forms were used on many sites, only to be combined and modified to make more elaborate forms when needed to respond to particular site conditions.

30. McCarter, *Aldo van Eyck.* As mentioned earlier, the initial idea comes from Jakoba Mulder and her work with the city and at BeatrixPark.

31. McCarter, *Aldo van Eyck.*

32. The largest circular sand pit had a diameter of 15 meters (50 feet), compared with 4.5 to 6 meters (16 to 20 feet) in the new housing districts.

33. The Dutch have developed a water square, most notably the Benthemplein in Rotterdam designed by De Urbanisten, which opened in 2013.

34. This makes Amsterdam an anomaly within this book, where the cities are experiencing population decline at the moment of the activation of the abandoned land. However, the strategy of pavement, play, and plaza—constructed with frugality—can conceivably be extrapolated to situations of increasing abandonment.

35. About 2.4 million babies were born in the Netherlands between 1945 and 1955, and the birthrate remained high through 1960 (Statistics Netherlands, "Baby Boomers"). This is particularly high among countries in Europe.

36. Rotterdam and Arnhem were particularly devastated by air raids.

37. Up to 60 percent of postwar housing in the Netherlands was built by the government.

38. Tzonis and Lefaivre, *Architecture in Europe since 1968.*

39. Amsterdam annexed a significant amount of land from nearby villages in 1921, nearly quadrupling the size of the city. The villages of Sloten, Watergraafsmeer, and part of Nieuwer Amstel became part of the city.

40. From 1930 to 1947, Cornelius van Eesteren chaired the Congrès Internationaux d'Architecture Moderne (CIAM), a series of conferences on architecture and urbanism. He organized the fourth CIAM congress on the functional city.

41. Together with fellow members of CIAM, Van Eesteren developed the four tenets of the functional city: dwelling, recreation, work and transportation. These were published in the 1933 Athens Charter.

42. Lefaivre, "Space, Place and Play," 16–57.

43. The decision in the mid-1950s to provide the new housing estates with playgrounds in their inner courtyards led to a burst of construction: 600 of the over 700 playgrounds were built between 1955 and 1970 (Strauven, "List of Playgrounds," 81). Tallies are taken from the list in Lefaivre, De Roode et al., *Aldo van Eyck.* Of the 734 designed, a few were not executed, resulting in a lower total here.

44. This is from a letter quoted in Lefaivre, "Space, Place and Play," 41.

45. Nieuwmarkt was used as a collection point for the Nazis.

46. The somersault frames are 80-, 90-, and 100-centimeter tall tubular steel bars that could be combined in different arrangements to form lines, circles, or bridges). The climbing frames are also made of tubular steel and have vertical forms as well as arches, domes, funnels, globes, and other abstract geometric configurations (De Roode, "Play Objects," 86).

47. Murals are often used to claim and animate fallow lands. When pockets open in the city, exposed party walls provide the perfect canvas for a mural. In Philadelphia, for example, the Mural Arts program creates between sixty and a hundred public art projects each year, including the mural at Liberty Lands described in chapter 1.

48. For an image of this, see Strauven, "Neglected Pearls," 79.

49. For reproductions of the before and after images, see Lefaivre, "Space, Place and Play," 32–33; 56–57. This information is also edited and represented in figure 54.

50. The 1970s in the Nieuwmarkt district were a time of controversy, a moment when inhabitants protested the proposed construction of a highway and metro through the neighborhood—designed to link the modern housing developments of Biljermeer on the city outskirts with the center. On May 11, 1968, the Amsterdam City Council approved the metro plan, which led to the demolition of a great

number of buildings in the old city, creating a linear cut through the Nieuwmarkt neighborhood. In the spring of 1975, local activists rioted in protest, and although the demolition occurred, the highway was never built. The neighborhood groups received some concessions during the metro construction, which did take place. The riots signaled a rupture in the focus of planning on the new districts, and subsequently greater attention was given to the condition of the historic fabric.

51. The Chinese population in the Netherlands is among the largest in Europe, with waves of immigration occurring from the early 1900s to the present.

52. For example, Lefaivre, Boterman, et al., "Psychogeographical Bicycle Tour," calls out tacky additions.

53. Lefaivre, "Space, Place and Play," 41.

54. The East End and Village neighborhoods were considered for clearance but faced local opposition and eventually gained substantial cultural and economic value. The West End was cleared.

55. Urban renewal is a program that arms governments with the tools to claim and demolish property deemed unsuitable for living. The result is a wholesale rebuilding that is often blind to local characteristics and populations. See chapter 5 on St. Louis for more on urban renewal.

56. For example, in Paris, it is well known that Baron Georges-Eugène Haussmann, under Napoléan III, led a large redevelopment scheme, cutting wide boulevards throughout the city. Under the auspices of improving health and sanitation, the plan effectively demolished the existing urban fabric and displaced populations and economic activities. For more on this and recent activities in Amsterdam, see Minkjan, "Haussmann and the Sanitisation of Amsterdam."

57. The Stedelijk Museum mounted an exhibit on the work in 2002, and a van Eyck–type playground is permanently installed on the Museumplein. Key writings over the past two decades include Lefaivre and Tzonis, *Aldo van Eyck;* De Roode, "Play Objects"; Fuchs, 2002; Lefaivre, De Roode, et al., *Aldo van Eyck;* Strauven, "Neglected Pearls"; Solomon, *American Playgrounds;* 2014; Jongeneel, Withagen, and Zaal, "Do Children Create Standardized Playgrounds?"; Lingen, Kollarova, and Geradts, *Aldo van Eyck;* Sporrel, Calijouw, and Withagen, "Children Prefer a Nonstandardized"; Withagen and Caljouw, "Aldo van Eyck's Playgrounds." See the following paragraph for more on the playground surveys, documentation, and tours.

58. Here I reference the conditions in parts of Philadelphia and St. Louis, among other places.

59. Lefaivre, Boterman, et al., "Psychogeographical Bicycle Tour," 129–35.

60. Campanini, "Archis as Guide."

61. Strauven, "Neglected Pearls," 66–84.

62. The land area is a quarter of the size of Chicago and smaller than the 150 largest US cities. It is similar in land size and density to Boston.

63. Eyck, "Child, the City and the Artist," 24.

5. FALLOW LAND

1. See Fullilove and Wallace, "Serial Forced Displacement."

2. Colin Gordon, *Mapping Decline,* 8.

3. St. Louis is an independent city and does not belong to any county.

4. I first explored the idea of the bridge in relation to the St. Louis landscape during the 2016 conference, Voices and Visions of St. Louis: Past, Present, Future, at the Harvard University Graduate School of Design. The concept came from discussions with the urban sociologist Diane Davis.

5. The Cahokian people, who hunted in the riverine forests and cultivated the rich bottomlands, built a sophisticated network of settlements in the region, ultimately leaving 120 dirt mounds. Many

have since been lost to future settlement, but several remain as part of a UNESCO World Heritage Site, National Historic Landmark, and State Historic Site (see Barnett, "Designing Indian Country").

6. I owe this argument to historian Walter Johnson, who has written extensively on the culture and history of slavery in North America, at many times with a particular interest in St. Louis and Missouri. His books include *River of Dark Dreams: Slavery and Imperialism in the Mississippi Valley* (2013) and *The Broken Heart of America* (2020).

7. The border here is the Missouri-Kansas border.

8. *Shelley v. Kraemer,* a 1948 Supreme Court decision that ended restrictive covenants and deeds promoting racial segregation, originated in St. Louis (Wolff, "Saint Louis, Brick City," 121).

9. However, it is interesting to note that St. Louis citizens did not take to the streets during the 1960s race riots. In fact, it was seen then as a place that does not riot. Urban planner Daniel D'Oca recently taught a studio course on St. Louis's Third Ward that he entitled "The New Selma." D'Oca borrows this term from the activist Rev. Clinton Stancil, who states, "St Louis is the new Selma," or as D'Oca paraphrases, "the new center of the ongoing struggle for civil rights and equality" (email to author, October 21, 2018).

10. Race, household income, education level, and health trends all show distinctions between the north and south sides of the city.

11. For more on the Mississippi River from a designer and landscape architecture perspective, see the work of Anuradha Mather and Dilip da Cunha, *Mississippi Floods* (2001), and Derek Hoeferlin on Watershed Architecture,

12. Petrin, "Historic Flood Projections Threaten Tourism."

13. For example, the area around Benton Park has numerous depressions. See the David Rumsey Map Collection (www.davidrumsey.com) for the Compton and Dry atlas and plate 29 for the topography near Benton Park; Missouri Department of Natural Resources, "MO 2018 Sinkholes," dataset, https://msdis.maps.arcgis.com/home/item.html?id=bb7ecb814719469a95151c2db3250397.

14. Mining began in Missouri in the mid-1800s. A 1904 map of quarries in the city of St. Louis shows over thirty active quarries within the city boundaries. The map is in *The Quarrying Industry of Missouri,* by E. R. Buckley, director and state geologist, and H. A. Buehler, Missouri Bureau of Geology and Mines, vol. 2, 2nd series, 1904. For more, the website "Stone Quarries and Beyond" (quarriesandbeyond.org) compiles key historical resources.

15. Several breweries, including the Lemp Brothers, use the caves for refrigeration. The Cherokee Caves, near the Lemp Brewery, were opened for public tours until they were partially filled with the construction of Interstate 55 nearby.

16. Wolff, "Saint Louis, Brick City," 117; Fenneman, *Geology and Mineral Resources,* 49–53.

17. The "fire line" did not include all of the city limits until after 1897, but it did reduce combustion in densely settled areas. According to Wolff: "The fire produced a law that changed the landscape's meaning again: a new city code said that buildings within the 'fire line' had to be made from masonry. Resource values shifted. The clay soils that lay beneath the ground were suddenly worth more than the trees that grew above the surface. Wealth had been created by the port and destroyed by the fire. Now it would come from clay mines and brick factories. History had intersected with geology: a moment in time created the demand for a material formed three hundred million years earlier" (Wolff, "Saint Louis, Brick City," 116).

18. This includes the sewer infrastructure. Some of the lateral pipes date to the nineteenth century and are made of sections of one- to two-foot long terracotta clay pipes linked together (Nafziger, "Closer Look at Sinkholes").

19. Anne Whiston Spirn describes this process in Boston and Philadelphia in her book *The Language of Landscape,* and Kofi Boone talks about it in his work on racialized topographies (Boone and Pasalar, "Racialized Topography"), which in turn references Jeff Ueland and Barney Warf's paper ("Racialized Topographies").

20. Henry Shaw, first as a visitor and later as a resident, fell in love with this place. He arrived from England to a land of marshy ground, sinkholes, and Indian burial mounds and managed to find himself with a distant perspective on the landscape, as a man from a very different terrain who, as legend has it, found an elevated plateau to overlook the prairie and never turned away. Shaw was a philanthropist for the city—and worked carefully to establish two of the city's great landscapes—but it must be noted that he hired slave labor and that, by ensuring the lasting greatness of his own institutions, he created insular resource-rich places whose influence rarely extended to the larger community. The models may work locally but they are not replicable or inclusive.

21. I have written about the spontaneous forest on the site of the notorious Captain Wendell O. Pruitt Homes and the William L. Igoe Apartments (Desimini, "To Multiply or Subdivide"). The contested site remained in limbo for forty years, long enough to grow into a substantial wild urban woodland. To add a chapter to the story, since my initial writing, much of the site has been cleared and graded again to make way for the National Geospatial Agency's West Campus (NGA West), once again a large federal investment—in acreage and dollars—on St. Louis's near north side. To experience the jarring transformation, see figure 64 for a photograph of the woodlands from above in 2011, figure 66 for the evolution of the site and Google Earth's historical imagery slider for the more recent growth and clearing. The Pruitt Igoe site is just southeast of the intersection of Cass Avenue and Jefferson Avenue, while the main NGA West site is to the northeast. You cannot miss them.

22. Its museum covers the historical highlights, including the Dred Scott case (Gateway Arch National Park, https://www.nps.gov/jeff/index.htm).

23. The park is on nearly the exact same site as the 1849 fire. For more on New Deal funding, see Mark Tranel, "Introduction: From Dreams to Reality: The Arch as a Metaphor for St. Louis Plans," in Tranel, *St. Louis Plans,* 1–16.

24. It was not completed until 1965.

25. Kiley's office also worked on the Mill Creek Housing project in Philadelphia; again see chapter 1.

26. Landscape Architecture Legacy of Dan Kiley, "Jefferson National Expansion Memorial."

27. Later highway development around the JNEM site cut off connections to the city and the river.

28. Some funding was raised through a sales tax increase to improve parks, trails, and the Gateway Arch grounds. The bill passed in April 2013.

29. Abbott, "Document That Changed America," 17–53; Heathcott, "Whole City Is Our Laboratory," 322–55. Missouri was the first state to receive federal highway funds for what was to become part of Interstate 44 in Laclede County, about 150 miles (or 240 kilometers) west of St. Louis.

30. See chapter 4 on Amsterdam and Chicago for more on Progressive Era planning. The St. Louis Civic League was formed in 1901 by Louis Marion McCall as the St. Louis Improvement Association. The group took interest in the 1904 Louisiana Purchase Exposition, an impressive world's fair that marked the centennial of the Louisiana purchase. The fair took place in present-day Forest Park on grounds designed by the landscape architect George Kessler; see subsequent note.

31. George Kessler (1862–1923) trained in Germany in forestry, botany, and design and then brought this knowledge to his practice designing boulevards and park systems for various southern and midwestern cities including St. Louis, Kansas City, and Cincinnati. He opened an office in St. Louis and is known for his work designing the fairgrounds for the 1904 Louisiana Purchase Exposition (see above). Henry Wright (1878–1936) worked with George Kessler in St. Louis and then, in 1923, moved to New

York to join Clarence Stein's office. Together, Stein (1882–1975) and Wright planned the new garden cities of Sunnyside, Queens, and Radburn, New Jersey. Here Wright applied his interests in the way physical space can (and more often cannot) inform social behavior (Cultural Landscape Foundation, "Henry Wright").

32. Only New York, Chicago, and Philadelphia are larger (U.S. Bureau of the Census).

33. Again see Abbott, "Document That Changed America," for more on the 1907 plan. The conclusions here are pulled from Abbott's clear analysis of the document.

34. On Bartholomew's career trajectory and on engineering's dominance, see Bartholomew, *Zoning for St. Louis.*

35. Bartholomew was listed as an engineer, and the staff team included a secretary, an architect, an architectural designer, a planning analyst, two draftspersons, an aide, and a stenographer. The City Plan Commission was chaired by E. J. Russell and had eight citizen members and five public official ex officio members (Abbott, "1947 *Comprehensive City Plan,*" 111. See St. Louis City Plan Commission, *Comprehensive City Plan.*

36. The city and the county remain staunchly separate, a fact many scholars argue contributes to the city's economic and social struggles.

37. Abbott, "1947 *Comprehensive City Plan,*" 109–49. See also Lovelace, *Harland Bartholomew.*

38. Bartholomew also famously included over thirty airports on plate 27, imagining an evolution of air travel to require different airports for different needs: three major airports, a feeder airport for overflow, fifteen fields for freight, thirteen private fields, and three airports for helicopters.

39. These are areas called "blighted" in other plans and planning verbiage.

40. Please refer to the discussion of blight in chapter 4 on playgrounds, note 18.

41. In 1946, Missouri Chapter 353 allowed the government to take blighted and obsolete land. Title I of the 1949 Housing Act authorized the housing and home finance administrator to make loans and grants to local public agencies for slum clearance and urban redevelopment (Hill, "Recent Slum Clearance," 173). For more on these and other polices that led to the city's decline, see Colin Gordon, *Mapping Decline.*

42. See Colin Gordon, "St. Louis Blues," for more on the political, legal, and spatial history of urban renewal in St. Louis.

43. Missouri is one of the first states to adopt blight legislation (Hill, "Recent Slum Clearance," 187–88). Missouri's Chapter 353 urban redevelopment law was enacted in 1945, and the state's Chapter 99 land clearance law passed in 1951.

44. St. Louis Development Program, "Technical Report," 6.

45. Once the law was amended to include commercial and industrial property, Mill Creek Valley met federal funding qualifications.

46. St. Louis Development Program, "Technical Report," 10.

47. In 1916, St. Louis passed a measure to restrict housing occupation, stating that blacks could not reside in areas that were 75 percent white, and vice versa. It was mutual exclusion. The law was overturned in 1917, but not without lasting damage (Colin Gordon, *Mapping Decline,* 69–71). A "restrictive covenant" is a contractual agreement between property owners in a given area prohibiting the sale of property to African Americans and other minorities. The agreements usually last twenty years. The covenants were deemed illegal in 1948, with the Supreme Court ruling in *Shelley v. Kraemer,* a case that originated in St. Louis (Gordon, *Mapping Decline,* 71–83; Wolff, "St. Louis, Brick City," 121). "Redlining" is extremely complex but refers to a process whereby federal agencies (the FHA and the HOLC) assign lending risk, prohibiting prospective homebuyers in certain areas from qualifying for necessary insurance and mortgages. Effectively, the policies devalue areas deemed substandard, including all areas

with significant black populations (K. T. Jackson, *Crabgrass Frontier;* Colin Gordon, *Mapping Decline;* Hillier, "Historical Redlining in Philadelphia"; Rothstein, *Color of Law*).

48. The LRA was founded in 1971 and claims to be the nation's first land bank, though critics point out that it is not a model of best practice. Krewson, "Plan to Reduce Vacant Lots."

49. The Team Four plan was a planning memo issued as part of the 1973 master planning process, where a local consultation proposed an urban triage, with "conservation" for areas attracting development, "redevelopment" for areas beginning to lose market value, and "depletion" for areas already with severe disinvestment. The areas for "depletion" were on the city's black north side. The plan received public outrage for its racist implications. The planners did not map the racial distribution of the city or address the correlation between physical condition, race, and socioeconomic indicators. See Cooper-McCann, "Trap of Triage," 149–69.

50. The large team of planners, engineers, artists, and other consultants incudes Lamar Johnson Collaborative, urbanAC, HR&A, Alta, Marlon Blackwell Architects, Civic Creatives, Heart Ache + Paint, Justice + Joy, David Mason and Associates, Lochmueller, Tillett Lighting Design Associates, DJM Ecological, and Bruce Mau Design.

51. The Bissell Point Watershed covers over half of the city, including all of north St. Louis. See figure 64.

52. The Chess International Hall of Fame is in St. Louis.

53. The Model Cities Program is part of President Lyndon B. Johnson's war on poverty legislation. Funding shifts with the change of political administrations.

54. Grace Hill Settlement House, affiliated with the Episcopal diocese, was founded in 1903 to provide community services for new immigrants.

55. The housing rehabilitation work is done in conjunction with the local nonprofit housing development organization RISE (formerly the Regional Housing and Community Development Alliance). The housing work began with projects along North Market Street and continues with the work at Crown Square.

56. UrbArts, "About UrbArts."

57. Political cycles are short, but the victory of Cori Bush in the 2020 election signals a changing tide. Bush represents the first congressional district in Missouri, which includes all of the city of St. Louis and part of the county. She is the first Black woman and first nurse to represent Missouri; the first woman to represent her district; and one of the first activists from the movement fighting for Black lives elected to the United States Congress. She spent four hundred days protesting the death of Michael Brown.

CONCLUSION

1. "Management" connotes process, the word's roots being in the act of training, by hand, from the Latin *manus.* Originally this meant the training of horses but also referred to gaining control, as in war. In the context of managing a common landscape, the word is separate from its linkages to private capital and power. Instead managed commons are realigned with the gradual human process of shaping, directing, and intervening in wild and conflicting circumstances. The strategies commonly employed to deal with abandoned lands—maintenance and conservation—both imply an arresting of time, an imposition of what I argue is an unnatural and unrealistic stasis. With guidelines and variable interjections, management is capable of embracing dynamic process.

2. As a biproduct of this research, I created a collection of ideas and potential transformations, illustrated in a range of potential contexts. I am constantly inspired by the ingenuity of citizens to invent and imagine, and *From Fallow* is an homage to these careful practices.

3. See Tuck, "Suspending Damage."

4. See note 51 on the commons in chapter 3.

5. Sometimes the projects occupy private sites, funded by a mix of private, public, and institutional funding. This is especially the case in the United States, where property tax structure incentivizes private ownership and where the truly public project is something of the past. As urban theorist and architect Charles Waldheim explains in an interview in *ArchitectureBoston* magazine, "in North America, we've generally lost faith in the ability of public institutions to deliver public space. Increasingly, we rely on private development—in the form of both the philanthropic donor culture and private real-estate development—to deliver not only private space but also the public realm" ("Groundswell," 40).

6. "Loose space" is the free, breathing room of the city, where resourceful and uncanny happenings such as ruderal vegetation experiments and farming blossom. For more on the concept, see Franck and Stevens, *Loose Space*.

7. Foster and Iaione, quoted in "The Co-City Methodology," LabGov Georgetown, Georgetown University, McCourt School of Public Policy, https://labgov.georgetown.edu/co-city_methodology/#. For the full article, see Foster and Iaione, "City as a Commons."

8. Jonkman and Janssen-Jansen, "Identifying Distributive Injustice," 353–77.

9. The quotes are taken from the Old North St. Louis Restoration Group, "About," https://www.onsl.org/about.

10. Here, I refer to the work of Design as Protest and Dark Matter University, as well as the writings, podcasts, and speaking engagements of De Nichols, Stephen Gray, Bryan Lee, Mabel O. Wilson, Charles Davis Jr., and others.

11. This is a different kind of "incomplete" than large projects that fail to be implemented due to lack of sustained political and economic support. Here the projects are incremental, small, and complete individually, but the strategy is incomplete and partial, allowing room for growth, evaluation, and multiplicity.

12. To be clear, the idea is to have a cohesive response and set of projects that can work together as a network as evidenced by the municipal efforts described in each of the previous chapters. As previously mentioned, the scale of the issue requires aggregation—rather than twenty thousand projects for twenty thousand abandoned parcels. Rather than many projects, the larger projects are diversified and multidimensional. Further, they are planned, designed, and executed by people representing many disciplines, rather than by few individuals with limited interests, training, and expertise.

BIBLIOGRAPHY

AAIC Conference. Hotel Divani, Athens, Greece, 16 September 2014.

Abbott, Mark. "A Document That Changed America: The 1907 *A City Plan for St. Louis.*" In Tranel, *St. Louis Plans,* 17–53.

———. "The 1947 *Comprehensive City Plan* and Harland Bartholomew's St. Louis." In Tranel, *St. Louis Plans,* 109–49.

Akers, Joshua, and Eric Seymour. "Instrumental Exploitation: Predatory Property Relations at City's End." *Geoforum* 91 (2018): 127–40.

Albro, Sandra L., Sean Burkholder, and Joseph Koonce. "Mind the Gap: Tools for a Parcel-Based Storm Water Management Approach." *Landscape Research* 42, no. 7 (2017): 747–60.

Alexander, Frank S. "Land Bank Strategies for Renewing Urban Land." *Journal of Affordable Housing & Community Development Law* 14, no. 2 (2015): 140–69.

Algemeen Uitbreidingsplan Van Amsterdam. Amsterdam, 1934.

Allen, Michael R. "Downtown St. Louis Is Rising; Black St. Louis Is Being Razed." *Citylab,* August 19, 2019. https://www.citylab.com/perspective/2019/08/square-expansion-st-louis-demolition-blight -vacant-dorsey/596299/.

Amaral, Francisco Pires Keil do, José Antunes da Silva, Raúl Hestnes Ferreira, Ana Isabel Ribeiro, and José Santa-Bárbara. *Keil Amaral: Arquitecto, 1910–1975.* Lisbon: Associação Dos Arquitectos Portugueses, 1992.

American Society of Civil Engineers. *2013 Report Card for America's Infrastructure, 2013.* Infrastructure Report Card. http://www.infrastructurereportcard.org/.

American Society of Landscape Architects, Professional Awards 2011. "GreenPlan Philadelphia." http://www.asla.org/2011awards/610.html.

Arnold Arboretum of Harvard University. "About Us: Our History." https://arboretum.harvard.edu /about/our-history/.

Asakura Robinson. "St. Louis Land Bank Assessment." September 2016. https://asakurarobinson.com /projects/st-louis-land-bank-assessment/.

"Assignment Detroit: Why Time Inc. Is in Motown." *Time,* 2009. http://content.time.com/time /magazine/article/0,9171,1926008,00.html.

Balmori, Diana, and Gaboury Benoit. *Land and Natural Development (LAND) Code: Guidelines for Sustainable Land Development.* Hoboken, N.J.: John Wiley, 2007.

Baptista, Idalina. "How Portugal Became an 'Unplanned Country': A Critique of Scholarship on Portuguese Urban Development and Planning." *International Journal of Urban and Regional Research* 36, no. 5 (2012): 1076–92.

Baptista, Luís, and Teresa Rodrigues. "Population and Urban Density: Lisbon in the 19th and 20th Centuries." In *Urban Dominance and Labour Market Differentiation of a European Capital City,* edited by P. T. Pereira and M. E. Mata. Dordrecht: Springer, 1996.

Barlow, Elizabeth. *The Forests and Wetlands of New York City.* New York: Little, Brown, 1969.

———. "Urban Wilds." In *Urban Open Spaces,* edited by Lisa Taylor. New York: Cooper-Hewitt Museum, 1979.

Barnett, Rod. "Designing Indian Country." *Places Journal,* October 2016.

Bartholomew, Harland. *Zoning for St. Louis: A Fundamental Part of the City Plan.* St. Louis: Nixon-Jones Printing, 1918.

Baybeck, Brady, and E. Terrence Jones. *St. Louis Metromorphosis: Past Trends and Future Directions.* St. Louis: University of Missouri Press, 2004.

Beauregard, Robert A. "Urban Population Loss in Historical Perspective: United States, 1820–2000." *Environment & Planning A* 41, no. 3 (2009): 514–28.

———. *Voices of Decline: The Postwar Fate of U.S. Cities.* New York: Routledge, 2003.

Bélanger, Pierre. *Landscape as Infrastructure: A Base Primer.* Abingdon, Oxon, UK: Routledge, 2017.

———. "Regionalisation: Probing the Urban Landscape of the Great Lakes Region." *Journal of Landscape Architecture* 5, no. 2 (2010): 6–23.

Benton, Gregor, and Frank N. Pieke. *The Chinese in Europe.* Houndmills, Basinstoke, UK: St. Martin's Press, 1998.

Berger, Alan. *Drosscape: Wasting Land in Urban America.* New York: Princeton Architectural Press, 2006.

Bernardo, João Manuel, and Isabel Lopes Cardoso. "O campo na cidade: As hortas e os hortelões de Lisboa." In *Paisagem e património: Aproximações pluridisciplinares,* edited by Isabel Lopes Cardoso, 195–219. Porto, Portugal: Dafne Editora, 2013.

Blanco, Hilda, Marina Alberti, Robert Olshansky, Stephanie Chang, Stephen M. Wheeler, John Randolph, James B. London, et al. "Shaken, Shrinking, Hot, Impoverished and Informal: Emerging Research Agendas in Planning." *Progress in Planning* 72, no. 4 (2009): 195–250.

Boone, Kofi, and Celen Pasalar. "Racialized Topography as a Generative Design Tool." Unpublished paper, CELA Conference, 2010.

Bowman, Ann O'M, and Michael A. Pagano. *Terra Incognita: Vacant Land and Urban Strategies.* Washington, D.C.: Georgetown University Press, 2004.

Bowring, Jacky. *A Field Guide to Melancholy.* Harpenden, UK: Oldcastle, 2008.

Brantz, Dorothee. "The Natural Space of Modernity: A Transatlantic Perspective on (Urban) Environmental History." In *Historians and Nature: Comparative Approaches to Environmental History,* edited by Ursula Lehmkuhl and Hermann Wellenreuther. New York: Berg, 2007.

Brash, Alexander, Jamie Hand, and Kate Orff. *Gateway: Visions for an Urban National Park.* New York: Princeton Architectural Press, 2011.

Brenner, Neil, and Christian Schmid. "Towards a New Epistemology of the Urban?" *City* 19, no. 2–3 (2015): 151–82.

Bronner, Edwin B. *William Penn's "holy experiment": The Founding of Pennsylvania, 1681–1701.* Westport, Conn.: Greenwood Press, 1978.

Bronner, Edwin B., David Fraser, and Edwin Blaine Dunn. *The Papers of William Penn.* Vol. 5, *William Penn's Published Writings, 1660–1726: An Interpretive Bibliography.* Philadelphia: University of Pennsylvania Press, 1986.

Burkholder, Sean. "The New Ecology of Vacancy: Rethinking Land Use in Shrinking Cities." *Sustainability* 4, no. 6 (2012): 1154–72.

Burns, Matthew J., Tim D. Fletcher, Christopher J. Walsh, Anthony R. Ladson, and Belinda E. Hatt. "Hydrologic Shortcomings of Conventional Urban Stormwater Management and Opportunities for Reform." *Landscape and Urban Planning* 105, no. 3 (2012): 230–40.

Cabannes, Yves, and Isabel Raposo. "Peri-urban Agriculture, Social Inclusion of Migrant Population and Right to the City." *City* 17, no. 2 (2013): 235–50.

Caeiro, Baltazar Mexia de Matos. *Os conventos de Lisboa.* Sacavém, Portugal: Distri Editora, 1989.

Cairns, J., Jr., and S. E. Palmer. "Restoration of Urban Waterways and Vacant Areas: The First Steps toward Sustainability." *Environmental Health Perspectives* 103, no. 5 (1995): 452–53.

Câmara Municipal de Lisboa. *Parque Hortícola da Quinta da Granja: Regras de acesso e utilização das hortas urbanas.* Lisbon: Câmara Municipal de Lisboa, n.d.

———. *Parque Hortícola do Vale de Chelas: Regras de acesso e utilização das hortas urbanas.* Lisbon: Câmara Municipal de Lisboa, n.d.

———. *Plan of Parque Hortícola do Vale de Chelas.* Lisbon: Câmara Municipal de Lisboa, n.d.

Campanini, Juan. "Archis as Guide: Aldo van Eyck Playground Tour 2009 1 1 5 5." https://www.academia.edu/15615940/ARCHIS_AS_GUIDE_Aldo_van_Eyck_Playground_Tour_2009_1_1_5_5.

Canada, Department of Agriculture, Research Branch. "Glossary of Terms in Soil Science." Ottawa: Department of Agriculture, 1976.

Cancela, Jorge Manuel Frazão. *A Agricultura Urbana na Operacionalização da Estrutura Ecológica Municipal: O Estudo de Caso do Parque Agrícola da Alta de Lisboa.* Lisbon: Universidade de Lisboa, April 2014.

Carita, Helder. "Une Influence islamique durable: Les palais et "quintas" des environs de Lisbonne." *Monuments Historiques* 194 (1994): 46.

Carmo, José Pedro do. "As hortas." In *Evocações do passado: O fado, touradas, tipos populares das ruas, bailes campestres, o carnaval, as hortas, as feiras e teatros,* 115–38. Lisbon: Empresa Nacional de Publicidade, 1943: 115–38.

Carter, R. W. "Magnitude and Frequency of Floods in Suburban Areas." *U.S. Geological Survey Paper* 424-B, B9-B11. Washington, D.C.: Government Printing Office, 1961.

Castro, João. Interview by Jill Desimini. September 10, 2015.

Cierjacks, Arne, Ingo Kowarik, Jasmin Joshi, Stefan Hempel, Michael Ristow, Moritz Lippe, and Ewald Weber. "Biological Flora of the British Isles: Robinia Pseudoacacia." *Journal of Ecology* 101, no. 6 (2013): 1623–40.

City of St. Louis. *Redevelopment Plan for Mill Creek Valley, Land Clearance for Redevelopment Authority of the City of St. Louis.* St. Louis: City of St. Louis, February 1958; revised August 1960.

Civic League of Saint Louis. *A City Plan for St. Louis; Reports of the Several Committees.* Saint Louis: Civic League of Saint Louis, 1907.

Clement, Daniel, Miguel Kanai, and Richard Grant. "The Detroit Future City: How Pervasive Neoliberal Urbanism Exacerbates Racialized Spatial Injustice." *American Behavioral Scientist* 59, no. 3 (2015): 369–85.

Clément, Gilles. "The Natural History of Forsaken Places." Translated by Adam Christian. *Harvard Design Magazine* 31 (2009): 40–43.

———. "The Third Landscape." 2003. http://www.gillesclement.com/art-454-tit-The-Third -Landscape.

Clément, Gilles, and Louisa Jones. *Une Écologie Humaniste.* Genève: Aubanel, 2006.

Coates, Peter A. *American Perceptions of Immigrant and Invasive Species: Strangers on the Land.* Berkeley: University of California Press, 2006.

Consiglieri, Carlos. *Pelas freguesias de Lisboa: O termo de Lisboa (Benfica, Carnide, Lumiar, Ameixoeira, Charneca).* Lisbon: Câmara Municipal de Lisboa, Pelouro da Educação, 1993.

Cooper-McCann, Patrick. "The Trap of Triage: Lessons from the 'Team Four Plan.'" *Journal of Planning History* 15, no. 2 (2016): 149–69.

Corbin, Carla I. "Vacancy and the Landscape: Cultural Context and Design Response." *Landscape Journal* 22, no. 1 (2003): 12–24.

Corner, James. "Terra Fluxus." In *The Landscape Urbanism Reader,* edited by Charles Waldheim, 21–33. New York: Princeton Architectural Press, 2006.

Costa, C., A. P. Reis, E. Ferreira da Silva, F. Rocha, C. Patinha, A. C. Dias, C. Sequeira, et al. "Assessing the Control Exerted by Soil Mineralogy in the Fixation of Potentially Harmful Elements in the Urban Soils of Lisbon, Portugal." *Environmental Earth Sciences* 65, no. 4 (2012): 1133–45.

"The Countryside I: Ruralism." Events, Harvard Graduate School of Design, September 21, 2015. https://www.gsd.harvard.edu/event/the-countryside-i-ruralism/.

Craig, Gordon A. "Berlin, the Hauptstadt: Back Where It Belongs." *Foreign Affairs* 77, no. 4 (July–August 1998): 161–70.

Criss, Robert E., Everett M. Criss, and G. R. Osburn. "Caves of St. Louis, Missouri." *Missouri Speleology Journal of the Missouri Speleological Survey* 45, no. 1 (2005): 1–17.

Cronon, William. "The Trouble with Wilderness; or, Getting Back to the Wrong Nature." In *Uncommon Ground: Toward Reinventing Nature,* edited by William Cronon. New York: W. W. Norton, 1995.

———. *Uncommon Ground: Toward Reinventing Nature.* New York: W. W. Norton, 1995.

Crutzen, Paul. "The 'Anthropocene.'" *Journal de Physique IV* 12, no. 10 (2002): 1–5.

The Cultural Landscape Foundation. "Henry Wright, 1878–1936." https://tclf.org/pioneer/henry -wright.

Cupers, Kenny, Markus Miessen, and Wendy James. *Spaces of Uncertainty.* Wuppertal, Germany: Müller und Busmann, 2002.

Curtis, Henry S. *The Play Movement and Its Significance.* Home and School Series, ed. by P. Monroe. New York: Macmillan, 1917.

Czerniak, Julia, ed. *Formerly Urban: Projecting Rust Belt Futures.* Syracuse: Syracuse University School of Architecture and Princeton Architectural Press, 2013.

Dark Matter University. https://darkmatteruniversity.org/.

Daskalakis, Georgia, Charles Waldheim, and Jason Young, eds. *Stalking Detroit.* Barcelona: Actar, 2001.

Davis, John E., ed. *The Community Land Trust Reader.* Cambridge, MA: Lincoln Institute of Land Policy, 2010.

Davis, Ujijji. "The Bottom: The Emergence and Erasure of Black American Urban Landscapes." *Avery Review* 34 (2018).

DeFilippis, James. *Unmaking Goliath: Community Control in the Face of Global Capital.* New York: Routledge, 2004.

Delgado, Cecilia. "Answer to the Portuguese Crisis: Turning Vacant Land into Urban Agriculture." *Cities and the Environment (CATE)* 8, no. 2, article 5 (2015). https://digitalcommons.lmu.edu/cate /vol8/iss2/5/.

Delimbeuf, Katya. "Um pouco mais de verde e era campo." June 13, 2008. http://katyadelimbeuf.com
/unica/hortas/Hortas.htm.

DeLoach, Ryan, and Jenn DeRose. "Urban Renewal and Mill Creek Valley." *Decoding the City.* http://
www.decodingstl.org/urban-renewal-and-mill-creek-valley/.

Del Tredici, Peter. "Spontaneous Urban Vegetation: Reflections of Change in a Globalized World."
Nature and Culture 5, no. 3 (2010): 299–315.

de Monchaux, Nicholas. *Local Code: 3,659 Proposals about Data, Design & the Nature of Cities.* New
York: Princeton Architectural Press, 2016.

Dennis Haugh Studio. https://www.dennishaugh.com/about-1.

Denton, Jill, and Senatsverwaltung für Stadtentwicklung (Berlin, Germany). *Urban Pioneers: Berlin
Stadtentwicklung Durch Zwischennutzung / Temporary Use and Urban Development in Berlin.* Berlin: Jovis, 2007.

Deriu, Davide, Krystallia Kamvasinou, and Eugenie Shinkle. *Emerging Landscapes: Between Production
and Representation.* New ed. Farnham, Surrey, UK: Ashgate, 2014.

de Roode, Ingeborg. "The Play Objects: More Durable than Snow." In Lefaivre, De Roode, et al., *Aldo
van Eyck.*

Design as Protest. "Anti-Racist Designers Dedicated to Design Justice in the Built Environment."
https://www.dapcollective.com/.

Desimini, Jill. "Blue Voids: Stormwater Strategies for Abandoned Lands." *Journal of Landscape Architecture* 8, no. 2, 64–73.

———. "Deciphering the Urban Wild: Remnant and Reemergent." In *Urban Landscape: Critical Concepts in Built Environment,* edited by Anita Berrizbeitia, 163–70. London: Routledge, 2015.

———. *From Fallow: 100 Ideas for Abandoned Urban Landscapes.* Novato, CA: ORO Editions, Spring
2019.

———. "From Fallow to Wild." In *New Geographies 10: Fallow,* edited by Michael Chieffalo and Julia
Smachylo, 99–103. Barcelona: ACTAR, 2019.

———. "Limitations of the Temporary: Landscape and Abandonment." In "Reinventing the American Postindustrial City," edited by Pamela Karimi and Thomas Stubblefield, special issue, *Journal of
Urban History* 41, no. 2 (2015): 279–93.

———. "The Power of the Incremental: Agronomic Investment in Lisbon's Chelas Valley." In *Landscape and Agency: Critical Essays,* edited by Ed Wall and Tim Waterman, 131–42. London: Routledge, 2017.

———. "To Multiply or Subdivide: Futures of a Modern Urban Woodland." "Building the Urban
Forest." Special issue of *Scenario Journal* 04 (Spring 2014). https://scenariojournal.com/article/to
-multiply-or-subdivide/.

Dewar, Margaret E., and June Manning Thomas. *The City after Abandonment.* Philadelphia: University
of Pennsylvania Press, 2013.

Dias, Marina Tavares. *Lisboa = Lisbon Past and Present = Lisboa historia y presente = Lissabon gestern
und heute.* Lisbon: Quimera Editores, 1998.

———. *Photographias de Lisboa, 1900.* Lisbon: Quimera Editores, 1989.

Diemer, Matthias, Martin Held, and Sabine Hofmeister. "Urban Wilderness in Central Europe." *International Journal of Wilderness* 9, no. 3 (2003): 7–11.

Diener, Roger, Jacques Herzog, and ETH Studio Basel, eds. *The Inevitable Specificity of Cities: Napoli,
Nile Valley, Belgrade, Nairobi, Hong Kong, Canary Islands, Beirut, Casablanca.* Zürich: Lars Müller,
2015.

Dimitri, Carolyn, Lydia Oberholtzer, and Andy Pressman. "The Promises of Farming in the City:

Introduction to the Urban Agriculture Themed Issue." *Renewable Agriculture and Food Systems* 30, no. 1 (2015): 1–2.

Di Palma, Vittoria. *Wasteland: A History.* New Haven, Conn.: Yale University Press, 2014.

Dougill, Wesley. "Amsterdam: General Extension Plan." *Town Planning Review* 17 (1936): 1–10.

Drake, Luke, and Laura Lawson. "Validating Verdancy or Vacancy? The Relationship of Community Gardens and Vacant Lands in the U.S." *Cities* 40, no. B (2014): 133–42.

Duffner, Fay, and Peter Wathern. "Building an Urban Wilderness." *Environment: Science and Policy for Sustainable Development* 30, no. 2 (1988): 12–34.

Dümpelmann, Sonja. "Aeroporti come prati comuni." In *Prati urbani: I prati collettivi nel paesaggio della città = City Meadows: Community Fields in Urban Landscapes,* edited by Franco Panzini. Treviso, Italy: Fondazione Benetton Studi Ricerche-Antiga, 2018. https://www.fbsr.it/en/publication/prati-urbani-city-meadows/.

———. *Flights of Imagination: Aviation, Landscape, Design.* Charlottesville: University of Virginia Press, 2014.

Dunnett, Nigel, and James Hitchmough. *The Dynamic Landscape: Design, Ecology and Management of Naturalistic Urban Planting.* London: Taylor & Francis, 2008.

Echols, Stuart, and Eliza Pennypacker. "From Stormwater Management to Artful Rainwater Design." *Landscape Journal* 27, no. 2 (2008): 268–90.

Eesteren, Cornelis van, and Vincent van Rossem. *Het idee van de functionele stad: Ein lezing met lichtbeelden, 1928.* Rotterdam: NAi Uitgevers, 1997. Distributed by Art Publishers.

European Ecological Symposium. *Urban Ecology.* Edited by R. (Reinhard) Bornkamm et al. Oxford: Blackwell Scientific, 1982. Distributed by Halsted Press.

Everard, Mark. *Common Ground: The Sharing of Land and Landscapes for Sustainability.* London: Zed Books, 2011.

Eyck, Aldo van. *The Child, the City and the Artist: An Essay on Architecture; The In-between Realm,* edited by Vincent Ligtelijn and Francis Strauven. Amsterdam: SUN, 2008.

———." The Child and the City." In *Playgrounds and Recreation Spaces,* edited by Alfred Ledermann, 34–37. London: Architectural Press, 1959.

Fainstein, Susan S. *The Just City.* Ithaca, N.Y.: Cornell University Press, 2010.

Fairfax, Sally K., Lauren Gwin, Mary Ann King, Leigh Raymond, and Laura A. Watt. *Buying Nature: The Limits of Land Acquisition as a Conservation Strategy, 1780–2004.* American and Comparative Environmental Policy. Cambridge, Mass.: MIT Press, 2005.

Falck, Zachary J. S. "Property Rights, Popular Ecology, and Problems with Wild Plants in Twentieth-Century American Cities." In *Greening the City: Urban Landscapes in the Twentieth Century,* edited by Dorothee Brantz and Sonja Dümpelmann, 159–80. Charlottesville: University of Virginia Press, 2011.

———. *Weeds: An Environmental History of Metropolitan America.* Pittsburgh: University of Pittsburgh Press, 2010.

Farr, Stephanie. "Mulch, Sinkholes, Even Tara Reid's Birthday: Is There Anything Philly Can't Throw a Party For?" *Philadelphia Inquirer,* June 14, 2019. https://www.inquirer.com/news/philadelphia/philadelphia-party-mulch-sinkhole-tara-reid-20190614.html?__vfz=medium%3Dsharebar.

Fenneman, N. M. *Geology and Mineral Resources of the St. Louis Quadrangle.* Geological Survey Bulletin no. 438. Washington, D.C.: Department of the Interior and Government Printing Office, 1911.

Finkel, Kenneth. *Philadelphia Almanac and Citizens Manual for 1994.* Philadelphia: Library Company of Philadelphia, 1993.

Fischer, Leonie K., Moritz von der Lippe, Matthias C. Rillig, and Ingo Kowarik. "Creating Novel

Urban Grasslands by Reintroducing Native Species in Wasteland Vegetation." *Biological Conservation* 159 (2013): 119–26.

Fishman, Robert. "The Fifth Migration." *Journal of the American Planning Association* 71, no. 4 (2005): 357–66.

Fleming, Ronald Lee, and Lauri A. Halderman. *On Common Ground: Caring for Shared Land from Town Common to Urban Park.* Cambridge, Mass: Harvard Common Press and Township Institute, 1982.

Fonseca, Maria Lucinda, Maria José Caldeira, Alina Esteves, Gabriella Lazaridis, and Allan M. Williams. "New Forms of Migration into the European South: Challenges for Citizenship and Governance—the Portuguese Case." *International Journal of Population Geography* 8, no. 2 (2002): 135–52.

Foster, Sheila R., and Christian Iaione. "The City as a Commons." *Yale Law & Policy Review* 34, no. 2 (2016): 301–11, 334–49.

Franck, Karen A., and Quentin Stevens. *Loose Space: Possibility and Diversity in Urban Life.* London: Routledge, 2007.

Fröbel, Friedrich, and Arnold H. Heinemann. *Froebel Letters.* Boston: Lee and Shepard, 1893.

Fröbel, Friedrich, Emilie Michaelis, and H. Keatley Moore. *Letters on the Kindergarten.* London: S. Sonnenschein, 1891.

Frost, Joe L. "Play Environments for Young Children in the USA: 1800–1990." *Children's Environments Quarterly* 6, no. 4 (1989): 17–24.

Fugmann, Harald. Interview by Jill Desimini, September 2, 2015.

Fullilove, Mindy Thompson. *Root Shock: How Tearing Up City Neighborhoods Hurts America, and What We Can Do about It.* New York: New Village Press, 2016.

Fullilove, Mindy Thompson, and Wallace, Rodrick. "Serial Forced Displacement in American Cities, 1916–2010." *Journal of Urban Health* 88, no. 3 (2011): 381–89.

Fundevila, Maria José. Interview by Jill Desimini. September 9, 2014, and September 10, 2015.

Gabinete Técnico da Habitação da Câmara Municipal de Lisboa (GTH). *Plano de urbanização de Chelas.* Lisbon: Câmara Municipal de Lisboa, 1965.

Gaillard, Karin, Betsy Dokter, and Vincent van Rossem. *Berlage en Amsterdam Zuid.* Amsterdam: Gemeentearchief; Rotterdam: Uitgeverij 010, 1992.

Gallagher, John. *Reimagining Detroit.* Detroit: Wayne State University Press, 2010.

Gandy, Matthew. "Entropy by Design: Gilles Clément, Parc Henri Matisse and the Limits to Avant-Garde Urbanism." *International Journal of Urban and Regional Research* 37, no. 1 (2013): 259–78.

Garrison, Noah, and Karen Hobbs. "Rooftops to Rivers II: Green Strategies for Controlling Stormwater and Combined Sewer Overflows." National Resources Defense Council, 2011. http://www.nrdc.org/water/pollution/rooftopsii/files/rooftopstoriversII.pdf.

Gesetz zum Schutz, zur Pflege und zur Entwicklung der öffentlichen Grün- und Erholungsanlagen (Grünanlagengesetz—GrünanlG), Vom 24. November 1997 (GVBl. S. 612), (1997).

Gibson-Graham, J. K. *A Postcapitalist Politics.* Minneapolis: University of Minnesota Press, 2006.

Gillerman, Margaret. "10,000 Sunflowers Brighten Delmar Boulevard and Spur Hope for Revitalization." *St. Louis Post Dispatch,* July 30, 2014. https://www.stltoday.com/news/local/metro/10-000-sunflowers-brighten-delmar-boulevard-and-spur-hope-for-revitalization/article_0d105083-7e66-54ac-b89b-0862b4643e2f.html.

Gissen, David. *Subnature: Architecture's Other Environments; Atmospheres, Matter, Life.* New York: Princeton Architectural Press, 2009.

Gonçalves, Rita Gonçalves Galvão. "HORTAS URBANAS. Estudo do Caso de Lisboa." PhD diss., Universidade de Lisboa, 2014.

Gordon, Colin. *Mapping Decline: St. Louis and the Fate of the American City.* Philadelphia: University of Pennsylvania Press, 2008.

———. "Patchwork Metropolis: Fragmented Governance and Urban Decline in Greater St. Louis." *Saint Louis University Public Law Review* 34, no. 1 (2014): 51–70.

———. "St. Louis Blues: The Urban Crisis in the Gateway City." *Saint Louis University Public Law Review* 33, no. 1 (2013): 81–92.

Gordon, Constance, and Kathy Hussey-Arnston, eds. *A Breath of Fresh Air: Chicago's Neighborhood Parks of the Progressive Reform Era, 1900–1925.* Chicago: Chicago Public Library Special Collections Division and Chicago Park District, 1989.

Gray, Stephen F. "COVID-19 Puts Structural Racism on Full Display—Will We Finally Do Something to Correct It?" *Next City,* Op-Ed, May 11, 2020. https://nextcity.org/daily/entry/covid-19-puts-structural-racism-on-full-display.

Great Rivers Greenway. "Making of Brickline Greenway: Project & Process." https://greatriversgreenway.org/making-of-a-greenway/.

———. "2016 Regional Plan Update: Action Plans to Create an Exceptional River Ring Experience." St. Louis: Great Rivers Greenway, 2016.

Great Rivers Greenway District. "Summary: Building the River Ring; A Citizen-Driven Regional Plan." St. Louis: Great Green Rivers Greenway District, 2004.

Green, Jared. "Interview with Anne Whiston Spirn on the 30th Anniversary of *The Granite Garden.*' *The Dirt,* January 7, 2015. http://dirt.asla.org/2015/01/07/interview-with-anne-whiston-spirn-on-the-30th-anniversary-of-the-granite-garden/.

Gross, Matthias. *Inventing Nature: Ecological Restoration by Public Experiments.* Lanham, Md.: Lexington Books, 2003.

Groth, Jacqueline, and Eric Corijn. "Reclaiming Urbanity: Indeterminate Spaces, Informal Actors and Urban Agenda Setting." *Urban Studies* 42, no. 3 (2005): 503–26.

"Groundswell: The Rise of Landscape Urbanism; Charles Waldheim Talks with Jeff Stein, AIA." *ArchitectureBoston* 13, no. 3 (Fall 2010); 38–43.

Hackworth, Jason. "The Limits to Market-Based Strategies for Addressing Land Abandonment in Shrinking American Cities." *Progress in Planning* 90 (2014): 1–37.

Hanahan, Jonathan, and Rory Hyde. "Archis as Guide: Aldo van Eyck Playground Tour, 2009." *Volume,* no. 22 (January 2010).

Hardin, Garrett. "The Tragedy of the Commons." *Science* 162, no. 3859 (December 13, 1968): 1243–48.

Harloe, Michael. *The People's Home? Social Rented Housing in Europe & America.* Studies in Urban and Social Change. Cambridge, Mass.: Blackwell, 1995.

Harvey, David. *Justice, Nature, and the Geography of Difference.* Cambridge, Mass.: Blackwell, 1996.

Heathcott, Joseph. "'The Whole City Is Our Laboratory': Harland Bartholomew and the Production of Urban Knowledge." *Journal of Planning History* 4, no. 4 (2005): 322–55.

Heffernan, Paul. "Tax Puzzle Posed by the Shrinking City." *New York Times,* June 1, 1947.

Heilbrun, James. "On the Theory and Policy of Neighborhood Consolidation." *Journal of the American Planning Association* 45, no. 4 (1979): 417–27.

Heimann, Dr. Jutta. "Naturerfahrungsraum 'Robinienwäldchen.'" *Umwelt- und Naturschutzam* (October 2014). https://digital.zlb.de/viewer/metadata/34089920/1/.

Heitor, Teresa Valsassina. "Olivais e Chelas: Operações urbanísticas de grande escala." University of Lisbon, 2004. https://www.researchgate.net/publication/237317952_OLIVAIS_E_CHELAS_OPERACOES_URBANISTICAS_DE_GRANDE_ESCALA.

Henriques, Jorge Castro. "Urban Agriculture and Resilience in Lisbon: The Role of the Municipal Government." *Urban Agriculture Magazine,* no. 22 (June 2009): 49–50.

Henry, Ruth Eleanor. "The Public Playground Movement in the United States." PhD diss., University of Southern California, 1939.

Herscher, Andrew. *The Unreal Estate Guide to Detroit.* Ann Arbor: University of Michigan Press, 2012.

Hester, Randolph T. *Design for Ecological Democracy.* Cambridge, Mass.: MIT Press, 2006.

Heynen, Hilde. "Belgium and the Netherlands: Two Different Ways of Coping with the Housing Crisis, 1945–70." *Home Cultures* 7, no. 2 (2010): 159–77.

Hill, Philip. "Recent Slum Clearance and Urban Redevelopment Laws." *Washington and Lee Law Review* 9 (1952): 173–88.

Hillier, Amy. "Historical Redlining in Philadelphia." 2008. http://works.bepress.com/amy_hillier/15/.

Hobbs, Richard J., Salvatore Arico, James Aronson, Jill S. Baron, Peter Bridgewater, Viki A. Cramer, Paul R. Epstein, et al. "Novel Ecosystems: Theoretical and Management Aspects of the New Ecological World Order." *Global Ecology and Biogeography* 15, no. 1 (2006): 1–7.

Hodgson, Kimberley, Marcia Caton Campbell, and Martin Bailkey. *Urban Agriculture: Growing Healthy, Sustainable Places.* Planning Advisory Service report no. 563. Chicago: American Planning Association, 2011.

Hoeferlin, Derek. "Chasing #Antidrone." In *Chasing the City: Models for Extra-Urban Investigations,* edited by Joshua M. Nason and Jeffrey S. Nesbit, 37–60. New York: Routledge, 2019.

Hofmeister, Sabine. "Natures Running Wild: A Social-Ecological Perspective on Wilderness? The Debate on Urban Restructuring and Restoration in Eastern Germany." *Nature and Culture* 43, no. 3 (2009): 293–315.

Hollander, Justin B., and Jeremy Németh. "The Bounds of Smart Decline: A Foundational Theory for Planning Shrinking Cities." *Housing Policy Debate* 21, no. 3 (2011): 349–67.

Holme, Thomas, Francis Lamb, Robert Greene, and John Thornton. *A map of the improved part of the Province of Pennsilvania in America: begun by Wil. Penn, Proprietary & Governour thereof anno 1681.* Map. Library of Congress. https://www.loc.gov/item/2006625100/.

Hough, Michael. *Cities and Natural Process: A Basis for Sustainability.* London: Routledge, 2004.

Hudson, Joanne, and Pamela Shaw. "As Found: Contested Uses within the 'Left-Over' Spaces of the City." Paper presented at conference of the Research Group for Landscape Architecture and Urbanism, Copenhagen, Copenhagen University, 2012. https://docplayer.net/59417043-As-found-contested-uses-within-the-left-over-spaces-of-the-city.html.

Hunt, John Dixon. *Historical Ground: The Role of History in Contemporary Landscape Architecture.* New York: Routledge, 2014.

Hurley, Andrew. *Common Fields: An Environmental History of St. Louis.* St. Louis: Missouri Historical Society Press, 1997.

Jack, Malcolm. *Lisbon, City of the Sea: A History.* London: I. B. Tauris, 2007.

Jackson, John Brinckerhoff. *The Necessity for Ruins, and Other Topics.* Amherst: University of Massachusetts Press, 1980.

Jackson, Kenneth T. *Crabgrass Frontier: The Suburbanization of the United States.* New York: Oxford University Press, 1985.

Jacobs, Harvey M. "Claiming the Site." In *Site Matters: Design Concepts, Histories, and Strategies,* edited by Carol Burns and Andrea Kahn. New York: Routledge, 2005.

Jirku, Almut. "Historic Transport Landscapes in Berlin." in *Historic Airports: Proceedings of the International "L'Europe de l'Air" Conferences on Aviation Architecture: Liverpool (1999), Berlin (2000),*

Paris (2001), edited by Bob Hawkins, Gabriele Lechner, and Paul Smith. London: English Heritage, 2005: 210–15.

———. Interview by Jill Desimini. September 3, 2015.

Jirku, Almut, Nicole Herr, and Moritz Ahlert. *Stadtgrün.* Stuttgart: Fraunhofer IRB Verlag, 2013.

Jolles, Allard., Erik Klusman, and Ben Teunissen. *Planning Amsterdam: Scenarios for Urban Development, 1928–2003.* Rotterdam: NAi, 2003.

Johnson, Walter. *The Broken Heart of America: St. Louis and the Violent History of the United States.* New York: Basic Books, 2020.

———. "What Do We Mean When We Say, 'Structural Racism'? A Walk down West Florissant Avenue, Ferguson, Missouri." *Kalfou* (Santa Barbara, Calif.) 3, no. 1 (2016): 36–62.

Jongeneel, Douwe, Rob Withagen, and Frank T. J. M. Zaal. "Do Children Create Standardized Playgrounds? A Study on the Gap-crossing Affordances of Jumping Stones." *Journal of Environmental Psychology* 44 (2015): 45–52.

Jonkman, Arend, and Leonie Janssen-Jansen. "Identifying Distributive Injustice through Housing (Mis)Match Analysis: The Case of Social Housing in Amsterdam." *Housing, Theory and Society* 35 (2018): 353–77.

Jordan, W. R. "Restoration Ecology: Ecological Restoration as a Technique for Basic Research." In *Restoration Ecology: A Synthetic Approach to Ecological Research,* edited by W. R. Jordan, M. E. Gilpin, and J. D. Aber. Cambridge: Cambridge University Press, 1987.

Jorgensen, Anna, and Richard Keenan. *Urban Wildscapes.* Abingdon, Oxon: Routledge, 2012.

Jorgensen, Anna, and Marian Tylecote. "Ambivalent Landscapes: Wilderness in the Urban Interstices." *Landscape Research* 32, no. 4 (2007): 443–62.

Kamvasinou, Krystallia. "The Public Value of Vacant Urban Land." Proceedings of the Institute of Civil Engineers (ICE). *Municipal Engineer* 164, no. 3 (2011): 157–66.

Kastner, Jeffrey, Sina Najafi, and Frances Richard. *Odd Lots: Revisiting Gordon Matta-Clark's "Fake Estates."* New York: Cabinet Books, in conjunction with the Queens Museum of Art and White Columns, 2005.

Kattwinkel, Mira, Robert Biedermann, and Michael Kleyer. "Temporary Conservation for Urban Biodiversity." *Biological Conservation* 144, no. 9 (2011): 2335–43.

Kelley, Robin D. G. "Getting to Freedom City." In *The Politics of Care: From COVID-19 to Black Lives Matter. Boston Review Forum* 15 (Summer 2020): 197–212. New York: Verso, 2020.

Kinchin, Juliet, Aidan O'Connor, Tanya Harrod, Medea Hoch, and Museum of Modern Art. *Century of the Child: Growing by Design, 1900–2000.* New York: Museum of Modern Art, 2012.

Kleijn, Koen, Rob Van Zoest, Ernest Kurpershoek, and Shinji Otani. *The Canals of Amsterdam: 400 Years of Building, Living and Working.* Bussum: Thoth, 2013.

Kondo, Michelle, Bernadette Hohl, SeungHoon Han, and Charles Branas. "Effects of Greening and Community Reuse of Vacant Lots on Crime." *Urban Studies* (Edinburgh, Scotland) 53, no. 15 (2016): 3279–95.

Konigen, Hein. "Creative Management." In *The Dynamic Landscape: Design, Ecology and Management of Naturalistic Urban Planting,* edited by Nigel Dunnett and James Hitchmough, 256–92. London: Taylor & Francis, 2008.

Koster, Don. The Sunflower+ Project: STL. Sustainable Land Lab, 2012. https://landlab.wustl.edu /projects/sunflower/.

Kowarik, Ingo. "Novel Urban Ecosystems, Biodiversity, and Conservation." *Environmental Pollution* 159, no. 8 (2011): 1974–83.

———. "On the Role of Alien Species in Urban Flora and Vegetation." In Marzluff et al., *Urban Ecology*, 321–38.

Kowarik, Ingo, and Stefan Körner. "Natur-Park Südgelände: Linking Conservation and Recreation in an Abandoned Railyard in Berlin." In Kowarik and Körner, *Wild Urban Woodlands*, 287–99.

———, eds. *Wild Urban Woodlands: New Perspectives for Urban Forestry*. Berlin: Springer Berlin Heidelberg, 2005.

———. "Wild Urban Woodlands: Towards a Conceptual Framework." In Kowarik and Körner, *Wild Urban Woodlands*, 1–32.

Krewson, Mayor Lyda. "A Plan to Reduce Vacant Lots and Buildings." Initiatives, City of St. Louis. https://www.stlouis-mo.gov/government/departments/mayor/initiatives/vacancy.cfm.

———. "Preliminary Resilience Assessment." In *Resilient St. Louis*. St. Louis: Rockefeller Foundation, 2018.

Kromer, John. *Fixing Broken Cities: The Implementation of Urban Development Strategies*. New York: Routledge, 2010.

Kühn, Norbert. "Intentions for the Unintentional Spontaneous Vegetation as the Basis for Innovative Planting Design in Urban Areas." *Journal of Landscape Architecture* 1, no. 2 (2006): 46–53.

Lachmund, Jens. "Exploring the City of Rubble: Botanical Fieldwork in Bombed Cities in Germany after World War II." *Osiris* 18, no. 1 (2003): 234–54.

———. *Greening Berlin: The Co-Production of Science, Politics, and Urban Nature*. Cambridge, Mass.: MIT Press, 2013.

———. "The Making of an Urban Ecology: Biological Expertise and Wildlife Preservation in West Berlin." In *Greening the City: Urban Landscapes in the Twentieth Century*, edited by Dorothee Brantz and Sonja Dümpelmann, 204–28. Charlottesville: University of Virginia Press, 2011.

Ladd, G. E. *The Clay, Stone, Lime and Sand Industries of St. Louis City and County*. Geological Survey of Missouri, Bulletin no. 3, Supplement. Jefferson City, Mo., December 1890.

The Landscape Architecture Legacy of Dan Kiley. "Jefferson National Expansion Memorial." History. https://tclf.org/sites/default/files/microsites/kiley-legacy/JeffersonNEM.html.

Lange, Alexandra. *The Design of Childhood: How the Material World Shapes Independent Kids*. New York: Bloomsbury, 2018.

Langner, Marcel, and Wilifried Endlicher, eds. *Shrinking Cities: Effects on Urban Ecology and Challenges for Urban Development*. Frankfurt am Main: Peter Lang, 2007.

Larrivee, Shaina D. "Playscapes: Isamu Noguchi's Designs for Play." *Public Art Dialogue* 1, no. 1 (2011): 53–80.

Latz, Peter. "The Idea of Making Time Visible." *TOPOS* 33 (December 2000): 94–99.

Laurie, Ian C. *Nature in Cities: The Natural Environment in the Design and Development of Urban Green Space*. Chichester, UK: Wiley, 1979.

Lawton, Philip, Karen E. Till, Sandra Jasper, Alexander Vasudevan, Sonja Dümpelmann, Michael Flitner, Matthew Beach, Catherine Nash, and Matthew Gandy. "Natura Urbana: The Brachen of Berlin." *AAG Review of Books* 7, no. 3 (2019): 214–27. https://doi.org/10.1080/2325548X.2019.1615328.

Leal, Ernesto Castro. "The Political and Ideological Origins of the Estado Novo in Portugal." Translated by Richard Correll. *Portuguese Studies 32*, no. 2 (2016): 128–48.

Leal, Gomes. "As hortas." In *Histórias de Lisboa: Antologia de textos sobre Lisboa,* compiled by Marina Tavares Dias, 178–79. Lisbon: Quimera, 2002.

Leal, Miguel, and Catarina Ramos. "Susceptibilidade às cheias na Área Metropolitana de Lisboa norte das mudanças de uso do solo. Factores de predisposição e impactes." *Finisterra* 48, no. 95 (2013): 17–40.

Leal, Miguel, Catarina Ramos, and Susana Pereira. "Different Types of Flooding Lead to Different Human and Material Damages: The Case of the Lisbon Metropolitan Area." *Natural Hazards* 91, no. 2 (2018): 735–58.

Ledermann, Alfred. *Creative Playgrounds and Recreation Centers.* Edited by Alfred Trachsel. Rev. ed. New York: Praeger, 1968.

———. *Playgrounds and Recreation Spaces.* London: Architectural Press, 1959.

Lefaivre, Liane, and Döll-Atelier voor Bouwkunst, eds. *Ground-Up City: Play as a Design Tool.* Edited by Atelier voor Bouwkunst Döll. Rotterdam: 010 Publishers, 2007.

———. "Ground-Up City, the Place of Play." In *Ground-Up City: Play as a Design Tool,* edited by Liane Lefaivre and Döll-Atelier voor Bouwkunst, 36–71. Rotterdam: 010 Publishers, 2007.

———. "Space, Place and Play." In Lefaivre, De Roode, et al., *Aldo van Eyck,* 16–57.

Lefaivre, Liane, Marlies Boterman, Suzanne Loen, and Merel Miedema. "A Psychogeographical Bicycle Tour of Aldo van Eyck's Amsterdam Playgrounds." In *Archis Is Paranoid,* no. 3 (2002): 129–35.

Lefaivre, Liane, Ingeborg de Roode, Rudi Fuchs, Lia Karsten, Anja Novak, Debbie Wilken, Erik Schmitz, and Francis Strauven. *Aldo van Eyck: The Playgrounds and the City.* English ed. Amsterdam: Stedelijk Museum; Rotterdam: NAi, 2002.

Lefaivre, Liane, and Alexander Tzonis. *Aldo van Eyck, Humanist Rebel: Inbetweening in a Post-War World.* Rotterdam: 010 Publishers, 1999.

Lehmkuhl, Ursula, and Hermann Wellenreuther. *Historians and Nature: Comparative Approaches to Environmental History.* English ed. Oxford: Berg, 2007.

Le Roy, Louis G. *Natuur Uitschakelen, Natuur Inschakelen.* 2nd. ed. Deventer: Ankh-Hermes, 1973.

Levine, Adam, comp. "Philly H_2O: The History of Philadelphia's Watersheds and Sewers." http://www.phillyh2o.org.

Lewis, John Frederick. *The Redemption of the Lower Schuylkill: The River As It Was, the River As It Is, the River As It Should Be.* Philadelphia: City Parks Association, 1924.

Lichtenstein, Andra, and Flavia Alice Mameli. *Gleisdreieck: Parklife Berlin.* Bielefeld, Germany: Transcript, 2015.

Lincoln Institute of Land Policy. *Land and Property Values in the US.* http://www.lincolninst.edu/subcenters/land-values/metro-area-land-prices.asp.

Lingen, Anna Van, Denisa Kollarova, and Donald Geradts. *Aldo Van Eyck: Seventeen Playgrounds, Amsterdam.* Eindhoven: Lecturis, 2016.

Lokman, Kees. "Vacancy as a Laboratory: Design Criteria for Reimagining Social-Ecological Systems on Vacant Urban Lands." *Landscape Research* 42, no. 7 (2017): 728–46.

López-Piñeiro, Sergio. *A Glossary of Urban Voids.* Berlin: Jovis Verlag, 2020.

Lovelace, Eldridge. *Harland Bartholomew: His Contributions to American Urban Planning.* Urbana: University of Illinois Press, 1992.

Lovelace, Eldridge. "Urban Renewal Process ?" Chapter 8 in *Harland Bartholomew and His Contributions to American Urban Planning,* 103–18. Urbana: Department of Urban and Regional Planning, University of Illinois, 1993.

Lynch, Kevin, and Michael Southworth. *Wasting Away.* San Francisco: Sierra Club Books, 1990.

MacFaden, Sean W., Jarlath P. M. O'Neil-Dunne, Anna R. Royar, Jacqueline W. T. Lu, and Andrew G. Rundle. "High-Resolution Tree Canopy Mapping for New York City Using LIDAR and Object-Based Image Analysis." *Journal of Applied Remote Sensing* 6, no. 1 (2012): 063567.

MacKaye, Benton. *The New Exploration: A Philosophy of Regional Planning.* New York: Harcourt, Brace, 1928.

Madaleno, Isabel Maria. "Urban Agriculture Supportive Policies from Two Distant Cities: Lisbon (Portugal) and Presidente Prudente (Brazil)." *UA-Magazine,* July 2001: 38–39.

Madeira da Silva, Teresa, and Marianna Monte. "Social Inclusion as a Collective Urban Project: Urban Farm in Lisbon and Street Vendors in Rio de Janeiro." Paper presented at CITIES ARE US, International Conference, "Rethinking Urban Inclusion: Spaces, Mobilisations, Interventions," Coimbra, Portugal, University of Coimbra, June 28–30, 2012.

Magalhaes, Manuela Raposo. "Ecological Structure for Lisbon." *Ekistics* 60, no. 360/361 (May/June–July/August 1993): 159–66.

———. Interview by Jill Desimini. September 9, 2015.

Marat-Mendes, Teresa. "Lisbon Territory from a Morphological and Environmental Approach: Lessons for a Sustainable Urban Agenda." *Cidades, Comunidades E Territórios* 22 (2011): 22–40.

Marat-Mendes, Teresa, and Mafalda Teixeira de Sampayo. "The Different Scales of the Urban Intervention in Lisbon Territory." Lisbon University Institute, 2010.

Marat-Mendes, Teresa, and Vítor Oliveira. "Urban Planners in Portugal in the Middle of the Twentieth Century: Étienne De Groër and Antão Almeida Garrett." *Planning Perspectives* 28, no. 1 (2013): 91–111.

Marques, Beatriz Rosa de Abreu Pereira. "O vale de Alcântara como caso de estudo: Evolução da morfologia urbana." PhD diss., Universidade Técnica de Lisboa, 2009.

Marris, Emma. "Ragamuffin Earth." *Nature* 460, no. 7254 (2009): 450–53.

Marsden, K. Gerald. "Philanthropy and the Boston Playground Movement, 1885–1907." *Social Service Review* 35, no. 1 (1961): 48–58.

Martinez-Fernandez, Cristina, Karina Pallagst, and Thorsten Wiechmann. *Shrinking Cities: International Perspectives and Policy Implications.* Routledge Advances in Geography, vol. 8. New York: Routledge, 2014.

Martins, João, Patrícia Pereira, Pedro Almeida, Paulo Machado, Domingos Vaz, and Luís V. Baptist. "Planning Lisbon at the Metropolitan Scale: Elements for an Historical Analysis of Urban Planning Programs (1950–2010)." Sociology Research Center of the New University of Lisbon (CESNOVA), 2010. https://fcsh.academia.edu/Jo%C3%A3oMartins.

Marzluff, John M., Eric Shulenberger, Wilfried Endlicher, Marina Alberti, Gordon Bradley, Clare Ryan, Ute Simon, and Craig ZumBrunnen, eds. *Urban Ecology: An International Perspective on the Interaction between Humans and Nature.* Boston: Springer Science + Business Media, 2008.

Mathur, Anuradha, and Dilip da Cunha. *Mississippi Floods: Designing a Shifting Landscape.* New Haven, Conn.: Yale University Press, 2001.

———. "Waters Everywhere." In *Design in the Terrain of Water,* edited by Anuradha Mathur and Dilip da Cunha, with Rebekah Meeks and Matthew Wiener. San Francisco: Applied Research + Design Publishing; Philadelphia: University of Pennsylvania School of Design, 2014.

Matos, Rute Sousa, and Desidério Sales Batista. "Urban Agriculture: The Allotment Gardens as Structures of Urban Sustainability." In *Advances in Landscape Architecture,* edited by Murat Ozyavuz. InTech Open Science, 2013. https://www.intechopen.com/books/advances-in-landscape-architecture.

Mattern, Shannon. "Maintenance and Care." *Places Journal,* November 2018. https://placesjournal.org/article/maintenance-and-care/.

McArthur, Benjamin. "The Chicago Playground Movement: A Neglected Feature of Social Justice." *Social Service Review* 49, no. 3 (1975): 376–95.

McCarter, Robert. *Aldo van Eyck.* New Haven, Conn.: Yale University Press, 2015.

McHarg, Ian L. *Design with Nature.* Garden City, N.Y.: Doubleday/Natural History Press, for the American Museum of Natural History, 1971.

———. "Open Space from Natural Processes." In *Metropolitan Open Space and Natural Process,* edited by David Wallace, 10–52. Philadelphia: University of Pennsylvania Press, 1970; repr., 2016.

———. *A Quest for Life: An Autobiography.* New York: John Wiley, 1996.

Meyer, Elizabeth K. "Sustaining Beauty: The Performance of Appearance; A Manifesto in Three Parts." *Journal of Landscape Architecture* 3, no. 1 (2008): 6–23.

Milligan, Brett. "Landscape Migration." *Places Journal,* June 2015. https://placesjournal.org/article/landscape-migration/.

Milroy, Elizabeth. *The Grid and the River: Philadelphia's Green Places, 1682–1876.* University Park: Pennsylvania State University Press, 2016.

Minkjan, Mark. "Haussmann and the Sanitisation of Amsterdam." Failed Architecture. https://failedarchitecture.com/haussmann-and-the-sanitisation-of-amsterdam/.

Mitchell, Don. *The Right to the City: Social Justice and the Fight for Public Space.* New York: Guilford Press, 2003.

Mullin, John R. "The Reconstruction of Lisbon following the Earthquake of 1755: A Study in Despotic Planning." *Planning Perspectives* 7, no. 2 (1992): 157–79.

Mumford, Lewis. "The Fourth Migration." *Survey Graphic* 7 (May 1925): 130–33.

Naffziger, Chris. "A Closer Look at Sinkholes and Former Quarries in St. Louis." *St. Louis Magazine,* August 1, 2018. https://www.stlmag.com/history/sinkholes-in-st-louis/.

Nash, Roderick. *Wilderness and the American Mind.* Edited by Char Miller. 5th ed. New Haven, Conn.: Yale University Press, 2014.

Nassauer, Joan I. "Messy Ecosystems, Orderly Frames." *Landscape Journal* 14, no. 2 (1995): 161–70.

Nassauer, Joan Iverson, and Julia Raskin. "Urban Vacancy and Land Use Legacies: A Frontier for Urban Ecological Research, Design, and Planning." *Landscape and Urban Planning* 125, no. C (2014): 245–53.

Nelson, Robert K., LaDale Winling, Richard Marciano, Nathan Connolly, et al. "Mapping Inequality." In *American Panorama: An Atlas of United States History,* edited by Robert K. Nelson and Edward L. Ayers. https://dsl.richmond.edu/panorama/redlining/#loc=4/36.71/-96.93&opacity=0.8&text=.

Netherlands. Rijks Geologische Dienst. *Geologische Kaart van Nederland, Schaal 1:50,000.* Amsterdam: Rijks Geologische Dienst, 1925.

Niza, Samuel, Daniela Ferreira, Joana Mourão, Patrícia D'Almeida, and Bento Marat-Mendes. "Lisbon's Womb: An Approach to the City Metabolism in the Turn to the Twentieth Century." *Regional Environmental Change* 16, no. 6 (2016): 1725–37.

Nunes, João Pedro Silva. "Le Gabinete Técnico de Habitação et la réforme du logement social à Lisbonne (1959–1974)." *Le Mouvement Social* 4, no. 245, 2013: 83–96.

———. "O programa 'Habitações de Renda Económica' e a constituição da metrópole de Lisboa (1959–1969)." *Análise Social* 48, no. 206 (2013): 80–100. http://www.jstor.org/stable/41959850.

Odum, Howard T., and Elisabeth C. Odum. *A Prosperous Way Down: Principles and Policies.* Boulder: University Press of Colorado, 2001.

Ogata, Amy Fumiko. *Designing the Creative Child: Playthings and Places in Midcentury America.* Architecture, Landscape, and American Culture series. Minneapolis: University of Minnesota Press, 2013.

Oliveira, Pedro Elias, and Catarina Ramos. "Inundações na Cidade de Lisboa durante o Século XX e os seus factores agraventes." *Finisterra* 37, no. 74 (2012).

Oliveira, Vítor, and Paulo Pinho, "Lisbon." *Cities* 27, no. 5 (2010): 405–19.

Ostrom, Elinor. *Governing the Commons: The Evolution of Institutions for Collective Action.* Political Economy of Institutions and Decisions series. Cambridge: Cambridge University Press, 1990.

Oswalt, Philipp. *Shrinking Cities.* Vol. 1, *International Research.* Ostfildern-Ruit, Germany: Hatje Cantz, 2005.

———. *Shrinking Cities.* Vol. 2, *Interventions.* Ostfildern-Ruit, Germany: Hatje Cantz, 2006.

Oswalt, Philipp, and Tim Rieniets. *Atlas of Shrinking Cities.* Ostfildern-Ruit, Germany: Hatje Cantz, 2006.

Oxford English Dictionary (OED). 2013. http://www.oed.com/.

Pallagst, Karina, Jasmin Aber, Ivonne Audirac, Emmanuele Cunningham-Sabot, Sylvie Fol, Cristina Martinez-Fernandez, Sergio Moraes, et al. *The Future of Shrinking Cities: Problems, Patterns and Strategies of Urban Transformation in a Global Context.* IURD Monograph series. Berkeley: University of California Berkeley, Institute of Urban and Regional Development, 2009.

Palomar, Colette. "From the Ground Up: Why Urban Ecological Restoration Needs Environmental Justice." *Nature and Culture* 5, no. 3 (2010): 277–98.

Park, Kyŏng., and International Center for Urban Ecology. *Urban Ecology: Detroit and Beyond.* Hong Kong: Map Book, 2005.

Payne, Jessica. Interview by Jill Desimini. August 29, 2019.

Perdue, Robert E., Jr. "Arundo donax: Source of Musical Reeds and Industrial Cellulose." *Economic Botany* 12, no. 4 (October–December 1958): 368–404.

Peterson, Sarah Jo. "Voting for Play: The Democratic Potential of Progressive Era Playgrounds." *Journal of the Gilded Age and Progressive Era* 3, no. 2 (2004): 145–75.

Petrin, Kae M. "Historic Flood Projections Threaten Tourism, Towns along Rivers in Missouri, Illinois." St. Louis Public Radio, May 29, 2019. https://news.stlpublicradio.org/post/historic-flood-projections-threaten-tourism-towns-along-rivers-missouri-illinois#stream/0.

Philadelphia Evening Bulletin. "Fulton Street Collapse 1961," George D. McDowell Collection, Special Collections Research Center, Temple University Libraries. https://collaborativehistory.gse.upenn.edu/media/funston-street-collapse-1961.

Philadelphia Transit Shelter Project. "New Transit Shelters in the City of Philadelphia." http://phillytransitshelters.com.

Philadelphia Water Department. *Green City, Clean Waters: Implementation and Adaptive Management Plan.* December 1, 2011. http://archive.phillywatersheds.org/ltcpu/IAMP_body.pdf.

———. "Green Stormwater Infrastructure Project Map." https://phl-water.maps.arcgis.com/apps/webappviewer/index.html?id=c5d43ba5291441dabbee5573a3f981d2.

———. "Mill Creek Sewer Collapse, 5000 Block of Funston St." Philadelphia Water Department. https://philawater.pastperfectonline.com/photo/839E5151-A257–43E0–8FEC-002530970450.

Pickett, S. T. A., M. L. Cadenasso, J. M. Grove, C. H. Nilon, R. V. Pouyat, W. C. Zipperer, and R. Costanza. "Urban Ecological Systems: Linking Terrestrial Ecological, Physical, and Socioeconomic Components of Metropolitan Areas." *Annual Review of Ecology and Systematics* 32 (2001): 127–57.

Pinto, Pedro Ramos. "Housing and Citizenship: Building Social Rights in Twentieth-Century Portugal." *Contemporary European History* 18, no. 2 (2009): 199–215.

Pobloth, Sonja. "Die Entwicklung der Landschaftsplanung in Berlin im Zeitraum 1979 bis 2004 unter besonderer Berücksichtigung der Stadtökologie." PhD diss., Technische Universität Berlin, 2008. ProQuest (AAT 3300426). https://depositonce.tu-berlin.de/bitstream/11303/2393/1/Dokument_13.pdf.

Popper, Deborah Epstein, and Frank J. Popper. "The Great Plains: From Dust to Dust; A Daring Proposal for Dealing with an Inevitable Disaster." *Planning* 53, no. 12 (1987): 12–18.

"Prémio Jellicoe para as 'utopias' de Gonçalo Ribeiro Telles," Arquitectura, Publico, April 10, 2013. http://www.publico.pt/culturaipsilon/noticia/goncalo-ribeiro-telles-distinguido-com-premio-da -arquitectura-paisagista-ifla2013–1590761.

Prener, Christopher G., Taylor Harris Braswell, and Daniel J. Monti. "St. Louis's 'Urban Prairie': Vacant Land and the Potential for Revitalization." *Journal of Urban Affairs* 42, no. 3 (2018): 1–19.

Price, Edward T. *Dividing the Land: Early American Beginnings of Our Private Property Mosaic.* Chicago: University of Chicago Press, 1995.

Pritchett, Wendell E. "The 'Public Menace' of Blight: Urban Renewal and the Private Uses of Eminent Domain." *Yale Law & Policy Review* 21, no. 1 (2003): 1–52.

Prominski, Martin. *Urbane Natur gestalten: Entwurfsperspektiven zur Verbindung von Naturschutz und Freiraumnutzung.* Edited by Malte Maass and Linda Funke. Boston: Birkhäuser, 2014.

Pulido, Laura. "Geographies of Race and Ethnicity 1." *Progress in Human Geography* 39, no. 6 (2015): 809–17.

———. "Geographies of Race and Ethnicity II." *Progress in Human Geography* 41, no. 4 (2017): 524–33.

Rae, Douglas W. *City: Urbanism and Its End.* New Haven, Conn.: Yale University Press, 2003.

Ramalhete, Filipa, Luís Marques, Nuno Leitão, Pedro Costa, Saudade Pontes, and Suzel Gary. "Corredores Verdes, Conceitos base e algumas propostas para a Área Metropolitana de Lisboa." Lisbon: Grupo de Estudos de Ordenamento do Território e Ambient, 2007.

Ramos, Ana Rita Alves. "A Integração de Espaços de Cultivo Agrícola em Contextos Urbanos, Proposta de Intervencao para a Requalificação Urbana do Vale de Chelas [Lisboa]." PhD diss., Universidade Técnica de Lisboa, 2011.

Ramos, Catarina, and Eusébio Reis. "Floods in Southern Portugal: Their Physical and Human Causes, Impacts and Human Response." *Mitigation and Adaptation Strategies for Global Change* 7, no. 3 (2002): 267–84.

Ranganathan, Malini, and Eve Bratman. "From Urban Resilience to Abolitionist Climate Justice in Washington, DC." *Antipode* 53, no. 1 (2021): 115–37.

Reed, Chris. "Public Works Practice." In *The Landscape Urbanism Reader,* edited by Charles Waldheim, 267–85. New York: Princeton Architectural Press, 2006.

Reed, Francis. *On Common Ground: De Prima Materia.* London: Working Press, 1991.

Reilly, Richard. Interview by Jill Desimini. September 11, 2019.

Reis, A. P., C. Patinha, J. Wragg, A. C. Dias, M. Cave, A. J. Sousa, C. Costa, et al. "Geochemistry, Mineralogy, Solid-Phase Fractionation and Oral Bioaccessibility of Lead in Urban Soils of Lisbon." *Environmental Geochemistry and Health* 36, no. 5 (2014): 867–81.

Rhodeside, Elliot. "Boston Urban Wilds: A Natural Conservation Program for City Neighborhoods." *Environmental Comment,* March 1977, 10–12.

Ribeiro Telles, Gonçalo. *Plano Verde de Lisboa.* Lisbon: Edições Colibri, 1997.

Rich, Adrienne, Claudia Rankine, and Pablo Conrad. *Collected Poems, 1950–2012.* New York: W. W. Norton, 2016.

Robinson, Jennifer. *Ordinary Cities: Between Modernity and Development.* London: Routledge, 2006.

Rogers, Elizabeth Barlow. *Green Metropolis: The Extraordinary Landscapes of New York City.* New York: Alfred A. Knopf, 2016.

Rossem, Vincent van. *The Rape of Cities: The Disastrous Impact of Urban Renewal.* Amsterdam: Architectura & Natura, 2014.

Rothstein, Richard. *The Color of Law: A Forgotten History of How Our Government Segregated America.* New York: Liveright, 2017.

———. "The Making of Ferguson: Public Policies at the Root of Its Troubles." Report. Economic Policy Institute, October 15, 2014.

Rouard, Marguerite. *Children's Play Spaces: From Sandbox to Adventure Playground*. Edited by Jacques Simon. Woodstock, N.Y.: Overlook Press, 1977.

Rouse, D. C. *Green Infrastructure: A Landscape Approach*. Chicago: American Planning Association, 2013.

Rusk, David. *Cities without Suburbs*. Washington, D.C.: Woodrow Wilson Center Press; distributed by the Johns Hopkins University Press, 1993.

Russell, Josiah Cox. "Late Ancient and Medieval Population." *Transactions of the American Philosophical Society* 48, no. 3 (1958).

Ryan, Brent D. *Design after Decline: How America Rebuilds Shrinking Cities*. Philadelphia: University of Pennsylvania Press, 2012.

Rybczynski, Witold, and Peter D. Linneman. "How to Save Our Shrinking Cities." *Public Interest* 135 (Spring 1999): 30.

Salisbury, Edward James. *Weeds and Aliens*. London: Collins, 1964.

Sandweiss, Eric. *St. Louis: The Evolution of an American Urban Landscape; Critical Perspectives on the Past*. Philadelphia: Temple University Press, 2001.

———. *St. Louis in the Century of Henry Shaw: A View beyond the Garden Wall*. Columbia: University of Missouri Press, 2003.

Schaumann, Martin. "Grünordnungsplan in Berlin-Kreuzberg (SO 36): Forsetzung und Schluß des im August-Heft 1986 begonnenen Beitrages." *Das Gartenamt* 35 (August 1986): 622–630.

———. Interview by Jill Desimini. September 3, 2015.

———. "Vergleichende Untersuchung von Unteren Naturschutzbehörden im Ländlichen und Grossstädtischen Bereich: Dargestellt am Beispiel des Landkreises Göttingen und des Berliner Bezirks Kreuzberg." PhD diss., Technische Universität Berlin, 1992.

Schetke, Sophie, and Dagmar Haase. "Multi-Criteria Assessment of Socio-Environmental Aspects in Shrinking Cities: Experiences from Eastern Germany." *Environmental Impact Assessment Review* 28, no. 7 (2008): 483–503.

Schetke, Sophie, Dagmar Haase, and Jurgen Breuste. "Green Space Functionality under Conditions of Uneven Urban Land Use Development." *Journal of Land Use Science* 5, no. 2 (2010): 143–58.

Schilling, Joseph, and Jonathan Logan. "Greening the Rust Belt: A Green Infrastructure Model for Right Sizing America's Shrinking Cities." *Journal of the American Planning Association* 74, no. 4 (2008): 451–66.

Schmid, Christian. "Specificity and Urbanization: A Theoretical Outlook." In *The Inevitable Specificity of Cities*, edited by ETH Studio Basel. Zürich: Lars Müller, 2015.

Schumacher, E. F. *Small Is Beautiful: Economics As If People Mattered; 25 Years Later . . . with Commentaries*. Point Roberts, Wash.: Hartley & Marks, 1999.

Schumpeter, Joseph Alois. *Capitalism, Socialism, and Democracy*. New York: Harper and Brothers, 1942; rev. ed., New York: Harper and Row, 1976.

Schwarz, Terry, and John Hoornbeek. "Sustainable Infrastructure in Shrinking Cities: Options for the Future." Kent State University, July 17, 2009. SSRN, March 6, 2012. http://ssrn.com/abstract =2016933 or http://dx.doi.org/10.2139/ssrn.2016933.

Scordia, Danilo, Giorgio Testa, Efthimia Alexopoulou, and Salvatore L. Cosentino. "The Promising Perennial Herbaceous Energy Crop for Mediterranean Area Giant Reed (Arundo donax l.)." Power-Point Presentation, 26th AAIC Conference, Hotel Divani, Athens, September 16, 2014.

Searing, Helen. "Betondorp: Amsterdam's Concrete Garden Suburb." *Assemblage,* no. 3 (July 1987): 109–43.

The Second Studio (David Lee and Marina Bourderonnet). Podcast #184, "Racism and Cities with Mabel O. Wilson, Akira Drake Rodriguez, and Bryan Lee." June 2020. https://www.secondstudiopod .com/podcasts-8/184-racism-and-cities-with-mabel-owilson-akira-drake-rodriguez-and-bryan-lee.

Segal, Rafi, and Els Verbakel. "Urbanism without Density." In *Cities of Dispersal,* edited by Rafi Segal and Els Verbakel, 6–11. Chichester, UK: Wiley, 2008.

Senatsverwaltung fur Stadtentwicklung. *Landschaftsprogramm Artenschutzprogramm: Ergänzung 2004.* Berlin, June 2004.

Sennett, Richard, *The Uses of Disorder: Personal Identity and City Life.* London: Allen Lane, 1971.

Shields, Rob. *Places on the Margin: Alternative Geographies of Modernity.* London: Routledge, 1992.

Shultz, Michael M., and F. Rebecca Sapp. "Urban Redevelopment and the Elimination of Blight: A Case Study of Missouri's Chapter 353." *Washington University Journal of Urban and Contemporary Law* 37 (1990): 3–95.

Sisti, Claudia. "Morfologia do território e paisagem. Marvila." *On the W@terfront,* no. 7 (2005): 7–17.

Solà-Morales Rubió, Ignasi. "Terrain Vague.". In *Anyplace,* edited by Cynthia C. Davidson, 118–23. New York: Anyone; and Cambridge, Mass.: MIT Press, 1995.

Solomon, Susan G. *American Playgrounds: Revitalizing Community Space.* Hanover, N.H.: University Press of New England, 2005.

Somer, Kees. *The Functional City: The CIAM and Cornelis van Eesteren, 1928–1960.* Edited by Ed Taverne, Van Eesteren-Fluck, and Van Lohuizen Stichting. Rotterdam: NAi; The Hague: EFL Foundation, 2007.

Spencer, Thomas. *The Other Missouri History: Populists, Prostitutes, and Regular Folk.* Columbia: University of Missouri Press, 2004.

Spirn, Anne Whiston. *The Granite Garden: Urban Nature and Human Design.* New York: Basic Books, 1984.

——. "Identity: The Power of Place." In *The Language of Landscape,* 160–63. New Haven, Conn.: Yale University Press, 1998.

——. "Reclaiming Common Ground: Water, Neighborhoods, and Public Spaces." In *The American Planning Tradition: Culture and Policy,* edited by Robert Fishman, 302. Washington, D.C.: Woodrow Wilson Center Press; Baltimore: Johns Hopkins University Press, 2000.

——. "Restoring Mill Creek: Landscape Literacy, Environmental Justice and City Planning and Design." *Landscape Research* 30, no. 3 (2005): 395–413.

Sporrel, Karlijn, Simone R. Caljouw, and Rob Withagen. "Children Prefer a Nonstandardized to a Standardized Jumping Stone Configuration: Playing Time and Judgments." *Journal of Environmental Psychology* 53 (2017): 131–37.

Starr, Roger. "Making New York Smaller." *New York Times,* November 14, 1976, 33, 99.

Statistics Netherlands. "Baby Boomers in the Netherlands: What the Statistics Say." The Hague/Heerlen: Statistics Netherlands, 2012.

Stieber, Nancy. *Housing Design and Society in Amsterdam: Reconfiguring Urban Order and Identity, 1900–1920.* Chicago: University of Chicago Press, 1998.

Stilgoe, John R. *Common Landscape of America, 1580 to 1845,* New Haven, Conn.: Yale University Press, 1982.

——. "Town Common and Village Green in New England: 1620–1981." In *On Common Ground: Caring for Shared Land from Town Common to Urban Park,* edited by Ronald Lee Fleming and Lauri A. Halderman. Cambridge, Mass.: Harvard Common Press and Township Institute, 1982.

St. Louis City Plan Commission. *Comprehensive City Plan: St. Louis, Missouri.* St. Louis: St. Louis City Plan Commission, 1947. https://www.stlouis-mo.gov/archive/1947-comprehensive-plan/.

———. "Obsolete & Blighted Districts." Map. 1947. https://www.stlouis-mo.gov/archive/1947-comprehensive-plan/images/plate13.GIF.

———. "Proposed Interstate and Urban Distributing Routes." Map. January 1947. https://www.stlouis-mo.gov/archive/1947-comprehensive-plan/images/plate20.GIF.

St. Louis Development Program. "Technical Report on the History of Renewal." St. Louis: City Planning Commission, 1971.

Stoss Landscape Urbanism. "Chouteau Greenway: The Loop + The Stitch." Chouteau Greenway Competition (April 2018). https://www.stoss.net/projects/greenways-streets/chouteau-brickline-greenway.

Strauven, Francis. "List of Playgrounds 1947–1978 in Amsterdam." In Lefaivre, De Roode, et al., *Aldo van Eyck,* 132–42.

———. "Neglected Pearls in the Fabric of the City." In Lefaivre, De Roode, et al., *Aldo van Eyck.*

Sugrue, Thomas J. *The Origins of the Urban Crisis: Race and Inequality in Postwar Detroit.* Princeton Studies in American Politics. Princeton, N.J.: Princeton University Press, 1996.

Sukopp, Herbert. "The City as a Subject for Ecological Research." In Marzluff et al., *Urban Ecology,* 281–98.

———. "On the Early History of Urban Ecology in Europe." In Marzluff et al., *Urban Ecology,* 79–97.

Sukopp, Herbert, Hans-Peter Blume, and Wolfram Kunick. "The Soil, Flora, and Vegetation of Berlin's Waste Lands." In *Nature in Cities: The Natural Environment in the Design and Development of Urban Green Space,* edited by Ian C. Laurie. Chichester, UK: Wiley, 1979.

Suttles, Gerald D. "The Cumulative Texture of Local Urban Culture." *American Journal of Sociology* 90, no. 2 (1984): 283.

TallBear, Kim. "Caretaking Relations, Not American Dreaming." *Kalfou* 6, no. 1 (2019): 24–41.

Tanner, Ogden. *Urban Wilds.* New York: Time-Life Books, 1975.

Taylor, Dorceta. *Toxic Communities: Environmental Racism, Industrial Pollution, and Residential Mobility.* New York: New York University Press, 2014.

Taylor, Keeanga-Yamahtta. "How Real Estate Segregated America." *Dissent* 65, no. 4 (2018): 23–32.

Thomas, Lewis F. "The Sequence of Areal Occupance in a Section of St. Louis, Missouri." *Annals of the Association of American Geographers* 21, no. 2 (1931): 75–90.

Torquato Luiz, Juliana, and Silvia Jorge. "Hortas urbanas cultivadas por populações Caboverdianas na área metropolitana de Lisboa: Entre a produção de alimentos e as sociabilidades no espaço urbano não legal." *Miradas en Movimiento* 1 (2012): 142–58.

Tostões, Ana. *Francisco Keil do Amaral.* Arquitectos Portugueses, series 2, no. 11. Aveleda, Vila do Conde, Portugal: Verso da História, 2013.

Tostões, Ana, and Manuel Silveira Ramos. *Do Estádio Nacional ao Jardim Gulbenkian: Francisco Caldeira Cabral e a primeira geração de arquitectos paisagistas (1940–1970).* Lisbon: Fundação Calouste Gulbenkian, 2003.

Toussaint, M., P. B. D'Almeida, and M. D. Alcântara. *Guia de arquitetura de Lisboa: Do movimento moderno à atualidade: 1948–2013,* Lisbon: A + A Books, 2013.

Tracey, David. *Urban Agriculture: Ideas and Designs for the New Food Revolution.* Gabriola Island, B.C.: New Society, 2011.

Tranel, Mark. "Introduction: From Dreams to Reality: The Arch as a Metaphor for St. Louis Plans." In Tranel, *St. Louis Plans,* 1–16.

———, ed. *St. Louis Plans: The Ideal and the Real St. Louis.* St. Louis Metromorphosis Series. St. Louis: Missouri Historical Society Press, 2007.

TRIP. *The Interstate Highway System in Missouri: Saving Lives, Time and Money.* June 2006. www
.tripnet.org.

Tsing, Anna Lowenhaupt. "On Nonscalability: The Living World Is Not Amenable to Precision-Nested
Scales." *Common Knowledge* 18, no. 3 (2012): 505–24.

Tuck, Eve. "Suspending Damage: A Letter to Communities." *Harvard Educational Review* 79, no. 3
(2009): 409–28.

Tulumello, Simone. "Fear and Urban Planning in Ordinary Cities: From Theory to Practice." *Planning
Practice and Research* 30, no. 5 (2015): 1–20.

Turner, Victor Witter. *The Ritual Process: Structure and Anti-Structure.* Ithaca, N.Y.: Cornell University
Press, 1969.

Tzonis, Alexander, and Liane Lefaivre. *Architecture in Europe since 1968: Memory and Invention.* New
York: Rizzoli, 1992.

Ueland, Jeff, and Barney Warf. "Racialized Topographies: Altitude and Race in Southern Cities." *Geographical Review* 96, no. 1 (2006): 50–78.

Ukeles, Mierle Laderman. "Manifesto for Maintenance Art 1969! Proposal for an Exhibition 'CARE.'" 1969.
https://static1.squarespace.com/static/5d67edcebcb9230001022a12/t/5eb5c7c199a7f767ae768754
/1588971457098/%5BFILE-+MAINTENANCE+ART+MANIFESTO+1969.pdf.

Ungers, Oswald Mathias and Rem Koolhaas, with Peter Riemann, Hans Kolhoff, and Arthur Ovaska.
The City in the City: Berlin; A Green Archipelago. Zürich: Lars Müller, 2013.

United States Congress. House of Representatives. Committee on Banking, Finance, and Urban Affairs. Subcommittee on the City. *How Cities Can Grow Old Gracefully.* Washington, D.C.: Government Printing Office, 1977.

United States Department of Agriculture. "National Resources Inventory Glossary." Natural Resources
Conservation Service, last updated August 26, 2015. https://www.nrcs.usda.gov/wps/portal/nrcs
/detail/national/technical/nra/nri/?cid=nrcs143_014127.

United States Environmental Protection Agency. "Old North St. Louis: Sustainably Developing a Historic District." Smart Growth, March 2016. https://www.epa.gov/smartgrowth/old-north-st-louis
-sustainably-developing-historic-district.

———. "Summary of the Clean Water Act," Laws & Regulations. https://www.epa.gov/laws
-regulations/summary-clean-water-act.

University of Michigan, A. Alfred Taubman College of Architecture and Urban Planning. "2021 MLK
Symposium: Building the Beloved Community through Trauma-Informed Design." January 21, 2021.

UrbArts. "About UrbArts." https://www.urbarts.org/abouturbarts/#more-79.

Van Valkenburgh, Michael, and William S. Saunders. "Landscapes over Time: The Maintenance Imperative." *Landscape Architecture Magazine* 103, no. 3 (2013): 106–15.

Verordnung zum Schutz des geschützten Landschaftsbestandteils Grünanlage Hallesche Straße / Möckernstraße im Bezirk Kreuzberg von Berlin Vom 15. December 1987.

Verstrate, Lianne, and Lia Karsten. "The Creation of Play Spaces in Twentieth-Century Amsterdam:
From an Intervention of Civil Actors to a Public Policy." *Landscape Research* 36, no. 1 (2011): 85–109.

Vieira, Alice, and António Pedro Ferreira. *Esta Lisboa.* Lisbon: Caminho, 1993.

Viljoen, Andre, and Joe Howe. *Continuous Productive Urban Landscapes: Designing Urban Agriculture
for Sustainable Cities.* Oxford: Architectural Press, 2005.

Vítková, Michaela, Jana Müllerová, Jiří Sádlo, Jan Pergl, and Petr Pyšek. "Black Locust (*Robinia pseudoacacia*) Beloved and Despised: A Story of an Invasive Tree in Central Europe." *Forest Ecology and
Management* 384 (January 2017): 287–302.

Von Hoffman, Alexander. "A Study in Contradictions: The Origins and Legacy of the Housing Act of 1949." *Housing Policy Debate* 11, no. 2 (2000): 299–326.

Wall, Derek. *The Commons in History: Culture, Conflict, and Ecology.* Cambridge, Mass.: MIT Press, 2014.

Wallace, David A. *Metropolitan Open Space and Natural Process.* Philadelphia: University of Pennsylvania, 1970.

Wallace Roberts & Todd. *GreenPlan Philadelphia: Our Guide to Achieving Vibrant and Sustainable Urban Places.* Prepared for the City of Philadelphia, 2010. https://theasthmafiles.org/sites/default/files/artifacts/media/pdf/greenplan_philadelphia.pdf.

Weaver, Robert C. "The Suburbanization of America, or the Shrinking of the Cities." *Civil Rights Digest* 9, no. 3 (1977): 2–11.

Wiggin, Kate Douglas Smith, and Nora Archibald Smith. *The Republic of Childhood.* Boston: Houghton, Mifflin, 1895.

Williams, Raymond. *The Country and the City.* London: Chatto and Windus, 1973.

Wilson, William J. *The Truly Disadvantaged: The Inner City, the Underclass, and Public Policy.* 2nd ed. Chicago: University of Chicago Press, 2012.

Withagen, Rob, and Simone R. Caljouw. "Aldo van Eyck's Playgrounds: Aesthetics, Affordances, and Creativity." *Frontiers in Psychology* 8 (2017): 1130.

Wolff, Jane. "Saint Louis, Brick City." In *Material Culture: Assembling and Disassembling Landscapes,* edited by Jane Hutton, 115–23. Landscript no. 5. Zurich: Jovis, 2018.

Zipp, Samuel. "The Roots and Routes of Urban Renewal." *Journal of Urban History* 39, no. 3 (2013): 366–91.

ILLUSTRATION CREDITS

Illustrations/photographs by the author: fig. 2, fig. 6 (data sources: U.S. Census; statistik-berlin -brandenburg.de; cbs.nl; Wikipedia; Russell, "Late Ancient and Medieval Population"), fig. 8, fig. 15, fig. 16, fig. 18, fig. 22, fig. 28, fig. 29, fig. 31, fig. 35, fig. 42, fig. 45 (*bottom*), fig. 49, fig. 55, fig. 59, fig. 61, fig. 64, fig. 72, fig. 73

Illustration by the author with Taylor Baer, Emmanuel Coloma, Angela Moreno-Long, and Ui Jun Song: fig. 27 (data sources: Del Tredici, "Spontaneous Urban Vegetation"; Cierjacks et al., "Biological Flora of the British Isles"; plants.usda.gov)

Illustrations by the author with Taylor Baer, Emmanuel Coloma, Tiffany Dang, Angela Moreno-Long, and Ui Jun Song: fig. 47 (data sources: Câmara Municipal de Lisboa; site visit; Scordia et al., "Promising Perennial Herbaceous Energy Crop")

Illustrations/maps by the author with Taylor Baer, Tiffany Dang, Angela Moreno-Long, and Ui Jun Song: fig. 23 (data sources: Senatsverwaltung für Stadtentwicklung und Wohnen, Berlin), fig. 24 (data sources: Senatsverwaltung für Stadtentwicklung und Wohnen, Berlin; Ungers, *City in the City*), fig. 25 (data sources: http://www.berlin.ucla.edu; photographs; site visit), fig. 26 (data sources: http://www.berlin.ucla.edu; photographs; site visit), fig. 30 (data source: Senatsverwaltung für Stadtentwicklung und Wohnen, Berlin), fig. 32 (data sources: Senatsverwaltung für Stadtentwicklung und Wohnen, Berlin; Atelier Loidl; Google Earth), fig. 33 (data sources: Senatsverwaltung für Stadtentwicklung und Wohnen, Berlin; Google Earth; site visits), fig. 36 (data source: Câmara Municipal de Lisboa), fig. 37 (data source: Câmara Municipal de Lisboa), fig. 39 (data sources: Câmara Municipal de Lisboa; Ribeiro Telles, *Plano Verde de Lisboa*), fig. 40 (data source: Câmara Municipal de Lisboa), fig. 43 (data sources: Câmara Municipal de Lisboa; Plano Urbanização de Chelas), fig. 44 (data sources: Câmara Municipal de Lisboa; Google Earth), fig. 46 (data source: Câmara Municipal de Lisboa)

Illustrations by the author with Taylor Baer, Angela Moreno-Long, and Ui Jun Song: fig. 9 (data sources: City of Philadelphia; State of New Jersey), fig. 10 (data sources: City of Philadelphia; State of New Jersey), fig. 11 (data sources: City of Philadelphia; State of New Jersey; McHarg, *Design with Nature,* 63), fig. 12 (data sources: City of Philadelphia; State of New Jersey), fig. 19, fig. 20, fig. 50 (data sources: dinoloket.nl/en/subsurface-models; Aldo van Eyck Archive), fig. 51 (data source: maps .amsterdam.nl/open_geodata), fig. 52 (data sources: maps.amsterdam.nl/open_geodata; http://

code.waag.org/buildings), fig. 54 (data source: Google Earth), fig. 56 (data source: http://maps
.amsterdam.nl/open_geodata/), fig. 57 (data source: http://maps.amsterdam.nl/open_geodata/),
fig. 58 (data source: Google Earth)

Illustration by the author with Taylor Baer, Angela Moreno-Long, Ui Jun Song, and Megan Jones Shiotani: fig. 53 (data sources: http://maps.amsterdam.nl/open_geodata/; Lefaivre, De Roode, et al.,
Aldo van Eyck)

Illustration by the author with Taylor Baer, Angela Moreno-Long, Hannah van der Eb, and Ui Jun
Song: fig. 13 (data sources: City of Philadelphia; State of New Jersey; U.S. Census; Google Earth;
dsl.richmond.edu)

Illustrations by the author with Taylor Baer and Ui Jun Song: fig. 14 (data sources: Sanborn Maps;
philageohistory.org; Louis I Kahn Mill Creek drawings)

Illustrations by the author with Emmanuel Coloma, Tiffany Dang, Angela Moreno-Long, and Ui Jun
Song: fig. 62 (data sources: City of St. Louis; U.S. Army Corps; Geological Survey of Missouri;
Missouri Department of Natural Resources), fig. 65 (data sources: City of St. Louis, 1947 Compre-
hensive Plan; Colin Gordon, map 4.2; major highway construction), fig. 66 (data sources: City of
St. Louis, *Comprehensive City Plan*; Google Earth), fig. 67 (data source: City of St. Louis)

Illustrations by the author with Angela Moreno-Long: fig. 7, fig. 21 (data sources: U.S. Federal Housing Finance Agency, All-Transactions House Price Index for Philadelphia; thebalance.com; weather
.gov), fig. 34 (data source: Federal Statistics Office Germany), fig. 38 (data source: Câmara Municipal
de Lisboa), fig. 48 (data sources: Climate-data.org; OECD.org), fig. 60 (data sources: Climate-data
.org; https://www.cbs.nl/; Federal Reserve economic data), fig. 71 (data sources: Missouri Digital
Heritage; Federal Reserve Economic Data; Missouri Department of Natural Resources)

Illustrations by the author with Angela Moreno-Long and Ui Jun Song: fig. 41 (data sources: Câmara
Municipal de Lisboa; Google Earth; site visit), fig. 63 (data sources: Preservation Research Office,
Missouri Department of Natural Resource; *Pioneer America*), fig. 68 (data sources: Compton and
Dry, *Pictorial St. Louis*; Sanborn Fire Insurance Maps; City of St. Louis; Google Earth; Unreal City:
Historic St. Louis Maps), fig. 70 (data sources: City of St. Louis; Google Earth)

Illustrations by the author with Angela Moreno-Long, Hannah van der Eb, and Ui Jun Song: fig. 17
(data sources: Sanborn Maps; philageohistory.org; Sanborn Fire Insurance Maps)

Illustrations by the author with Lane Raffaldini Rubin: fig. 3, fig. 4 (data sources: Forbes Magazine; U.S.
Census), fig. 5 (data sources: Forbes Magazine; U.S. Census)

Illustrations by the author with A. Gracie Villa: fig. 1, fig. 74 (data sources: Google Earth; site visits)

Photograph by Maria José Fundevila: fig. 45 (*top*)

Photograph courtesy of Richard Reilly: fig. 69

INDEX

Italicized page numbers refer to illustrations.

abandonment/abandoned land: of community gardens, 22; in disenfranchised neighborhoods, 19; as driver of ecological successions, 73; etymology, 8; factors affecting, 5; holder of, in St. Louis, 190, 240n48; increase in, in St. Louis, 172, *173;* and land values, 8, 12, 222nn11–12; and reparations, 214; requirements for designing landscape from, 205; and social spaces, 24; time as affecting, 10, *10, 11, 12,* 221n9; and urbanization, 12–14; urban wild as description of human, 85–86; urban wild as valued outcome of, 77, 78. *See also* vacant spaces

aesthetics: of Berlin parks, 96; murals in vacant spaces, 235n47; Parque Hortícola projects, 132–33; Philadelphia murals, 56, *57,* 226n54, 235n47; *Speelplaatsen,* 156, 170; and sustainability, 40, 225n27; urban wilds as, of natural development of controlled unruliness, 72

agriculture: abandoned land and community gardens, 22; cycles of, in Lisbon, 120, *137;* fallowness in, 223n32; floodplains soil, 106, *107;* hortas and economy, 22; as ingrained part of culture, 23; Lisbon's strategy for, 116–18, *119,* 231nn24–25; quintas, 118, 121, 130–31; and recreational spaces, 117, 122; in St. Louis, 192; as temporary answer to vacant spaces, 22;

tradition in Lisbon, 23, 104, *104,* 106, 109, 118, 121, 126, 130, 131, 231n24; and water, 106, 108

Alfaiate, Maria Teresa, 113, 115, 116

allotment gardens. *See* hortas (food gardens; Lisbon)

American Wilderness series (Time-Life Books), 75

Amsterdam: annexation of land, 151, 235n39; highways, 235n50; the Jordaan neighborhood, 159–60, 162, *163, 164, 165,* 165–66; key structuring elements, *7;* Laagte Kadijk, *150,* 156–57, *158,* 159, *159,* 165–66; land reclaimed from canals and sea, 149, 151, *159,* 162; number of *Speelplaatsen* in, 141, 233n8; Plan Zuid, 147; population, 156, 213, 236n51; population fluctuations, *13;* population growth, 149, 235n34; in post–World War II, 139–40; post–World War II housing needs, 151, 235n37; ring layout, *150, 153,* 154–55; size of, and scale of projects, 168, 170; social housing in, 151; stormwater management, 149, 235n33; topography, 167; World War II damage, 149, 151. See also *Speelplaatsen* (playgrounds; Amsterdam)

Anhalter Banhof (Berlin), *95*

aqueduct and reservoir systems, 34, 224n11

ArchitectureBoston, 241n5

Chicago: Olmsted and, 144; playgrounds, 143–45, 234n17, 234n20; population in early 1900s, 239n32

City in the City, The: Berlin; A Green Archipelago, 68, 227n4

City Plan for St. Louis, A, 184–85

Clean Water Act (1972), 39, 224n22

climate crisis: and increase in more frequent, intense, and erratic storms, 59; land use and resource management, 30; sea level rise, 227n60; and urban wilds, 100; and water management, 19

clustered network systems, *204,* 204–5. *See also* St. Louis

Co-City Methodology, 210–11

commons, the: basic facts about, 232n51; management of, 210–11, 226n48, 240n1; parameters necessary for effective governance of, 62, 227n61; Parque Hortícola projects as, 134; in Philadelphia, 36; planned, managed stormwater meadows as, 61, *61;* rights traditional to, 49, 226n47; as shared public good, 49; urban wilds as, 100, 102

Comprehensive City Plan (St. Louis, Missouri, 1947), 185

Congrès Internationaux d'Architecture Moderne (CIAM), 235nn40–41

connected network systems, 204, *204. See also* Berlin; Lisbon

conservation and urban wild, 76–77

"continuum culturale," 113

Corredor Verde de Monsanto (Lisbon), 115, 116, 231n18

Crane, David, 223n2

Creative Playgrounds and Recreational Centers (Ledermann and Traschel), 146–47

Cronon, William, 77

culture: agriculture as ingrained part of, 23; of agriculture in Lisbon, 23, 104, *104,* 106, 109, 118, 121, 126, 130, 131, 231n24; as antithesis of wild, 75; hortas in *Evocações do Passado,* 136; landscape and communal values, 210; and land values, 8; population decline and practice, 17; and sandboxes in Amsterdam, 152, 154; and *Speelplaatsen,* 170–71; Stolperstein ("stumbling stones"/"setting stones") in

Berlin, 211–12, 229n56; and urban wilds, 74, 81, 96; weeds as construct of, 79

"Cumulative Texture of Local Culture" (Suttles), 222n13

Cunha, Dilip da, 227n60

cycles: of agriculture in Lisbon, *137;* defining, 15; evolution of landscape and housing, 211; examples, 14, 15, *16, 64;* fallow, in St. Louis, *201;* and nature of transformation, 5; playgrounds and population, 168, *169; Speelplaatsen* as part of Amsterdam, 147, 154–55; in urban wilds, 100, *101,* 102

Davis, Ujiji, 222n21

Delaware River: bridge to connect highways, 1; connection to Schuylkill, 54; and location of Philadelphia, 32; rail lines crossing, 2; sewage overflows into, 34; wastewater management and streams between, and Schuylkill, 45; watershed drainage, 54

Demnig, Guenther, 229n56

Dentinho, Álvaro, 112, 220

Design in the Terrain of Water (Mathur and Cunha), 227n60

Design with Nature (McHarg), 37

destruction, as requirement of reinvention and progression, 221n10

detention ponds, 28, 226n44

Detroit: land values, 8; population fluctuations, 14, 222n13; skyscrapers and woodlands cycle, 14, 15

Dijkstraat (Amsterdam), 147, 154, 166

disenfranchised neighborhoods: abandoned land in, 19; Chelas as, 126, 131, 232n39, 232n45; difficulties of investing in, 203; fighting speculation in, 196; and hortas, 117, 120, 134; and investment of government resources, 214; and low ground, 180–81; playgrounds in, 145; and practice of dwelling on statistical and figure-ground comparisons, 215; projects in, 48, 49; "redlining," 239n47; replicating successful programs in, 195–96, 199; and social spaces, 24; St. Louis north of Delmar Avenue divide, 177–78, 237n10; system strategies to address needs of, 203–5, *204. See also* Old North neighborhood (St. Louis); race and racism: in St. Louis

Merion Friends Meeting House (West Philadelphia), 29, 223n4
Metropolitan Open Space and Natural Process (Philadelphia), 27, 28, 36–37
Meyer, Elizabeth, 225n27, 227n60
Michael Van Valkenburgh Associates, 183
Miedema, Merel, 165
migrations, *10, 11*
Mill Creek Apartments (Philadelphia), *47,* 48, 238n25
Mill Creek neighborhood (Philadelphia), *53;* development of, 46; land values, 45–46; public housing, *47,* 48, 238n25; and Spirn, 223n6; wastewater management, 35, 224n14; water management projects in, *49,* 49–50, 226nn50–51; watershed, 29–30
Mill Creek Valley (St. Louis) renewal: demographics, 189; displacement of residents, 189; funding, 239n45; highways, *187,* 189; and racism, *187,* 189, 239n45; vacant spaces, *187,* 189
mining in St. Louis, 179, *180,* 237n14, 237nn17–18
Mississippi River: bridges spanning in St. Louis city and St. Louis County, 173–74, *175;* flooding of, 178; St. Louis as divide between managed and unmanaged, 178
Missouri Compromise, 176–77
Monchaux, Nicholas de, 226n59
Moshassuck River (Providence), 49
Mulder, Jakoba, 139, 140, 145
Mumford, Lewis, 221n9
Mural Arts Philadelphia, 226n54, 235n47

"nature-culture hybrid," 78
nature-culture system, 68, *69*
Nature in Cities: The Natural Environment in the Design and Development of Urban Green Space (Laurie), 97
Natur-Parks, 229n57
Natur-Park Schöneberger Südgelände (Berlin), *88,* 88–90, *95,* 96, 206
Netherlands, recognition of ruderal wilds in, 74
Neukrug, Howard, 39, 48
New York City: areas of urban wild, 75, 76, 228n21; percent built environment, 227n6;

population in early 1900s, 239n32; urban wild connections, 97, 99; water for drinking, 224n11
New York Times, 14
nonscalability, 40, 225n29
Northern Liberties neighborhood (Philadelphia), 51, 54
Northern Liberties Neighborhood Association (NLNA), 56
Norton de Matos, Inês, 113, 115, 116
nostalgia, 14
"novel ecosystem," 77, 78
Nutter, Michael, 39

Oberlander, Cornelia Hahn, 48
obsolete areas, 188
ÖkoCon & Planland, 89
Old North neighborhood (St. Louis), *200;* history, 194–95, *197,* 240n54; Old North St. Louis Restoration Group (ONSLRG), 195–96, 214; strategy for revitalization, 199; success of revitalization, 192, 194, 202; Sunflower+ Project: STL, 192, 196, *198,* 198–99
Olivais Norte, 126, 232n38
Olivais Sul, 126, 232n38
Olmsted, Frederick Law, 9, 144
open space. *See* vacant spaces
Ostrum, Elinor, 49, 227n61
Oswalt, Philipp, 17–18, 222nn18–19

Pacheco, Duarte, 109
Pagano, Michael A., 222n12
pandemics, 145
Paris redevelopment, 236n56
Park am Gleisdreieck (Berlin), 87, 90, 92–94, *93, 95,* 96
parklands: in Chicago as social centers for immigrants, 144, 145; Liberty Lands, 20, 54–57, *55, 57, 58;* Lucien Blackwell Park and Recreation Center before development, *53;* and Olmsted, 9, 144; as part of Philadelphia's 2015 Green Plan, 226n52; to preserve drinking water, 34; in St. Louis based on filled quarries, 179. *See also* recreational spaces *and specific parks by name*
Parque de Bela Vista (Lisbon), *110,* 111, 112

237nn9–10; rain gardens on abandoned land, 191–92, 240n51; sewer infrastructure, 191, 237n18; sinkholes, 179, 237n13; topography, 180–81; Tower Grove Park, 181; as urban crisis, 172; urban renewal, *187,* 188; urban wild in, 181, *182. See also* Old North neighborhood (St. Louis); race and racism: in St. Louis

St. Louis Civic League, 184, 238n30

St. Louis Improvement Association, 238n30

St. Louis Limestone, 179

Stolperstein ("stumbling stones"/"setting stones"), 211–12, 229n56

stormwater: age of and redesign of management systems, 44, 225n32; Amsterdam, 149, 235n33; Bussey Brook Meadow (Boston), stormwater impoundment, 222n24; defining, 224n9; and increase in more frequent, intense, and erratic storms, 59; land use strategies to impound, 19, 222n24; management combined with waste-water management systems, 225n33; management in Philadelphia, 39–40, *41, 42–43,* 44; overflow, 224n9; planned, managed meadows, 60–61, *61;* rain gardens in Philadelphia, 52–53, 56; rain gardens on abandoned land in St. Louis, 191–92, 240n51; stormwater basins, 52–53, 54, *58*

Stoss Landscape Urbanism, 190

Strauven, Francis, 162, 165

Strong, Ann Louise, 223n1

Sukopp, Herbert: and Berlin School of Urban Ecology, 80–81, 229n46; biotype classification system, 67–68; ecological documentation of ruderal species, 66–67; heberomy, 73; influence of, 97, 227n3; and McHarg, 97; urban wild as typology in urban matrix, 80

Sunflower+ Project: STL (St. Louis), 192, 196, *198,* 198–99

sustainability and aesthetics, 40, 225n27

Suttles, Gerald D., 222n13

Tagus River: Lisbon's valleys, 103, 108; and *Plano Verde,* 113; soil, 106, 113

Tanner, Ogden, 75–76

Team Four Plan (St. Louis), 190, 240n49

Telles, Gonçalo Ribeiro: basic facts about, 103; and Cabral, 231n17; "continuum culturale"

and "genius loci," 113; Corredor Verde de Monsanto (Green Corridor of Monsanto), 115, 116, 231n18; hortas, 23; and Mata de Alvalade, 112. See also *Plano Verde de Lisboa* (Telles)

temporality, Sunflower+ Project: STL, 198

Terra Incognita (Bowman and Pagano), 222n12

"Terrain Vague" (Solà-Morales Rubió), 222nn11–12

"third wilderness," 77, 78

Time-Life Books, American Wilderness series, 75

Tomazinis, Anthony R., 223n1

Toulan, Nohad A., 223n1

"Tragedy of the Commons, The" (Hardin), 226n48

transformation: cyclical nature of, 5; and economics, 6, 10, 12; measuring, 12; private, nongovernmental efforts, 195–96, 213–14; response rates to growth and decline, 14; of *Speelplaatsen,* 147, 154–55, 156, 157, 160, 166, 167; translocation versus, 12

translocations: American, *10,* 12, 221n9; transformation versus, 12

transportation: flooding of corridors for, 105; railroads, 2, *69;* St. Louis airports planned by Bartholomew, 239n38. *See also* highways

Traschel, Alfred, 146–47

Tredici, Peter del, 221n8

Trelease, William, 183

Tsing, Anna Lowenhaupt, 225n28

Ungers, Oswald Mathias, 66, 68, 86, 227n4

United States: housing and GI Bill, 2; migrations, *10,* 12, 221n9; national highways program (1957–80), 1, 221n1 (prologue); Progressive Era, 143–44, 184, 233n14, 238n30. *See also specific cities by name*

urban: ecological definition of, 227n62; milieu as mirror of society, 171

"urban blight," 144, 188, 234n18

urbanization: development of peri-urban areas, 122, 231n29; ethnicity and race, 46; role of water in, 30, *31,* 32, 37–38, 46; urban wild(s) developmental pressure on, 99, 230n68; vacant spaces as driver of development, 27 urban renewal: described, 236n55; in Mill Creek Valley (St. Louis), *187,* 189, 239n45; Model Cities Program, 240nn53–54; in Old North neighborhood (St. Louis), 195; opposition to, 160, 239n45; US federal and Missouri state laws, 239n41

urban wild(s): activity within, 181; adapting to changing needs of residents, 99–100; as aesthetic of natural development of controlled unruliness, 72; in Berlin, *70;* in Boston, 77; as catch phrase to support conservation, 76–77; and climate crisis, 100; as the commons, 100, 102; as cultural entity, 74, 96; cyclical nature of, 100, *101,* 102; defining, 73; degrees of human intervention, 79–80, 89–90; developmental pressure on, 99, 230n68; development of idea of, 75; and ecological succession, 73, 74, 77, 78, 89, 96; and history of built environment, 77, 211–12; impact of, on landscape, 79; as legitimate open space typology, 68; as material condition to be nurtured, 74; as minimal-maintenance landscape, 79; in New York City, 75, 76, 228n21; as part of Berlin culture, 81; and planning, 99–100; as reactive classification, 85–86; role of, 76; in San Francisco, 75; species protection and human use, 93, 96; in St. Louis, 181, *182;* structural linkage of parcels, 97, *98,* 99, 230n67; as typology in urban matrix, 80; as valued outcome of abandonment or degradation, 77, 78; vegetation of, 78–79; vilification of, 79; wild meadows compared to, 79

Urban Wilds (Tanner), 75–76

"urban wildscape," 77–78

Urban Wilds program (Boston), 77

vacant spaces: agriculture as temporary answer, 22; barriers associated with and planning for, 226n49; created by urban withdrawal, 222n19; curation of ruderal plants in, 21; defining, 222n12; as driver of development, 27; general characteristics, 18; gradations of solutions for, in terms of management and time, 206–7; *Green City, Clean Waters* projects on, 60, 63; as islands of ruderal vegetation, 68, *69,* 72; land values of, 8, 12, 222nn11–12; Mill Creek

Valley (St. Louis) renewal, *187,* 189; murals in, 235n47; number of, in St. Louis, 190; paved, as social spaces, 24; for playgrounds, 144; and retention of existing wilds, 99; as ruderal vegetation islands, 68, 72; ruderal vegetation mapped in Berlin, *69;* as *Speelplaatsen* sites, 146, 155; as in use and not truly abandoned, 205; and water management, 20, 32, 226n55; and waterways in Philadelphia, *31,* 39. *See also* hortas (food gardens; Lisbon)

van Eesteren, Cornelis: basic facts about, 151, 235nn40–41; and Bertelmanplein, 140–41; characteristics of, 152; and CIAM, 235nn40–41; on "cleaning up" the Jordaan neighborhood, 160; and garden cities, 151; and General Extension Plan of Amsterdam, 151, 152; and mutability of *Speelplaatsen,* 154; *Speelplaatsen* collaborators, 25; *Speelplaatsen* locations, 145, *150,* 152; tenets of functional city, 235n41

van Epen, Johannes C., 147

van Eyck, Aldo: basic facts about, 141, 146; Bertelmanplein design, 147, 149; cities as mirror of society, 171; description of playgrounds by, 171; kit of playground parts developed by, 146; materials used by, 146; site assessments for *Speelplaatsen,* 162; Zeedijk *Speelplaatsen,* 155–56

van Lingen, Anna, 165

van Lohuizen, Theo K., 151

van Roojen, Joost, 156

vegetation: for planned, managed stormwater meadows, 61, *61;* urban wild, as native ecological community, 76; weeds, 78–79. *See also* ruderal vegetation

Venice, population fluctuations, 14

Victory Gardens, 223n28

von Arnswald, Hermann, 142

Waldheim, Charles, 241n5

Wallace, David A., 223n1

Wallace Roberts & Todd, 39–40

wastewater management: and built environment, 32; in Philadelphia, 35, 46, 224n14; sewage overflows into Delaware River, 34; in St. Louis, 191, 237n18; stormwater management combined with, 225n33; and streams between Schuylkill and Delaware Rivers, 45

water: Amsterdam land reclaimed from, 149, 151, *159,* 162; and built environment, 32, 211; captured and cleansed on the surface of vacant spaces, 20; as common resource again manifest, 48–49; for drinking, 34, 39, 224nn10–12; as driver of human settlement, 28; for hortas, 122, 124, 131, 132, 231n33; land values and buried, 45–46; and Lisbon agriculture, 106, 108; Lisbon drainage, 103, 104; Philadelphia as hydrological innovator, 32, 224n10; in Philadelphia's history, 28, 44–45, *64;* and Philadelphia's vacant lands, *31,* 39; as public good and utility, 59, 226n57; and public health, 35; as recreational destinations, 56; regulation of pollutants in open, 39, 224n22; rights and commons, 49; rivers, 36, 37, 90, 229n59; role of, in urbanization, 30, *31,* 32; runoff management systems, 56; as traditional right in the commons, 49; underground, and ability to build, 29; as unifying process and primary agent in structuring landscape, 28.

See also stormwater; water management; *and specific rivers by name*

WaterFire (Evans), 226n45

water management: and climate crisis, 19; imagined future of, 49–50; Mill Creek neighborhood projects, *49,* 49–50, 226nn50–51; Philadelphia, *33,* 36, 224n14; and vacant spaces, 32, 226n55. *See also* wastewater management

water squares, 226n46, 235n33

weeds, 78–79

West Philadelphia Landscape Project, 224n6

West Philadelphia study, 27–28

Wheaton, William L. C., 223n1

wilderness: defining, 74–75; wildscape versus, 78

wild plants. *See* ruderal vegetation

wildscape versus wilderness, 78

Wolff, Jane, 179, 237n17

Woonasquatucket River (Providence), 48–59

Wright, Henry, 183, 238n31

Youngstown (Ohio), *6*

Zeedijk (Amsterdam), 155–56, 235nn46–47